Why Democracies Develop and Decline

The Varieties of Democracy project (V-Dem) pioneered new ways to conceptualize and measure democracy, producing a multidimensional and disaggregated data set on democracy around the world that is now widely used by researchers, activists, and governments. *Why Democracies Develop and Decline* draws on this data to present a comprehensive overview and rigorous empirical tests of the factors that contribute to democratization and democratic decline, looking at economic, social, institutional, geographic, and international factors. It is the most authoritative and encompassing empirical analysis of the causes of democratization and reversals. The volume also proposes a comprehensive theoretical framework and presents an up-to-date description of global democratic developments from the French Revolution to the present. Each chapter leverages the specialized expertise of its authors, yet their sustained collaboration lends the book an unusually unified approach and a coherent theory and narrative.

Michael Coppedge is Professor of Political Science at the University of Notre Dame. He is a principal investigator of the Varieties of Democracy project, the author of *Democratization and Research Methods* (2012), and co-author of *Varieties of Democracy: Measuring Two Centuries of Political Change* (2020).

Amanda B. Edgell is Assistant Professor of Political Science at the University of Alabama. She works on the politics of regime transformation, authoritarianism, political inclusion, and African politics. Her work has appeared in several peer-reviewed journals, including the *British Journal of Political Science, European Journal of Political Research, Democratization*, and *African Studies Review*.

Carl Henrik Knutsen is Professor of Political Science at the University of Oslo and leads the Comparative Institutions and Regimes (CIR) research group. He is also Research Professor at PRIO, and a principal investigator of Varieties of Democracy and several research projects, including an ERC Consolidator Grant on autocratic politics, and co-author of *Varieties of Democracy: Measuring Two Centuries of Political Change* (2020).

Staffan I. Lindberg is Professor of Political Science and Director of the V-Dem Institute at the University of Gothenburg, Sweden. He is a principal Investigator of the Varieties of Democracy project as well as several other projects, a Wallenberg Academy Fellow, author of *Democracy and Elections in Africa* (2006), and co-author of *Varieties of Democracy: Measuring Two Centuries of Political Change* (2020).

Why Democracies Develop and Decline

Edited by

MICHAEL COPPEDGE
University of Notre Dame

AMANDA B. EDGELL
University of Alabama

CARL HENRIK KNUTSEN
University of Oslo

STAFFAN I. LINDBERG
V-Dem Institute, University of Gothenburg

CAMBRIDGE
UNIVERSITY PRESS

CAMBRIDGE
UNIVERSITY PRESS

Shaftesbury Road, Cambridge CB2 8EA, United Kingdom

One Liberty Plaza, 20th Floor, New York, NY 10006, USA

477 Williamstown Road, Port Melbourne, VIC 3207, Australia

314–321, 3rd Floor, Plot 3, Splendor Forum, Jasola District Centre, New Delhi – 110025, India

103 Penang Road, #05–06/07, Visioncrest Commercial, Singapore 238467

Cambridge University Press is part of Cambridge University Press & Assessment, a department of the University of Cambridge.

We share the University's mission to contribute to society through the pursuit of education, learning and research at the highest international levels of excellence.

www.cambridge.org
Information on this title: www.cambridge.org/9781009078238

DOI: 10.1017/9781009086974

First published 2022
First paperback edition 2023

A catalogue record for this publication is available from the British Library

ISBN   978-1-316-51441-2   Hardback
ISBN   978-1-009-07823-8   Paperback

Contents

Figures

Tables

Acknowledgements

"Bernard of Chartres used to compare us to dwarfs perched on the shoulders of giants. He pointed out that we see more and farther than our predecessors, not because we have keener vision or greater height, but because we are lifted up and borne aloft on their gigantic stature"[1]

From the very inception of the Varieties of Democracy-project (V-Dem) through now over decade, Bernard of Chartres' point has been true for everything we managed to accomplish. This volume is no exception. While the volume has editors and each chapter has named authors, the intellectual content contained therewithin is not only ours. We are the fortunate ones in the development of the social sciences, bestowed with so many insights and advancements made by those who came before us, and, more specifically, by the many who worked with us in V-Dem. We are grateful if readers appreciate how preciously little we as individual scholars contribute and recognize that the advancements of knowledge found in this volume really are realizations of being "perched on the shoulders of giants".

We will undoubtedly fail in the effort to acknowledge all whom we are indebted to. Quite beyond the innumerable individuals and institutions making V-Dem possible and thrive, even a more limited effort to recognize those who were invaluable in the process leading to this volume will ultimately fall short. We ask all to know that we express our sincerest gratitude to undergraduate and graduate students, postdocs, visiting and affiliate scholars, colleagues, as well as institutions and practitioners in the policy community,

---

[1] This is believed to be the first formulation of "standing on the shoulders of giants" and is found in John of Salisbury. 1159. *Metalogicon*. folio 217 recto (f 217r), Cambridge, Corpus Christi College, MS 046, Book III, Chapter 4, original translated to English by MacGarry, Daniel Doyle, ed. (1955). *The Metalogicon of John Salisbury: A Twelfth-century Defense of the Verbal and Logical Arts of the Trivium*. Berkeley: University of California Press. p. 167. Bernard of Chartres was a twelfth century philosopher, scholar, and administrator.

who at some point invited us to share our preliminary ideas or were involved in activities contributing to the ideas shared in this volume.

The volume is a principal outcome of the six-year "Varieties of Democracy Research Program" funded by Riksbankens Jubileumsfond (Grant M13-0559:1, PI: Staffan I. Lindberg) from 2014 to 2019. As editors of this volume, we would like to express our gratitude for this generous contribution. The program's main objective was to build and test a comprehensive theory of democratization integrating endogenous as well as exogenous explanatory factors. Naturally, we cannot claim to have fully achieved that somewhat unrealistic goal. We are nonetheless very proud of the advances the V-Dem team has made over these years with some 120 scientific working papers, of which more than 60 are now published as peer-reviewed articles, and the first book, *Varieties of Democracy: Measuring Two Centuries of Political Change*, published by Cambridge University Press in 2020. This volume is the culmination, for now, of our efforts as members of the V-Dem team, to produce a comprehensive account of why democracies develop and decline.

The editors and all co-authors thank funders who made it possible for us to hold three book workshops, and for all the terrific comments and suggestions provided by commentators during these workshops, which have been indispensable for us to reach this final outcome. A first book workshop was held in October 2017 in Rome to plan and discuss initial drafts of this volume. Funders for that workshop include the V-Dem Institute; the Helen Kellogg Institute for International Studies; the Nanovic Institute for European Studies; and Notre Dame International, which manages the University of Notre Dame's Rome Global Gateway. Therese Hanlon ably handled travel and other logistics for this workshop. A second book workshop was organized by Michael Bernhard at University of Florida in February 2019, sponsored by the University of Florida Foundation. A third and final workshop was organized by the V-Dem Institute and held at Vann Hotel outside of Gothenburg in conjunction with the V-Dem annual conference in May 2019, funded by the large grant from Riksbankens Jubileumsfond mentioned above.

In addition to organizers and participants at these workshops, several others deserve to be mentioned for their contributions to individual chapters of this book:

As authors of Chapter 2, Carl Henrik Knutsen and Svend-Erik Skaaning would like to thank Lasse Aaskovsen, Larry Diamond, Johannes Lindvall, the participants at the, the Historical V-Dem Workshop at the University of Oslo (2018), the APSA Annual Meeting in Boston (2018), and the Annual Meeting of the Danish Political Science Association at Hotel Vejlefjord (2019) as well as the other contributors to this volume for excellent comments and suggestions. They would especially like to thank Tore Wig, both for excellent comments and for creating Figure 2.4.

As author of Chapter 3, John Gerring wishes to acknowledge that the chapter builds on work conducted in collaboration with Brendan Apfeld, Tore Wig, and Andreas Tollefsen.

As authors of Chapter 4, Michael Coppedge, Benjamin Denison, Paul Friesen, Lucía Tiscornia, and Yang Xu feel deeply indebted to Robert Franzese for his ICPSR workshop on "Spatial Econometrics," including permission to adapt a post-estimation Stata do-file he wrote with Jude Hays and Scott Cook; and to Nick Ottone, Jack Stump, and Jacob Turner for research assistance. The authors are also grateful to the Kellogg Institute's Research Cluster on Democratization Theory for many discussions. As always, Notre Dame's Center for Research Computing provided high-performance computing, without which Chapter 4 would not have been possible.

As authors of Chapter 5, Carl Henrik Knutsen and Sirianne Dahlum would like to thank Vanessa Boese as well as the other contributors to this volume for excellent comments and suggestions. They would especially like to thank Laura Maxwell for help with identifying and gathering data for many of the indicators used in this chapter.

As authors of Chapter 6, Allen Hicken, Samuel Baltz, and Fabricio Vasselai acknowledge excellent feedback on previous iterations of the text and analyses at book workshops.

As authors of Chapter 7, Michael Bernhard and Amanda Edgell are grateful for the feedback provided by participants in seminars at the University of California at Irvine, the State University of New York in Binghamton, and Gothenburg University. The authors are also grateful to Rachel Sigman for comments on our presentation of the Social Forces chapter at an internal V-Dem meeting. Michael Bernhard's work was supported by the University of Florida Foundation.

The three editors who are also co-authors of Chapter 8 (Amanda Edgell, Carl Henrik Knutsen, and Staffan I. Lindberg) wish to recognize Michael Coppedge as the principal author of this chapter. Michael's insistence that it could be done despite our explicit doubts is the main reason that we have this chapter, which includes what we consider to be unique contributions in piecing together and assessing different links in the complex network of factors influencing democratic development and decline.

Michael Coppedge thanks the Kellogg Institute for its multiyear support of the Democratization Theory Research Cluster and its other principal investigators J. Samuel Valenzuela, Dianne Pinderhughes, Aníbal Pérez-Liñán, and Gary Goertz for serving as a sounding board for many of the ideas in several chapters. Coppedge also thanks the College of Arts and Letters at Notre Dame for supporting his research leave in 2020–2021, and Political Science Department Chair Dave Campbell for being an enthusiastic and effective advocate. Great thanks are due also to the Center for the Study of Democratic Institutions at Vanderbilt University, which provided Coppedge with a visiting appointment in spring 2021 despite social distancing; and to CSDI and Political Science colleagues and staff at Vanderbilt, especially Joshua Clinton, Shannon Meldon-Corney, John Sides, Noam Lupu, Kristin Michelitch, Elizabeth Zechmeister, Keith Weghorst, David Lewis, and Guillermo Toral. Coppedge expresses personal thanks to his wife, Lynn McDonald, for graciously tolerating his absence from home that semester.

Amanda B. Edgell is indebted to colleagues at the University of Florida, the V-Dem Institute, the University of Gothenburg, and the University of Alabama for countless hours of conversation over the contents of this volume. In particular, she would like to thank three graduate students - Myles Williamson, Scott Corso, and Kim Jacks for their feedback - and Michael Bernhard for always treating his research assistants as colleagues and co-authors.

Carl Henrik Knutsen also wishes to express a large thank you to several colleagues, at the University of Oslo and elsewhere, and co-authors of previous publication on the topics analyzed and discussed also in this book; their ideas have been vital for shaping the analysis and discussions in different chapters. He also wishes to sincerely thank his family for their patience and support throughout the process.

Staffan I. Lindberg wishes in particular to also recognize the Knut and Alice Wallenberg Foundation's five-year Wallenberg Academy Fellowship (KAW 2013.0166) and five-year prolongation (KAW 2018.0144) that were essential in supporting the building of the V-Dem Institute and its team of assistant professors and postdocs. Everyone (23 past and present members) have made incredible contributions to our research collaborations, which in turn have made invaluable stepping-stones also towards the research presented in this volume. This is true not the least for Amanda Edgell who first participated in the V-Dem research program as a graduate student with Michael Bernhard as her committee chair, then joined the V-Dem Institute as a postdoctoral research fellow, and now is a much appreciated colleague and co-editor of this volume.

The larger V-Dem research agenda and therefore also this volume, was supported by a series of other grants not explicitly mentioned above. A full list of funders of various aspects (research, the infrastructure and data collection, outreach, collaborations, and other activities) can be found at the V-Dem website: https://www.v-dem.net/en/about/funders/. We are all very grateful for all the support that has helped build V-Dem, the advanced research infrastructure for data collection and curation, the research projects and programs, as well as the V-Dem Institute.

The Editors

V-Dem Reconsiders Democratization

Michael Coppedge, Amanda B. Edgell, Carl Henrik Knutsen, and Staffan I. Lindberg

Why do some countries manage to escape autocratic rule and become democratic, whereas others remain trapped? And why do some democracies remain stable or improve their level of democracy while others "backslide" or even die? These are the big questions this book seeks to answer.

Advances and setbacks in democracy are among the most important events in modern world history, as consequential as wars, economic recessions, and pandemics. Democracy is the only political regime that is designed to foster human dignity and individual freedoms for all citizens. Recent studies also provide rigorous evidence that democracy promotes economic growth (Acemoglu et al. 2019), helps prevent catastrophic economic outcomes (Knutsen 2021), and lowers infant mortality (Wang et al. 2019). Transitions to democracy more than double spending on poverty alleviation (Murshed et al. 2020), increase life expectancy, reduce child mortality, and lower deaths from noncommunicable diseases (Bollyky et al. 2019). In contrast, autocratizing countries have substantially lower estimated life expectancy, less effective health service coverage, and higher levels of out-of-pocket health spending than they would have had without erosion of democratic rights and freedoms (Wigley et al. 2020). Furthermore, the democratic peace axiom – that democracies do not fight wars against each other and that the spread of democracy reduces armed disputes and wars – is soundly confirmed by recent rigorous studies (e.g., Altman et al. 2021; Hegre et al. 2020); and other studies demonstrate that democracies are less prone to civil war and domestic volatility compared to less democratic regimes (Fjelde et al. 2021; Hegre 2014). In short, advances and setbacks have real implications for the well-being and freedom of millions of people.

As we write this book, the world is experiencing a "wave of autocratization," with a third of the population living under "autocratizing" conditions (Lührmann and Lindberg 2019). People across the world currently endure severe deterioration of civil liberties and political rights. Given the inherent normative importance of democracy as well as its wider implications for the well-being of citizens, it is important to understand why these processes happen. However, sixty years of scholarship on democratization has produced an immense, unwieldy, and bewildering literature. By one count, there are at least fifty-five competing explanations in the literature on democratization (Coppedge 2012, Chapter 4). It is especially difficult to make sense of so many arguments because they emerged from varied and incompatible research programs and methodologies, including historiography, comparative sociology, macroeconomics, institutionalism, geography, game theory, statistical analysis, and dozens of influential case studies.

This volume proposes a series of tests and eventually a synthesis of the leading explanations for why democracy develops and declines. We develop a unifying framework by (1) distinguishing among democratization outcomes, (2) ruling out explanations that are incompatible with the best empirical evidence, and (3) regarding explanations as complementary rather than competing. Following the lead of Teorell (2010) and theory going back at least as far as Rustow (1970), we are persuaded that conditions that explain levels of democracy are often different from those that explain change; and that explanations for advances in democracy are probably different from those that explain setbacks. We believe that treating levels of democracy as essentially the same as positive change, and treating negative change as nothing more than the absence or negation of positive change, has been a frequent source of confusion in the literature. The empirical analyses in this volume confirm this approach. High levels of democracy, upturns in democracy, and downturns in democracy often require different explanations.

We rely on wide-ranging empirical testing to winnow the relevant explanations down to a manageable number. After a series of detailed descriptive analyses of trends in democracy and autocracy since 1789 in Chapter 2, our testing proceeds in two phases. First, the five thematic chapters examine groups of related hypotheses: geography and demographics (Chapter 3); international influences (Chapter 4); economics (Chapter 5); institutions (Chapter 6); and social forces (Chapter 7). Each of these chapters begins with a thorough survey and critique of its family of hypotheses, then tests them using the best available measures (including Varieties of Democracy data) on global samples, typically covering most countries in the world sometimes for more than two centuries of history.

Although these analyses confirm many familiar beliefs about democratization and democratic reversals, they cast doubt on others. Gerring (Chapter 3), for example, rules out population and small territory as explanatory factors of variation in levels of democracy. Coppedge et al. (Chapter 4) report that although democracy is internationally "contagious" in the long run, ignoring its effects does not appear to exaggerate the short-run influence of domestic conditions. Knutsen and Dahlum (Chapter 5) add to the evolving debate about income and democracy: while per capita income correlates positively with level of democracy and makes downturns less severe, it does not boost upturns. Hicken et al. (Chapter 6) find no consistent support for the perils of presidentialism or party-system fragmentation. Bernhard and Edgell (Chapter 7) report evidence that right-wing anti-system movements harm democracy but left-wing anti-system movements do not.

Second, in Chapter 8 we test the most promising remaining hypotheses from each school of thought, reducing the number of viable hypotheses further by using a multi-equation path analysis. Because we are open to the possibility that many of the relevant explanatory factors represent complementary rather than competing explanations, we consider more complex causal chains and distinguish between direct and indirect effects. This contrasts with most prior quantitative research that pits these factors against one another in additive single-equation models. Multi-equation path analysis gives us the freedom to stipulate that some variables mediate the effects of others on democracy outcomes. In this way, we can test the causal sequences of all the promising factors where some have direct effects on the outcome while others only affect the outcome indirectly through their influence on factors with direct effects. The very different timescales in which the processes tested in Chapters 3–7 operate suggest a theoretical framework centered on causal sequences.

Some explanatory factors are "distal" in that they assumed their values long ago, in a pre-democratic era, and changed very little in subsequent years. Distal factors that remain significant in the conclusion include distance from natural harbors (a measure of difficult communication and trade, which hurts democracy), Protestant and European-descended population (which help democracy, although we regard them as proxies for some kind of long-run European influence), and economic dependence on exports of natural resources such as oil and minerals (a harmful influence).

Distal variables can also have indirect effects through intervening or "intermediate" variables, which do change, but only incrementally or episodically. Some of them are well-known elements of modernization theory: literacy, the share of national income produced by agriculture, and income level. We find that agricultural income share negatively and directly affects electoral democracy levels, upturns, and downturns; but literacy and income matter only indirectly for these outcomes.

The other intermediate variables that matter are a healthy civil society, the rule of law, and institutionalized political parties. We find that these features of organizations, institutions, and the state form a "protective belt" that tends to keep a country's level of democracy from changing very much, regardless of whether it is high or low. These three factors are sticky and tend to reinforce one another. They are influenced by development variables such as income and literacy, which are also sticky. In turn, practically invariant, distal variables such as natural harbors, natural resources, and European influence condition these development variables. The relationship between levels of democracy and these mutually reinforcing slowly or barely changing intermediate and distal variables help explain why most countries' democracy levels change very little in

most years. Most of the time, an equilibrium prevails. Chapter 4 suggests that
neighboring countries with similar democracy levels tend to reinforce the
equilibrium, too, although we do not model international influences in
Chapter 8.

Other forces, however, can punctuate the equilibrium. Occasionally, some
countries do experience large upturns (democratization) or downturns
(autocratization) in electoral democracy. Proximate variables that are much
more dynamic are most useful for explaining the upturns and downturns of
electoral democracy. Upturns tend to be larger after nonviolent opposition
campaigns and when the global economy is growing strongly. By contrast,
downturns in electoral democracy tend to be more severe when there is a
strong anti-system movement and when national economic growth is weak or
negative. These scenarios are powerful enough to disrupt the protective belt and
overcome the equilibrium sustained by intermediate and distal variables. Our
models also suggest that long-term reversals of development or of the strength
of civil society, the state, and party organizations can upset the equilibrium as
well, making a large downturn or upturn possible.

In the remainder of this introductory chapter, we address the motivations for
this volume and give a brief overview of the democratization research program,
including its many achievements, limitations, and impasses. Next, we describe
the Varieties of Democracy dataset and the methodology underpinning the data
collection. We discuss some limitations but also several of the advantages
associated with using these data to study democracy. Thereafter, we discuss
methodological aspects of the empirical analyses conducted in this book,
acknowledging threats to causal inference and describing the specific
dependent variables that are used throughout the volume. Then, we provide
an overview of the main argument by summarizing the remaining chapters of
the volume.

1.1 MOTIVATIONS FOR THIS VOLUME

Variation in countries' political systems and regime change is among the oldest
and most studied fields of political science. Numerous theories provide
explanations of how different geographic, demographic, international,
economic, social, and institutional factors influence democratization and
reversals.[1] Thousands of empirical studies assess these theories with methods
ranging from country-specific case studies to statistical analyses on global
samples (see Pelke and Friesen 2019 for a recent overview).

Despite these efforts, political scientists are still uncertain, and often in
disagreement, about the direction or even existence of key relationships that

---

[1] Because our methodological approach requires large-sample historical data, we cannot retest
explanations from at least two schools of thought: political culture (Inglehart and Welzel 2005)
and strategic bargaining among elites (Acemoglu and Robinson 2006; O'Donnell et al. 1986).

help explain regimes and regime transitions. For example, debates over the effects of economic development on democratization remain unresolved. Some studies indicate that higher income levels make countries more likely to democratize, whereas others find no relationship and yet others a negative one (see Chapter 5). There are especially few robust findings on the determinants of democratic decline and breakdown, (see, e.g., Gassebner et al. 2013; Rød et al. 2020). For instance, researchers strongly disagree on whether presidential forms of government make democracies more vulnerable to breakdown when compared to parliamentary regimes (see Chapter 6). Even after several decades of systematic research (see, e.g., Coppedge and Kuehn 2019; Geddes 1999; Munck 2019), democracy researchers are far from reaching any full understanding or consensus on the key drivers of democratization and democratic decline.

The described state of knowledge in democracy research provides two motivations for this volume. First, inconclusive findings on key relationships call for an up-to-date, critical, and comprehensive reassessment. The chapters in this volume provide such summaries and discussions, focusing on the various clusters of proposed determinants of democracy. Second, methodological differences often explain why previous studies have diverged so dramatically. Some studies may come to different conclusions, for instance, on the relationship between economic development and democratization, simply because of a short time series, low-powered tests, imprecise or inconsistent measures, and/or the omission of relevant variables. When equipped with more precise measures, long time series covering most countries in the world, and an appropriate model specification, we can develop more credible conclusions about the general relationships between the various proposed causal factors and democratic outcomes (Coppedge and Kuehn 2019).

To achieve the second ambition of this volume, the contributing authors – after having reviewed the relevant literatures – conduct empirical analyses that draw on extensive samples and new measures from the Varieties of Democracy (V-Dem) dataset (Coppedge et al. 2019b; Pemstein et al. 2019. As a disclaimer, most of the contributors to this book were involved in the development of the V-Dem dataset. Naturally, we and the other contributors want to use our data. However, the motivation for this book should not be misconstrued as data-driven. Rather, we created the V-Dem data so that we could explore answers to important questions about, among others, the determinants of democratization and the survival of democratic regimes.

The V-Dem dataset has unprecedented detail, as well as geographic and temporal coverage, which allows us to test key hypotheses about democratization across a wide range of contexts and to obtain more precise estimates of these relationships. The long time series – covering more than 200 political units (including both countries and colonies) from 1789 to 2018 – allows us to account for several sources of possible confounding, including country- and time-specific global factors that influence democratization or democratic survival. The contributors to this book typically draw on more than a century of global data, sometimes more than two centuries, in the search for robust, general relationships.

One caveat, however, is that this type of analysis masks substantial heterogeneity in some relationships, if they differ across or operate only in certain geographical contexts or particular periods. When such heterogeneity is theoretically expected, researchers can benefit from focusing their analyses on more limited but relevant samples despite the loss in statistical power. Oftentimes, theoretical expectations are less clear, but there is still a good reason to expect, for instance, time-varying effects. Then, researchers will probably also gain from using the extensive samples offered by V-Dem data to carefully assess the extent and nature of heterogeneous treatment effects. Given the large number of theories and relationships already covered, we do not engage in such extensive testing here, but limit our discussions and tests mainly to assessing the robustness of general relationships. However, we refer readers to Chapter 7 in Coppedge et al. (2020) for methodological discussions on how V-Dem data can be used to assess heterogeneous relationships.

Drawing on the V-Dem data, the contributors to this book revisit key proposed determinants of democracy – geographic and demographic, international, economic, social, and institutional – in separate chapters. Finally, we build on these different results and develop an empirically informed and coherent theoretical framework for understanding democratization in the concluding chapter. We begin our investigation by detailing what V-Dem data tells us about the trajectories of (different aspects of) democratization over the past 230 years. Chapter 2 of this volume describes the broad historical and regional trends in democracy since 1789. It mainly draws on the V-Dem Electoral Democracy Index (EDI), which is constructed to capture Robert Dahl's (1971) concept of "polyarchy" and its core institutional guarantees. However, the chapter also drills down into the institutional components of polyarchy to depict what drives global and regional changes in particular time periods and considers the trajectories of non-electoral aspects of democracy.

The second, and principal, issue of the volume centers on empirically testing different types of determinants of democracy measured with the EDI. This question occupies the bulk of the book and entails investigating which aspects of societies and their institutions hinder or trigger democratization, as well as what factors lead to or prevent erosion (or "autocratization") and breakdown. Hence, most of the chapters in the book take an incremental approach using four dependent variables, building on the approach taken in Teorell's (2010) *Determinants of Democratization*: (1) level of democracy, (2) annual change in democracy, (3) annual upturns, and (4) annual downturns. Chapter 6 also takes a more discrete approach, modeling the effects of institutions on the likelihood of regime change.

We organize the investigation by testing clusters of variables, one at a time, associated with the established dominant schools of thought regarding key explanations. Importantly, these proposed explanations are often not orthogonal and may be causally related. For example, different chapters discuss how access to natural harbors and economic development may independently enhance democracy levels, but natural harbors may also influence economic development, such as, by facilitating trade (another proposed determinant of democracy studied in this volume). Hence, we order the chapters from those determinants that are relatively exogenous and placed early on in the proposed causal chain (geography) to fairly endogenous factors placed later in the causal chain (social forces and institutions) that culminate in regime outcomes. We discuss this ordering and assess it in more detail in the concluding chapter, which serves as a theory building exercise drawing on the extensive reviews of theories and empirical analyses of the preceding chapters.

I.2 SETTING THE STAGE

We do not intend to provide a comprehensive overview of the field often referred to as "democracy research" here, but rather highlight some key developments in order to set the stage for clarifying how the current volume contributes to this literature.[2] Several researchers note how the field has moved from being centered on qualitative single and comparative case studies to increasingly including statistical studies on global and regional samples, supplemented by survey and experimental projects.[3] This, we surmise, reflects the reality that many, if not most, phenomena of interest to democratization scholars, such as national-level political institutions, are difficult to research without drawing on observational data. Substantively, the field has moved from

---

[2] Other books (Coppedge 2012; Geddes 2003; Mainwaring and Pérez-Liñán 2013; Møller and Skanning 2011; Przeworski et al. 2000) and articles (e.g., the special issue of *Democratization* edited by Coppedge and Kuehn 2019; Geddes 2007) describe the history and (methodological and substantive) trends of democratization research. Teorell (2010) summarizes the literature on several types of determinants of democracy and provides a comprehensive empirical analysis of these various factors under a common framework. Recent works also provide extensive sensitivity analysis (Gassebner et al. 2013; Rød et al. 2020) and meta-analysis (Saghaug Broderstad 2018) with systematic and condensed overviews of the state of knowledge for several empirical relationships. For some of the subliteratures in this field, including on the widely studied modernization hypothesis discussed in Chapter 5, there are also available accounts on the development of the literature (e.g., Munck (2019) and the recent issue edited by Dahlum (2018).

[3] A recent analysis of published articles in three top comparative politics journals (*Comparative Political Studies, Comparative Politics*, and *World Politics*) and the two top subfield journals (*Democratization, Journal of Democracy*) show that the use of statistical analyses in democratization-related topics increased from around 11 percent in 1990–1995 to 24 percent in 2010–2016 (Pelke and Friesen 2019). While the share of articles using experiments has also increased in recent years (to about 3 percent according to Pelke and Friesen (2019)), most empirical studies in democratization research still draw on observational data. In fact, according to the same article, over 70 percent of the sampled articles using experiments focused not on regime change but on democratic consolidation, with a secondary emphasis on ethnicity, citizen attitudes, policies, electoral behavior, and clientelism.

an early focus on democratic transitions from the 1970s, to studies of democratic consolidation, to a recent focus on authoritarianism (Pelke and Friesen 2019). This field of research remains one of the most heterogeneous within political science in its geographic scope and the diversity of national contexts from which data are drawn (Wilson and Knutsen 2020).[4]

The field is also eclectic in the types of theories that researchers develop to explain the emergence, functioning, and effects of democratic or autocratic institutions. While some theories focus on particular actors, notably leaders and regime elites, or particular social classes, others focus on how structural conditions shape political outcomes. Some theories highlight the relevance of economic factors in shaping regime outcomes, whereas others point to historical and institutional legacies, and yet others emphasize features of the international system. This richness in theoretical accounts, and the many different types of explanatory factors under focus, is reflected in this volume. Yet, the richness and variety in theoretical accounts also implies particular challenges. As noted by both Gassebner et al. (2013) and Rød et al. (2020), this theoretical heterogeneity results in a lack of consensus about the appropriate empirical models for large-N cross-national studies of democratization and autocratization. For statistical tests of theories in the field, this often means that models fail to account for alternative arguments about why democracies arise, erode, or break down.[5]

This issue speaks to the importance of thinking carefully about how different theories of democracy-related outcomes complement each other or pose contrasting explanations, and the implications for research design and specifying appropriate tests. Avoiding the compartmentalization of democracy research is thus important not only for diffusing results and insights from certain parts of the field to other parts but also for achieving consistent estimates, across the board, of the different determinants and effects of democracy. This suggests that more comprehensive treatments incorporating multiple families of causal factors in one study have advantages for understanding democracy-related outcomes.

Nevertheless, quantitative democracy research over the last forty years has benefited from methodological advances and new measures with improved validity, reliability, and coverage. Such developments have allowed researchers to test more nuanced hypotheses on an extensive number of countries in a careful manner. Next, we give a brief history of the type of empirical democratization research that we are conducting in this book: research that uses statistical tools to analyze data from a broad range of countries over time. We thus describe a

---

[4] For instance, studies of democratic transitions frequently feature cases from Eastern Europe and sub-Saharan Africa, democratic consolidation research often draws on Western Europe and Latin America contexts, and the study of authoritarian politics commonly addresses countries in the Middle East and North Africa (MENA) and East Asia (Pelke and Friesen 2019: 149).

[5] To take one example, geographic and political–historical factors may be omitted confounders in designs constructed to study the influence of, say, domestic political institutions such as presidentialism on democratic breakdown (see Cheibub 2007 and Chapter 6 of this volume).

central part of the research agenda on democratization and democracy-related topics, and in doing so, clarify our own contribution to this literature using V-Dem data.

1.3   IMPROVING DATA

The development of datasets incorporating democracy measures with extensive coverage across countries and over time has contributed greatly to understanding the causes of democracy and different types of regime change. Consider, for example, the modernization hypothesis, which is detailed and retested in Chapter 5 of this volume.[6] For several decades, quantitative tests of the relationship between economic development and democracy consisted of cross-sectional associations between levels of development (often measured as GDP per capita) and levels of democracy, following Lipset (1959). The development of annual cross-country measures of democracy covering a fairly long time series, beginning in the 1980s, opened up opportunities to empirically disentangle the underlying links that generated this correlation and thus, to test more specific theories about the mechanisms linking development to democracy (Burkhart and Lewis-Beck 1994). Notable in this regard were the Freedom House Political Rights and Civil Liberties measures (updated annually since 1972), the Polity Democracy and Autocracy indices (going back to 1800), and the ACLP (after the original authors, Alvarez, Cheibub, Limongi, and Przeworski (1996); later called DD – Democracy and Dictatorship) binary measure of democracy with time series coverage (initially from 1950 to 1990) across a large sample of countries. These datasets resulted in seminal contributions highlighting how income may correlate with democracy not because it enhances the probability of democratization but because it greatly mitigates the danger of democratic breakdown (cf. Boix and Stokes 2003; Przeworski and Limongi 1997; Przeworski et al. 2000).

Binary democracy measures are well suited for studies that consider autocracies and democracies as qualitatively distinct categories and that investigate the transition between such categories as discrete events (see, e.g., Przeworski and Limongi 1997). Yet many democracy scholars consider democracy to be a matter of degree. In their view, regimes often become slightly more or less democratic over a limited period of time, even if no change occurs on a binary democracy measure. In other instances, regimes can become much more or less democratic but do so through a protracted and gradual process rather than in one discrete event. Therefore, for those who

---

[6] Another important example is how the dataset on autocracy types and autocratic breakdown provided by Geddes (1999), and subsequently updated by Geddes et al (2014), has helped shape the study and understanding of how autocratic politics works in, for example, party-based, military, and personalist regimes.

conceive of democracy as a continuous dimension, there are limits to the types of analysis that can be conducted using binary regime indicators.

The development of interval measures of democracy has further refined our knowledge of democratization processes. For example, Kennedy (2010) demonstrates how the Polity2 index (from Marshall et al. 2013) can improve our understanding of the development–democracy relationship. By leveraging small changes on the Polity scale as indicators of institutional change, Kennedy makes the key distinction between those factors that influence whether a regime breaks down and those factors that influence whether the new regime that replaces the old one is more or less democratic. He finds that rich autocracies are less likely to experience regime change, but when they do, they typically move toward democracy. This may contribute to explaining the null relationship between income and democratization reported by Przeworski and colleagues (1997, 2000) using the binary democracy measure.

To finalize the illustration of how refined measures of democracy with more extensive time series coverage can provide new insights into substantive causal relationships, we turn to Knutsen et al. (2019a). This recent study utilizes V-Dem data to consider even more nuanced relationships between development and different aspects of democracy. The authors theorize that economic development may have distinct effects on different aspects of democracy, highlighting the particular institutional and other features of electoral democracy that may facilitate a strong link. Testing the related expectations by drawing on various V-Dem measures, the authors find a clear link between development and *electoral* democracy but not with several other varieties of democracy, such as participatory and deliberative democracy. The relationship between development and electoral democracy survives even when accounting for time-invariant, country-specific factors that may confound the relationship (cf. Acemoglu et al. 2008), and the relationship is stronger when considering how income mitigates democratic downturns, as opposed to facilitating democratic upturns. This is just one illustration of how rich, disaggregated democracy data with extensive coverage has helped democracy researchers achieve more nuanced and empirically founded insights into the determinants of democracy.

We could also turn this presentation on its head and focus on the limitations placed on our understanding of the causes and consequences of democracy in the absence of datasets such as V-Dem. Increasingly, one might argue, the limitations of extant democracy measures were responsible for impasses in this research program. Even the most widely used cross-national measures of democracy are problematic (see, e.g., Coppedge et al. 2020, 149–158; Munck and Verkuilen 2002). It has, for example, never been very clear what concept of democracy the alternative graded measures are capturing. They are highly aggregated and the procedures for aggregation are opaque (for Freedom House) or are of murky variables (for Polity). Further, the reliability and precision of these measures is unknown, aside from those generated by combining many measures in a latent-variable analysis (as in Coppedge et al. 2008; Pemstein et al. 2010; Treier and Jackman 2008).

As a result, when different researchers reach different conclusions about whether some predictor has a significant effect, there is always some concern that the outcome (whether significant or not) is due to how democracy is defined; the extent to which the democracy measure might be biased by attributes unrelated to democracy such as income, corruption, or a vague national reputation; noise, that is, random measurement error; or the limited geographic and historical coverage of the sample due to missing democracy values. Our hope is that V-Dem data – given the attributes that are described later in the text – can lessen such sources of uncertainty about findings.[7]

The best, most recent book-length synthesis is Teorell (2010), which is now more than a decade old and relied solely on Freedom House data for 1972–2006. It also predates V-Dem, which expanded the quantitative evidence, improved its quality, and distinguished among hundreds of distinct institutions and aspects of democracy. It is time for a fresh effort to retest all the major hypotheses about democratization so that we can update our understanding of which conditions matter, which do not, and which questions remain open and need to be addressed by other approaches. However, before summarizing the contributions made by the various chapters of this book, and the overall argument, we provide a description of V-Dem.

1.4 VARIETIES OF DEMOCRACY DATA

One motivation for writing this book is the belief that V-Dem data make it possible to do a better job of quantitatively testing the many hypotheses about democratization than has been possible heretofore.[8] What justifies this belief? We and others in the V-Dem project have written a separate book that addresses these questions exhaustively (Coppedge et al. 2020). Here we highlight some of the key arguments. The V-Dem dataset currently comprises over 27 million data points covering over 450 indicators – both factual indicators as well as more evaluative ones pertaining to how institutions work in practice – for 202 political units, with the longest time series extending from 1789 to the present. Hence, as the description of trends in Chapter 2 of this volume illustrates, the dataset covers the entirety of modern history. This includes a somewhat longer time period and more countries than the most complete alternatives – Polity (Marshall et al. 2013) and Boix et al. (2013). Given that democracy has evolved over long spans of time, a long time series is essential for a full understanding of this evolution.

---

[7] For a more thorough investigation of how different features of the V-Dem data present opportunities for drawing stronger inferences about the causes and consequences of democracy, see Coppedge et al. (2020, Chapter 7).

[8] Although we recognize qualitative and multimethod research as valuable in complementary ways, doing a good job with quantitative methods in this book requires us to leave them aside for now.

Behind these data lies a new approach to conceptualizing and measuring democracy. The core principle is that "democracy" is a multidimensional concept. As such, the indicators collected and indices constructed to measure democracy should reflect the concept's complexity. V-Dem distinguishes between and measures five high-level principles of democracy, namely electoral, liberal, participatory, deliberative, and egalitarian democracy. These democracy measures are described in Chapter 2 and in even greater detail in Coppedge et al. (2020).[9] The data are also far more fine-grained than any alternative: V-Dem provides not just one or a few measures of democracy, but hundreds of indicators on key political institutions and aspects of politics even beyond the dozens included in the indices capturing the democracy principles (e. g., corruption, gender-specific protection of civil liberties, electoral systems, social identity of the regime's support groups, the types of legitimacy claims that regimes make, state bureaucracies, and the use of social media in politics).[10]

This book does not begin to make full use of this distinctiveness, as most of our analyses concern the most conventional EDI, which we often refer to as a measure of "polyarchy," as it was designed to hew closely to Robert Dahl's concept. However, the distinctiveness is crucial for generating new insights in certain analyses, especially those concerning the relationship between civil society and electoral democracy in Chapter 6 as well as the descriptive overview, which distinguishes trends in components of democracy and varieties of democracy, in Chapter 2. Likewise, in Chapter 6 of this volume, Hicken et al. draw on measures capturing key aspects of how state-bureaucratic institutions function, proxying for state capacity.

With 202 political units, including independent states (both current and some historical ones), semi-sovereign entities, and colonies, the V-Dem data cover more countries than Polity, the next closest alternative, even though some microstates are still missing. The inclusion of colonies means that V-Dem data can be used to address several key questions pertaining to colonial politics – for example, how colonial networks facilitate the diffusion of regime characteristics (see Chapter 4) – that previous democracy datasets covering only independent states have been unable to address.[11] Often a country's first experiences with elections, legislatures, a free press, civil society (see Chapter 7), and other components of democracy began before it was a sovereign, self-governing state. Ignoring that experience often means overlooking the beginning of the story.

---

[9] Another source is the V-Dem Working Paper "Comparisons and Contrasts" where these principles are discussed and V-Dem's data is discussed in relation to essentially all other data sources on democracy. See Coppedge et al. (2017).

[10] For an extensive discussion on some of the different sets of indicators contained in V-Dem that are not part of any of the democracy indices, see, Teorell and Lindberg (2019), Djuve et al. (2020), and the Digital Society Project, http://digitalsocietyproject.org/.

[11] Freedom House rates the few remaining colonies from 1972.

The extensive cross-country and time series coverage, in addition to the large number of indicators, means that V-Dem is one of the largest social science data collection efforts in the world. This is also reflected in the number of people involved in the construction of the dataset. V-Dem relies on an extensive, global network of democracy researchers to create the V-Dem dataset.[12] In addition to all the researchers in the wider V-Dem team and the large number of Research Assistants (RAs) and others involved in the coding of factual indicators, more than 3,000 country-experts are involved in coding V-Dem's evaluative indicators, each of which are typically scored by five or more experts per country-year.

Despite being only a few years old, the V-Dem dataset is already widely used by academics, journalists, policymakers, and the general public. Since its first public release in 2016 through early 2020, the V-Dem dataset and documentation were downloaded over 182,000 times by users in 176 countries or territories. The data have been featured in several high-profile publications on various topics pertaining to democracy and political institutions more broadly. For example, studies concerning recent global regime developments and patterns of autocratization (Lührman and Lindberg 2019), how the granting of civil liberties to women precedes broader and more successful democratization (Wang et al. 2017), how party institutionalization enhances economic growth (Bizzarro et al. 2018), and how democracy and media freedom mitigates the construction of skyscrapers (Gjerløw and Knutsen 2019), all draw insights from V-Dem data. Beyond academia, the V-Dem Institute's annual Democracy Report, which draws exclusively on the V-Dem data, is now a leading authoritative source on global trends for democracy and autocracy among international organizations, governments, and (I)NGOs.[13]

In many ways, V-Dem is redefining how we measure and study democracy. Its variety of measures, transparent construction of indices, and attention to concept-measure consistency means that V-Dem measures score high in terms of validity relative to other cross-country indices such as those from the Polity Project and Freedom House (see Boese 2019.) The long time series and the multiple measures for different political institutions also allow us to better account for various types of confounding related to both observable and unobservable factors, while simultaneously obtaining efficient estimates.[14] When key relationships between regime outcomes and different international, economic, and other causal factors are context-dependent (see, e.g., Boix 2011), V-Dem data allow researchers to empirically assess temporal heterogeneity.

---

[12] We refer to various chapters in Coppedge et al. (2020) for more detailed discussions on the process of constructing the V-Dem dataset, as well as its contents, methodology, benefits, and limitations.

[13] The Democracy Reports as well as the V-Dem data can be downloaded from the V-Dem website: https://v-dem.net

[14] For discussions on this topic, see Chapter 7, Coppedge et al. (2020).

Finally, the large number of indices and measures pertaining to different varieties of democracy allow us to consider whether potential determinants have heterogeneous effects on different aspects of democracy. This edited volume brings to the fore an initial set of substantive findings from analyses using these new and unique data. These extensive data allow us to draw information from and to generalize to most countries using a nearly complete range of years during which anything resembling modern democracy existed.

Despite the extensive scope and unparalleled validity of the V-Dem data, there are still some issues that we cannot address with these data. First, the data are observational – as are all data that we know of at a similar level of analysis. It is neither practically feasible nor normatively desirable to run experiments that alter the core national institutional structure of a country. Therefore, despite our best efforts, some confounding necessarily remains when we investigate relationships between V-Dem measures of democracy and plausible determinants. Second, because all our indicators are at the national level, in practice often coded with annual granularity, the data are not as fine-grained as qualitative data used in process-tracing case studies.

Third, one key concern with any cross-national measure of democracy, and which also presents particular challenges to V-Dem given its reliance on several thousand different country experts, is how to ensure comparability in scores across countries and over time. The primary tool for addressing this comparability issue in V-Dem is its measurement model, which is described in detail elsewhere (see Coppedge et al. 2020, Chapter 4; Marquardt and Pemstein 2018; Pemstein et al. 2019).[15] Although there is no way to prove definitively that

---

[15] In brief, this Bayesian item response theory (IRT) model is based on the assumption that there is a continuous underlying reality for each indicator that all country experts rating the same country-years on that indicator perceive. They rate their evaluations as "raw scores" on the various (ordinal-level, typically five-point scale) questions in the V-Dem survey. The measurement model estimates the extent to which disagreements among country experts are the result of differential item function (DIF) – one expert's "2" being equivalent to another expert's "3," and so on – and corrects for it, so that scores become more comparable. For example, if an expert for Russia scores her country as considerably less free in terms of media censorship than an expert for France scores his country, we cannot immediately know how much of this difference is due to differences in the country context and how much is due to experts' differential understanding of the ordinal scale. By drawing information from each expert's coding of many years, some experts' coding across countries (bridging), and their responses to identical hypothetical scenarios (vignettes), the measurement model can estimate differences in how experts understand the response scales, thus making scores more comparable across countries and over time. Drawing also on coders' ratings of several countries and on experts' ratings of anchoring vignettes, it weights the contributions by different experts according to their estimated (question-specific) reliability and considers various patterns, such as overlap with other experts' ratings, to provide uncertainty estimates of the scores contained in V-Dem. The final outcome is a dataset with measures that are much more comparable across countries and over time – despite drawing on the context-specific knowledge of different experts for each country – and more reliable and valid than simple averages of raw scores. V-Dem also provides estimates of the uncertainty of the scores alongside their point estimates.

V-Dem data are more valid and reliable than other democracy measures, there are good reasons to believe that they are, on average, better than the alternatives.

At the same time, we are the first to recognize that our data contain measurement uncertainty. For that reason, we release measures of the uncertainty. We actually make little use of the uncertainty estimates in this book, but the data to incorporate uncertainty into the analysis are publicly available to anyone who wishes to use them.

1.5 METHODOLOGICAL CONSIDERATIONS

All scientific research must confront the fundamental problem of causal inference: that we can never observe what happens both when a case is treated and when it is not (Imbens and Rubin 2015). It helps – in the sense that we can draw inferences about causal relationships with greater certainty – if the researcher can manipulate the treatment. Experimentalists working with a large sample of cases base their causal inferences on the difference between the average outcome in cases that were randomly assigned to receive treatment and cases that were randomly assigned to a control group.[16] Yet, for many of the phenomena of interest to democracy scholars, experimental data cannot (and often should not) be produced. Democracy scholars therefore typically rely on different types of observational data, as is the case in this book. We see a trade-off. Experimental methods typically provide greater certainty about causal inference and less certainty about generalization, while large-N regressions on observational data typically provide less certainty about causal inference but greater certainty about general tendencies and greater external validity (Coppedge and Kuehn 2019; Findley et al. 2021). Therefore, researchers must still learn important lessons from large-N panel regressions on observational data (and other methods).

In fact, one may go even further: there are certain research questions and relationships of great interest that simply cannot be adequately addressed by experiments or quasi-experiments in practice (Gerring 2012). We seek to understand processes of democratization that are relevant across a very general sample of countries covering more than a century. Experimental methods are inappropriate for understanding complex processes that unfold over long periods of time in wildly different contexts, which are exactly the kinds of processes that we study. Well-designed experiments rely on researchers being able to

---

[16] Although they enhance internal validity, experiments often possess little external validity: generalizations from their conclusions are confounded by elements of the context in which the experiment was conducted, which is held constant by design. This is an issue even in the natural sciences: a drug shown to be effective in experiments conducted on men will not necessarily bring the same benefit to women. In comparative politics, experiments and the question of external validity often pose an even more serious issue. We cannot assume, for example, that the result of an election-observation experiment in Armenia in 2003 (Hyde 2007) would be the same in Armenia in 2018, much less in Finland, Haiti, or Mongolia in 2018. Replication in many countries and clear rules for aggregating across results from such exercises are required for generalization.

manipulate one treatment (or sometimes a small number of treatments) in meticulously controlled environments in which every other condition that might affect the outcome is randomized.

Democratization is manifestly not such a process. Few determinants of democracy can be manipulated by researchers. Sometimes there are plausible natural experiments, but they are also rare and certainly not available in all the countries we wish to understand, for many time periods, or for many hypotheses we need to test. Moreover, even where natural experiments are available, limiting the focus to one or a few determinants necessarily eliminates from consideration all the other likely determinants of democracy. An experimental approach may enable us to understand a small piece of the puzzle, but only by ignoring the whole. Other methods must be used to put all the pieces together.

Although we often use the language of causal inference when we speak of "effects," "determinants," "impacts," and "influence" in this book, we acknowledge that alternative explanations for the patterns that we observe (other than a causal effect of X on Y) inevitably remain. We can often exclude a number of threats to our causal inferences but never get rid of them completely. Hence, the nature of the knowledge that we aspire to would be more properly called "robust dependence" (Goldthorpe 2001).[17] We do not claim that robust dependence is the best, much less the only, way to understand democratization. We believe that the truth lies at the confluence of multiple streams of evidence. We urge social scientists who are adept in other approaches such as qualitative historical case studies or experiments to, wherever possible, subject our findings to other kinds of evidence and testing, and thus complement the analysis that we are doing with country-level data and panel regressions.[18]

---

[17] This means that we provisionally believe findings that (1) have well developed and plausible theoretical rationales; (2) fit the evidence better than alternative hypotheses suggested by competing theories; (3) fit the evidence robustly, that is, even when we use different controls, measures, samples, and estimators; and (4) if they do not hold in very large samples, we are able to show where and when they do fit the evidence, and we have persuasive theoretical reasons for these scope conditions.

[18] Even if we limit our ambition to inferring robust dependence, we face a daunting gauntlet of pivotal and often consequential choices concerning model specification. The quantitative literature on democratization is littered with inconsistent findings, many of which depend on how the dependent variable is defined, which predictors are included in the model, whether the dependent variable is lagged, how long the lags are, which countries and time periods are included in the sample, whether the model uses country or year fixed effects or both, which statistical estimator is used, what assumptions one makes about the distribution of the errors, and so on (see, e.g., Gassebner et al. 2013; Rød et al. 2020). Given that there is a good reason to believe that our findings hinge on the specification choices we have made, we describe and defend those choices here. The authors of the different chapters in this book have made every effort to coordinate their work so that, as much as possible, the findings would be comparable across chapters and the most compelling findings of each chapter could be tested against one another in the conclusion. This was – due to differences in the type of independent variables and relationships studied across the chapters – not possible in every instance. For an overview, we have specified our core models as shown in Table 1.1.

1.6 DEMOCRACY AS OUTCOME: FOUR DEPENDENT VARIABLES

We primarily use the V-Dem's EDI for constructing our dependent variables. There are four main dependent variables used in different chapters of this book: the level, annual change, the magnitude of upturns (annual positive changes), and the magnitude of downturns (annual negative changes). A substantial literature suggests that the factors that explain levels of democracy do not necessarily explain the dynamics of democratization and that the factors that explain changes toward greater democracy do not necessarily explain democratic decline (autocratization). Each of these types of change requires a different theory and a different model. Chapter 5 explains all four outcomes straightforwardly, but each of the other chapters makes some adjustments.

Chapter 3 tests the most exogenous determinants (geography and demography), which are often historically fixed or slowly changing. The relationships are therefore primarily cross-sectional, so these models include year dummies to hold time constant and focus on the differences across countries. Because this chapter sets time aside, it explains only levels of democracy, not changes, upturns, or downturns.

Chapter 4 on international factors faces computational challenges because it attempts to explain not just the effect of some variables on democracy in each country-year but also the impact of each country-year on every other country-year. This chapter makes the computational task feasible by modeling two-year averages rather than annual levels and changes. It does explain levels, changes, upturns, and downturns, but all the lags are over two years rather than one. Furthermore, because modeling spatial dependence forces one to pay attention to thorny problems of endogeneity, the analyses in this chapter employ an instrumental-variables version of spatiotemporal regression.

Chapter 6, which deals with institutions, relies on hazard models because much of the relevant literature examines the possibility that institutions affect probabilities of transition and breakdown. Unlike most of this literature, however, Chapter 6 tests transitions above and below every possible threshold of electoral democracy – an innovative and revealing exercise.

Chapter 7 on civil society and social forces models all four dependent variables, but for some models cannot use the EDI because it contains some of V-Dem's civil society indicators; these indicators would appear both on the right- and left-hand side of the equation if EDI were to be used, thus giving endogeneity by construction. Instead, this chapter uses a custom-built index of "procedural" democracy that excludes the civil society components when measuring social forces using V-Dem variables. This chapter therefore explains variation in a minimalist version of democracy, capturing core features of electoral competition and participation.

Although the chapters reflect somewhat different modeling choices, all of them increase our understanding of the factors that affect levels of democracy and the dynamics of democratization and reversals. In fact, the variety of

TABLE 1.1 *Model specification by chapter*

Chapter	3 Geography	4 Space	5 Economics	6 Institutions	7 Society	8 Conclusion
Estimator						
Panel regression	x	x	x	x	x	x
Hazard model				x		
Spatiotemporal IV panel regression		x				
Dependent variables						
Electoral Democracy Index	x	x	x	x		x
Minimal Democracy Index					x	
Level	x	x	x		x	x
Change			x		x	
Upturn		x	x		x	x
Downturn		x	x		x	x
Step-up (across c.74 thresholds)				x		
Step-down (across c.74 thresholds)				x		
Minimum sample	5,703	6,753*	3,693	2,229	9,265	5,127
Maximum sample	24,205	6,855*	16,978	6,825	10,205	8,301
Fixed effects (in any model)						
countries			x		x	x

(*continued*)

					decades
regions	x		x		
years			x	x	x
Lags (number of years)					
Dependent variable		2	1 (& 5, 10)**	1	1
Independent variables	1 or 100	0 or 2	1 (& 5, 10)**	1	1 & 2
Clustered standard errors in any model	x		x	x	x
Spatially correlated errors		x			

Notes: * Units are two-year averages. ** Numbers in parentheses are for robustness checks in an appendix.

approaches adds more nuance to this understanding than would have been possible if each chapter had conformed to a standard base model. The conclusion (Chapter 8) provides a theoretical and empirical synthesis of this new understanding of democratization.[19]

We use the largest samples that the data permit. As noted earlier, V-Dem's EDI furnishes scores for practically all countries, including most colonies, from 1900 to 2018, and for more than 202 countries since the first year of their existence, as far back as 1789. If we could use all of this data (as Chapters 2 and 3 nearly do for some analyses), there would be less risk of sample bias. The constraints come from missingness in the predictors. Sample sizes therefore unavoidably vary from chapter to chapter, and the varying sample can still produce sample bias. We have tried to be conscientious about how these changing sample sizes affect the generality of our conclusions; here and there we check some conclusions by expanding coverage with multiple imputations (Honaker and King 2010).

Another problem that we face is that the controls employed in our statistical analyses are inadequate: some variables that are correlated with the dependent variable and one or more predictors have been omitted, biasing the estimates. This has been a problem in democratization research historically, as in many other social science research fields. For example, what used to be universally accepted received wisdom – that per capita GDP is the single most robust predictor of democracy – has been questioned on the grounds that it is largely a spurious relationship between unobserved slowly changing conditions that determine both income and democracy (Acemoglu et al. 2008). Observational studies cannot eliminate omitted variable bias completely, but they must reduce this risk as much as possible.

Our models do this, first, by specifying selected control variables that are the most plausible confounders of the variables of interest in each chapter. Second, however, because it is not possible to anticipate and measure all possible omitted variables in a large sample, we take the extra precaution of controlling for country or region fixed effects when possible. This procedure holds each country's mean level of democracy constant. In effect, it controls in a rough way for all the omitted determinants of democracy that vary across countries but not within them; examples could be geographical factors or events and developments in a country's deep political history that affect its modern development. The current practice in much of the quantitative democratization literature is therefore to use country fixed effects in panel

---

[19] Apart from the different modeling approaches, the contributors to this book share a vision of how best to minimize confounding while striving for generality. This vision includes – whenever possible – using large samples with carefully chosen control variables, a lagged dependent variable, lagged predictors, country (or, alternatively, region) fixed effects, clustered standard errors, and year fixed effects. The shared vision also includes paying attention to endogeneity biases of different kinds (e.g., stemming from reverse causality) and carrying out extensive robustness checks to ensure that results are not driven by particular specification choices.

models. Most of our chapters do this. However, Chapter 3 examines long-run factors, which are often fixed themselves and would be dropped with fixed-effect estimation. Some models in that chapter, therefore, control for regional fixed effects instead, and other models estimate random effects (Chapter 8, Table 8.1).[20] Some other omitted variables might be associated with time rather than space. One possibility is that there are period effects reflecting, for example, the impact of the Great Depression, world wars, or the coronavirus pandemic on democratization. Chapter 4 models some possible period effects as exogenous shocks; most other chapters control for year dummies or splines.[21]

Another kind of issue related to time is serial autocorrelation: the fact (in this application) that the past weighs heavily on the unexplained variation in our democracy variables. Having long time series at our disposal gives us the leverage to learn about and model the influence of the past. However, there is no reliable guidance about how long temporal lags should be, and we recognize that these choices can have major consequences. Our default is to lag all predictors by one year, include the lagged dependent variable as a regressor, and cluster errors by country, but there are several exceptions that we document and justify in each chapter. With panel data on levels of democracy, the coefficient on the lagged dependent variable tends to be around 0.9, which raises concerns about non-stationarity and the "washing out" of other time-trended variables (Achen 2000). Our models of change, upturns, and downturns are other ways of dealing with serial autocorrelation and yield insights about the dynamics of regime change.

Lagging our independent variables and adding the lagged dependent variable has the added benefit of increasing confidence in the direction of the causal arrows. It helps reduce the possibility that democracy causes our predictor variables rather than the reverse. Simple lags can take us only so far; it may, for some relationships studied in this book, be better to add Granger causality tests, structural equation models, and mediation analyses to study proposed complex causal chains. Our concluding chapter takes steps toward implementing these strategies. However, there is a limit to what we can accomplish in one volume. We and other researchers will certainly follow up the results presented in this book with more rigorous analyses in the future. In sum, by adding lagged dependent variables, it is possible that we over-correct for serial dependence, making it too hard to identify true relationships. However, we think it is best to be cautious: following this strategy increases confidence in the

[20] Chapter 4 on spatial dependence faces computational challenges in including a large number of country or year dummies, so omits them.

[21] While these strategies deal with time-varying confounders that affect all countries similarly on the dependent variable, we remind readers that they are insufficient for dealing with *causal relationships* between particular independent variables of interest and our dependent variables varying over time. As discussed earlier in this chapter, addressing such temporally heterogeneous effects lies outside the scope of this book, which focuses on the robustness of general relationships.

predictors that robustly survive these severe corrections, even if we do this at the risk of failing to pick up some relevant relationships.

Another type of confounding that we address is spatial dependence. It is likely that democracy in each country depends partly on democracy in other countries: they are not independent observations. Where there is spatial dependence, one of the requirements for causal identification, the Stable Unit Treatment Value Assumption (SUTVA), does not hold. Units interfere with each other, and a treatment applied to one unit can spill over to other units. Dealing with this, even imperfectly, is complicated enough in an observational setting; dealing with it perfectly in an experimental setting is many times harder (Aronow and Samii 2013). Chapter 4 assesses how much of a threat to inference spatial dependence poses for democratization research and concludes, reassuringly, that although there is significant spatiotemporal independence, in the short term it is too small to noticeably affect estimates of the effects of domestic variables on the level of electoral democracy. In the long run, however, spatial dependence – particularly among neighboring countries – makes a large difference for levels of EDI in the more democratic regions of the world.

Endogeneity is typically rampant in complex processes that unfold over centuries. Partly for this reason, we thought it important to include Chapter 3 on geography, the most distal and exogenous of all determinants of democratization, and demographic characteristics of society such as population and European migration, which follow paths laid down long before modern democratic regimes emerged. We can often be relatively certain that the estimated "effects" of these distant features, as captured by our regression coefficients, are causal, but much less certain of the mechanisms through which they operate. At the other extreme of the funnel of causality, we test very proximate determinants such as anti-system movements, internal war, and economic growth. It is harder to assess their causal significance in part because they may be endogenous to prior developments such as per capita income, ethnic fractionalization, and long-standing institutional arrangements, but if they matter, the mechanisms through which they act often narrow to a smaller set of possibilities.

Aside from Chapter 8, we have not attempted more complex and sophisticated empirical tests of the sequencing of our many determinants of democratization such as structural equation modeling. Instead, we simply take care to interpret each variable of interest properly given the covariates in each chapter. If the variable is probably endogenous to an omitted exogenous variable, we exercise caution about its independent contribution to the outcome. If we do control for known exogenous factors, we report more confidence in how much the variable in focus matters. We avoid including posttreatment confounders because they can obscure the full impact of the variables exogenous to them. However, what is a posttreatment confounder in one model may be the variable of interest in another, in which case we are careful to interpret its effect as an effect above and beyond the contributions of the conditions that preceded it. For these reasons, in Chapter 8, we use path-analytic structural equations to appropriately specify and test endogenous relationships among the most promising variables from Chapters 3 to 7.

It would certainly be possible to make any of these analyses more rigorous. For example, one complication of having long time series, which we have already indicated, is that they give the world a long time to change in fundamental ways, raising questions about whether it is fair to subject a hypothesis to a test that assumes that the relationship is the same in 1918 and 2018. Ideally, we would conduct robustness checks to discover the ways in which our conclusions are limited to specific historical periods. We could also make more frequent use of alternative estimators such as two stage least squares (2SLS) or the generalized method of moments (GMM), which might increase the rigor of our estimates under certain conditions; be more adventurous in our testing of interactions; and so forth. However, it is not possible to eliminate all uncertainty or explore all possible nuances to the many relationships studied in this book. Regarding the former, we are comfortable with uncertainty, including looking beyond the p-values to consider also specification uncertainty, selection bias, spatial confounding, and so on. Regarding the latter, we hope that future research on democracy will follow up and suggest nuances on the many relationships under study in this volume, both through the development of more detailed theory but also various empirical tests of effect heterogeneity and interactive relationships.

Ultimately, the findings we offer are provisional. As in all sciences, they are subject to revision when others have better data, better models, or better methods. There are never any guarantees that our findings will stand the test of time. Nevertheless, V-Dem data marks such an advance that it is worthwhile to conduct a comprehensive, new analysis using these extensive data and to state a rough-hewn but new and ambitious vision of what we provisionally understand about the causes of democratization.

1.7 OVERVIEW

Chapter 2, by Knutsen and Skaaning, describes "The Ups and Downs of Democracy, 1789–2018," tracking the spread of democracy globally across modern history using different indicators and indices from V-Dem. The chapter speaks to several prominent debates about patterns of regime development. The authors begin by focusing on electoral democracy and consider its spread from the American constitution and the French Revolution in 1789 until the present day. Over this period, the world has witnessed a massive but uneven spread of electoral democracy. Some periods have seen more change than others: substantial upturns and downturns have tended to cluster in different parts of the world in different periods. Thereafter, Knutsen and Skaaning take a disaggregated perspective, discussing trends in the subcomponents of electoral democracy, that is, adult suffrage, elected officials, clean elections, freedom of association, and freedom of expression. By doing so, they reveal that these aspects of democracy did not develop in parallel and that their covariation has changed substantially over time. In the final part of the chapter, Knutsen and Skaaning change the focus from electoral democracy to supplementary components associated with "thicker" understandings of democracy, namely the liberal, deliberative, participatory, and egalitarian components of democracy. These comparisons show that their respective trends are fairly similar to that of electoral democracy, with the exception of a steadier increase in the egalitarian component after World War II.

The subsequent five chapters of the volume assess the relationships between different clusters of potential determinants and democracy. Chapter 3 by Gerring focuses on the long-run factors that include various geographic, historical, and demographic determinants of regime types. The chapter begins with what is surely the most distal set of potential causes of democracy, namely those rooted in geography, such as climate, soil, topography, and waterways. Section 3.2 discusses Islam, which many believe to have a negative effect on prospects for democracy. Section 3.3 considers influences related to the spread of Europeans throughout the world, including colonialism (especially the English colonial experience), religion (especially the various Protestant sects), and Europeans themselves (who had a dramatic impact on the demographic composition of the New World, in particular). Section 3.4 explores the role of population, population density, and urbanization. Section 3.5 examines the diversity of populations with respect to ethnicity and religion. Gerring finds that distance from nearest natural harbor and temperature are negatively correlated with democracy in all model specifications. Among the factors associated with European colonialism, Protestantism and Europeans (both measured as a share of population) are positively associated with democracy in all model specifications. However, none of the other demographic factors are strongly associated with the level of electoral democracy. Gerring finds a weak positive relationship for ethnic heterogeneity and a weak negative relationship for religious heterogeneity, but neither is very robust. Finally, although Islam is a robust predictor of democracy, Gerring discusses plausible reasons to suspect this relationship is spurious.

Chapter 4 by Coppedge, Denison, Friesen, Tiscornia, and Xu develops and tests hypotheses about possible causes of democratization that lie beyond national borders, starting from a theoretical framework that systematically catalogues most of the plausible international hypotheses. Employing the best available spatial econometric methods, these authors find that international shocks such as war and global economic expansion affect levels of electoral democracy, upturns, and downturns. All four of the international networks that Coppedge et al. test – contiguity, alliances, current colonial ties, and former colonial ties – channel contagion for at least one of the four outcomes, and contiguity matters for all of them. The contagion effects that they report appear small as short-term, global averages, but are larger in some regions and in the long term, after they have reverberated through the international system and accumulated over many years. Hence, the authors find that for researchers who limit their attention to global averages of short-term relationships, it is probably unnecessary to account for any international influences other than exogenous shocks. However, the authors caution that a fuller understanding of democratization requires taking long-term, regional relationships into account.

Chapter 5 by Knutsen and Dahlum maintains a focus on time-varying and fairly proximate determinants of democracy but shifts the focus to domestic economic determinants. The authors note that despite an extensive body of literature on the economic explanations of democracy, robust findings are relatively rare. They review relevant literatures and retest various relationships between democracy and (1) indicators of economic development, (2) structural features of the economy, (3) short-term economic performance, and (4) economic inequality. The authors discuss why the economic determinants of democratization may differ from those of democratic decline, and therefore distinguish between positive and negative changes in democracy in their empirical analyses. Their analyses also account for potential omitted time-invariant, country-specific factors that simultaneously affect democracy and economic variables. Knutsen and Dahlum's analysis lends support to revisionism regarding the modernization thesis: when properly modeled, per capita income (usually logged) is associated with higher levels of electoral democracy and less severe downturns. They do not find support for an impact of income on upturns. However, they do identify other robust predictors of both democratic upturns and downturns. Notably, they find evidence that a high share of agricultural production is negatively linked to democratic upturns and that good short-term economic performance reduces the magnitude of democratic downturns.

Chapter 6, by Hicken, Baltz, and Vasselai, considers the relationship between political institutions and democracy. These authors ask the following questions: Do certain kinds of political institutions – state capacity, executive regime type (presidentialism vs. parliamentarism), and the party system – make democracy more or less durable? Are some configurations of institutions more or less conducive to democracy? To what extent do political institutions influence the degree or quality of democracy? The authors review some of the prominent arguments regarding the relationship between different types of political institutions and democracy. In their empirical analysis, Hicken et al. use the long time series data from V-Dem to reevaluate the leading arguments. Specifically, they focus on two primary outcomes of interest – probability of breakdown or survival of democracy and the level of democracy. The authors find strong support for the positive influence of state capacity on these outcomes, but mixed or no support for executive regime type or party system variables. The authors then conclude by discussing the important role of electoral experience in many of their statistical model specifications.

Chapter 7 by Bernhard and Edgell considers the role of social forces. Their point of departure is the notion that new social forces emerging through economic development act as the chief agents translating structural change into political change. These popular struggles for representation and incorporation have long occupied a prominent place in our understanding of regime change. Even elite-driven democratic transitions are often thought to require moments of mass mobilization that push liberalization over the threshold into regime change. Many scholars also contend that after the installation of democracy, an active citizenry leads to democratic stability through more effective government. Yet, other scholars warn that a mobilized and polarized civil society can *undermine* democracy – particularly if the demands of social forces outstrip the capacity of institutions to process these demands. After an extensive review of the existing literature and arguments, the authors proceed to explore empirically the role of social organization and mobilization on democracy. The role of social forces in democracy and democratization has until recently been difficult to study in a large-N framework. This was, in part, due to the scarcity of comparable cross-national data covering a large number of countries over an extended time. It was also due to the distinct ontology found in theorizing about social forces. While it remains impossible in a large-N setup to track and measure social forces in the same ways that small-N researchers do, V-Dem and the Nonviolent and Violent Campaigns and Outcomes (NAVCO) project provide new measures of civil society organization and mobilization. These measures enable Bernhard and Edgell to gauge the extent to which organized and mobilized social forces are responsible for levels, upturns, and downturns of democracy. Based on a sample of 156 countries from 1900 to 2014, the authors find evidence that both civil society organizations and nonviolent protest affect democracy in positive ways, and that, among a range of different political actors, right-wing anti-system movements may constitute a threat to democracy.

As our summary of the individual chapters indicates, the proposed determinants of democracy vary in scope and proximity to the outcome. Some factors are widely anticipated to (mainly) influence processes of democratization, or democratic upturns, such as the mobilization of urban mass protests dealt with in Chapter 7, whereas others are most likely to affect only downturns, such as presidential versus parliamentary systems of government studied in Chapter 6. Some pertain to more structural features such as the geographical factors discussed in Chapter 3, whereas others are clearly linked to collective action by particular groups of actors, such as the nonviolent campaigns discussed in Chapter 7.

Another distinguishing feature of this book is the time dimension, which is more often overlooked in the democracy literature than, for example, the distinction between structure- versus agency-related factors. Yet researchers do tend to assume that some determinants of democracy work with a long time lag (such as effects of geographical factors like natural harbors or some economic factors like land inequality), while others unfold and affect regime change very quickly (such as episodes of hyperinflation, studied in Chapter 4). In other words, determinants of democratization operate on vastly different timescales.

Despite the large number and diversity of these "explanations of democracy," we strive to show how many partial and incomplete determinants and explanations can fit together in a more comprehensive and coherent whole. In the concluding chapter, we detail how different sets of determinants are linked together in long causal chains – sometimes with feedback loops between the different determinants. Hence, factors that, at first glance, seem to be rival explanations turn out to be complementary explanations tied to different links in the same long causal chains. Some factors are more exogenous in the sense that they are less influenced by other determinants of democracy, whereas more endogenous factors can be treated as intermediate variables that are important in transmitting the effect from the more exogenous factors on democratic upturns or downturns, as well as contributing independent influences of their own.

Building comprehensive and more elaborate explanations of democracy requires that we specify the causal sequence and possible feedback mechanisms, not only between the different proposed determinants of democratic upturns and downturns but also the feedback mechanisms between these various determinants within the causal sequence. Further, the range of temporal lags and different time scales also points to the need to explicitly discuss the time dimension with which these different determinants affect *each other* in addition to the main outcome of interest, democracy.

Finally, the seemingly sharp distinction between structure- and agency-centered explanations of democracy can be overcome by taking a more comprehensive view and building broader explanations that explicitly consider the relationships between different determinants of democracy. Such comprehensive explanations would consider how structural factors that correlate with democracy – whether natural harbors, high income levels, or urbanization – influence the power resources or incentives of very different actors in society – the urban middle classes, labor unions, political party operatives, parliamentarians, and the incumbent leader – to either work for regime change or to stabilize the existing regime. Changes to structural factors may thus spur different social groups or organized actors to double down on their efforts to engage in collective action that may lead to democratization (or stabilizing existing democracy, e.g., by thwarting military coups or self-coups by sitting leaders). Alternatively, these actors may choose to work to maintain nondemocratic regimes that may benefit the empowered group. Structure- and agency-centered factors are nested and they interact to affect democracy levels and change.

Most of the independent variables used in this book will be familiar to students of democratization. However, many researchers have studied them selectively, paying close attention to one school of thought while relegating other variables to the background. The contributions of the concluding chapter are, first, to test the best variables from each school of thought against the others; second, to propose how to place each variable properly in causal sequences; and third, to demonstrate that these sequences make theoretical sense and are consistent with the most abundant empirical evidence attainable today. This exercise is as much about building theory as it is about testing it. We hope that many scholars will follow these lines of inquiry, testing them in different ways and contributing to a more comprehensive theory of democratization.

2

The Ups and Downs of Democracy, 1789–2018

Carl Henrik Knutsen and Svend-Erik Skaaning

2.1 INTRODUCTION

The democratic ideal – or ideals, if we take on V-Dem's pluralistic view of the core concept – will never be fully achieved. But variations in the degree of democracy, however understood, within the range of regimes that we observe throughout the world are not hard to spot. According to any plausible definition of democracy that we know of, North Korea is less democratic than Norway, and Eritrea is less democratic than Estonia. Such variation in the degree of democracy matters. It matters because of the intrinsic value of democracy. No other form of political rule recognizes the fundamental rights of citizens to free and equal participation in making collectively binding decisions for a society (Dahl 1989). It also matters because how democratic a political regime is seems to influence a range of other outcomes that we care about, such as economic growth (Gerring et al. 2005; Knutsen 2012), human development (Gerring et al. 2012, 2021), happiness (Inglehart et al. 2008; Rahman and Venhoven 2018), domestic peace (Bartucevicius and Skaaning 2018; Davenport 2007; Rummel 1997), international peace (Maoz & Russett 1993; Weart 1998; Hegre 2014), and environmental protection (Bättig and Bernauer 2009; Li and Reuveny 2006).

It is therefore not surprising that global trends in democratic development have drawn a great deal of attention from scholars and others and been the topic of intense debates. Notably, the focus on global patterns of upturns and downturns in democracy was reinforced when Huntington (1991) published his classic statement on the "waves" and "reverse waves" of democratization. The shape of these trends, for instance related to the number of waves or the exact start and end dates of a particular wave, has been intensely discussed ever since (e.g., Berg-Schlosser 2009; Doorenspleet 2000; Lührmann and Lindberg 2019; Møller and Skaaning 2013; Skaaning 2020). At present, the discussion – both in academia and in the public sphere – centers on the question of whether we are currently witnessing a global reverse wave or not (e.g., Carothers and Young 2017; Diamond and Plattner 2015; Lührmann et al. 2018; Skaaning and Jeminez 2017).

In this chapter, we draw on data from V-Dem to revisit these issues and other descriptive questions related to the global spread of democratic institutions. Our point of departure is that previous overviews and analyses of the global upturns and downturns of democracy have suffered from several shortcomings. First, many such analyses have only covered recent decades rather than the whole period of modern democracy. Second, they have mostly relied on measures with less fine-grained scales (often binary) and questionable methodologies (see Coppedge et al. 2011; Munck 2009). Third, scrutiny of democratic development has generally been based on aggregate measures rather than measures of democratic subcomponents. Fourth, extant measures have only captured a single understanding of democracy – typically centering on notions of electoral democracy, although sometimes involving liberal or participatory elements such as the rule of law and electoral turnout.

Against this backdrop, we present and discuss new overviews of trends in global democratization. Our agenda in this chapter is mainly to describe rather than to explain. Causal explanations have a high priority in political science, for good reasons. Yet, good descriptions are crucial, too (Gerring 2012). We care about *how* democracy has spread and contracted around the world and not only *why*. Moreover, descriptive analysis is a fruitful way to set the stage for subsequent attempts to explain some of the interesting spatial and temporal variations, which is the aim of the subsequent chapters.

All empirical analyses are based on V-Dem data (see Coppedge et al. 2019a, 2019b), which allow us to provide a comprehensive overview of trends in global democratization from 1789 to 2018. Our assessment should help reveal whether *what we think we know* about global democratic trends is valid if we base our assessment on more comprehensive, nuanced, and disaggregated data. Besides shedding new light on old questions, we are also able to address some new questions because of the broad coverage and fine-grained nature of V-Dem data. The questions and patterns addressed in the remainder of the chapter are as follows.

We start out by focusing on a common notion of democracy, namely electoral democracy or "polyarchy," as defined by Dahl (1989; see also Dahl 1971). We first consider the spread of electoral democracy, as measured by V-Dem's Polyarchy index (Teorell et al. 2019), covering the whole period of modern democracy from its beginning with the French Revolution and the American Constitution in 1789 until the present day (see also Knutsen et al. 2019a). Over this period, the world has obviously witnessed a massive spread of electoral democracy. However, the spread has been uneven. Some periods have seen more change than others, and substantial upturns and downturns have tended to cluster in different parts of the world in different periods: Abrupt improvements happened in Europe with the liberal revolutions in 1848–1849 as well as right after World War I, in Europe and Latin America after World War II, and in all regions of the world but Western Europe, North America, and the Middle East at the end of the Cold War. The only major downturn took place in the 1930s in Europe and Latin America. When placed in a historical context and judged by average scores across countries, several recent claims about the magnitude or early onset of a current reverse wave or wave of autocratization seem to be exaggerated. Moreover, there have continuously been noteworthy differences in the level of electoral democracy across regions and countries, where North America, Australasia, and Western and Central Europe have typically achieved the highest levels of electoral democracy and Central Asia and the Middle East (broadly understood) the lowest.

In Section 2.4, we take on a disaggregate perspective and look at trends in the subcomponents of the Polyarchy measure, that is, adult suffrage, elected officials, clean elections, freedom of association, and freedom of expression. We do this to reveal any idiosyncratic patterns pertaining to how the institutions and practices associated with electoral democracy have developed historically. More specifically, we investigate whether covariations among particular subcomponents of democracy have changed over time. Our findings demonstrate that there are noteworthy differences in the disaggregate trends: The presence of elected parliaments and government responsibility (directly or indirectly) to the electorate trended upward before suffrage and clean elections until World War I. Today, just a few countries do not have elected parliaments and electorally responsible governments. Also, universal suffrage has gradually become the rule with only a few exceptions, while the level of clean elections has experienced more modest increases since the interwar years and still has left much room for improvement. The global averages for freedom of expression and freedom of association have historically followed each other, largely corresponding to the overall democratization trends. Like clean elections, there is still substantial room for improvements in respect to these freedoms, despite the substantial increases.

In Section 2.5, we change our focus from electoral democracy to supplementary components associated with "thicker" understandings of democracy, that is, "liberal democracy," "deliberative democracy," "participatory democracy," and "egalitarian democracy." When doing so, we compare trends in these components with each other and with that of the electoral core shared by all. The results indicate that performance of the different components tends to be highly correlated. That said, some countries do show different performance and trends across components. In particular, performance on the egalitarian component tends to deviate from the other components, as changes are typically more incremental. We also demonstrate that the variance of the components, across countries, are different and have changed over time: Changes in standard deviations of scores on the different components, globally, were not very marked in the twentieth century, apart from electoral democracy around the end of World Wars I and II. All components show more variance in the middle of that century than at the beginning and end. Particularly, electoral democracy and the deliberative component have experienced reduced variation across countries since the early 1980s.

2.2 V-DEM DATA

Before using the data from V-Dem to describe historical trends in democracy, we want to highlight an important methodological point. As for other measures of democracy, the scores provided by V-Dem indicators and indices are associated with uncertainty and potential measurement error. In a given year, research assistants, country experts,[1] or others who code features of democracy may over- or underestimate the scores for certain countries. Such errors can have different sources. They could be the product of conceptual misunderstandings, different standards being applied by different coders/to different cases, flawed interpretations of facts, scarcity of historical records, ambiguous evidence, inattentiveness by the coders, or random mistakes (Coppedge et al. 2019d: 32). Random errors only affect the precision of our estimates, while systematic errors introduce biases.

One benefit with V-Dem indices, compared to most other democracy indices, is that this uncertainty is modeled explicitly. To this end, various sources of information – most notably the degree of agreement among the various experts and the number of coders for a given year, and also personal characteristics of the coders and their self-reported uncertainty estimates and responses to vignettes – are taken into account by V-Dem's Bayesian measurement model (see Coppedge et al. 2020; Pemstein et al. 2019). To highlight this feature of the V-Dem data, Figure 2.1 displays time series for three large countries, two of which were among the countries with the highest Polyarchy score in 1789 (the USA and France) and one with a very low score in 1789 (Brazil). In this figure, we report not only our "best estimates" but also the so-called low scores and high scores given in the V-Dem dataset as uncertainty bounds around the best estimate. These low and high scores provide the bounds for 68 percent of the probability mass of the Polyarchy score, implying that the low/high scores are about one standard deviation below/above the best point estimate.[2]

---

[1] Regarding the number of country experts, the goal for the data collection in the years from 1900 to the present has been to have a minimum of five to code each country-year for every indicator. For different reasons (see Knutsen et al. 2019a), the equivalent number has been one or two for the historical part, where the coding has covered 1789–1920. The overlap of twenty-one years helps the V-Dem measurement model (Pemstein et al. 2019) linking the time series (in addition to other sources of information, including anchoring vignettes).

[2] We note that the uncertainty bounds vary across time and that for Brazil, for example, uncertainty is somewhat higher in the 2000s than for most of the eighteenth and early nineteenth centuries. There could be several underlying reasons for this peculiar pattern. First, uncertainty (in absolute numbers) is typically lower for very low scores on Polyarchy than for intermediate and high

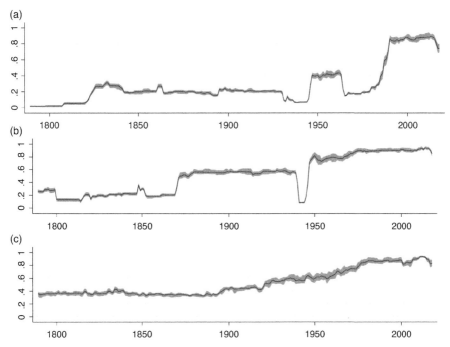

FIGURE 2.1 Polyarchy scores for Brazil (a), France (b), and the USA (c)
Notes: The middle lines represent best estimates, and upper/lower bounds represent scores that are located about ± one standard deviation from the best estimates.

When we consider global trends, as we do for most of this chapter, uncertainty is typically much lower than when we consider trends for particular countries. The reason that the global average is fairly precisely estimated is that countries that are given a too high score are mixed together with and balanced out by other countries with a too low score. In Figure 2.2, we report uncertainty intervals for the global mean on the Polyarchy scale, where the upper bound is created by assuming that all countries receive their "high scores" – one standard deviation above the best estimate in the year – and then taking the average, whereas the lower bound is created by averaging the low scores of all countries. Since these "high" and "low" scenarios where all countries end up at one extreme are unrealistic, the uncertainty intervals in Figure 2.2 thus probably underestimate uncertainty, even if we only consider scenarios where countries are within one standard deviation of their best estimates from the V-Dem measurement model. With these caveats concerning

scores. Second, inter-coder disagreement on the democratic features of a polity may sometimes be especially high for very recent years, before social scientists and historians have settled on an authoritative interpretation of the political system. In addition, inter-coder disagreement is a major source of the uncertainty estimates from the V-Dem measurement model.

uncertainty in global trends in mind, we do not report uncertainty intervals in the rest of this chapter. The reason is simply that we present graphs with multiple trend lines, and adding uncertainty intervals tends to clutter the visual impression. In this regard, we also note that for very long periods, trends do not really differ by much when we consider the best estimates or upper or lower bounds, which generally move in parallel.[3]

2.3 TRENDS IN ELECTORAL DEMOCRACY

We first make use of V-Dem's index for electoral democracy, also known as the Polyarchy index, to identify patterns in democratic development. This measure captures the institutional guarantees of Dahl's (1989: 221) concept of polyarchy: adult suffrage, free and fair elections, elected officials, freedom of political parties and civil society organizations, and freedom of expression and access to alternative sources of information. It builds on information from a large number of indicators, some of which are based on an expert survey, while others are in-house coded by V-Dem researchers and research assistants. The main index is constructed by taking the average of two subindices: (1) the weighted average of the subindices for the five institutional guarantees, where elected officials and suffrage receive half the weight of the other components, and (2) the five-way multiplicative interaction between the subindices. The latter (multiplicative) part of the formula reflects that the components are complements in terms of producing democracy (e.g., clean elections matter more for democracy if suffrage is high), whereas the former (additive) part reflects that all components carry some independent weight (for a detailed description and discussion of the measure, see Teorell et al. 2019).

The theoretical range of the index goes from 0 to 1, and the empirical range in version 9 of the V-Dem dataset goes from 0.01 (Guinea-Bissau in the early 1930s under Portuguese colonial rule as well as nineteenth-century Nepal) to 0.95 (the United Kingdom in 2012). The truncated empirical range reflects that it is hard to achieve high scores on this measure. The fact that countries are not clustered at the "floor" or "ceiling" of the measure also indicates that it separates well between polities lumped together by dichotomous measures of democracy (see, e.g., Boix et al. 2013; Cheibub et al. 2010). The median score across 24,995 observations is 0.17 (Serbia in 1914), whereas the mean is 0.26 (about the score of France in 1790, Uruguay in 1859, or Niger in 2010).[4] The index covers 183 sovereign or semi-sovereign countries since 1900 and onward

[3] A country's trend line may, naturally, also be affected by a country moving within the uncertainty bounds (e.g., from the lower bound in year *t* to the upper bound in year *t* +$_i$). Yet, for longer time intervals, such movements are often small when compared to the differences in the point estimates at the beginning and end of a time series.
[4] In contrast, many other democracy indices, such as Polity and the Freedom House Index, separate less well between fairly democratic countries, leading to a pattern where several countries cluster on the maximum score on the index. This not only is an issue for describing differences and

and 78 historical units that have been coded back into the late eighteenth or nineteenth century, often to the year they gained autonomy or all the way back to 1789.

We begin with an overview of aggregated global trends in Polyarchy. The standard way to assess the trends in democracy globally is to only incorporate independent countries and assign equal weight to all of these countries and calculate average scores. We follow this standard approach but supplement the yearly estimates with uncertainty intervals, as mentioned previously, and later also consider alternative ways of aggregating global democracy scores.

Figure 2.2 shows the average democracy score globally for all independent countries, together with uncertainty estimates. The figure lends support to Huntington's (1991) notion of the so-called three waves of democratization in modern history. A long first wave of democratization was characterized by gradual, global improvements apart from two conjunctions – a small one followed the liberal revolutions in 1848–1849, and a larger one is identifiable by the end of World War I. The second, shorter wave then took off with a dramatic increase right after World War II. The third wave is recognizable

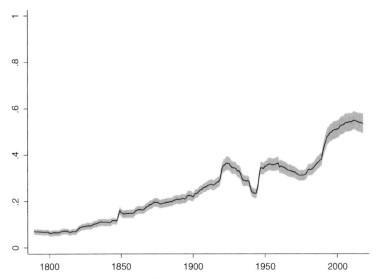

FIGURE 2.2 Global trend in Polyarchy from 1789 to 2018 for all independent countries
Notes: The line represents best estimates of the global mean of Polyarchy, and the gray area shows the scores within the uncertainty bounds calculated from taking the global averages of, respectively, the "low" and "high" scores of Polyarchy (±1 standard deviation) from the V-Dem version 9 dataset.

developments in fairly democratic countries but also has problematic consequences for the analysis of the causes and consequences of democracy (see, e.g., Knutsen and Nygård 2015).

from the late 1970s with a short-term, but substantial, escalation around the end of the Cold War, followed by more moderate increases until 2012.

What about the situation today? Much has been written in recent years about the halt, or even decline, of democracy in the twenty-first century. Some observers have proposed that we have faced a (dramatic) drop in global democracy levels since the mid-2000s. They have declared that we are witnessing a substantial decline and maybe even an outright reverse wave of democratization (e.g., Diamond 2016; EIU 2017; Klaas 2016; Kurlantzick 2014; Lührmann and Lindberg 2019; Puddington and Roylance 2017). Others are less pessimistic and argue that democratization has only very recently come to a global halt and that the current situation is better described as one of overall stability and trendless fluctuations (Carothers and Young 2017; Levitsky and Way 2015; Mechkova et al. 2017; Skaaning and Jeminez 2017).

V-Dem's Polyarchy measure shows no large decline in the global average since the mid-2000s. However, over the past five years, there has been a slight decrease. The most recent (2018) value for the global average among all independent states (0.535) is smaller than the peak value (0.549 in 2012). This situation *could* indicate the beginning of a downward trend. Yet, one should note that the change is clearly within our uncertainty bounds, which account for possible measurement error. There are also recent cases of positive developments in countries such as Armenia, Ecuador, Gambia, Malaysia, Nigeria, and Tunisia.

However, there are currently some disturbing circumstances that deserve to be taken into account when we speculate about the future trajectories of democracy globally. First, major and strategically important countries, such as Brazil, India, Turkey, and the USA, have recently experienced democratic declines, and it is plausible to assume that spillover effects from such countries on the democracy levels of, for instance, regional neighbors are stronger than those from smaller, less powerful countries. A number of EU members and candidate countries, such as Hungary, Poland, and Serbia, have also experienced declines. Moreover, China, Russia, and Saudi Arabia continue to be ruled by oppressive regimes, which are directly or indirectly involved in undermining democracy abroad.

Nonetheless, the global decline in the average democracy score is so far very small compared to previous reverse waves identified by Huntington. The first of these began in the 1920s and culminated during World War II when a number of countries with initially very high levels of electoral democracy, such as Belgium, Czechoslovakia, France, the Netherlands, and Norway, experienced temporary setbacks because of the German occupation. The second global swing away from electoral democracy in the 1960s and early 1970s is smaller. Notable for this reverse wave is the many military coups in Latin America and the fact that the newly independent states – most of them in sub-Saharan

Africa – were from the beginning (or quickly became) quite authoritarian, with Botswana as one noteworthy exception.

However, it is important to note that interpretations of trends must take into account that the set of independent countries has changed over the time period under study. Processes of decolonization increased the number of independent Latin American states in the early nineteenth century, while smaller states were united to form Germany and Italy in the second half of the nineteenth century. After World War I, the dissolution of the Ottoman and Habsburg empires resulted in a larger number of independent countries. Also, after World War II, more countries became independent as a result of decolonization in Asia and Africa, especially in the early 1960s. More recently, quite a few new independent states emerged when the Soviet Union and Yugoslavia collapsed in the early 1990s.

These developments imply, first, that the average associated with independent countries is somewhat misleading when the goal is to capture the typical political regime that global citizens experience because some areas are excluded from the calculation, at least up until recent decades. These excluded areas have typically been less democratic than the average independent country, as many of them have been subjected to colonial rule. To exemplify, the average Polyarchy score in 1950 across the eighty-one countries with data that were independent was 0.35, whereas the corresponding number for the seventy-four nonindependent polities covered by the V-Dem data was 0.12. Second, increases or decreases in the global average displayed in Figure 2.2 can thus either come from changes in democracy levels in the "original" countries or from the fact that the new countries differ on average, positively or negatively, from the global mean. We shall see that the dip in the global level associated with the second reverse wave is largely a product of this latter logic, as the new countries emerging after decolonization were generally less democratic than the older countries.

Fortunately, the V-Dem dataset also covers many nonautonomous or semiautonomous units (colonies, dependencies, and protectorates), such as many African states before decolonization in the late 1950s, Norway during the union with Denmark and personal union with Sweden, and the Palestinian territories (Gaza and the West Bank). If we include all units in the dataset in the overview, that is, 24,995 polity-year observations, the picture largely remains the same (see Figure 2.3). Note in this connection that the abrupt downturn in 1900 is due to the exclusion of many (although far from all) colonies, particularly in Asia and sub-Saharan Africa, from the historical part (pre-1900) of the data collection. The average level of electoral democracy is lower when we include all polities because the colonies, unsurprisingly, tended to be less democratic than independent countries. With extensive decolonization, the difference has decreased over time and is negligible from around 1980. It is interesting to note that the global increase in democracy since 1945 is much larger when we also take into account the political developments in colonies and

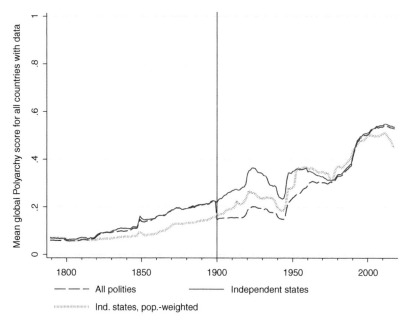

FIGURE 2.3 Mean global democracy scores, 1789–2018

Notes: The figure displays global means for Polyarchy for all units, for only independent countries, and for independent countries population-weighted, 1789–2018. Independent countries are identified by Gleditsch and Ward's (1999) list of independent countries, updated by us to cover all units and years included in the V-Dem dataset. A horizontal line is added to the year 1900 to highlight that several polities, mainly Asian and African colonies, enter the dataset this year.

semi-sovereign polities. No previous measures of democracy have been able to display this empirical pattern, although a large chunk of the world's population lived in colonies until the 1960s.

Apropos of population size, we also add a line to Figure 2.3 that weighs the democracy scores by the population size of each (independent) country. This specification is inspired by the frequently raised critique that – from a "global citizen perspective" – assigning, say, Mauritius with the same weight as China despite the huge difference in population size gives a biased picture of global developments. Nonetheless, the population-weighted average rather closely follows that of the country-based average for most of modern history. The population-weighted average was a fair amount lower than the non-weighted average for independent states from the early century, and especially after 1850, until about 1960. Since 2000, a new gap has been noticeable, coming on the heels of recent reductions in Polyarchy scores in populous countries such as India, the USA, Brazil, and Turkey. The difference between the two measures has increased and is now comparable to the size it had from about 1850 to 1950.

Yet, global averages collapse a great deal of information. If we only rely on such crude summary statistics, we cannot get a good impression of the cross-country variation in democracy scores, at any given point in time. Neither can we identify where in the world the best- and worst-performing countries are situated. As a complement to the global timelines, we have therefore added global heat maps of Polyarchy levels for the first and last year covered and for a year (1899) in the middle of the first wave of democratization, and the last year before the V-Dem sample is expanded to include a number of additional colonies in Africa and Asia.

Figure 2.4a reflects that at the end of 1789, the year of the French Revolution and the American Constitution, polyarchical institutions were totally absent in virtually all parts of the world, apart from a few countries such as the USA (0.36), France (0.26), the United Kingdom (0.23), Poland (0.21), and Sweden (0.20). About fifty years later, in the aftermath of the liberal revolutions of 1848, a number of European countries, in particular, made noteworthy improvements. While several of these cases, such as France and most of the German states, experienced setbacks shortly after (Weyland 2014), others maintained a relatively high degree of Polyarchy. In 1850, Switzerland, for example, maintained a Polyarchy score of 0.55, whereas the Netherlands scored 0.38 and Denmark 0.37. By the end of the century, the global mean of democracy had improved further, to above 0.2, after a slow, steady rise. Figure 2.4b shows that the most democratic countries in the world in 1899 according to Polyarchy, were, inter alia, New Zealand (where women were now allowed to vote), Australia, Canada, and France. Also Uruguay and Argentina, scored relatively high.

The end of World War I saw increased democracy scores in several European countries in particular – including new countries that had previously been part of larger empires, especially the Austro-Hungarian one. By 1921, formal democratic institutions had spread to most European and Latin American countries. However, the level of democracy was generally very low apart from a few countries in Northwestern Europe and the former British settler colonies with long traditions of liberal rights and representative government (i.e., Australia, Canada, New Zealand, and the USA). Moreover, many of the new gains were quickly rolled back when fascists and other antidemocratic forces gained momentum in the interwar years.

When comparing the maps in Figure 2.4, we may observe that democratic institutions and practices have gone from being esoteric and rare, to becoming a broader Western phenomenon in connection with the first wave of democratization, and later to gaining ground in other parts of the world as well. When the most recent wave of decolonization was almost completed in 1968, Western Europe, North America, and Oceania (Australia and New Zealand) continued to stand out as particularly democratic. A high degree of electoral democracy could only be found in a few spots in other parts of the world. To exemplify by using the value of 0.5 on the index as a yardstick, only

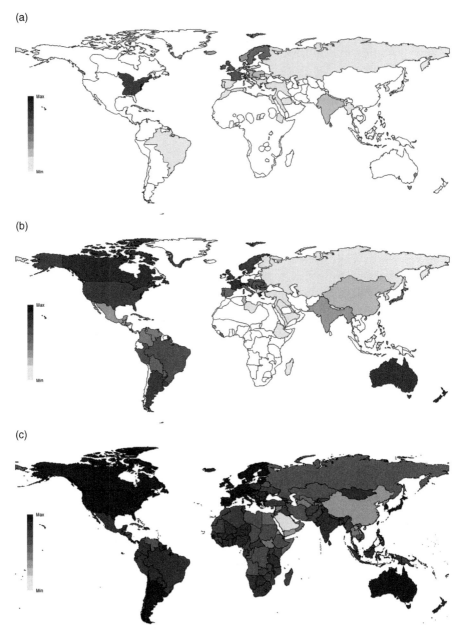

FIGURE 2.4 Global heat maps of electoral democracy: 1789 (a), 1899 (b), and 2018 (c)

five countries outside these regions scored above this value in 1950 (Uruguay, 0.79; Sri Lanka, 0.74; Israel 0.61; Costa Rica, 0.56; Suriname, 0.53). Countries in different regions of the world have subsequently improved their electoral democracy scores, albeit at different points in time in different regions. For example, large improvements were made in the late 1970s and 1980s in Latin America and in the 1990s in Eastern Europe and sub-Saharan Africa. However, as it is clear from the bottom map in Figure 2.4, for 2018, many countries in these regions still belong to an intermediate "grey zone" of hybrid regimes, where formal democratic institutions are typically in place but where there are important problems in how they work in practice (Carothers 2002; Diamond 2002).

When we consider the variation in scores globally, one unsurprising finding is that the variance tended to increase as the world went from a largely undemocratic place in 1789 (standard deviation = 0.08) to a situation in 1921 (standard deviation = 0.23), where some (Western) parts of the world had become rather democratic, while democratic institutions had not been introduced elsewhere. Since then, the global variance moved up and down, largely following the trends in the mean until the 1970s, and peaking at around 0.3 in the ensuing decade. Thereafter, widespread democratization resulted in a stage where further progress actually went hand in hand with a reduction in the global variance (standard deviation = 0.25 in 2018).

Returning to the discussion on global democratization waves, Figure 2.5 provides some more detail by showing the mean global upturns and downturns, respectively, in any given year in Polyarchy. Negative changes are counted as 0 when we calculate the mean global upturns, and positive changes are counted as 0 when we calculate the downturns. Hence, the figure allows us to capture the fact that, at any given point in time, there are movements in "both directions" for different sets of countries; some countries are democratizing whereas others are experiencing reverse processes.

Figure 2.5 supports the descriptions of "conjunctures" (sudden spikes) and waves of democratization (substantially larger grey areas than black areas over delimited periods) identified earlier, but the figure also provides additional information. Note that only small positive and negative changes (on average) took place in the period until 1848–1849 – and subsequently until the interwar years. In contrast, the relatively constant global levels in Polyarchy between the mid-1950s and mid-1970s and, again, since 2000 are associated with larger average changes in both directions. That said, the relatively small average changes on the (0–1 scaled) Polyarchy measure that are mapped in the figure reflect that the democracy level in most countries is very stable from year to year. Another observation is that it might seem surprising that the largest positive peak is just after World War II in connection with the second wave rather than the third wave, which tended to be larger in some of the previous graphs. The reason is primarily that a number of European countries went through abrupt re-democratization – going swiftly from very low to very high levels of democracy – at the same time, after being liberated from Nazi occupation.

However, which countries have experienced the largest upturns and downturns in particular periods? From Figure 2.6, we see that the interwar wave of autocratization – referred to by Huntington (1991) as the first reverse

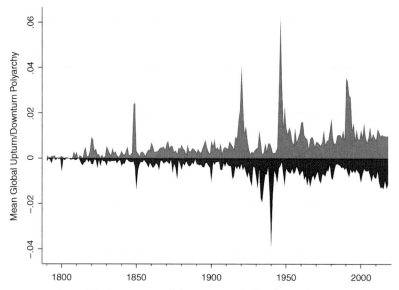

FIGURE 2.5 Mean global upturns and downturns of all independent states, 1789–2018

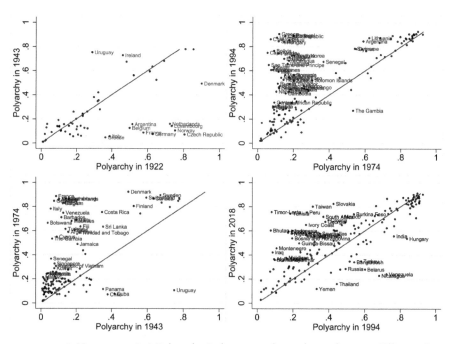

FIGURE 2.6 How countries' Polyarchy index scores have changed across different time intervals

Note: Country names are only included for countries that experienced a change > ±0.2 on Polyarchy across the relevant time interval.

wave of democratization – was mainly a European phenomenon. Argentina is the only country outside of Europe with a major decline from 1922 to 1944. Uruguay experienced the biggest increase in electoral democracy score over this period, but it also represents the biggest decline in the period from 1943 to 1974, followed by a number of other Latin American countries. Many Western European countries improved their scores in the same period, not least because of the end of World War II and the introduction of female suffrage in Belgium, France, and Italy. However, also countries from other parts of the world, such as Venezuela, Gambia, and Sri Lanka, experienced substantial increases.

Nonetheless, only during the subsequent period, 1974–1994, does democratization become a truly global phenomenon. Numerous countries from all parts of the world, with the Middle East as a flagrant exception, experienced democratic progress, while only a handful of countries became less democratic. The picture is more blurred when we look at the most recent decades. Most countries have approximately the same democracy score in 2018 as they had in 1994. In addition, there are more countries above the diagonal than below, which indicates that recent setbacks for many countries during this twenty-four-year period have not totally undermined previous gains. Timor-Leste, Bhutan, Tunisia, Taiwan, and Peru make up the principal democratic achievements. That being said, the well-known cases of Venezuela, Nicaragua, Poland, Hungary, Thailand, Turkey, Belarus, Russia, and India have gone through democratic regressions to various degrees.

2.4 TRENDS IN SUBCOMPONENTS OF ELECTORAL DEMOCRACY

When considering developments in aggregated democracy indices such as Polyarchy across time, we cannot disclose whether trends vary across the components of electoral democracy.[5] In Figure 2.7, we investigate this possibility more closely by mapping out more nuanced descriptions of how different aspects of democracy have changed over time. More specifically, this figure maps the average global score, across independent states for the five subcomponents of Polyarchy.[6]

---

[5] The subcomponents of Polyarchy also lend themselves to further disaggregation. For example, the clean elections index is based on eight indicators, two general ones on the Election Management Board's (EMB's) autonomy and capacity and six election-specific indicators. Some of them tend to be partly substitutable (such as government intimidation and manipulation with voter registration), and the capacities and willingness to fulfill or oppose each of them vary. Consequently, not all of them are highly correlated, and some of them follow different patterns, as indicated by diverging trends in average global scores. Given the sheer number of indicators that enter the Polyarchy index, not to speak of V-Dem's other democracy component indices, we will not dwell on and discuss particular time trends or correlations between specific indicators here.

[6] While all subcomponents are scaled to go from 0 to 1, these are different indices drawing on very different indicators. We thus caution against putting too much weight on the comparison of exact scores across these indices.

All the subcomponents directly related to elections started out at very low levels. This of course reflects the fact that hardly any countries held elections in the late eighteenth and early nineteenth centuries. The elected officials index, capturing to what degree members of parliament are elected and the degree to which the government is responsible to an elected parliament or directly to the electorate, began an upward trend shortly before suffrage and clean elections – and the increases continued at a higher pace until World War I (see Figure 2.7). More and more countries have introduced elections as a means to fill political offices, the share of appointed seats in parliaments has been reduced, and the role of monarchs in the appointment and dismissal of governments has declined. The high global average today indicates that only a few countries lack elected parliaments and governments, which are at least formally responsible to the electorate.

The average levels of clean elections and inclusive (de jure) suffrage followed each other closely until the interwar period. Hereafter, voting rights continued to expand immensely. This upturn continued until the stage where almost all countries, at least formally, granted all their adult citizens voting rights. There are almost no states left where virtually all adult citizens are not enfranchised, Saudi Arabia being the most well-known exception to the rule.

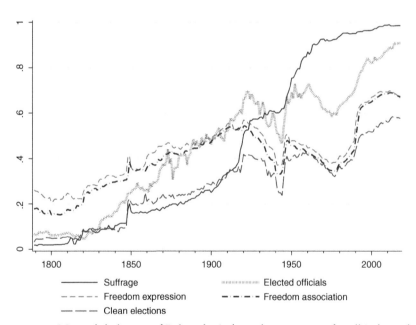

FIGURE 2.7 Mean global score of Polyarchy index subcomponents for all independent states

Early on in modern history, suffrage extensions generally followed patterns similar to the waves of democratization. However, the spike around the liberal revolutions in 1848–1849 is more noteworthy. Quite a few of the independent states at the time went from no or very restrictive suffrage criteria to rather inclusive criteria, although everywhere still excluding women. With the conservative restorations around 1850, which undermined many of the gains achieved in connection with the liberal revolutions in the previous years, the average global score on suffrage declined markedly (although not back to pre-1848 levels). Noteworthy gains were also associated with the extension of the franchise to women in the early twentieth century, the many democratic openings after World War I, and decolonization in the late 1950s and early 1960s. Since then, upturns in suffrage have almost died out because universal suffrage has been introduced in almost all countries. Moreover, and in contrast to other subcomponents of Polyarchy, contractions have generally been the exception (over the whole period, except for, e.g., the early 1850s) for global suffrage scores. Suffrage restrictions have not tended to be reintroduced or replaced by new ones once they have been lifted, although exceptions do exist. Even in connection to coups, civil wars, and executive arrogations, the formal suffrage regulations are generally left untouched.

The global averages on the freedoms of expression and association have tended to move in tandem, largely following overall democratization trends. While also clean elections have followed the overall democratization trends, we note that the global average score on this component was relatively low until the second wave of democratization. Moreover, the increase in the average score on this component has also been less marked than for the two freedom components after the 1980s.

Despite remarkable positive developments over the long term, we still find significant problems not only regarding clean elections but also regarding freedom of association and freedom of speech. Furthermore, Figure 2.7 suggests that current democratic deficits, and the latest dip in the average global scores on measures such as Polyarchy, are due to shortcomings and backlashes on these dimensions.[7] Indeed, Lührmann et al. (2018) demonstrate that between 2007 and 2017, the countries experiencing significant decreases on freedom of expression and freedom of association outnumbered those with significant increases, while the opposite pattern was the case with respect to clean elections and elected officials.

Another intriguing question is whether the countries that tend to score high on one component also tend to score high on the others and vice versa. An additional and related question is to what degree these correlations are stable across time. Figure 2.8 reflects that, in general, the answer to the first question is yes.

---

[7] Note again, however, that while we do not display confidence bounds for the components in Figure 2.7, the apparent decline in some of the subcomponents is not statistically significant at conventional levels.

For this figure, we use the Spearman's rho correlation coefficient, which calculates the correlation based on the similarities in the rank ordering of units (here, countries) across the two measures. A perfect correlation of 1 results from identical rank orderings on the two measures, 0 reflects no relationship between the two rank orderings, and −1 indicates that the rankings are perfectly inverted.[8] The Spearman's rho rank-order correlation coefficient for two variables is 1 if all countries are identically rank ordered on both variables, and 0 if there is no relationship at all between the rank orderings. As Figure 2.8 shows, for all country-year observations, rho is almost 0.7 for clean elections, on the one hand, and suffrage and freedom of expression, respectively, on the other hand. This represents a fairly high, although far from perfect, rank-order correlation. The similar coefficient for clean elections and elected officials is 0.68.[9]

Yet, a closer look at the correlation patterns decade by decade reveals that the extent to which these democratic institutions tend to come together "in packages" varies dramatically across time. For clean elections and suffrage, the rho value hovered around 0.7 across the entire nineteenth century but increased to around 0.8 during the first decades of the twentieth century. Suffrage was expanded to working class men and to women in many Western countries, and regimes with the most extensive suffrage were typically among the regimes with the cleanest multiparty elections during this period. In addition, quite a few countries had not yet introduced elections and therefore scored low on both. As universal suffrage expanded to characterize almost all countries in the world in recent decades, panel a of Figure 2.8 shows that the correlation with clean elections has vanished to almost zero. The pattern is very similar if we investigate the development over time for Pearson's r rather than Spearman's rho.

Panel b of Figure 2.8 shows that the correlation between clean elections and freedom of expression has followed a very different trajectory. In the late eighteenth and early nineteenth centuries, the correlation hovered around 0.4. This was a period when hardly any countries displayed free and fair multiparty elections, but several countries in Europe and the old British settler colonies of Australia, Canada, New Zealand, and the USA showed decent protections of freedom of speech. In the latter half of the nineteenth century, this correlation increased to about 0.7 and kept relatively stable for about one and a half century. Over the last couple of decades, however, the correlation has increased even further to above 0.8. In today's world, the countries that score

---

[8] This correlation coefficient, in contrast to the more conventional Pearson's r coefficient, only needs to assume ordinal measurement levels, and is thus less sensitive to potential differences in scaling properties on the different component indices.

[9] For the relationship between clean elections and suffrage, the corresponding (more conventional) Pearson's r coefficient is closer to 0.6, whereas the Pearson's r coefficient between clean elections and freedom of expression is closer to 0.8 and that between clean elections and elected officials is 0.62.

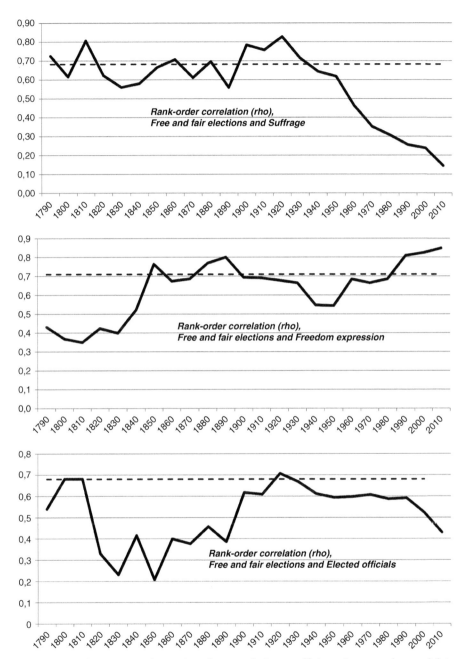

FIGURE 2.8 Spearman's rho rank-order correlation coefficients between free and fair elections, on the one hand, and suffrage (a), freedom of expression (b), or elected officials (c) on the other, by decade. Dotted lines show rho values for the entire sample

relatively high on free and fair elections thus also tend to score relatively high on freedom of expression.

Divergence in the developments of different components of electoral democracy over time is also recognizable from the pattern for the correlation between clean elections and elected officials. In this case, a third pattern is revealed. An initial high level (driven by the fact that only very few countries held national elections) is followed by a major drop in the covariation, which fluctuates between 0.2 and 0.45 for the period between the 1820s and the 1890s. Formally elected offices were combined with elections of low quality in large parts of Latin America (Drake 2009), and in a number of European monarchies, relatively clean elections took place, but parliamentary control with the appointment and dismissal of governments was not established (Congleton 2011). Especially, the latter combination gradually became less frequent, and in the aftermath of World War I, the association reaches an all-time high (rho = 0.71). Thereafter, it stays close to 0.6 until the two most recent decades, where national elections are formally used to fill political offices in most countries but where there is (still) much variation in how clean the elections are.

2.5   TRENDS IN THICKER ASPECTS OF DEMOCRACY

Comprehensive coverage and disaggregation are only some of the advantages of V-Dem data. Another is the ability to capture additional components of democracy that go beyond the electoral core. While the Polyarchy index is – for the sake of comparability – the democracy measure used in the following chapters, we here also show the trends associated with four distinct V-Dem high-level components associated with more comprehensive principles of democracy (see Coppedge et al. 2020):

> *Liberal component*: This component embodies the ideal of protecting liberty and security of individuals against state repression. It is based on the subcomponents equality before the law and individual liberty, judicial constraints on the executive, and legislative constraints on the executive.
>
> *Participatory component*: This component embodies the ideal of active political participation – in various ways – by citizens in all political processes at different levels. It is based on the three subcomponents popular participation in civil society organizations, mechanisms of direct democracy (i.e., initiatives, referenda, and plebiscites), and elected decision-making bodies at the local and regional levels.
>
> *Deliberative component*: This component embodies the ideal of respectful and reasonable dialogue and the pursuit of the public good in connection with political decision-making. Core features of this component are public justifications for political positions on matters of public policy,

justification of political positions in terms of the public good, acknowledgment of and respect for counterarguments, and extensive consultation.

Egalitarian component: This component embodies the ideal that the capacity to influence political decisions should be distributed equally among all citizens regardless of class, ethnicity, sexual orientation, and other social identities. It is based on two subcomponents: Rights and freedoms of individuals are protected equally across all social groups, and resources relevant for political influence are distributed equally across all social groups.

Different scholars have made arguments implying that different components of democracy should reinforce each other or be mutually constitutive (see, e.g., Dworkin 1996; Habermas 1996; Rawls 1971; Rousseau 1993[1762]; Sen 1993). Moreover, it is highly likely that the components are jointly influenced by factors that pull them in the same direction, such as socioeconomic modernization, social diversity and inequality, and state capacity. This would mean that we should see fairly similar patterns across the components over time in global aggregates and that countries doing well on one component should also tend to do well on other components.

Then again, scholars have also produced arguments suggesting that there may be a potential tension between some of these components, such as between liberal rights and social equality (see, e.g., Berlin 2002[1958]; von Hayek 1960; Tocqueville 1988[1835/40]).[10] If this is correct, very similar trends on all of the different components are unlikely, and – for any given year – we would not expect that the exact same countries should be able to perform very well on all of them.

When considering trends in the global averages for the different components in Figure 2.9a, we see that this exercise largely points in favor of the perspective arguing for a positive relationship between the components. The trend lines for the electoral, liberal, egalitarian, participatory, and deliberative components mostly follow parallel tracks, as displayed in Figure 2.9a, although there are small deviations. For instance, we note that the deliberative component has had the most noteworthy decline among the democracy components over the past few years. Another interesting deviation is that the egalitarian component after 1960 tends to increase gradually in a close to linear fashion. As signified by the example of the Nordic countries over the last century, this does not necessarily reflect an ingrained trade-off between egalitarian vis-à-vis other high-level components of democracy. However, this pattern does indicate that the

---

[10] Diamond and Morlino (2004) tend to be somewhat ambivalent on this issue as they state that the "dimensions are closely linked and tend to move together, either toward democratic improvement and deepening or toward decay" (28–29), but also that "it is impossible to maximize all [components] at once. . . . every democratic country must make an inherently value-laden choice about what kind of democracy it wishes to be" (21). On potential trade-offs, see also Lauth (2016).

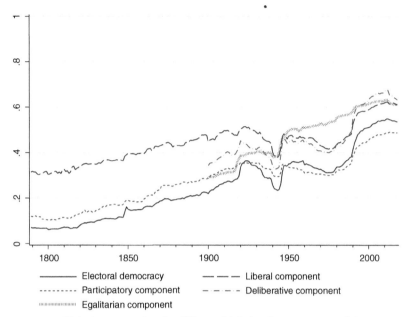

FIGURE 2.9a Global averages for the different high-level components of democracy for all independent countries with relevant V-Dem data

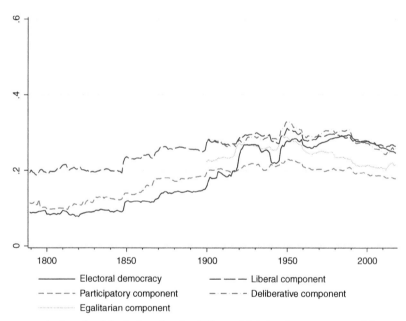

FIGURE 2.9b Standard deviations for the different high-level components of democracy for all independent countries with relevant V-Dem data

dynamics of this aspect is somewhat different and that they are – at least partly – driven by other factors.

Figure 2.9b displays the standard deviation, by year, in the different component indices, measured across all independent countries. As for the global averages across the nineteenth century, we observe a very gradual increase in the variation in scores on the three components with data. This reflects the fact that more democratic regimes over time populated the international system of independent states, which had started out as fairly homogeneously authoritarian in the late eighteenth and early nineteenth centuries. Interestingly, however, the standard deviation was, already from 1789, much higher for liberal aspects of democracy than for electoral and participatory aspects of democracy – reflecting that many otherwise authoritarian states had notable checks on the chief executive and rule of law early on. Hence, the increase in the variance was also less marked for the liberal component than for the others.

Across the twentieth century, changes in standard deviations were not very marked for most components, with some exceptions around the end of the two world wars – especially for electoral democracy, which observes large increases in variance after these major events. Interestingly, all five high-level components displayed greater variance globally in 1950 than in 1900 but also lower variance in 2000 than in 1950. Especially since 1980 (after which averages have mostly continued to grow), the trend has been toward less cross-country variance in democracy scores, particularly in terms of electoral democracy and the deliberative component.

The countries that, at any given point in time, tend to score relatively high (low) on one component also tend to score relatively high (low) on the other components. This is illustrated in Figure 2.10, which shows the Spearman's rank order correlation coefficient, rho, for electoral democracy (Polyarchy) and the Liberal component, which both have time series extending back to 1789. For the entire sample, rho is 0.83 – and Pearson's r is even higher at 0.86 – but Figure 2.10 also shows that the coefficient has exceeded 0.9 over the last couple of decades. We note that these rank-order correlations are stronger than the ones we observed between different subcomponents of the Polyarchy measure.[11]

Rho was about as strong in the latter half of the nineteenth century as it has been in recent years (around 0.9). Yet, the correspondence was the lowest (around 0.7) in the first few decades after the French Revolution, where liberal constitutionalism gained strength in some countries without a broad representation. This combination is not really a viable option today, where universal suffrage is basically taken for given under most circumstances.

---

[11] Rho coefficients between electoral democracy, on the one hand, and the participatory and deliberative components on the other are, respectively, 0.85 and 0.86 (Pearson's r coefficients are virtually similar). The egalitarian component correlates less strongly with the electoral democracy measure (rho = 0.73, r = 0.76).

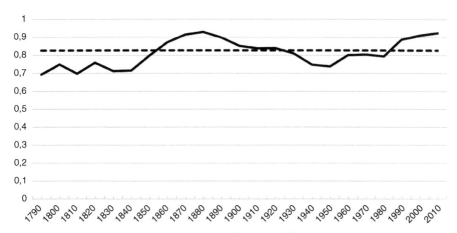

FIGURE 2.10 Spearman's rank-order correlation coefficient between Polyarchy index and the Liberal Component index by year (first year of decade reported). The dotted line displays the coefficient for the entire sample.

In sum, while there are certainly countries that perform differently on the different components of democracy measured by V-Dem – and closer scrutiny suggests that deviations are somewhat larger between the egalitarian components and other democracy components – the main picture is one of consistency. That is, the countries that perform well on one aspect of democracy tend to perform well also on other aspects and vice versa. Accordingly, there is more support for the above-described perspective that envisions complementarities (or at least concurrence) rather than trade-offs between the high-level components.

We note that the distinctions between different aspects of democracy rest on conceptual and theoretical differences. V-Dem now enables us to also distinguish these phenomena empirically. Given the high correlations among most of the components, some could legitimately ask whether it is meaningful and worthwhile to distinguish among varieties of democracy at all. Providing a general answer to such question is not easy – the correlations are not perfectly stable over time (and across regions). Moreover, there are clear deviations from the general tendency, which might be important for particular questions, and the high correlations are to a large extent driven by observations at the extremes, whereas the picture is more muddy when it comes to the correspondence in rankings of countries that are located somewhere "in the middle" on the different dimensions. That said, for many research questions, it will often be more interesting and relevant to apply even more disaggregate measures than these democracy components – for instance, as captured by the various V-Dem indicators, which tend to be more empirically distinct.

2.6 CONCLUSION

Achieving high-quality democracy on all relevant components of democracy is hard, at least judging by the relative infrequency of such regimes throughout modern history. Electoral malpractices, corruption, and restrictions on fundamental civil liberties are common, even in today's world. Likewise, shortcomings exist for deliberative practices, equal treatment of social groups, and political participation. When we take a long perspective, however, our descriptive analysis shows that the world has improved tremendously in many important aspects of democracy.

This overall trend across modern history has been spurred by liberal revolutions, victories by the democratic allies in the two world wars (and the Cold War), and decolonization. It has coincided with the decline of traditional monarchical rule as well as dominant party, military, and (to a lesser extent) personalist dictatorships more recently. However, as the numerous time trends displayed in this chapter make clear, progress has not been linear or even monotonic. Some aspects of democracy largely display similar patterns of change from 1789 until today, while others differ from each other both regarding average levels and tendencies. Particularly, suffrage and elected offices deviate from the trends of the other subcomponents of electoral democracy, and equality does follow a somewhat different trajectory than the other high-level components.

Moreover, progress has not been evenly distributed across the globe, and it has varied across different aspects of democracy and continues to do so. It is also evident that there is much room for further improvements regarding most aspects of democracy in most countries of the world, although the right to suffrage for adult citizens and the recognition of elections as the principal means to fill political offices are today formally recognized in virtually all corners of the globe.

Despite these long-term improvements across the board – and notable gains in some specific areas, primarily related to the conduct of elections, even in recent years – democratic regression continues to be a viable threat. Moreover, if we consider the strategic importance of some countries experiencing democratic decline and put less weight on conservative confidence intervals, there are some negative tendencies, which could indicate the beginnings of a reverse wave of democratization. The controversies associated with the recent presidential elections in the USA, democratic regression in some EU member states and major countries (including Brazil, Turkey, and India), and increasingly self-confident autocratic great powers (Russia and China), which are actively engaged in undermining democratic forces at home and abroad, point in the same direction. Nonetheless, we contend that the most pessimistic assessments of the global state of democracy tend to paint an overly gloomy picture. We are, arguably, not yet in a full-blown reverse wave of democratization, and some aspects of democracy have been stable or even improved lately. Ordinary citizens generally do not favor alternatives to democracy and only few are openly rejecting democratic principles. The view that, as expressed by Winston Churchill, "democracy is the worst form of Government except for all those other forms that have been tried from time to time" continues to be shared by many people around the world.[12]

However, even as relative "optimists," we want to end with a cautionary note. Despite the many positive developments since the initial stages of modern democracy, we should not be lulled into a false sense of security on behalf of democracy. Democratic principles are not fulfilled in any country, and many places – including some of the most populous countries in the world – the access to, and exercise of, political power are further away from these ideals today than only a few years ago.

---

[12] See PEW (2017). *Globally, Broad Support for Representative and Direct Democracy*, www .pewresearch.org/global/2017/10/16/globally-broad-support-for-representative-and-direct-democracy/; Latana (2021). *Democracy Perception Index 2021*, www.latana.com/democracy-perception-index/

3

Long-Run Factors

John Gerring

The immense body of work devoted to explaining regime types is focused primarily on proximal causes, where a change in X at time t is thought to lead to a change in a country's regime status at $t+1$. Structural causes, which operate quietly over long periods of time, are generally ignored or treated as background covariates of no theoretical interest. In this chapter we address structural factors that may affect the fate of regimes across the world in the modern era. A structural factor is understood as one that changes slowly, if at all during the modern era, and one that is likely to have long-term effects on a country's propensity to democratize or consolidate a democratic form of rule.

We begin with what are surely the most structural causes of all, those that are geographically based, for example, in climate, soil, topography, or waterways.[1] Section 3.2 discusses Islam. Section 3.3 looks at the spread of Europeans throughout the world through colonialism, religion, language, and demography. Section 3.4 explores the role of population. Section 3.5 examines the diversity of populations, understood ethnically and religiously. Readers should be aware that our discussion of these multifarious factors will be scandalously brief. We offer a concise statement of the argument along with citations to the literature, to which readers can repair for further details.

Empirical tests adopt a cross-sectional mode of analysis that treats countries in a pooled fashion. This is because the variables of theoretical interest do not change appreciably over the observed period (as noted). Consequently, the available leverage is primarily across countries rather than through time. Nonetheless, it is vital to include all available data, stretching back to 1789 wherever possible. Only in this fashion can we generalize across the modern era and minimize problems of stochastic error. Year dummies are included to

---

[1] We do not touch upon the so-called resource curse, as this factor seems to have had its greatest impact on regimes in the late-twentieth century (Andersen, Ross 2014) and hence falls outside the long-term temporal framework adopted in this chapter. This topic is taken up in Chapter 5.

control for time effects, and standard errors are clustered by country to mitigate serial autocorrelation.

We find that two geographic factors – distance from equator (+) and distance from nearest natural harbor (–) – are strongly correlated with democracy. Among factors associated with European diffusion, Protestantism and Europeans (both measured as a share of population) are positively correlated with democracy. Islam – understood as share of population of Muslim descent or share of territory conquered by Arab armies – is negatively associated with democracy. Other factors tested in this chapter do not bear a robust empirical relationship to democracy. That does not eliminate them from consideration; but it does cast doubt on the likelihood that they are very important causes of democracy in the modern era.

3.1   GEOGRAPHY

Recent years have seen a resurgence in the study of geography, with numerous studies devoted to some aspect of the natural landscape and its impact on social or economic development.[2] A much smaller corpus focuses on democracy. Here, several arguments deserve attention. These center on (a) climate, (b) irrigation, (c) agriculture, (d) mountains, (e) islands, and (f) natural harbors.[3]

3.1.1   Climate

A number of factors may conspire (individually or collectively) to diminish the prospects of democracy in tropical areas, that is, in low-lying areas close to the equator that receive abundant rainfall. Most of these factors also affect economic development, which one may view as a proximal cause of democracy (see Chapter 5). Tropical climates affect the epidemiological environment. Specifically, malaria and many other communicable diseases are fostered by hot, humid climates. This limits human capital and economic productivity at large (Mellinger et al. 2000).

Where disease vectors were rampant, European settlers were less likely to tread – or at least less likely to settle in large numbers (Curtin 1989, 1998). This, in turn, may have had important repercussions for the sort of regimes that developed in the modern world, as discussed in Section 3.3 later. Tropical climates also condition the sort of crops that can be grown. Crops requiring massive labor inputs – and therefore suitable for a plantation mode of production – are often viable in a hot, humid climate. This includes coffee, cotton, rubber, sugarcane, tobacco, and other highly profitable cash crops, which formed – and to a large extent still form – the basis of economies in the

---

[2] See Buhaug and Gates (2002), Diamond (1992), Mellinger et al. (2000), Michalopoulos (2012), Nunn and Puga (2012).
[3] This section builds on Gerring, Apfeld, Wig, Tollefsen (2022: Chapters 3–7, 12).

tropics. Labor extraction of this sort fostered the slave trade, vast inequality in landholding and wealth, and poor institutions in subsequent centuries (Engerman and Sokoloff 2012).

By contrast, too *little* rainfall – or unpredictable rainfall – may be an invitation for centralized control, as farmers need the state to assist them in times of drought and may also need a centralized political organization to develop and maintain irrigation systems, as discussed later. It follows that the sort of climate most conducive to democracy is one featuring regular rainfall – neither scarce nor torrential and occurring at predictable intervals. Regular rainfall is likely to generate a trajectory of economic development based on independent family farms (as opposed to large plantations), which are often viewed as a social foundation of democracy. This, in turn, obviates the need for state intervention and impedes the consolidation of power in the capital.[4] A similar set of arguments have been made about agricultural potential, which of course rests crucially upon rainfall. Consequently, this argument is similar conceptually and empirically (Ang et al. 2020).

3.1.2   Irrigation

One may trace back the notion of "hydraulic" autocracy as far back as Adam Smith, Karl Marx, and various followers of the latter. For Marxists, the idea was wedded to the theory of an "Asiatic mode of production" (Sawer 2012). Max Weber (2013[1909]: 84) also identified irrigation as a potential source of despotism. Thus, the notion of irrigation fostering autocracy was by no means new when Karl Wittfogel (1957) turned his attention to the thesis in a lengthy book that has become a classic reference point. For Wittfogel, areas where there was a strong need for irrigation and flood control would also see a consequent need for the development of centralized states to provide those public goods. Because there were no mechanisms of popular accountability operable at large scale in premodern societies, this led to authoritarian states, whose legacies extend to the present-day.

More recently, Bentzen et al. (2016) build on this thesis, offering a subtle twist – that irrigation required major investments and as such gave crucial advantages to local elites who were in a position to build and maintain those systems. This led to greater inequality and, in turn, encouraged the formation of autocratic governments.

3.1.3   Agriculture

Early states were generally situated on a rich agricultural base. Surplus from the land provided revenue for the state, and sedentary, densely settled areas provided fodder for armies and bureaucracies. Thus, where geographic

---

[4] See Elis et al. (2017), Midlarsky (1995), Welzel (2013, 2014).

conditions – soil, climate, topography – are conducive to a single, dominant crop, serving as the staple diet in a community, this probably encouraged the rise of highly centralized, agrarian states. Cereals, in particular, seem to be susceptible to hierarchy and centralized control.[5] To begin with, they offer a predictable source of revenue. They are also highly transparent – visible to the tax collector and hard to hide, whether in the field or in the silo. Accordingly, cereals offer a rich harvest for the state, one that can be collected cheaply in a coercive fashion, without need for consent.

By contrast, where the environment is unpropitious for agriculture – excessively dry, cold, or hot – states are likely to develop much later and will be weaker and less prone to authoritarian rule. Likewise, where the climate is wet and humid, nature provides an abundance of food that can be gathered easily but is difficult to preserve. In this fashion, a geography of perishable plenty discourages the adoption of sedentary agriculture, urbanization, and state formation. Here, we can expect power to be exercised in a more diffuse fashion.

A closely related approach to this subject examines agricultural *variability* as a key to political development. Where the geographic conditions of an area encourage the development of a wide array of agricultural products, strong states may develop but their structure is likely to differ from the prototypical agrarian state. This is because in a situation of agricultural diversity it is more difficult for elites to appropriate surplus revenue. In this vein, Mayshar et al. (2017) contrast the monoculture of Egypt with the more diverse agricultural portfolio of Northern Mesopotamia, arguing that the former provided easy revenue – revenue that could be garnered without negotiation or consent – while the latter environment made it difficult for statemakers to extract revenue at a distance, leading to nucleated settlements and decentralized political control. Ahmed and Stasavage (2020) build on this idea, showing that variability in agricultural potential is correlated with early democracy.

In addition to a territory's own agricultural fertility, one might also consider the surrounding environment. If a fertile region is surrounded by less fertile regions (e.g., mountains, deserts, or dense tropical forests), the latter may serve to *circumscribe* the fertile territory.[6] This, in turn, may enhance the power of statebuilders, as they can more easily define and control the fertile territory, within which citizens are effectively "caged" (Mann 1986). From this perspective, it is the environmental differential between adjacent regions that leads to authoritarian outcomes. Egypt, once again, serves as a point of reference.[7]

A final agricultural argument about long-term economic development concerns aquaculture. Dalgaard et al. (2020) argue that countries bordering on fertile shoreline offered a bounty of the sea, which served as a source of

[5] See Mayshar. et al. (2017), Mayshar. et al. (2019), Scott (2017), Stasavage (2020).
[6] See Carneiro (1970, 1988, 2012), Mayoral and Olsson (2019), Schönholzer (2020).
[7] See Jones (1981: 10–11), Stasavage (2020).

nutrition and agricultural surplus, leading to long-term economic development. They do not make a case for the impact of fish on political development, but one can easily imagine that economic development might have spillover effects on politics.

3.1.4   Mountains

Mountains are often regarded as a redoubt of democracy.[8] Plutarch remarked upon "the Men of the Hills, who were the most democratic party, the Men of the Plain, who were the most oligarchic, and thirdly the Men of the Coast, who favored an intermediate, mixed kind of system."[9] Much later, Fernand Braudel (1972[1949]: 38–39) draws quotations from early modern writers, who also commented on the vigor and liberty of mountain folk. The most recent study to take on this subject concludes that mountain communities are more likely to sustain political structures "reminiscent of those of the Classical polis" (Korotayev 1995: 61–63). Yet, there is no comprehensive study of mountain communities that we are aware of that might allow us to evaluate these claims in a systematic fashion.

3.1.5   Islands

Many writers regard island status as a force in favor of democratic outcomes in the modern era.[10] A number of reasons have been (or might be) offered. First, island-states are exposed to oceans and this may influence the propensity of a state to democratize. Second, islands offered appealing ports of call and colonies of settlement for Europeans, including Britishers and Protestants (Anckar 2008; Hadenius 1992: 126–127), and they were often subjected to an extensive tutelary relationship with a European power, culminating in many years' experience with electoral politics and semiautonomous governance prior to independence. For a variety of reasons, one may suppose that the colonial experience was more transformative for island-states than for other states (Caldwell et al. 1980; Srebrnik 2004).

Third, most islands depend upon international trade or tourism for a large share of their national income. This may encourage a more open attitude toward democracy, though the point is disputed (Milner and Mukherjee 2009). Fourth, islands tend to be small, limiting the population. With natural borders provided by the sea, island living may foster a greater sense of national community than one finds in land-based states.[11] These features are often

---

[8] Braudel (1972[1949]: 38–39), Hechter (1975: 50–51), Korotayev (1995), Leach (1960), Matloff (2017), Peattie (1936), Scott (2009), Wolf (1982: 57, 221–222).
[9] Quoted in Acemoglu, Robinson (2019: ch 2).
[10] See C. Anckar (2008), Baldacchino (2012), Congdon Fors (2014), Dommen (1980), Doumenge (1985), Srebrnik (2004), Sutton and Payne (1993).
[11] Anckar and Anckar (1995: 213, 220–222), Congdon Fors (2014), Royle (2001).

regarded as conducive to democracy. Finally, being geographically isolated, island-states may be less militarist because their sovereignty is more secure than land-based states and because expansionist policies are more difficult to pursue (Clague et al. 2001: 22–23).

3.1.6 Natural Harbors

Recently, it has been argued that the existence of natural harbors has a long-run influence on democracy. Harbors enhance mobility – of people, goods, and ideas. The extraordinary connectivity of harbor regions may have fostered economic development, altered the structure of the military (toward a reliance on naval rather than land-based forces), small states (in the premodern era), and a stance of openness to the world. Through these pathways, operating over many centuries, maritime geography placed its imprint on political institutions. As a consequence, territories blessed with natural harbors may have been more likely to develop democratic forms of government than territories surrounded by large land masses or inaccessible coasts (Gerring et al. 2022: Part II).

3.1.7 Tests

To provide adequate empirical tests for each of the myriad geographic factors vetted earlier would be a monumental endeavor. Nonetheless, it is possible to measure many of these factors in a provisional fashion drawing on extant work or readily available datasets. As measures of climate, we include (a) distance from the equator (absolute latitude), (b) tropical (share of territory classified as tropical), (c) temperature (annual mean temperature), (d) frost days (number of days where the temperature dips below freezing), and (e) precipitation (annual rainfall plus its quadratic, allowing for a non-monotonic functional form).[12]

As a measure of irrigation potential, we adopt a variable developed by Bentzen and associates (2016) that identifies areas where irrigation could make a big impact on agricultural productivity. Specifically, the authors calculate the share of land suitable for agriculture where irrigation can more than double agricultural production. As measures of agriculture, we include (a) soil quality, (b) overall agricultural suitability, (c) caloric suitability (the calories an area would yield if farmed to its potential), (d) caloric variability (the standard deviation of caloric suitability across a grid-cell, averaged across grid-cells in a state), and (e) fish (the "bounty of the sea" index developed by Dalgaard et al. 2020).

As measures of mountains, we employ a coding of territory classified as mountainous as a share of all territory within a grid-cell (Tollefsen et al.

---

[12] Measuring rainfall and its quadratic achieves much the same thing as measuring potential crop yield and its quadratic (Ang et al. 2020) and is more robust according to our measure of the latter.

2012), aggregated up to state levels. We also employ a ruggedness variable from Nunn and Puga (2012) that calculates differences in elevation across grid-cells, aggregated to states. To code islands, we examine whether a state is attached to a continental land mass or not. Typically, states that conform to one or several small plots of land surrounded by sea or ocean are classified as islands. Finally, we include a variable measuring distance from the nearest natural harbor, where the latter is identified by the configuration of coastlines throughout the world (Gerring et al. 2022: ch 4).

In Table 3.1, we examine the possible impact of these predictors on democracy in the modern era. Column 2 indicates the expected relationship between each of these geographic factors and democracy, based on the discussion aforementioned and literature cited therein. In the next column, we show the results of fifteen bivariate models in which democracy is regressed against each of these variables individually, along with year dummies. In Model 16, we test all factors together in a single specification. Our assumption is that they are all exogenous (or mostly so) and therefore independent of each other. There is little risk of posttreatment bias. Several factors survive this packed specification test, as judged by t statistics and conventional thresholds of statistical significance. These are included in Model 17. In Model 18, we continue the winnowing process, dropping factors that do not perform well in the preceding test. In Model 19, we repeat the same specification with the addition of a vector of regional dummies. In Model 20, the specification is restricted to variables that pass all previous tests with flying colors.

It will be seen that most of the theories vetted earlier do not receive much empirical support from the tests shown in Table 3.1. Stronger relationships might appear if we had chosen different model specifications, different indicators, or different temporal or spatial contexts. Note that our measure of regimes begins in 1789, limiting our analysis to the modern era, while some of the theories seem more suited to the premodern era. All we can report is that this particular set of tests, focused on the modern era and on a global sample, does not offer strong corroboration for most geographically based theories of democracy. Precipitation is a partial exception – showing the expected curvilinear relationship to democracy in all specifications. However, the relationship attenuates significantly when a vector of regional dummies is included (Model 19), suggesting that precipitation may be proxying for regional effects. Only two predictors are highly robust in all specification tests: equator distance (+) and natural harbor distance (−). These are the geographic factors whose impact on modern democracy is greatest, bearing in mind all the usual caveats.

3.2 ISLAM

It is often noted that countries with a predominantly Islamic population are less likely to be democratic in the contemporary era than countries with other religious heritages. To be sure, some Islamic societies are fairly democratic, at

TABLE 3.1 *Geographic factors*

	E		16.	17.	18.	19.	20.
Equator distance	←	1. 0.005*** (7.333)	0.003* (2.178)	0.006*** (3.382)	0.007*** (10.089)	0.006*** (4.694)	0.005*** (7.938)
Tropical	→	2. -0.001*** (-3.378)	-0.002*** (-2.742)	-0.001 (-1.280)			
Temperature	→	3. -0.011*** (-5.434)	-0.008 (-1.414)	-0.001 (-0.138)			
Frost days	←	4. 0.007*** (4.322)	-0.005 (-1.241)				
Precipitation	←	5. 0.001*** (2.781)	0.001*** (3.069)	0.001*** (4.222)	0.001*** (4.872)	0.000** (2.306)	
Precipitation^2	→	-0.000** (-2.421)	-0.000* (-2.090)	-0.000*** (-3.288)	-0.000*** (-2.889)	-0.000* (-1.663)	
Irrigation potential	→	6. -0.201*** (-5.135)	-0.029 (-0.506)				
Soil quality	←	7. 0.002*** (3.068)	0.001* (1.825)				
Agricultural suitability	→	8. 0.075 (1.319)	0.089 (1.365)				
Caloric suitability	→	9. 0.000 (0.954)	-0.000*** (-3.783)	-0.000* (-1.777)			

(*continued*)

	E	(10)	(11)	(12)	(13)	(14)	(15)
Caloric variability	←	0.000 (0.581)	0.000 (1.447)				
Fish	←	0.710*** (4.793)	0.093 (0.942)				
Mountains	←	−0.059 (−0.869)	−0.164* (−1.757)				
Rugged	→	−0.008 (−0.574)	−0.026 (−1.290)				
Island	←	0.066 (1.639)	0.063 (1.517)				
Natural harbor distance	→	−0.016*** (−5.709)	−0.009*** (−3.179)	−0.010*** (−3.395)	−0.008*** (−2.956)	−0.009*** (−3.266)	−0.014*** (−5.427)
Region dummies						✓	✓
Countries			142	162	179	179	179
Years			231	231	231	231	231
Observations			19,966	22,312	24,095	24,095	24,096
R-squared			0.597	0.551	0.522	0.558	0.469

Notes: Outcome: Polyarchy index of electoral democracy. *E:* expected direction of the relationship. Models 1–15 are shown in a single column (model-fit statistics omitted). Not shown: Year dummies, Constant. Ordinary least squares, standard errors clustered by country, *t* statistics in parentheses. ***p < 0.01 **p < 0.05 *p < 0.10.

least in the sense of allowing for multiparty elections and change in control of the executive (e.g., Albania, Bangladesh, Bosnia-Herzegovina, Indonesia, Kosovo, Malaysia, and Tunisia) and many feature competitive elections for top policymaking offices even if those elections are not entirely free and fair and are not always accompanied by liberal rights (e.g., Iran, Iraq, Kyrgyzstan, Lebanon, Maldives, Pakistan, Palestine, Senegal, Turkey, and until recently Mali). In a third group of countries (e.g., Jordan, Kuwait, and Morocco) parliamentary elections are competitive but executive power is wielded by hereditary monarchs. Furthermore, in two countries (Saudi Arabia and Brunei) there are no national-level elections at all, a rarity in the contemporary world.

The popular Western image of an unrelieved Islamic autocracy, while once plausible, is clearly false today (Nasr 2005). Yet, over the past several centuries it seems that Islamic societies have been less likely to democratize than non-Islamic societies. Accordingly, many studies have focused on the question of Islam's compatibility or incompatibility with democracy.[13] A review of this literature reveals a large number of plausible hypotheses that might explain this relationship. There may be doctrinal features of Islam that make it inhospitable for democracy (Huntington 1996), for example, a lack of separation between religion and politics (Lewis 2002), repression of religious freedom (Rowley and Smith 2009), or centralized financing of religious authorities (Rothstein and Broms 2013). Domestic politics in many Muslim countries pits authoritarian rulers against perceived threats posed by Islamic militants, a dynamic that is not favorable to democracy (Lust 2011). Islamic conquest may have brought with it a particular approach to autocratic rule, that is, slave soldiers and bureaucrats (*mamluks*) and landholdings concentrated in the hands of the ruler (*iqta*), which had greater endurance than autocratic institutions elsewhere (Ahmed 2018; Blaydes 2017; Blaydes and Chaney 2013; Chaney 2012; Crone 1980; Kuran 2011). Whether by virtue of well-developed states (Hariri 2012, 2015) or strong religious bonds, Muslim cultural areas were – and are – resistant to European influence (Burke 1972), which means that the pathway from European settlement to democracy (discussed later) may have been blocked. Most Muslim polities are located in the Arabic linguistic and cultural zone, a cultural heritage that may stand in the way of democratization (Noland 2008; Sharabi 1988). The ongoing Arab–Israeli conflict may serve to entrench autocratic leaders in the Arab world (Diamond 2010; El Badawi, Makdisi 2007; Stepan and Robertson 2003). US foreign policy, oriented toward defending energy sources deemed essential for the US economy, protecting Israel, and deterring the Soviet Union (or, latterly, Iran), may have hindered the development of democracy in the Middle East (Jamal 2012). Many Muslim polities are located in areas with hot, arid climates and few natural harbors – geographic factors that may be

---

[13] See Brumberg, Diamond, and Plattner (2003), Esposito and Voll (1996), Hefner (2009), Platteau (2008), Potrafke (2012), along with studies cited later.

unfavorable to democracy (as discussed). Most Muslim polities are located in or near the oil-rich Middle East, which may have stimulated a "resource curse" (Ross 2001). Since the oil-rich countries are also influential – a by-product of their wealth – the impact of the resource curse may have extended throughout the region, even to those countries with no mineral resources (Kuru 2014). In many Muslim societies, women are forced to accept a subordinate role, which may also inhibit the development and flourishing of democracy (Fish 2002). The Middle East is home to many of the world's last remaining monarchs – autocrats who rule rather than merely reign. Insofar as this form of government has staying power, it may be credited as a factor in the endurance of autocracy throughout the region (Menaldo 2012). Finally, there may be a regional effect centered on the Middle East and North Africa (MENA), which one may interpret as the confluence of a number of factors – including, but not limited to, those listed earlier (Bellin 2004; Lewis 1993).

Interestingly, public opinion research suggests that support for democracy is no weaker among Muslims, or residents of the MENA region, than elsewhere (Rowley, Smith 2009), and support among observant Muslims is no weaker than among less observant or lapsed Muslims (Tessler 2002). So, the democracy deficit may not be due to a lack of demand. Even so, there are many potential explanations for the negative relationship between Islam and democracy. Each presupposes a somewhat different treatment and causal interpretation. Fortunately, many of these alternate hypotheses are measurable on a global scale so it is possible to test them side by side (with the usual caveats about potential measurement error and specification error).

Table 3.2 begins with what is perhaps the most commonly used variable in cross-national regression analyses: the share of population that is Muslim by descent (Alesina et al. 2003).[14] In Model 1, the Polyarchy index is regressed against this variable along with annual dummies. In Model 2, we add those geographic factors that proved most robust in our earlier analysis (Table 3.1): equator distance and natural harbor distance. Model 3 adds a second measure that is closely related to Muslim: the share of territory of present-day countries that was conquered by Arab armies in the period after the death of Prophet Muhammad (Chaney 2012). Model 4 adds a variable measuring the share of present-day populations speaking Arabic. Model 5 adds a dummy variable measuring presence in the MENA region. These four variables – Muslim, Islamic conquest, Arabic, and MENA – are fairly highly correlated with each other (Pearson's r ranges from 0.6 to 0.8), as one might expect.

---

[14] Another approach is to dichotomize the variable, separating majority-Muslim societies from the rest (Ahmed 2018; Chaney 2012; Hariri 2015). This approach yields weaker results, presumably because of information loss. We see no compelling reason to dichotomize this variable, especially as comparable measures – for example, of Protestants, Catholics, Europeans – are almost always operationalized with interval scales.

Subsequent models add covariates that might be interpreted as potential mechanisms or confounders, depending upon one's reconstruction of the data-generating process. Model 6 includes state history, a measure of the strength of states up to 1500 CE (Borcan et al. 2018). Model 7 adds three measures of European influence from Table 3.3: English colonial duration, Protestant (%), and European ancestry (%). Model 8 adds oil income per capita (Haber and Menaldo 2011). Model 9 adds a dummy variable measuring the existence of a hereditary monarchy who rules, not merely reigns (Gerring et al. 2021). Model 10 adds a measure of gender equality from the Varieties of Democracy project (Coppedge et al. 2020).

Results posted in Table 3.2 show that Muslim (%) is a robust predictor of autocracy in the modern era. Islamic conquest is correctly signed but loses strength as covariates are added – perhaps because the latter are downstream. Arabic shows a strong correlation with autocracy only in certain specifications; since these are likely to be downstream, we do not regard this as providing very strong evidence for the proposition. MENA, finally, carries the wrong sign in most of our analyses, vitiating the argument that there is a regional effect.

Taken together, these analyses corroborate the common view that Islam has served as a barrier to democracy in the modern era. Though we cannot definitively specify a mechanism(s), we can conclude that this effect is not entirely explained by state history, European influence, a resource curse, monarchical traditions, or female oppression – singly, or in combination. Having said this, it is important to recognize that there are many varieties of Islam, and many sorts of political movements that purport to carry out an Islamic mission (Sadowski 2006). Treating them together in a single index lumps together heterogeneous phenomena with divergent effects. As with other composite indices – for example, of European ancestry, colonialism, Protestantism – one must be careful not to confuse general causal effects with uniform causal effects. A good deal of noise accompanies these estimates.

3.3 EUROPEANS

Europeans were the first to develop representative institutions, to hold elections for public office, and to constrain the use of political power by constitutional rules. Exactly why democracy arose in Europe and not elsewhere is a conundrum that we shall not attempt to unravel. We know that it was a long, slow, and halting development, with many reversals and many shifts of course across the continent. Nonetheless, democracy has deep roots in Europe, which remains the most democratic region of the world today.[15]

Europe also became the first (and, to date, the only) global hegemon, controlling vast portions of the planet during the age of imperialism and

[15] This section builds on Gerring, Apfeld, Wig and Tollefsen (2022: Chapters 8–11, 13).

TABLE 3.2 *Islam*

Model	1	2	3	4	5	6	7	8	9	10
Muslim (%)	-0.002***	-0.002***	-0.001***	-0.001***	-0.001***	-0.001***	-0.001***	-0.001**	-0.001**	-0.001***
	(0.000)	(0.000)	(0.000)	(0.000)	(0.000)	(0.000)	(0.000)	(0.000)	(0.000)	(0.000)
Islamic conquest			-0.082***	-0.084**	-0.079**	-0.060	-0.037	-0.066	-0.054	-0.017
			(0.026)	(0.035)	(0.039)	(0.039)	(0.041)	(0.052)	(0.046)	(0.038)
Arabic (%)				-0.000	0.000	-0.000	-0.001	-0.001**	-0.001***	-0.001*
				(0.000)	(0.000)	(0.000)	(0.000)	(0.001)	(0.000)	(0.000)
MENA					-0.015	0.039	0.122***	0.193***	0.183***	0.182***
					(0.044)	(0.040)	(0.044)	(0.056)	(0.049)	(0.045)
Equator distance		✓	✓	✓	✓	✓	✓	✓	✓	✓
Natural harbor distance		✓	✓	✓	✓	✓	✓	✓	✓	✓
State history (to 1500)						✓	✓	✓	✓	✓
English colonial dur.							✓	✓	✓	✓
Protestant (%)							✓	✓	✓	✓
European ancestry (%)							✓	✓	✓	✓
Oil income per cap								✓	✓	✓
Monarchy									✓	✓
Gender equality										✓
Countries	194	177	177	170	170	154	152	148	148	148
Years	231	231	231	231	231	231	222	207	207	207
Observations	24,852	23,790	23,790	23,206	23,206	21,488	19,664	13,142	12,834	12,834
R-squared (within)	0.417	0.537	0.541	0.542	0.543	0.560	0.633	0.584	0.621	0.653

Notes: Outcome variable: democracy, measured by the Polyarchy index. Not shown: annual dummies, constant. Ordinary least squares regression, country clustered standard errors in parentheses. ***p < 0.01 **p < 0.05 *p < 0.10.

spreading its languages (especially English, French, Spanish, and Portuguese), its religions (variants of Christianity), its technologies (military, agricultural, industrial), and its germs (smallpox, influenza et al.). In the wake of European contact, populations around the world were variously decimated, displaced, enslaved, and colonized. Given the extraordinary impact of Europeans on the modern world, it is plausible to suppose that they also affected the development of political institutions, including regime types. Four arguments may be fruitfully distinguished.

3.3.1 Colonialism

The most obvious way in which Europeans influenced the world was through their overt control of territory and peoples, that is, *colonialism*. Colonies modeled their political institutions after the metropole, and these institutions often survived long into the postcolonial era. This includes the form of the executive (e.g., parliamentary or presidential), the electoral system (e.g., proportional or majoritarian), the judiciary, the legal system (e.g., common law or civil law), the regulatory system (e.g., mercantilist or liberal), and so forth.[16] In this light, it would not be surprising to find a legacy effect of colonialism on regimes.

It is now well documented that English colonies offered greater scope for the development of democratic institutions than other European colonies (Lee and Paine 2020; Paine 2019). With respect to the postindependence legacy of colonial rule the verdict is less clear. Some studies find that colonial heritage – and especially British colonial heritage – is associated with greater democracy.[17] Other studies report weaker relationships, relationships that attenuate over time, or no relationship at all.[18]

3.3.2 Religion

Religion establishes a sense of community around a shared set of religious practices and membership in a single organization. If the religion is global, as is the case for Christianity, it provides a ready-made transnational civil society (Rudolph 1997). There are many examples of Christian activists defending the rights of indigenous peoples, most prominently the antislavery movement (Stamatov 2010). With this in mind, it is plausible to suppose that religion might serve as a mechanism of global diffusion (Beyer 2001). Since Europe was

[16] See De Juan and Pierskalla (2017), Fieldhouse (1966), Go (2003), Klerman, Mahoney, Spamann and Weinstein (2011), Krieckhaus (2006), La Porta, Lopez-de-Silanes, Shleifer, and Vishny (1998), Mahoney (2010).
[17] See Bernhard et al. (2004), Hariri (2012), Lange, Mahoney, and Vom Hau (2006), Lee and Paine (2020), Narizny (2012), Olsson (2009), Paine (2019).
[18] See Goldring and Greitens (2019), Gunitsky (2014: Table 14), Houle, Kayser, and Xiang (2016), Lee, Paine (2019), Miller (2012), Przeworski et al. (2000), Woodberry (2012).

the leading exemplar of representative democracy, it is plausible to suppose that Christian churches and Christian missionaries might have instilled democratic values (Anckar 2011). The influence of Protestantism on democracy is a longstanding hypothesis.[19] In addition to serving as a platform for diffusion of the idea of democracy, Woodberry (2012: 244–245) argues that "conversionary Protestants … were a crucial catalyst initiating the development and spread of religious liberty, mass education, mass printing, newspapers, voluntary organizations, most major colonial reforms, and the codification of legal protections for nonwhites in the nineteenth and early twentieth centuries." Others, following Weber, have noted Protestantism's effect on overarching values such as individualism and universalism (Eisenstadt 1968), which may have spillover effects on democracy.

A few studies explore a possible relationship between Catholicism and modern democracy.[20] Originally, the Catholic Church, that is, the Papacy and church officialdom, was no friend to democracy. Troy (2009) reports, "the Church opposed the first attempts to establish the 'rights of man' and democracy as a political system as this very process threatened the Church's unity and questioned its claim of holding absolute truths such as moral values as well as political convictions such as its claims of regulating political and social life." However, over the course of the twentieth century – and at an accelerated pace after Vatican II – the Church embraced democratic institutions in Eastern Europe (where this tendency was bolstered by the Church's historic animosity to communism), in Latin America, and in other regions with significant Catholic populations. The "third wave" of democratization centered on predominantly Catholic societies both in Europe (Portugal, Spain) and outside Europe.[21]

3.3.3 Language

Ideas encoded in a text, a recording, or a film are most likely to reach those fluent in the language in which that artifact was produced (Weyland 2007). Moreover, language plays a critical role in establishing and maintaining a sense of community.[22] Speakers of the same language find it easier to establish friendships and professional bonds, while those with different native tongues must struggle to communicate, and are hence excluded (Marquardt 2018).

---

[19] See Anderson (2004), Bollen and Jackman (1985), Brown (1944), Bruce (2004), Hadenius (1992), Lankina and Getachew (2012), Tusalem (2009), Woodberry (2012). Lee, Paine (2019) find that the influence of Protestantism on democracy attenuates in the late twentieth century.

[20] A much longer-range view of Catholicism, discussed in Chapter 8, argues that by changing family structures and fertility rates it paved the way for Europe's Sonderweg. Here, we are concerned with Catholicism as a global factor.

[21] See Anderson (2007), Chu (2011), Corrin (2010), Huntington (1991), Mantilla (2010), Philpott (2004), Troy (2009).

[22] See Barbour and Carmichael (2000), De Swaan (2001), Joseph (2004).

In this fashion, learning a European language may open an enduring link to an international network, centered – at least initially – on Europe. Francophones were connected to France, Lusophones to Portugal, Hispanics to Spain, Anglophones to England, and so forth. By virtue of speaking a European language, people around the world were presumably drawn into a social network centered on Europe and its offshoots, aka "the West." Although these polyglot individuals were initially elites, they probably served as transmission belts for ideas and practices that diffused broadly throughout societies in the non-European world. Thus, in states where significant numbers of citizens are conversant with a European language they are more likely to feel connected to Europe – to travel there, to be educated there, to have business contacts there, and to absorb ideas from there. Accordingly, one may conjecture that democracy, as an idea and an institution, diffused through linguistic networks across the world.

3.3.4   Demography

A fourth line of work focuses on demography. Beginning about 1500 CE, with the advent of sailing vessels capable of circumnavigating the globe, Europeans began to populate the distant abroad. Gerring et al. (2022: Part III) argue that the resulting ratio of Europeans/non-Europeans ("European ancestry") structured the fate of democracy around the world. Where Europeans were numerous (relative to indigenes and migrants from elsewhere), they championed some form of popular sovereignty, though often with restrictions limiting suffrage or office-holding to those of European heritage. Where they were in the minority, they were more reticent and often actively resisted democratization. Where Europeans were entirely absent, there was no one – at least initially – to carry the democratic torch.

The logic of this argument becomes clearer if we regard democracy as a *club* and its policies as *club goods*. Where Europeans composed a majority of the population, democracy offered a convenient system for monopolizing political power. Rule by the people meant rule by Europeans, who had the infrastructure (education, wealth, etc.) to make it work. Where Europeans composed a substantial minority they might still achieve this result, but to do so they needed to prevent the majority from participating or successfully coerce/coopt their political opponents, a precarious feat that was difficult to sustain. Where Europeans composed a tiny fraction of the population, establishing a democratic system of rule was neither practicable nor necessary, as European interests could be coordinated through informal channels within a small (and generally tightly knit) community. Regime types therefore evolved from the intersection of European ideas and interests with varying demographic realities.

3.3.5 Tests

We have now introduced multiple modalities of potential European influence. Our empirical tests, displayed in Table 3.3, privilege measures of these concepts that offer extensive coverage and perform reasonably well in tests conducted elsewhere (see Gerring et al. 2022: chapter 13). This narrows the field to six indicators: English colonial duration (years), European colonial duration (years), Protestants (%), Catholics (%), European language (% speaking), and European ancestry (%). As it happens, these pathways from Europe are only weakly correlated with each other, suggesting that Europe's presence throughout the world was not all of a piece.

In Model 1, all six variables are included on the right side, along with year dummies. Model 2 is limited to variables that are somewhat robust in Model 1. The remaining models focus on variables that are robust in Model 2, which narrows the field to English colonial duration, Protestants, and European ancestry. Model 3 broadens the sample to include Europe, and thus a global reach. Model 4 is restricted to the postwar era (1950-). Model 5 adds geographic covariates to the specification. Model 6 adds Muslim (the share of populations with an Islamic heritage, as discussed earlier) and a vector of regional dummies. Model 7 is a one-period cross-section, centered on the year 2000. These tests demonstrate that among a wide variety of indicators intended to measure European influence on democracy, there are three strong performers: English colonial duration, Protestantism, and European ancestry. Of these, only the latter is robust in all tests.

3.4 POPULATION

We now turn to the role of population in structuring political institutions.[23]

Examples of the dangers of scale were abundant in the premodern era. City-states were always small and sometimes democratic (at least by the standards of the day), while empires were large and made little pretense of representing popular opinion. A case in point is the transition of Rome from republic to empire, which was accompanied by an enlargement of territory and peoples and loss of popular control over the apparatus of government. These examples seem to confirm that when it comes to democracy, small is beautiful. Of course, communications and transport infrastructure were primitive in the premodern era and the principle of representation undeveloped. Under the circumstances, it is not surprising that writers like Plato, Aristotle, Montesquieu, and Rousseau expressed reservations about the impact of a growing population on politics.

Contemporary researchers often adopt this "classical" view of the subject. They, too, are skeptical about the capacity of communities to cope with the challenges of scale within a democratic framework (C. Anckar 2008; D. Anckar

---

[23] This section builds on Gerring and Veenendaal (2020: ch 16).

TABLE 3.3 Europeans

States	Europe	Europe	Full	Europe	Europe	Europe	Full
Time-period	Full	Full	Full	1950-	Full	Full	2000
Lag (years)	0	0	0	0	0	0	0
Model	1	2	3	4	5	6	7
English colonial duration	0.000	0.000	0.000***	0.000***	0.000*	0.000*	0.000
	(1.339)	(1.591)	(2.838)	(2.790)	(1.949)	(1.677)	(1.358)
European colonial duration	0.000**	0.000***					
	(2.007)	(2.952)					
Protestant (%)	0.003***	0.003***	0.002***	0.003***	0.003***	0.003***	0.001
	(3.326)	(3.812)	(3.286)	(3.416)	(3.678)	(3.286)	(1.149)
Catholic (%)	-0.000						
	(-0.839)						
European language (%)	0.001*						
	(1.819)						
European ancestry (%)	0.004***	0.004***	0.003***	0.005***	0.004***	0.004***	0.005***
	(7.672)	(9.221)	(10.069)	(8.462)	(9.051)	(5.571)	(5.210)
Equator distance					✓	✓	✓
Natural harbor distance					✓	✓	✓
Muslim						✓	✓
Region dummies						✓	✓
Countries	134	139	193	139	137	136	135
Years	222	229	229	67	229	229	1
Observations	16,892	17,289	23,033	7,766	17,123	17,012	135
R2	0.602	0.600	0.564	0.439	0.599	0.614	0.411

Notes: Outcome: Polyarchy index of electoral democracy. Not shown: Year dummies (except Model 7), Constant. Ordinary least squares, standard errors clustered by country, t statistics in parentheses. ***p < 0.01 **p < 0.05 *p < 0.10.

2002, 2004; Anckar and Anckar 1995, 2000; Diamond and Tsalik 1999; Hadenius 1992; Ott 2000; Srebrnik 2004). As an empirical point of departure, writers note the many microstates throughout the world that now qualify as democracies. A short list includes Andorra, Antigua and Barbuda, the Bahamas, Barbados, Belize, Dominica, Grenada, Kiribati, Liechtenstein, Marshall Islands, Micronesia, Monaco, Nauru, Palau, Saint Kitts & Nevis, Saint Lucia, Saint Vincent & Grenadines, Samoa, San Marino, Sao Tome & Principe, Tuvalu, and Vanuatu. Regression tests, as well as informal comparisons, seem to confirm a negative association between size and democracy.[24]

However, these regressions rely mostly on bivariate models or very limited specification tests and are usually focused on a narrow slice of time in the contemporary era. Note also that while many microstates do indeed achieve free and fair elections, a close look at their domestic politics suggests that smallness does not always lead to increased cooperation, harmony, or consensual politics. Instead, many microstates experience sharply polarized and personalistic politics, coupled with pervasive patronage, clientelism, and nepotism.[25] These dynamics, which (arguably) stem from the diminutive size of microstates, may undermine prospects for free and fair elections. Accordingly, the survival of electoral politics in microstates may be a by-product of colonial history, geographic location, or international politics rather than size per se (Veenendaal 2014). Anecdotally, one may counter lists of microstates with lists of macro-states, which are also predominantly democratic. A casual glance at the world's ten largest countries – China, India, the United States, Indonesia, Brazil, Pakistan, Bangladesh, Russia, Nigeria, and Mexico – reveals that all but one feature multiparty contestation, even if they are not perfectly democratic in other respects. A "Madisonian" view of politics suggests that larger states may enjoy advantages that small states lack, for example, greater tolerance for differences and greater stability, stemming from the fact that no single group is capable of monopolizing power.

3.4.1 Tests

To test the relationship, we regress Polyarchy on population (log) along with year dummies, as shown in Table 3.4. Model 1 includes only the regressor of theoretical interest. Model 2 adds the two geographic variables found to be robust in the previous analysis – equator distance and natural harbor distance. Model 3 adds several additional factors that may affect regime type along with a panel of regional dummies. Model 4 tests a different measure of scale. Instead of measuring population in a logarithmic fashion, we distinguish small states from all others. This accords with a threshold view of

---

[24] See Clague et al. (2001), Colomer (2007), Diamond and Tsalik (1999), Hadenius (1992), Ott (2000), Srebrnik (2004).

[25] See Richards (1982), Sutton (2007), Veenendaal (2013).

causal effects: size matters, but only up to a point. Typically, this threshold is set at a fairly low level, for example, a half million or one million. We test both options, but show only the latter. (There is little difference in results.)

Model 5 employs a fixed-effect estimator along with a covariate measuring per capita GDP. We do not regard this as a very plausible approach to estimation given that population is sluggish, highly trended, and subject to short-term perturbations (civil war, repression, famine, migration) that may serve as confounders. It is informative, nonetheless, since we have a long time series at our disposal. In Models 6 and 7 we explore several factors that are closely related – both theoretically and empirically – to population: *urbanization* (the share of population living in cities) and *population density* (transformed by the natural logarithm). Arguably, urbanization and population density should foster democracy as citizens living in close proximity are in a better position to solve coordination problems. Our test of urbanization includes per capita GDP, so as to distinguish between demography and economic development (for which urbanization is often regarded as a proxy).

Results posted in Table 3.4 show that population and its various analogs bear no relationship to regime type in the modern era. Signs on the coefficient for population switch and are nowhere near statistical significance. Likewise, the coefficient for the small state dummy is positive but not significant. Granted, the Polyarchy index excludes many microstates, often regarded as the strongest evidence for the classical view. However, additional tests using the Lexical index of electoral democracy (Skaaning et al. 2015) or the Freedom House Political rights index – both of which offer a comprehensive coding of countries, including all microstates – bears out the same story (Gerring and Veenendaal 2020: ch 16). Likewise, there is no change in results when the sample is restricted to contemporary years.

We therefore conclude that there is no perceivable relationship between population and regime type. States that are small seem to be about as likely to develop and maintain multiparty contestation, universal suffrage, and civil liberty as states that are large. Whatever negative impact a large population might have on prospects for democracy are countered by positive effects, generating a null result.

3.5 DIVERSITY

Diverse social identities coexisting within the same society are often viewed as problematic for economic and political development. Diversity is said to provide a focal point for conflict (Hegre and Sambanis 2006; Montalvo and Reynal-Querol 2005b; Reynal-Querol 2002; Sambanis 2001; Vanhanen 1999; Varshney 2007; Wilkinson 2009), poor governance (Alesina et al. 1999; Englebert 2000; Lieberman 2009), low social capital (Alesina and LaFerrara 2005), and poor economic performance (Alesina and LaFerrara 2005; Easterly and Levine 1997; Montalvo and Reynal-Querol 2005a).[26]

---

[26] This section builds on Gerring, Hoffman, and Zarecki (2018).

TABLE 3.4 *Population*

Estimator	OLS	OLS	OLS	OLS	OLS, FE	OLS	OLS
Model	1	2	3	4	5	6	7
Population (ln)	0.002	−0.001	0.004		−0.009		
	(0.009)	(0.008)	(0.009)		(0.020)		
Small state (dummy)				0.025			
				(0.023)			
Urbanization						0.085	
						(0.081)	
Population density (ln)							−0.008
							(0.010)
Equator distance		✓	✓	✓		✓	✓
Natural harbor distance		✓	✓	✓		✓	✓
Muslim (%)			✓				
English colonial duration			✓				
Protestant (%)			✓				
European ancestry (%)			✓				
GDP pc (ln)			✓		✓	✓	
Natural resources per cap			✓				
Regional dummies			✓				
Country dummies					✓		
Countries	183	173	159	175	183	165	149
Years	226	221	107	221	226	110	195
Observations	19,659	15,651	9,990	18,131	19,659	11,974	14,272
R-squared (within)	0.258	0.408	0.639	0.449	(0.605)	0.481	0.476

Notes: Outcome: Democracy, measured by the Polyarchy index. Right-side variables lagged one year in Model 5. Not shown: annual dummies, constant. Ordinary least squares regression, country clustered standard errors in parentheses. ***p < 0.01 **p < 0.05 *p < 0.10.

For similar reasons, diversity is also generally viewed as problematic for the establishment and consolidation of democratic political institutions. Arguably, social diversity provides the basis for enduring conflicts and clientelistic relationships, which impede the development of more encompassing attachments to the state and nation. It may also pose coordination problems for opposition groups (Arriol 2013), leading to outbidding (Rabushka and Shepsle 1972), None of this seems propitious for democracy (Anckar 1999;

Diamond and Plattner 1994; Epstein et al. 2012; Horowitz 1985; Lijphart 1977; Mill 1958[1861], 230; Rabushka and Shepsle 1972; Snyder 2000; Weingast 1997).

In addressing this issue, scholars usually regard social identity as a unified concept. At the same time, few would maintain that cleavages grounded in ethnic, linguistic, and religious identities are interchangeable. This, in turn, suggests that different types of diversity might have divergent effects. Gerring et al. (2018) argue that religious diversity has a negative impact, and ethnolinguistic diversity a *positive* impact, on a polity's propensity to develop and maintain a democratic system of government. Specifically, they suggest that religious diversity imposes a barrier to the development of a democratic form of government because it discourages toleration and compromise. By contrast, ethnic diversity may facilitate democracy by virtue of making it more difficult for a single clique to monopolize power over the *longue duree*.

3.5.1   Tests

To test these hypotheses, we enlist a set of cross-national regression tests displayed in Table 3.5. These are limited to the postwar period, as comprehensive cross-national data for ethnic and religious fractionalization indices is available only for this restricted period. We shall assume that these measures are sticky enough to justify holding them constant across a half-century period of observation. Fractionalization is measured in standard fashion with the Herfindahl index, which measures the probability that two randomly chosen individuals from a population belong to the same social group. To measure ethnolinguistic fractionalization we draw on an index used by Easterly and Levine (1997), based on data gathered in the 1950s and 1960s for the Soviet-sponsored *Atlas Narodov Mira*. Missing data is imputed for several countries omitted in the survey. To measure religious fractionalization we draw on an index constructed by Alesina et al. (2003), drawing on data recorded in *Encyclopedia Britannica*. (Additional measures of ethnic and religious fractionalization and polarization are tested in Gerring et al. 2018.)

Model 1 builds on previous sections of this chapter, including covariates that have proven their worth in previous tests – Protestant (%), Europeans (%), temperature, and natural harbor distance – along with year dummies. Model 2 adds several additional covariates identified by previous work, including distance from equator (latitude), island, Muslim (%), and per capita GDP. Results are equivocal. Model 1 shows no trace of a causal effect, while Model 2 corroborates arguments made by Gerring et al. (2018) – ethnic fractionalization appears to have a positive effect on prospects for democracy, while religious fractionalization appears to have a negative effect.

TABLE 3.5 *Diversity*

Model	1	2
Ethnic fractionalization	–0.004	0.101**
	(0.050)	(0.051)
Religious fractionalization	0.021	–0.111**
	(0.056)	(0.052)
Equator distance	✓	✓
Natural harbor distance	✓	✓
Muslim (%)		✓
Protestant (%)		✓
Europeans (%)		✓
Island		✓
GDP pc (ln)		✓
Countries	157	154
Years	44	44
Observations	5,825	5,703
R-squared (within)	0.533	0.603

Notes: Outcome: Democracy, measured by the Polyarchy index. Not shown: annual dummies, constant. Ordinary least squares regression, country clustered standard errors in parentheses. ***p < 0.01 **p < 0.05 *p < 0.10.

Under normal circumstances, one might prefer the pared down specification, which mitigates the potential of posttreatment bias. However, it is important to bear in mind that the cultural diversity of a country is likely to be affected by many factors that may also affect its regime type; unless conditioned, these factors pose a problem of confounding. For example, diversity seems more extreme near the equator (latitude), in large land masses (non-islands), and in less developed countries (as proxied by GDP). Likewise, any measure of religious fractionalization is likely to be correlated with particular religions, including those that are suspected to influence regime types such as Protestantism and Islam, as well as with the share of the population that is of European ancestry. So, there is a rationale for more fully specified models, even at the risk of including posttreatment confounders.

There is no obvious way out of this specification problem, which is considerably more severe than for other factors tested in this chapter by reason of the endogenous nature of cultural diversity. Gerring et al. (2018) explore various robustness tests including an instrumental variable model (where topographic contours of the landscape instrument for ethnic fractionalization) and a fixed-effect model (where a sluggish, though not entirely static, measure of ethnic fractionalization is employed on the right side). However, these are not ideal solutions, requiring fairly strong assumptions. Note also that since measures of ethnic and religious fractionalization are available only for a limited period of time we cannot test the entire time series of democracy (back to 1789), as we have for other outcomes in this chapter. For all these reasons, we conclude that the relationship between diversity and democracy is impossible to resolve.

3.6 CONCLUSIONS

In this chapter we surveyed factors that may have contributed to the long-run development of democracy or autocracy in the modern world.

It is important to remind ourselves that these are very brief empirical exercises. Helpfully, work published elsewhere (cited in the text) provides more extensive empirical support for most of these conclusions. This includes instrumental variables (where warranted), additional specifications, alternative measures of the predictor and the outcome (democracy), different right-side lags, different country samples (some of which encompass countries outside the V-Dem dataset), and different time-periods. It also includes qualitative and quantitative data drawn from more specific settings, and thus departing from our cross-national research design. Since these supplementary analyses generally support the propositions put forth in this chapter, we have more faith in our conclusions than we might if they reflected only those analyses appearing in preceding tables.

Our own analyses offer a mixed set of results, which is perhaps not surprising given the wide range of factors under investigation. Among geographic factors, distance from equator (+) and distance from nearest natural harbor (−) are strongly correlated with democracy. Among factors associated with European diffusion, Protestantism and Europeans (both measured as a share of population) are positively correlated with democracy. Population (along with associated concepts such as urbanization and population density) is not correlated with regime type. Among measures of cultural diversity we find different relationships between democracy and ethnic heterogeneity (+) and religious heterogeneity (−), though neither is very strong. Islam – understood as share of population of Muslim descent or share of territory conquered by Arab armies – is negatively associated with democracy. Other factors tested in this chapter do not bear a strong empirical relationship to democracy.

How much of the variability in regime types can these factors explain? In Table 3.6, we limit ourselves to those variables with the greatest predictive power and (in our view) the strongest claims to causal inference. To simplify the interpretation, we adopt a single cross-section of the world in 2000 CE. Model 1 includes the two geographic factors – equator distance and natural harbor distance – which, together, explain about a quarter of the variability in regimes across the world. Model 2 adds variables measuring religion – share of Muslims and Protestants – and European ancestry. All together, these five variables explain over 50 percent of the variability in our outcome.

TABLE 3.6 *A parsimonious model*

Model	1	2
Equator distance	0.006***	0.001
	(0.001)	(0.001)
Natural harbor distance	–0.021***	–0.006
	(0.004)	(0.004)
Muslim (%)		–0.002***
		(0.001)
Protestant (%)		0.001**
		(0.001)
European ancestry (%)		0.003***
		(0.001)
Observations (countries)	176	171
R2	0.242	0.550

Notes: Outcome: Democracy, measured by the Polyarchy index. Year: 2000. Not shown: Constant. Ordinary least squares, standard errors clustered by country, ***$p < 0.01$ **$p < 0.05$ *$p < 0.10$.

This exercise demonstrates that a nontrivial portion of the variance in regime types across the world today can be explained by structural factors that extend back for a century or more. Democracy has deep roots. At the same time, it shows that there is a good deal of variation left to explain. Structural factors are not determinative, as witnessed by the many regime transitions in the modern era. This chapter thus serves as a fitting segue to later chapters, which focus on more proximal factors.

4

International Influence

The Hidden Dimension

Michael Coppedge, Benjamin Denison, Paul Friesen, Lucía Tiscornia, and Yang Xu[*]

The other chapters of this book, like the majority of quantitative analyses of democratization, examine domestic determinants: geography, economic factors, institutions, and civil society. In this chapter we develop and test hypotheses about possible influences that lie outside national borders. We find that levels of electoral democracy are contagious among neighboring countries. Although contagion among neighbors is a small influence year-to-year, it compounds like the principal in an interest-bearing bank account. Over several decades, the cumulative effect is substantial: enough to help create and sustain very democratic regions such as Western Europe and North America. Contagion among neighbors also helps spread short-term upturns and downturns in democracy. A different network that links colonizers and their current and former colonies also spreads upturns. Networks linking military allies appear to help make both upturns and downturns contagious, although these effects are less certain because democracies tend to join the same alliances. We also find that exogenous shocks such as war and the expansion of the global economy affect democracy. Taken together, our results suggest that the international system is an important long-term influence on democratization even when its effects are barely perceptible in the short term.

[*] Coppedge and Friesen: Department of Political Science, University of Notre Dame; Denison, Notre Dame International Security Center; Tiscornia, Centro de Investigación y Docencia Económicas (CIDE): Yang Xu, Center for Social Science Research, University of Notre Dame. We are deeply indebted to Robert Franzese for his ICPSR workshop on "Spatial Econometrics," including permission to adapt a post-estimation Stata do-file he wrote with Jude Hays and Scott Cook; and to Nick Ottone, Jack Stump, and Jacob Turner for research assistance. We are also grateful to the Kellogg Institute's Research Cluster on Democratization Theory for many discussions and to Vanderbilt University's Center for the Study of Democratic Institutions for support during Coppedge's research leave in spring 2021, in particular to Vanderbilt colleagues Joshua Clinton, John Sides, Kristin Michelitch, Noam Lupu, and David Lewis.

A major reason for studying international influences is Galton's problem, which inspires cautions that domestic determinants may receive too much credit for democratization if we ignore international determinants. For example, Brinks and Coppedge argued that "If, as all the prior research and our own results suggest, diffusion is an important phenomenon, then researchers who ignore diffusion risk exaggerating the impact of domestic determinants" (Brinks and Coppedge 2006, 466). There are many good reasons to expect that domestic factors are not the sole determinants. We lay out a theoretical framework that systematically catalogues most of the possible international hypotheses. We then test selected hypotheses about exogenous shocks and contagion – the spread of democracy outcomes from country to country through various international networks. Surprisingly, contagion at first appears to be real but so small that it could be ignored when studying domestic influences. However, some of these effects grow as time passes. In fact, our estimates suggest that the average West European/North American country was about 0.20 points more democratic (on a 0–1 scale) over the 1900–2010 period than it would have been without other democracies as neighbors. This paradox leads us to conclude that international influences are a hidden dimension of democratization.

Although some hypotheses about international influence have been tested repeatedly, very few of the tests have employed the most rigorous methods from spatial econometrics. We use the best currently available methods to test a handful of hypotheses about international sources of democratization and erosion. There are many other hypotheses about international factors that remain to be tested. These findings are therefore preliminary and provisional even though we consider them an advance beyond the previous literature.

Some of the contagion effects that we report here are large in the long term. However, their importance is difficult to discern from the regression results, for two reasons. First, the regressions report only average effects over a very large sample with sparse linkages. Each country has only a few neighbors, a few alliance partners, a few or no colonies, and one or no colonizer. As a result, the estimated effects are averages that include many zeroes. These averages can hide local effects that can be larger. For example, later in the text we show that contagion among neighbors is stronger and more certain in some regions than it is in others, and the implications of these relationships are quite different for different countries even in the same region.

Second, the small effects reported in regression tables are just the most proximate and immediate effects; they grow stronger as they reverberate through their extended networks and accumulate over several years. The long-term effects become evident only when we simulate the predictions of our regressions. Paradoxically, as long as researchers limit their attention to global averages of short-term relationships, it is probably unnecessary to take any international influences other than exogenous shocks into account: estimates of domestic determinants are not likely to be biased in such models. However, a fuller understanding of democratization requires taking the long-term and local relationships into account.

4.1   RATIONALE

There are at least three good reasons to expect international influences to matter. First, it should be obvious that democracy did not evolve independently in each country. Many ideas rooted in principles of self-government, political equality, and inclusion sprouted in different regions of the world at different times – ancient Athens, the Roman republic, Italian city-states, ecclesiastical institutions, Western European feudalism, Enlightenment norms, resistance to absolute monarchy, the French Revolution, independence struggles, mass conscription, socialist writings, civil rights movements, feminism, and technological innovations. These ideas gradually but incompletely blended together into several varieties of democracy that are practiced in about half of the countries in the world today (Coppedge et al. 2011; Held 2006). In addition, we know that countries are bound together in many ways: through trade and investment, migration, shared news and entertainment, international organizations, transnational NGOs, diplomacy and treaties, and military alliances. Furthermore, these ties tend to follow shared languages, religion, linked histories, and so on. It seems likely that these networks convey norms about desirable political regimes whether the networks were constructed to shape political regimes or not. Moreover, many democratic countries make active efforts to spread democratic practices to other countries in their international networks. Some non-democracies attempt to prevent or undermine democracy abroad by encouraging nondemocratic forms of government, too.

The second reason to expect international influence is the empirical evidence that is consistent with such influence. Spatial patterns suggest that geographic proximity matters. A map of degrees of democracy in any decade since 1900 makes it evident that the most democratic countries tend to be found persistently in the northwest quadrant of the world and in Oceania (O'Loughlin et al. 1998). This clustering is statistically significant.[1] Moreover, when democracy becomes more common, it tends to arise next in countries adjacent to these regions, such as Latin America and Eastern Europe, with a few exceptions such as Japan, India, South Africa, and Mongolia. In addition, historical changes in the proportion of countries that are democratic tend to occur in waves and reverse waves (Diamond 1999; Huntington 1991). As Chapter 2 shows, there was a long, slow process of gradual movement toward electoral democracy among sovereign countries in the nineteenth century, with perhaps a small sudden improvement around 1848. This process was followed by some dramatic improvement after World War I; then the well-known setbacks of the Interwar Period and a new wave of democratization after World War II; then another reverse wave starting around 1960, followed by

[1] Following a regression of V-Dem's polyarchy index for 2017 (v8) on an intercept, Moran's test of spatial independence decisively rejects the null hypothesis of no spatial autocorrelation based on latitude and longitude (Chi-sq$_{1, 169}$ = 188.16, p<0.00005).

the celebrated Third Wave starting in the late 1970s, with great acceleration from 1989 until 1993. We may now be at the beginning of a new reverse wave (Lührmann and Lindberg 2019). There are always countries that swim against these tides, but the average trends are clear. It is extremely unlikely that these spatial and temporal patterns could be purely the products of domestic forces working independently within each country, separate from domestic processes in any other country. There must be some kind of linkage among countries.

Third, several scholars have developed arguments about the channels and mechanisms through which countries affect democracy, or components of democracy, in other countries. Although these works tend not to offer general tests, they have documented the workings of these mechanisms in qualitative case studies. Keck and Sikkink (1998), for example, show how transnational issue networks helped abolish slavery, win women's suffrage, and protect women's rights. Whitehead (2001), although he takes a sober, cautionary view of international influences, distills lessons from a collection of regional surveys and case studies, and distinguishes among three processes: contagion among neighbors (Li and Thompson 1975), control (or imposition or occupation) by a single foreign power, and consent (the interaction of internal and external conditions favoring democracy). Huntington (1991) argues that the Catholic Church's shift in favor of democracy and human rights helped drive the third wave of democratization. It is hard to find a study arguing that international influences do not matter, although it is possible that researchers bury null findings in the proverbial file drawer.

4.2 THEORETICAL FRAMEWORK

Theories about how and why external factors matter for democratization – the causal mechanisms – are rarely well developed. Perhaps it is not surprising that the theories are vague, given that these are claims about the impact of distant, diffuse causes on a complex macro-phenomenon, democracy, in many diverse global and historical contexts. It is a challenge to reduce the process to just one causal mechanism, much less to specify who the actors are, what motivates them, what resources they command, and why they are successful or not. The most common response to this challenge has been to settle for documenting empirical generalizations that are compatible with multiple mechanisms, while leaving theoretical precision for later (Brinks and Coppedge 2006). Several articles develop more specific hypotheses about international influences. Among the better examples are Mainwaring and Pérez-Liñán's discussion of the ideas shared in the international left in Latin America, Woodberry's arguments about how mission schools indirectly promoted democracy, and Pevehouse's reasoning about how belonging to a regional organization might influence regime change (Mainwaring and Pérez-Liñán 2013, 93–123; Pevehouse 2002; Woodberry 2012). While these are important contributions, they do not claim to provide a comprehensive inventory of other pathways for international influence.

In principle, it is always prudent to aim to be comprehensive in order to avoid omitted variable bias, but in practice it is especially necessary to avoid it when studying international influences because so many of these potential pathways are correlated and believed to produce similar outcomes. Otherwise, the effect of being trading partners or military allies, for example, could easily be mistaken as an effect of merely being neighbors or sharing a language or religion or a level of income. In this section, we make an inventory of practically all the possible kinds of international influence as a sobering reminder of how much remains to be tested.[2]

We now describe our theoretical framework in order to contrast our approach with other research on international influences on democratization. In this chapter, "international influences" are hypothesized causes of democracy in a country that originate outside that country's borders. This definition excludes hypotheses about domestic causes even if they cluster in certain regions and therefore contribute to regional clusters of democracy. These exclusions make a long list comprising most of the hypotheses that the rest of this book and, indeed, the bulk of the democratization literature, takes most seriously: hypotheses about income, inequality, education, social cleavages, state strength, culture, institutions, latitude, climate, and so on. How domestic causes, such as high income, strong states, and relative social equality, came to be concentrated in certain regions is an interesting question, but it is not the question we pose here. Spatially clustered domestic causes and strictly international causes are easily confused because they often have very similar effects. Distinguishing between them is therefore an essential goal of our analysis (Houle et al. 2016).

We make further distinctions between exogenous shocks, endogenous networks, and exogenous networks. Exogenous shocks are international influences that are not easily attributable to a specific source country; rather, they are emergent properties of the international system.[3] This kind of influence leads countries to act in similar ways around the same time, but not because they are influencing one another; they are all simply reacting to the same external stimulus. Good examples of shocks from the international system are global economic crises, world wars, and pandemics. These are unidirectional relationships in which influence flows only from a diffuse international source to a group of countries, never – even indirectly – from targets to sources. This is why they are safely treated as exogenous.

---

[2] Many of the elements of this framework were originally laid out by Starr (1991).

[3] "Exogenous shock" is a term of art in econometrics for a stimulus that is assumed to originate outside the unit that receives it and is therefore not caused by characteristics of the unit itself. That assumption may not be perfectly true. In a world war, each combatant probably played a role in initiating or responding to attacks; in a global depression, each country's economic decline contributes to the shrinking of the world economy; in a pandemic, each country plays a role in spreading or containing the sickness. However, when such outbreaks of war, depression, or illness involve many countries and develop in a year or two, each country's contribution to the process is small, and in a century-long panel study the outbreaks happen relatively suddenly, in one or two years. For these reasons, we think it a reasonable simplification to treat such shocks as exogenous.

Networks are sets of ties linking countries. Normally, they are multidirectional relationships in which countries are both sources and targets, so their outcomes are therefore endogenous. The simplest example is when country A affects country B and country B affects country A. However, the relationship is also endogenous when the feedback is indirect, as when A affects B, which affects C, which affects A. Endogeneity requires us to think about, and model, exogenous and endogenous international relationships differently. All endogenous relationships can be conceptualized and modeled as networks linking countries. As with exogenous relationships, we can distinguish networks by the structure of the linkages: which countries, and how many countries, are linked together. Some networks consist of mutually exclusive groups of countries, all of which affect each other. Examples include international organizations, alliances, and geographic regions. NATO members presumably affect one another, as did members of the Warsaw Pact before the breakup of the Soviet Union. A group could be as small as two countries, such as North and South Korea, which illustrates the fact that groups need not correspond to a formal organization; rather, which groups matter is a theoretical supposition that we must test.[4] Perhaps, countries adopting Huawei's 5G network will be connected in politically relevant ways. The Organization of African Unity probably matters more for democratization than Association of Southeast Asian Nations (ASEAN) does, but probably less than the European Union.

Some networks, by contrast, are not mutually exclusive: countries that are linked to one group are also linked to other groups. These are networks of overlapping networks in which every country that is connected to any other country is indirectly linked to every other country in the network. A good example is the network of contiguous neighbors, which is complex because each country is directly linked to only a handful of other countries, but because every country's direct network is slightly different from its neighbors', every country is indirectly linked to all other countries (assuming that we define neighbors linking islands to a mainland and continents to each other, as we do). Other examples are multidirectional colonial relationships, trading partners, and linkages formed by investment flows. Some networks reach the extreme of being global, linking every country to every other one, such as a network defined by the distance between every possible pair of countries.

However, some networks are exogenous. This is possible when a dominant country in a network affects all the other countries but they do not affect either the dominant country or one another: it is a single hierarchy. Exogenous networks, which are not tested here, would include democracy promotion programs, sanctions, occupation, and unilateral domination of colonies by a colonizer.

---

[4] In this regard, our approach differs fundamentally from the fast-growing inferential network analysis approach, which uses exponential random graph models (ERGMs) primarily to explain network structures (Cranmer et al. 2021). We take the networks as theoretically given and focus on estimating their effects on outcomes.

86

Michael Coppedge, et al.

Beyond the direction and structure of the linkages between sources and targets, a framework for classifying types of international influence must consider the nature of the stimulus that sources send to targets. For exogenous shocks, what matters is usually the magnitude of the shock that each country experiences: in war, lives lost, territory surrendered, resources spent; in an economic crisis, the unemployment rate, shrinkage of GDP, and loss of access to capital markets; in pandemics, numbers of infections, hospitalizations, and deaths. For international influences channeled by networks, we think it is useful to use the outcome in the source countries – here, levels, upturns, and downturns in electoral democracy – as the stimulus. Therefore, we use our networks to model "contagion," a common term for outcomes "there" affecting outcomes "here" (Li and Thompson 1975). If we modeled independent variables in one country affecting outcomes in other countries, a different term, such as "spillovers," would apply.

However, whether the stimulus is an exogenous shock or a democracy outcome, there is still an undertheorized linkage between the stimulus and the response. In this chapter, the stimulus is an increment to the democracy level or upturn or downturn in another country. Researchers must supply additional theory to flesh out causal mechanisms. One way to get closer to mechanisms is to specify which countries carry more weight, and why. Is a country's international influence proportional to population? Income? Economic growth? Military capabilities? Population flows? Volume of investment? Media production? Internet presence? Assigning weights to countries based on such variables can narrow down the kinds of mechanisms to a few possibilities. For example, the hypothesis that countries emulate the political regimes of economically successful countries could be modeled by weighting influence by per capita GDP or economic growth rates (which are two different implications of this idea). By contrast, a more coercive kind of diffusion would be better modeled with networks among countries whose weights are proportional to military power. A softer, more ideational kind of diffusion could be represented by networks linking countries speaking the same language, which encourages flows of information, news, entertainment, and social media. This kind of diffusion could be compatible with an equal weighting of countries, which would permit the examples set by smaller, less important countries to matter as much as the experiences of large, important countries. Although we consider network weighting a promising avenue for future research, all analyses in this chapter are unweighted.[5]

This theoretical framework is fairly comprehensive in scope. In principle, one could translate any hypothesis found in the literature on international

---

[5] Technically, our spatial weights are row-weighted, meaning that each source country's weight is divided by the number of countries directly linked with the target country so that the sum of the weights of source countries is 1 and the effect can be interpreted as the effect of the average linked country. Row weighting is not the only or necessarily the best weighting scheme, but because of its simplicity it is the most common one.

influences on democracy into some combination of (1) either an exogenous impact or a network (2) in one or multiple directions (3) with a certain stimulus and (4) an appropriate weighting scheme.[6] The earliest hypotheses proposed exogenous impacts of belonging to one international group or another. For some it was the group of former colonies, or of former colonies of Great Britain, or another great power (Bernhard et al. 2004; Bollen and Jackman 1985; Gassebner et al. 2009; Gunitsky 2014; Miller 2012; Woodberry 2012). For others (Bollen 1983; Burkhart and Lewis-Beck 1994), it was the group of countries in the periphery or semi-periphery of the world economy. For Pevehouse (2002), it is membership in regional organizations. Similarly, some scholars have controlled for the average democracy level or the proportion of democracies in a country's geographic region or the globe, which is an exogenous impact of membership in an informal geographic group (Gunitsky 2014; Starr and Lindborg 2003). Miller (2016) weights mean democracy (Polity) at the regional and global levels by economic growth, concluding that democracy is more likely to spread when democracies are experiencing economic growth. This model, too, is treated as an exogenous group effect.

Others have proposed that democracy promotion efforts have had bilateral, unidirectional exogenous impacts (Finkel et al. 2007; Mainwaring and Pérez-Liñán 2013, 93–123; Miller 2012). Woodberry (2012) argued that prolonged early exposure to Protestant missions aided later democratization, a thesis that translates into an exogenous impact of a linkage to colonizers weighted by mission exposure.

A common strategy has been to construct networks derived from geography, whether based on contiguity (Brinks and Coppedge 2006; Leeson and Dean 2009; O'Loughlin et al. 1998; Starr 2001) or proximity (Gleditsch and Ward 2006).[7] Miller (2016) also tests his growth-weighted model for contiguous countries, but finds no significant relationship at that level. As we argue later in the text, there is a conflict between the assumption of multidirectional linkages in geographic networks and the tests these studies report, which treat these relationships as exogenous. A well-executed application of spatial econometrics to democratization using distance is Cook et al. (2020). The authors find that the results depend crucially on model specification, and in their preferred model, there is no significant country-to-country influence. Spatial econometrics is a recent adoption in political science, but it is increasingly used in democratization research (Goldring and Greitens 2019; Goodliffe and Hawkins 2015; Leeson and Dean 2009; Zhukov and Stewart 2013).

---

[6] It may be necessary to add a time parameter to specify lag lengths and cumulative exposure to the stimulus. In addition, the dependent variable could be categorical, a continuous magnitude of change, upturns or downturns, the probability of change, or the cumulative hazard of change.

[7] O'Loughlin et al. (1998) were early adopters of some of the spatial econometric techniques we use, but used them only in a descriptive way, to test for significant spatial clustering of democracy.

Levitsky and Way's (2006) argument that transitions from competitive authoritarian regimes are determined by linkage and leverage also fits in our framework. Which countries are linked together is a matter of being included in the western or eastern network. Linking is the strength of the economic and technological ties, and leverage is the degree of asymmetry of those ties. Both linkage and leverage can be expressed as weights for each direction of a dyadic relationship: linkage by the absolute size of each country's weight, leverage by the ratio of their weights.

Gunitsky (2014, 2017) proposes that several international conditions work in combination. He argues that regime transitions are more likely when there are "hegemonic shocks": "abrupt shifts in the distribution of power among leading states"; but that other factors – British colonial legacies, the proportion of democratic neighbors in the region and globally and recent neighbor transitions – also have exogenous impacts, alone and in interaction with hegemonic shocks. Furthermore, he finds that average trade with the United States in the previous five years also matters. Trade is, in effect, a weight in each country's bilateral relationship with the United States. Finally, Gunitsky allows for some countries to influence others, sometimes in the aftermath of a hegemonic shock. However, Gunitsky treats all of these linkages as unidirectional and therefore exogenous.

Teorell (2010, 77–99) tested the greatest variety of international influences: total trade volume; democratization among neighbors; level of democracy among neighbors, in the region, and in the world; democratization and prior level of democracy in regional organization; flows of portfolio and foreign direct investment; economic sanctions; and military interventions. Furthermore, Teorell estimated the impact of each of these factors on the short-term level of democracy, upturns and downturns, and the long-run level of democracy, and complemented the quantitative analysis with several case studies. However, he specified all of these factors as unidirectional, and therefore exogenous, relationships. Sanctions and occupations probably are, but others probably involve some endogeneity.

One of the best-known typologies of international influence is Elkins and Simmons's set of distinctions between hard coercion, soft coercion, competitive advantage-seeking, learning, and emulation (2005). These are better seen as broad categories of explanation rather than specific explanations that have empirically distinguishable observable implications. Nevertheless, each type is compatible with one or more combinations of possibilities in our theoretical framework. Most of the emphasis in their typology is on the nature of the stimuli and the weights, without precisely specifying the structure of the network. Soft coercion could take the form of aid conditionality, economic sanctions, withdrawing an ambassador, sponsoring a censure vote in an international organization, or secret diplomacy. "Learning" does not specify who learns what from whom. Is it the executive, party leaders, military officers, jurists, journalists, NGOs, or the mass public that learns? Do they learn to emulate positive examples abroad (which raises the question of how learning differs from emulation) or to avoid mistakes? This chapter will not answer these questions, but neither does any other large-sample research project. Some clues can be found in small-sample qualitative studies (Elkins 2013, González Ocantos 2016; Madrid 2003), but more general answers will have to wait.

This list is not exhaustive, but it serves to support the point that all the major hypotheses readily translate into our theoretical framework. It should be clear that there is a world of hypotheses about international influences on democratization, too many to test in a single chapter. In Section 4.4 we develop the hypotheses we have chosen to test here. But first, in Section 4.3 we explain the methodological problems with previous research designs and how we seek to get better estimates.

4.3 METHODOLOGICAL CONSIDERATIONS

As long as a variable in the model is exogenous, no special handling is needed: it becomes a right-hand-side variable and its coefficient has a straightforward interpretation, exactly like the coefficients of domestic variables. War and international economic shocks, and if we included them here, invasions, occupations, and sanctions, fall under this heading. If a variable represents a spatially endogenous explanatory factor, however, it requires a much more elaborate procedure to obtain accurate estimates and meaningful interpretations. In fact, processes with spatial endogeneity necessarily violate Rubin's SUTVA, the Stable Unit Treatment Value Assumption, because (a) units interfere with each other – this is what interests us! – and (b) potential outcomes are not uniquely defined.[8] As we will see, the same model implies different effect sizes for different countries, depending on how they are linked to other cases. We expect the impact of the erosion of democracy in Hungary to be different for Ukraine than it is for Austria, because it makes a difference that Austria's other neighbors are Slovakia, Czechia, Germany, Italy, and Slovenia, while Ukraine's other neighbors are Poland, Slovakia, Romania, Moldova, Russia, and Belarus. From a potential outcomes perspective, it is doubtful whether one can make any meaningful causal inference in such situations.[9] Yet, we believe that spatial dependence exists and must be understood if we

---

[8] The problem is not utterly hopeless: Aronow and Samii (2013), among others, have offered advice on how to design experiments that achieve causal identification when interference among units is likely. However, research applications in this area have so far been confined to controlled experiments on individuals or small communities. No one has attempted to apply such an approach to the study of countries over more than a century of history, for which it is impossible to randomize any sort of treatment. Natural or quasi-experiments may be found, but they would exclude most of the cases, many of which must be included in any valid study of international influence.

[9] However, even Imbens and Rubin (2015, p. 10 of advance typescript) acknowledge that "(...) SUTVA is only one candidate exclusion restriction for modelling the potentially complex

are to achieve unbiased estimates of the effects of domestic conditions. Therefore, rather than give up, we use the best alternative observational methods from spatial econometrics.

We must use such methods for all of the variables that use democracy "there" (in country$_j$) to explain democracy "here" (in country$_i$). They include terms for the effects of contiguity or distance, trade and investment flows, membership in alliances and other international organizations, regional location, and status in the world economy. It also includes the effects of colonial rule, invasion, or occupation if there is reason to believe that these actions spur a backlash on the colonizer, invader, or occupying power. These variables are endogenous because every country in the network is both a source and a target.

In a South American neighbor network, for example, we cannot take democracy in Argentina at face value and use it to explain democracy in its neighbor, Brazil, because democracy in Brazil presumably affects democracy in Argentina. Our estimate of democracy in Argentina must be purged of Brazil's influence (and the influence of Chile, Bolivia, Paraguay, and Uruguay) before we use it to explain democracy in Brazil. We must also purge Brazil's democracy of the influence of its ten neighbors before testing for its influence on Argentina. Our solution is to use instrumental variables to approximate what the level of democracy would have been in each country if it had no neighbors and then use those instruments to try to explain democracy in the other countries. The same precaution is necessary when the explanatory variable is the regional or global mean or the mean score for members of an alliance or international organization, or any network in which influence directly or indirectly flows in both directions.

As far as we know, no other published work has yet used instrumental variables to correct for endogeneity when analyzing international influences on democracy. At best, others have used a temporal lag of other countries' scores to lessen the threat of endogeneity, but given the very strong serial autocorrelation in democracy scores it is far from clear that lagging an independent democracy variable is an adequate solution. Appendix A explains models of spatial dependence in greater detail.

There are two additional limitations of the existing research. First, much of the quantitative research considers only the long-term effects of international factors. This is implied, for example, by Woodberry's analysis of the consequences of Protestant missions (Woodberry 2012). His analysis uses missions data from 1900 to 1923 to explain mean levels of democracy in 1955–1994, a cross-section observed more than three decades later. Long-term effects are also implied when a panel analysis uses dummy variables to represent an experience in a country's distant past, such as colonial experience (Barro 1999; Bollen and Jackman 1985; Burkhart 1997; Gassebner et al. 2009;

interactions between units and the entire set of treatment levels in a particular experiment," while adding that "In many settings, however, it appears that SUTVA is the leading choice."

Lipset et al. 1993; Muller 1995). Is this a problem? Certainly there can be long-term consequences of past experiences, and they need to be studied. However, we are too easily impressed by empirical relationships that persist over long spans of time. Cross-sectional differences can be persistent even if they are spurious. Cross-sectional regression assumes that differences between countries are equivalent to changes over time, which would be more valid evidence of causation. These are not sufficiently rigorous tests; they cannot distinguish well between the past experience one is interested in and all the other experiences the country had in the distant past. If differences rooted in the past are persistent, they are relatively fixed effects for these countries that would appear to have the same consequences. Short-term effects would be much less confounded. We therefore estimate short-term effects and simulate their long-term consequences, which decay as time passes.

Second, a subset of studies uses a binary dependent variable. For example, some researchers model the difference between democracies and dictatorships (Londregan and Poole 1996), or the probability of a transition or breakdown (Bernhard et al. 2004; Przeworski et al. 2000), or of a coup (Li and Thompson 1975). These are valid, interesting questions. However, they are also dramatic, rare, low-probability events that are hard to model. Only 565 of the 24,751 country-years in v9 of the V-Dem dataset, or 2.3 percent, registered an absolute change of at least 0.1 on the 0–1 polyarchy index. Regime changes as measured by a binary indicator are much rarer than this. Models of continuous outcomes, or changes in continuous outcomes, are more sensitive to the modest effects that international factors are likely to have.

We cannot completely eliminate all the competing explanations. One, as we have noted, is Galton's problem: the difficulty of distinguishing truly international causes from domestic causes that happen to be geographically clustered. We address this threat to inference in two ways. First, we control for selected domestic predictors whether they are spatially correlated or not. Second, our models also correct for network-correlated errors, which helps mop up variance that is due to omitted variables that are geographically clustered. For example, why are so many Western European countries democratic today? Neighbor influence may play a role, but it is important to distinguish it from the fact that these countries tend to be wealthy, highly educated, Christian or secular, and so on. Countries like these may have been democratic even if they were surrounded by authoritarian regimes. Our models control explicitly for literacy, income, Protestant population, and/or European population, but we cannot control for everything that Western European countries have in common. An error term that is designed to be correlated with contiguity helps correct for the influence of the variables that happen to be spatially clustered but are not included in the model. These two strategies are uninformative about the nature of any spillovers from domestic variables "there" to democracy outcomes "here." However, if there are such spillovers, our models help prevent them from biasing our estimates of contagion.

Another competing explanation is that our networks are effects rather than causes of the other variables in the models, a phenomenon called "endogenous network formation." Techniques exist to model network formation (Hays et al. 2010 in spatial econometrics; Cranmer et al. 2021 in inferential network analysis) but we have not availed ourselves of them. However, we think it safe to treat neighbors as an exogenous network. No modern political science variable placed France next to Germany or Burma far from Bolivia. The exploitability of natural and human resources certainly did influence which territories European powers chose to colonize, but colonizers in the proto-democratic eighteenth and nineteenth centuries could not have weighed democracy heavily in these choices. Even so, we include Heckman corrections for membership in the two colonial networks in the upturns and downturns models. However, endogenous network formation is a real concern that could bias our estimates of the effects of alliance membership. Homophily, including similar levels of democracy and shared values, is a known determinant of alliance membership. We therefore interpret effects of alliances cautiously.

4.4   OUR HYPOTHESES

4.4.1   Exogenous Shocks

Exogenous shocks originate outside a target country's borders, but not from any specific country. They are emergent properties of the international system.[10] We consider shocks produced by either violent conflict or by the international economy. Both of these can have a negative manifestation – war or economic contraction – or a positive manifestation – peace or economic expansion. Each of these four scenarios could affect democratization in a different way, for different reasons.

Wartime threatens democracy in several ways. Most obviously, some countries can be conquered and occupied by others, and typically the conqueror governs the occupied territory undemocratically. Even if a more-democratic country occupies a less-democratic one, it will not immediately allow the occupied country to govern itself by electing leaders with real power. However, occupations are the most extreme form of country-to-country coercive diffusion. War can also act as an exogenous shock that can weaken democracy in more subtle ways. The sense of foreign threat, the heightened nationalism, the need for mobilization, and the imperative of national security and secrecy encourage and empower domestic actors who are inclined to suppress dissent, muzzle the media, or curtail the rights of groups suspected of being disloyal. The degree of damage probably

---

[10] Climate change may eventually be the best example of an exogenous shock, but we think it is probably too recent to be an important determinant of political change in most of the world. Pandemics (AIDS, SARS, the Spanish Flu of 1918) could be historical examples and COVID-19 is the obvious current example.

ranges widely, from barely perceptible changes to genocide, but we expect the average impact to be harmful to democracy.

The aftermath of war, however, sometimes has the opposite effect, even beyond the recovery of any rights that were suppressed during wartime (Gunitsky 2017). It is no accident that the most dramatic expansions of the suffrage took place soon after World War I. Mass conscription gave millions of veterans the authority to demand the right to vote, and the economic contributions of women during the war helped secure their calls for suffrage (Dahl 1989). Similar consequences have been attributed to the end of the Napoleonic Wars, World War II, the Vietnam War, and other conflicts. Wars tend to have a leveling effect that is realized only after the peace is won.[11]

The economic expansions and contractions that we treat as exogenous shocks are not the routine, year-to-year fluctuations of the economy captured by national economic growth rates, which often follow different trends in different countries and are therefore better treated as domestic variables. Rather, the exogenous economic shocks are the major shifts that affect many countries at the same time, for an extended period, such as the Great Depression, the long post-World-War-II expansion, and the financial crisis of 2007. These shocks, we believe, are more consequential for political regimes than the routine ups and downs of individual national economies. Deep, lasting economic decline prompts politicians and publics to search for fundamental flaws in the economy and the political system. When this self-questioning takes place in the most democratic and economically advanced countries in the world, the legitimacy of the democratic ideal (as it is understood at the time) is tarnished. The advocates of democracy are put on the defensive and advocates of alternatives such as communism, fascism, technocratic authoritarianism, Islamist fundamentalism, and populism are taken more seriously. However, this works both ways: the economic decline of nondemocratic rule, such as the collapse of communism, can undermine that form of rule and enhance the legitimacy of democrats. The impact of the economic shock is conditional on the regime where it hits: a good example of what Franzese and Hays (2008a) called "context-conditional exogenous shocks." Politicians and publics tend to interpret sustained prosperity as a vindication of their political system, whether it is democratic or not. Prosperity can therefore encourage both the improvement of democracy and the entrenchment of nondemocratic regimes (Haggard and Kaufman 1995). We expect that exogenous economic expansions are also context-conditional, although we do not model them here.

4.4.2   Endogenous Influences

In this chapter we focus on four kinds of networks: neighbors, military alliances, and current and former colonial networks. Our expectations about

---

[11] We plan to estimate the impact of the aftermath of war in future research.

how and why they matter are different for each kind of network. Neighbor networks are the most frequently tested kind, but are also least informative. The proximity of neighbors is probably a proxy for many more specific relationships that would tell us more about how contagion works. Neighbors are more likely to share languages and religions, to experience migration, to trade and invest, to go to war, and (paradoxically) to be allies. Some of what appears to be contagion among neighbors is probably actually contagion within more meaningful networks that happen to be regionally clustered. Ideally, the estimated contagion due to proximity would disappear if we could fully specify all these other networks. Until then, we interpret neighbor effects as a residual category of unspecified mechanisms that follow contiguity. Appendix B develops the theoretical expectations about military alliances, current colonial ties, and former colonial ties. We emphasize the neighbor networks throughout this chapter to illustrate endogenous network dependence.

4.5 OPERATIONALIZING THE HYPOTHESES

4.5.1 The Dependent Variable and the Sample

Our outcome variables are the V-Dem Electoral Democracy Index, also known as polyarchy (*v2x_polyarchy*), and two transformations of it: upturns and downturns.[12] Upturns are the positive period-to-period changes in *v2x_polyarchy*; negative changes are recoded to zero. Downturns are the negative changes, with positive changes recoded to zero. The full v9 dataset consists of 26,834 country-year observations, divided into 202 countries over 8 to 230 years, or on average 132.8 years. This full dataset includes many colonies prior to independence. However, we use data only from 1900 to 2010 due to missing data on key variables such as literacy. This cuts the baseline number of countries to 181. Furthermore, the computational limits of our software (Stata) forced us to aggregate all observations into 60 two-year periods (except for 1900, which is one year). Missing values for some analysis variables further reduces the sample size to 6,755–7,170, which still covers a range equivalent to more than 13,000 country-years.

4.5.2 Exogenous Shocks

To measure international war, we use a dummy that captures cases of interstate war with at least 1,000 battle deaths, recoded from the UCDP/PRIO Armed Conflict Dataset (Gleditsch et al. 2002; Pettersson 2019; Pettersson et al. 2019) and the Correlates of War project (Sarkees and Wayman 2010).

---

[12] Unlike some of the other chapters in this book, we omit the change outcome because coefficients of the variables explaining it are almost always very close to the sum of the coefficients of the variables explaining upturns and downturns.

To measure exogenous global economic expansions and contractions, we averaged the annual growth rates of per capita GDP for all available countries in each year, using the "GDP growth" variable *e_migdpgro*.[13] This variable does not cover all countries, especially before 1950, but we deem this only a small problem because the fluctuations we need to capture are those that affect a very large number of countries in the same way. We can therefore assume that trends that affect the available countries affected the countries with missing data as well. If in reality some national economies expanded and others contracted, this indicator should produce mean growth or decline rates closer to zero. The only problem would be if growth rates were correlated with missingness, which we think is unlikely. Because annual average global growth is still quite volatile, we smoothed these values with a three-year centered moving average and then calculated the first difference of the moving average.[14] The result is a series with a mean of less than 0.0001 and a standard deviation of 0.009 and that has its largest declines (–0.032 to –0.025) in 1930–1931 and 2008 and its largest increases (0.025 to 0.045) in 1945–1947 and 1933–1934. Because we assume that expansions and contractions do not necessarily have opposite effects, we split this into two series: one for negative values and one for positive values, with values of the opposite sign set to zero. The economic shocks are lagged one period. See Appendix D for descriptive information about all the variables used in this chapter.

4.5.3 Endogenous Hypotheses

We test four networks that link countries in different ways: contiguous neighbors, military allies, current colonies and their colonizers, and former colonies and their colonizers. We operationalize each network as a spatial weights matrix, conventionally denoted by "**W**." Each **W** is a square matrix (like a spreadsheet) with a column for each country-period and a row for the same country-periods. The cells of each **W** therefore identify the strength of the linkage between each column country-period and each row country-period. Neighbor "weights" may be a misleading term in our analysis because they are binary: either a country is a neighbor (weight = 1) or it is not (weight = 0). However, during the analysis, this matrix is row-standardized so that the influence on each country is an average of the influence coming from all immediate neighbors. To define neighbors, we use the criteria of contiguity used in Brinks and Coppedge (2006), with a few amendments.[15] Neighbor

---

[13] V-Dem estimates this variable using the "GDP per capita" variable from the Maddison Project (2013).

[14] This formula simplifies to $(growth_{t+1} - growth_{t-2})/3$, where *growth* is the global average by year.

[15] Countries on continents are neighbors if they share a border; Australia is counted as an island, rather than a continent. If an island is close to a continent, its neighbors are the closest neighbor on that continent and any island nations in between. If an island is about equally close to any continent, or to multiple countries on the same continent, it has as neighbors all nearly equally

dyads are bidirectional. That is, if country A is a neighbor of country B, then country B is also a neighbor of country A.[16]

To test our hypotheses about contagion through military alliance networks, we constructed a matrix that specifies every pair of countries that are members of a shared alliance. Similar to the neighbor network weights mentioned earlier, alliance network weights are binary but row-standardized. If two countries are in multiple military alliances, the network weight remains one. There is no additional weight for multiple alliance memberships. We also do not distinguish between bilateral alliances and multilateral alliances, coding all members of multilateral alliances as in bilateral alliances with every other member of the alliance. To construct our alliance network variables, we use the formal alliances data set from the Correlates of War project (Gibler 2009). In both datasets, countries and their allies are coded on a yearly basis and for every year they code a dyad as being in an alliance, the dyad is given a one in the alliance network variable. When the alliance ends, the dyad reverts back to 0.

Importantly, we only code membership in what Gibler calls defensive alliances and what Leeds et al. (2002) call offensive or defensive alliances. These are military alliances that obligate the members of the alliance to aid in the defense of their alliance members if attacked militarily, and sometimes also compel alliance members to aid an alliance member with offensive military operations. These are distinct from nonaggression pacts, which are coded separately, and do not meet the full definition of military alliances.[17] Nonaggression pacts do not operate in the same manner as military alliances and as such we do not expect them to impact the diffusion of democracy.[18]

Our approach is unlike any other in several respects. First, we use V-Dem electoral democracy data (version 9). V-Dem data does not just provide extensive geographic and historical coverage; it is the only dataset that

---

close mainland countries and any islands in between. If an island is not close to any continent it has as neighbors islands within 150 percent of the nearest neighbor. For example, we classify Cuba and the Dominican Republic as neighbors of the United States.

[16] We have yet to exploit the potential of weighting neighbors by population, GDP, military capabilities, and so on, to learn more about why neighbors matter. However, Brinks and Coppedge (2006) found that various weighting schemes performed no better than unweighted neighbor networks.

[17] Leeds et al. (2002) define alliances as "written agreements, signed by official representatives of at least two independent states, that include promises to aid a partner in the event of military conflict, to remain neutral in the event of conflict, to refrain from military conflict with one another, or to consult/cooperate in the event of international crises that create a potential for military conflict."

[18] This chapter excludes tests that weight military alliances by capabilities and explore the timing of diffusion through alliances. However, elsewhere we have reported that (a) much of the convergence on levels of democracy takes place in the lead-up to alliance membership, (b) countries with strong military capabilities exercise more influence in diffusion within alliances, and (c) convergence is much more rapid among neighboring allies than among distant ones (Denison and Coppedge 2017).

measures electoral democracy (and other types of democracy) for most colonies before independence, which is crucial for this analysis. Second, the Electoral Democracy Index (or "polyarchy") we use is constructed from variables measured on a true interval scale, unlike most democracy measures, which are ordinal. Interval-level measurement is especially important for calculating democracy gaps between countries, as it is meaningful to subtract equal-interval values but not ordinal ranks – an advantage that ordinal Freedom House data did not afford to Brinks and Coppedge (2006). Third, we operationalize diffusion paths separately before and after independence.[19] Therefore, we use a "former colonies" **W** matrix for linkages between former colonizers and former colonies after independence and a "current colonies" **W** matrix for linkages between colonizers and colonies before independence. Both colonial matrices have a radial structure in which colonies are linked to their colonizer but not to one another. All nine colonial networks – Belgian, British, Dutch, French, German, Italian, Portuguese, Spanish, and the United States – are included in each matrix. We therefore estimate spatial dependence as a weighted average across all the colonizers and colonies.[20]

We used information in the V-Dem Country Coding Units document to define colonies (Coppedge et al. 2014). We coded these networks for the period from 1900 to 2016. A network weight of 1 (before row standardization) represents the existence of a relationship for the two corresponding countries in a given year, and 0 represents the absence of such relationship.

4.5.4 Controls

The only variables of real interest in our models are the two exogenous shocks and the spatially lagged dependent variable. However, we necessarily include several domestic determinants in the analysis that serve as control variables for the domestic part of the analysis (effects on country$_i$) and instrumental variables in the international part of the analysis (effects of country$_j$ on country$_i$). The

---

[19] In earlier versions of this analysis, we tested more than fifty colonial hypotheses that yielded separate estimates not only for current and former colonies but also for each of nine colonizers, three types of colony (occupation, settlement, and forced settlement) for four of the colonizers (Britain, France, Spain, and Portugal), and two directions of influence: from periphery to center and from center to periphery. For now estimating so many relationships with spatial econometrics tools is not feasible unless we treat them all as unidirectional, exogenous influences.

[20] The colonial networks are set up as dyads with the colonizer. For example, France has a tie with Benin and Mali, and Benin and Mali have ties with France, but Benin and Mali do not have ties with each other. Row normalization divides the weight of each colony by the number of colonies for that colonizer, so the effect is the mean of (a) the effect of the colonizers on all of their colonies and (b) the effect of the average colony on its colonizer. In effect, the center→periphery side gets much more weight than the periphery→center side. Colonizers have disproportionate influence within their networks compared to their colonies, and the disproportion is a function of the number of colonies they dominate.

model of levels of polyarchy employs a different selection of variables than the models of upturns and downturns because the latter are much more dynamic outcomes; levels are better explained by less dynamic variables. For example, the model of levels of polyarchy includes measures of the Protestant and European percentages of the population, which regard as proxies for many possible explanations associated with ties to Europe.

We use two controls for economic development: estimates of per capita GDP (for upturns and downturns only) and the adult literacy rate.[21] Many have argued that literacy has a relationship with economic development, as increased levels of literacy and schooling produce higher levels of human capital inside a country (Barro 1992, Benhabib and Spiegel 1994; Blaug 1966). The country can then convert human capital into tangible economic growth. Our measure of literacy is the adult literacy rate, which measures the percentage of the population age fifteen or older who are literate. We use the percent literate variable from Vanhanen (2003) and merge it with the World Bank's (2016) adult literacy variable for country-years not covered by Vanhanen. Both variables measure the adult literacy rate in the same percentage format. Many colonizers kept records of the literacy rate and education in their colonies, which gives greater data coverage for the literacy variable. Since both data sources have gaps in their coverage of the literacy rate, however, we interpolated the data after combining them into one measure. After interpolation, the literacy variable has 3,577 more observations than the most comprehensive GDP per capita measure and covers almost all of the colonial cases we are interested in. Finally, we used multiple imputation to fill in the 1,441 remaining missing values (most of which are for nonexistent country-periods that are not used in the analysis).[22] We also use a measure of GDP per capita in the upturns and downturns models, based heavily on Fariss et al. (2017). See Chapter 5 for details.

For the upturns and downturns models, we include Election year: a dummy for a presidential, legislative, or constituent assembly election taking place in a given year. We include this because we consistently find that democracy scores tend to change more at the time of these high-profile events. For more severe shocks, we use measures of economic shocks. We also include latitude and distance from natural harbors. See Chapter 3 for sources. Following the work of

---

[21] Because literacy and income are both usually proxies for the same concept – either economic development or some version of modernization – it may seem odd to include both as domestic predictors. However, empirically these two indicators are correlated at only 0.70 in this sample, probably not strongly enough to risk multicollinearity. More importantly, they are not the variables of interest here. Even if they are collinear, it is not a problem because their role in the model is to serve as two of the nine instruments for polyarchy. If either one explains some additional variance in polyarchy, it is all to the good.

[22] Although it would be better to generate many imputed values, run our model many times to generate many parameter estimates, and then report their medians and confidence intervals, it is not feasible to multiply this amount of computation by the hours it takes to run each model once on high-performance computing machines.

Miller (2012) and Teorell (2010), we use a dummy variable for incidents of hyperinflation. We also use a dummy that captures cases of internal war which, like international war, we recoded from the UCDP/PRIO Armed Conflict Dataset and the Correlates of War project (Sarkees and Wayman 2010). In both cases, the dummy variables have some values of 0.5 that we created when we aggregated all the data to averages for two-year periods. Unfortunately, listwise deletion in analyses with these measures reduces our sample to fewer than 8,327 country-periods. Finally, our models incorporate one or two variables that correct for selection into the set of colonizers and colonies. These corrections are included to prevent biased estimates for the two colonial networks.

4.6 ESTIMATION

We estimate the aforementioned relationships with a spatiotemporal autoregressive (STAR) model, which is described in detail in Appendix C. It models democracy outcomes in each country as a function of exogenous shocks (international war and global economic expansions and contractions), a set of domestic determinants, and democracy outcomes in other countries that are linked through the four networks. To deal with the complication that democracy in every country is potentially endogenous to democracy in every other country, we use the domestic determinants as instruments for democracy. This reassures us that we have a good idea of what democracy in each country would have been if there were no such international influences, and therefore enables us to estimate influence through networks with less bias. We also correct for the possibility that countries that appear to affect one another may be merely similar with respect to some omitted domestic determinants. We estimate this model three times, once for each of the dependent variables: level of polyarchy, upturns, and downturns.

Figure 4.1 makes the structure of the model more concrete with a simplified depiction of these relationships in a hypothetical world with a target country, i, and source countries j, which are linked to each other through our four networks. (The four **W** matrices appear twice to prevent arrows from crossing in the figure, but the two sets of matrices are the same in the actual model.) Every country is country$_i$ and every country is a country$_j$ with respect to some other countries, but for simplicity Figure 4.2 focuses attention on one dyad. Each country has a polyarchy score, Polyarchy$_{it}$ or Polyarchy$_{jt}$, which the model attempts to explain. The model specifies several exogenous drivers of the process: a lagged outcome variable, a set of instrumental variables, and exogenous shocks. All predictors of endogenous variables are lagged one period.[23] It also has Heckman

---

[23] Recall that all variables are aggregated into two-year periods after 1900. Therefore, t_0 is the mean of year 1 and year 2, t_{-1} is the mean of year$_{t-1}$ and year$_{t-2}$, and t_{-2} is the mean of year t_{-3} and year t_{-4}.

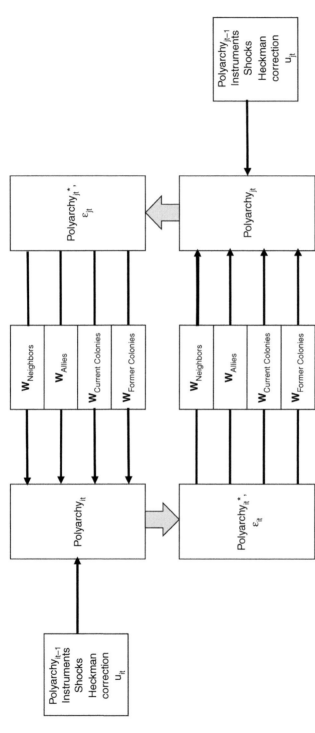

FIGURE 4.1 The full STAR model

Notes: Wide arrows represent the first-stage estimation of the instruments Polyarchy$_{it}$* and Polyarchy$_{it}$*. The four **W** matrices appear twice to prevent arrows from crossing, but the two sets of matrices are the same.

correction factors for the probability of being "selected" into the group of colonizers, the group of colonies, or neither.[24]

The model structures the way in which polyarchy in one country depends on polyarchy in other countries. Country$_i$ influences country$_j$ and vice versa. Arrows drawn through the four **W** networks indicate that countries influence each other only if they are connected by the network in question. However, polyarchy in one country does not directly influence polyarchy in the other. Rather, the instrument of Polyarchy$_{it}$, Polyarchy$_{it}$*, influences Polyarchy$_{jt}$ while the instrument of Polyarchy$_{ijt}$, Polyarchy$_{jt}$*, influences Polyarchy$_{it}$. The wide arrows represent the first-stage estimation of the instruments. Overall, it is a partially circular process driven by the exogenous shocks and domestic determinants.

Arrows drawn through the matrices indicate interactions between the matrices, on the one hand, and on the other, the errors and the instruments for polyarchy, producing estimates of spatial autocorrelation of polyarchy and spatial error correlation.

4.7 RESULTS

Table 4.1 compiles the coefficients for all the STAR regressions and compares them with estimates from models without networks. We modeled three of the four dependent variables that most of the other chapters of this book analyze, with the probably unimportant difference that our observations are aggregated into two-year averages. Models 1 and 2 explain the level of polyarchy, which is most relevant for understanding long-term trends in democracy and cross-national differences. Models 3–6 analyze upturns and downturns, which reveal more about short-term, within-country dynamics.

The odd-numbered models are simple panel regressions with exogenous shocks but without contagion through networks; the even-numbered STAR models include the four contagion networks.[25] This comparison is important because one of the concerns about models that ignore spatial relationships has been that they may yield exaggerated estimates of the effect of domestic determinants. Our comparisons suggest that there is little basis for this concern, at least in this application. Although each of these four networks is statistically significant in at least one STAR model, they appear to make very little difference in the impact of the other factors. There is little reason, for example, to discount the estimates in the other chapters in this book on the grounds that they usually do not take interference among units into account. We cannot generalize this conclusion to all large-N quantitative analyses of democratization; strictly speaking, it is limited to explaining these three variables, with these measures,

[24] Details about how the Heckman corrections for selection into membership into colonizers and colonies are described in Coppedge et al. (2016).
[25] The simple panel regressions use random effects. They do not use fixed effects or clustered standard errors in order to maximize comparability with the STAR models.

TABLE 4.1 *Comparison of models with and without network relationships*

	Level		Upturns		Downturns	
	without networks	with networks	without networks	with networks	without networks	with networks
Domestic covariates						
Lagged DV	0.9518	0.9382	0.2504	0.240	0.208	0.200
Literacy/1000	0.1731	0.2015	0.1382	0.131	−0.080	−0.076
Colony selection/1000	−4.2266	−3.7104	−0.5387	−0.450	−0.487	−0.476
Protestant population	0.0001	0.0001				
European population	0.0001	0.0001				
Election year			0.0144	0.014	0.001	0.001
GDP per capita			−0.0034	−0.003	0.002	0.002
Hyperinflation			0.0151	0.014	−0.002	−0.002
Internal war			−0.0026	−0.003	−0.004	−0.004
Colonizer selection/1000			0.0837	0.121	−0.212	−0.211
Latitude			−0.0080	−0.007	0.004	0.004
Port distance/ 1000			−0.0018	−0.002	0.002	0.001
Exogenous shocks						
International war			−0.0068	−0.006	−0.002	−0.002
Global GDP expansion	0.9802	0.6542	0.5075	0.478	0.055	0.062
Global GDP contraction			−0.0921	−0.057	0.136	0.137
Decade dummies	yes (not shown)		no		no	
Constant	0.0106	0.0031	0.0287	0.022	−0.016	−0.013
Endogenous networks and spatially correlated errors						
Current colony network						
Lagged instrument		0.0017		0.075		0.015
Network error term		0.0182		−0.063		−0.023
Former colony network						
Lagged instrument		0.0003		0.054		−0.008
Network error term		−0.0021		−0.058		0.012

(continued)

TABLE 4.1 *(continued)*

	Level		Upturns		Downturns	
	without networks	with networks	without networks	with networks	without networks	with networks
Neighbor network						
Lagged instrument		0.0250		0.350		0.335
Network error term		0.1473		−0.325		−0.373
Alliance network						
Lagged instrument		0.0032		0.192		0.140
Network error term		0.2177		−0.253		−0.168
N		7170		6755		6756
Wald chi^2 for spatial terms:		295.82		152.52		107.93

Notes: Coefficients in bold are significant at the 95 percent level or better.

using this set of independent variables, and every other specification decision that undergirds this analysis. Nevertheless, it is at least possible that Galton's problem is less problematic for democratization analysis than many (including us!) have warned as long as we confine our attention to short-term effects.

Not much needs to be said about the domestic covariates because they are not the variables of interest. Lagged outcomes are always the strongest variables in each model, although more for levels than for the more dynamic dependent variables. Election years and, strangely, episodes of hyperinflation, are associated with more positive upturns.[26] Internal war tends to increase the magnitude of downturns but does not affect levels or upturns. Controls for latitude, port distance, and being a likely colonizer are all insignificant. Not surprisingly, being a likely colony is associated with lower levels of polyarchy on average. It is interesting that literacy and income have positive effects on level, but opposite-signed coefficients for the two dynamic variables. If there is a substantive reason for this pattern, it may be that income affects polyarchy with diminishing returns but literacy does not. It is also possible that these two variables are collinear, making their coefficients unstable. However, as noted previously, it does not matter because these domestic covariates serve as instruments for domestic-driven polyarchy, not as variables of interest.

In four of the six models, exogenous shocks affect polyarchy in expected ways. First, international war makes upturns smaller, shifting them toward

[26] One possibility is that hyperinflation is correlated with economic crisis, making the input of big players more important when inflation does occur. For example, developing countries that need a bailout from the IMF or World Bank and are subject to conditionality to respect the rule of law and democracy. Aid comes with strings attached.

zero. Global economic expansion has the opposite effects. First, it raises the level of democracy. Although the coefficient is large, the substantive effect is modest because the average rate of global expansion is 0.037. Multiplied by the coefficient, it would raise the level by 0.036 on average. Expansion makes the average upturn in polyarchy about 0.018 points more positive on the 0–1 scale. Neither war nor economic expansion has a significant effect on downturns. However, global economic contractions do not hurt, on average.

The four networks channel different contagion effects for different dependent variables. The neighbor network is significant for all three outcomes, which may indicate either that we have not yet adequately specified all the meaningful linkages that are correlated with geography or that space just intrinsically matters and no specific reason can be given for this phenomenon. The other networks matter only for some of the dynamic dependent variables. The alliances network channels polyarchy contagion significantly for upturns and downturns. This tendency suggests that the causal mechanisms that alliances employ – diplomacy, bargaining, carrots in the form of inducements and sticks in the form of sanctions and the threat of expulsion – operate primarily in the short term. All networks have significant effects on upturns. The former colonial network has a significant positive impact on upturns. The same is true for current colonial ties (the "current" signifies the pre-independence period, when colonial rule was still ongoing). These estimates suggest that an upturn in one country tends to add a small increment to upturns in other countries with which it is linked by contiguity, military alliance, or colonial ties.

We present simulations later, but first there is one more model to discuss. As we noted, one possible reason for the small contagion coefficients is that they are the average effect for the entire globe over more than a century. It seems likely that we would find some variation in these effects if we obtained estimates for specific regions or historical periods; or for specific alliances rather than treating all alliances as interchangeable. In this spirit, in Table 4.2 we report estimates for six regional networks consisting of neighbors in sub-Saharan Africa, Eastern Europe, Latin America, Asia and the Pacific, Western Europe and North America (and Australia and New Zealand) or "WENA," and the Middle East and North Africa ("MENA"). This table confirms our intuitions. First, all of the regional neighbor networks are significant except for the Middle East and North Africa. They are significant even though the model also shows that there is significant spatial clustering of omitted variables in Africa, Eastern Europe, and WENA. Moreover, the magnitude of the network coefficients ranges from 0.016 in Asia to twice that, 0.032, in sub-Saharan Africa. The effects of neighbors on contagion are not homogeneous across regions.

However, how large any of these effects are, how certain they are, and how long they persist must be explored through simulations that go beyond the immediate, first-order effects represented by regression coefficients.

TABLE 4.2 *STAR estimates for a model of Polyarchy levels with six regional neighbor networks*

region	contagion	se	z	p	spatial error	se	z	p
Africa	**0.0332**	0.0087	3.793	0.0001	0.1548	0.0411	3.765	0.0002
E. Europe	**0.0271**	0.0083	3.273	0.0011	0.3480	0.0302	11.533	0.0000
Latin America	**0.0263**	0.0057	4.588	0.0000	0.0469	0.0249	1.883	0.0598
WENA	**0.0173**	0.0051	3.389	0.0007	0.1984	0.0256	7.743	0.0000
Asia	**0.0161**	0.0072	2.222	0.0263	0.0219	0.0459	0.476	0.6338
MENA	0.0071	0.0098	0.725	0.4686	−0.1069	0.0771	−1.387	0.1656

Notes. Figures in bold are statistically significant at the 95 percent level or better. Temporal lag = 0.9456, se = 0.0042. Covariates (not shown) are ten decade dummies, Protestant population, European population, adult literacy, and global economic expansion. $N = 7,170$. Wald test of spatial terms: $chi^2(12) = 357.32$, p> $chi^2 = 0.0000$.

4.8 INTERPRETATION

It is a paradox that Table 4.1 shows multiple significant network effects, yet the coefficients of the domestic determinants and exogenous shocks are practically the same whether our models include networks or not. The most obvious resolution of the paradox would be that the network effects are small (which is true), and they are significant only because the sample is very large. Another possible reason is that our instruments for outcomes "there" are the same domestic variables that are specified in the nonspatial models (albeit for different countries). A third possible reason is that because the domestic instruments take on values in countries "there," their contributions are practically uncorrelated with the values of these domestic variables "here." However, there is a less obvious reason, too: the full effects are larger than the coefficients indicate. In order to understand how this is possible, it is important to know how to simulate the magnitudes of these effects.

The network effects reported in Table 4.1 are only the immediate first-order effects: that is, the effect of the source country's polyarchy on the first band of contiguous countries' polyarchy in the next period. However, these are not the full effects. In time series analysis, it is customary to report a long-run effect, which is the limit of the sum of the effects of all previous years. There is a spatial analogue to this: the "steady-state" effect, which is the limit of the sum of all the first- and higher-order spatial effects. The effects of each country on itself are largest, then they decay exponentially for each successive network lag. In the neighbor network, for example, neighbors have stronger effects than the neighbors of neighbors, and so on.[27] In models with both spatial and temporal lags, combined long-run steady-state (LRSS) effects are most relevant. Appendix C contains further explanation.

Because it is difficult to understand what the model says simply by inspecting the network coefficients, simulations are required to interpret STAR model estimates properly.[28] We perform three kinds of simulation: (1) LRSS estimates of the full effect of a hypothetical shock emanating from one country; (2) dynamically evolving effects of shocks from every country on neighbors in each period; and (3) a snapshot map of the "front lines" of polyarchy contagion among regional neighbors all over the world in a single period.[29]

4.8.1 LRSS Estimates

LRSS estimates show the full effect of contagion after a single hypothetical shock has propagated through the network and decayed over time. The steady-state part is the total of all the first-order (immediate neighbors), second-order (neighbors of neighbors), third-order (neighbors of neighbors of neighbors)

[27] A common way to present the steady-state effects in a spatial analysis is to distinguish between a "direct" effect, which is the average steady-state effect of each country on itself, and an "indirect" effect, which is the average effect of every other country on each country (LeSage and Pace 2009). These are meaningful summary statistics for compact networks, that is, ones with relatively few higher-order linkages, such as a regional organization that indirectly links every member to every other member. Indirect effects are less meaningful for the highly dispersed neighbor network, in which every country is linked to every other country but the vast majority of the linkages are high-order linkages that are very close to zero. The indirect effects in such networks will vary over a wide range that makes the average much less meaningful, and the average will tend to be very small.

[28] Strictly speaking, the contributions of each network included in the same model are not separable, as they interact with one another to produce the combined effect. However, we do separate simulations of the effects of each of our four networks even when we estimated them in the same model because the total effect becomes uncertain when some of the networks are not statistically significant. The "noise" of the nonsignificant networks overwhelms the effects of the significant ones. These simulations therefore model the *marginal* effects for a hypothetical world in which all countries were members of only the one network that is the focus of the simulation: for example, a world in which countries were neighbors but none were allies or ever colonies. Simulated effects would be somewhat different if they were based on a model of only one network at a time. For example, neighbor coefficients for all three outcomes modeled separately would be within 27 percent (sometimes larger, sometimes smaller) of the coefficients from a model that included all four networks. See Table 4.A1 for all the comparisons. Given that the significant coefficients are usually fairly similar in magnitude whether they are estimated separately or together, we use the pooled-model coefficient estimates in our simulations. In our view, the benefits of controlling rigorously for other networks outweigh the drawbacks of simulating a world that is marginally less realistic.

[29] The simulation with six regional networks is done properly. Countries with neighbors from one region show the effect of that region; countries with neighbors in more than one region show the effects of all the regions they are linked to.

effects, and beyond to infinity. With each remove from the first shock, the effect decays exponentially. Because the first-order effects tend to be small to begin with, they decay fast. The spatial propagation is assumed to happen instantaneously in the first period. The long-run part of the LRSS effect is a similar process, but playing forward in time rather than space. However, because the temporal lag coefficient is much larger (around 0.90) in models of levels of polyarchy, this process decays more slowly and therefore cumulates much more. The long-run steady-state impact of an initial shock can be much larger than the coefficient reported by the regression. As LeSage and Pace (2009) have shown, "A process with low spatial dependence and high positive temporal dependence implies a long-run equilibrium with high levels of spatial dependence" (p. 197).

The notion of a "half-life," borrowed from the physics of radioactive decay, gives us a useful way to understand the long-run impact of an initial shock. The half-life of an effect is the time it takes for half of the long-run effect to be realized. The half-life of the effects of contagion on levels of polyarchy in Table 4.1 is more than twenty years.[30] Because there is tremendous inertia in the levels of polyarchy, the influence of contagion is analogous to the pull of a tugboat on an oil tanker: when a country is very undemocratic, it takes a long time to get things moving and make noticeable progress; but once a country gains momentum toward democracy, it also takes a long time for contagion to slow it down and reverse direction. (Other determinants can have larger and more immediate effects.) The temporal lag coefficients in upturns and downturns models are much smaller (0.25 and 0.20) and therefore the temporal effects decay very quickly: half of the effect is realized within a year, 90 percent of it within about three years. These more dynamic processes ramp up and die down quickly.

This calculation of the LRSS effect of a hypothetical shock yields nonsensical predictions if the shocks are unrealistic or out-of-sample.[31] Conventional interpretations of the network coefficient based on the notion of a "unit change" are out of the question, as the theoretical range of the polyarchy level variable is 0–1, the real-life range is a bit less, and most actual values are much smaller than one: a level of polyarchy of 0.314 on average over the whole sample; much smaller for upturns and downturns. In our simulations, therefore, we use a typical value of the polyarchy level, upturn, or downturn, depending on the model, for each category of network membership.

---

[30] A half-life of a temporal lag can be calculated as $\ln(1 - \text{proportion of effect remaining})/\ln$ (temporal lag coefficient). In the levels model, this works out to $\ln(1 - 0.5)/\ln(0.938) = 10.87$ two-year periods, or 21.74 years. It takes more than seventy years for 90 percent of the effect to be realized.

[31] This is because the LRSS multiplier is $1/(1 - \rho\mathbf{W} - \varphi)$, where ρ is the spatial lag coefficient, φ is the temporal lag coefficient, and $\mathbf{W}$ is the spatial weights matrix. With row-standardization we can replace $\mathbf{W}$ with 1 for a simple calculation, which makes it easy to see that the multiplier becomes extremely large as $\rho + \varphi$ approaches 1.

However, the average outcomes that we can observe for neighbors, allies, and current or former colonies are posttreatment: they already include the cumulative earlier effects of network membership that we are trying to estimate. Therefore, we compare the observed outcomes to a simulation of what the outcomes would have been without the network contagion.[32] The differences between the simulated pre-contagion outcome and the actual outcome with contagion show how much contagion matters.

Figures 4.2–4.5 show that in the long run (decades), contagion matters quite a bit for neighbors, less for alliances, and not significantly for colonial ties. The LRSS effects are significant whenever the observed values are outside the range of estimated averages excluding contagion. Specifically,

- Figure 4.2: The neighbor network is the only significant one in the long run for explaining mean levels of polyarchy.
- Figure 4.3: Contagion in the neighbor network nearly doubles the size of upturns. The alliance network has a significant positive effect as well, but not as large. Contrary to the short-term coefficients in Table 4.1, the current and former colonial networks have no significant impact on upturns in the long run.
- Figure 4.4: Both alliances and neighbors increase the size of the average downturn, this time making them larger negative changes. In the neighbor network, contagion once again doubles the effect. Consistent with Table 4.1, neither colonial network significantly augments these changes.
- Figure 4.5: In the long run, contagion among neighbors significantly raises levels of democracy in all six regions, including the Middle East and North Africa despite its nonsignificant short-run coefficient in Table 4.2
- The size of the effect increases nonlinearly as the mean regional democracy level increases. For the least-democratic regions, MENA and Asia, contagion raises the mean democracy level by less than 0.10; for the most-democratic region (Western Europe, Canada, the USA, Australia, and New Zealand), the increase is nearly 0.22.

The significant LRSS effects are much larger than the immediate pre-spatial effects shown in Tables 4.1 and 4.2. Propagation of a shock through space and time augments the effect of network membership. The LRSS effect increases nonlinearly with higher mean outcome values: the more democratic network members are on average, the more of a boost they get. This tendency helps explain the persistent geographic clustering of both democracy and non-democracy. Undemocratic countries are more likely to be stuck at a low level

---

[32] We can conceive of the observed level of polyarchy as the level before contagion plus the LRSS effect due to contagion. Therefore, we can calculate the counterfactual shock before contagion as $\rho * $observed shock$/[1 + (1 - \rho W - \varphi)]$. We bootstrap these estimates with 5,000 draws from the distributions of ρ and φ to get 95 percent confidence intervals for the outcomes excluding contagion.

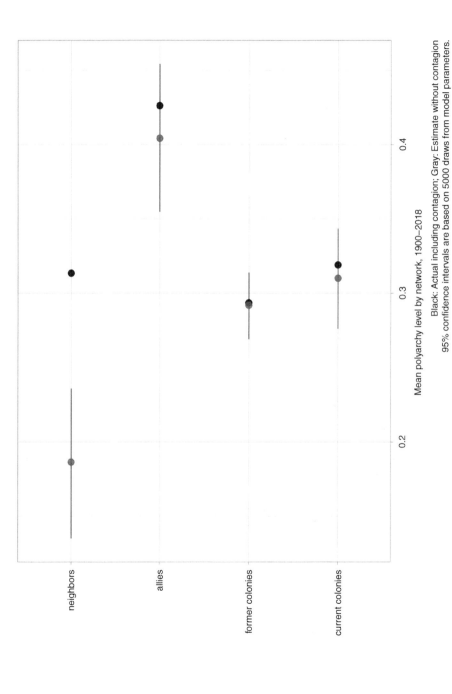

Mean polyarchy level by network, 1900–2018

Black: Actual including contagion; Gray: Estimate without contagion
95% confidence intervals are based on 5000 draws from model parameters.

FIGURE 4.2 Long-run steady-state impact of contagion on mean polyarchy by network

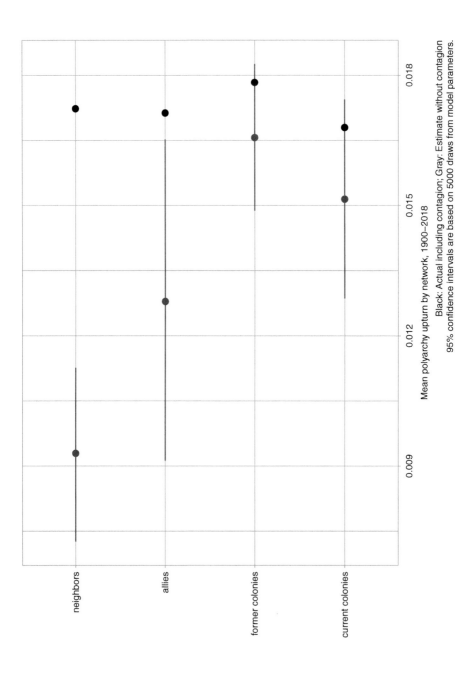

FIGURE 4.3 Long-run steady-state impact of contagion on mean upturns by network

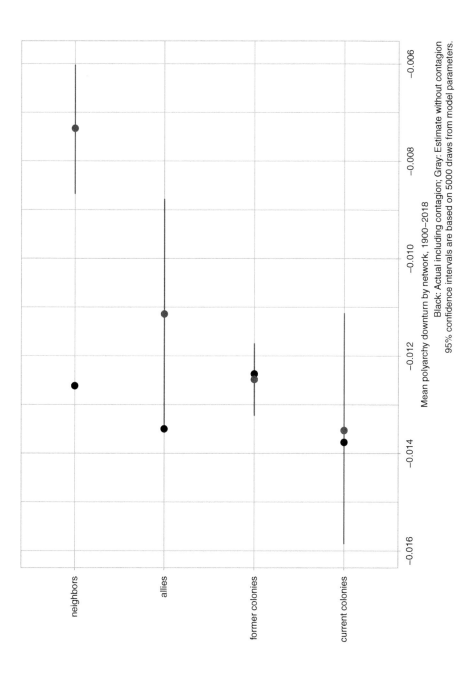

FIGURE 4.4 Long-run steady-state impact of contagion on mean downturns by network

Mean polyarchy downturn by network, 1900–2018
Black: Actual including contagion; Gray: Estimate without contagion
95% confidence intervals are based on 5000 draws from model parameters.

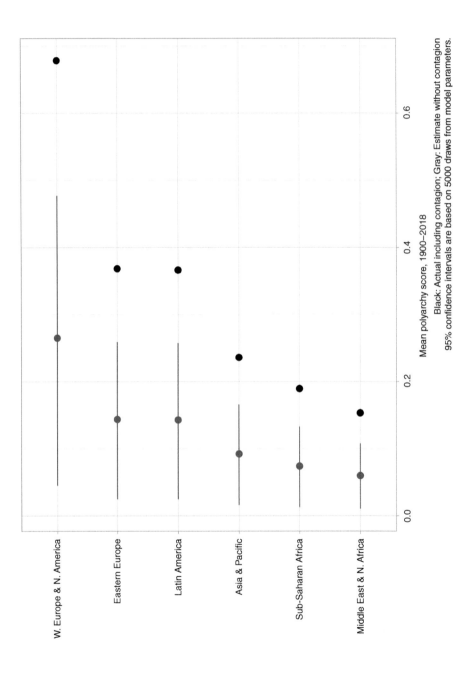

Mean polyarchy score, 1900–2018

Black: Actual including contagion; Gray: Estimate without contagion
95% confidence intervals are based on 5000 draws from model parameters.

FIGURE 4.5 Long-run steady-state impact of contagion on regional polyarchy means

of democracy when they are surrounded by other undemocratic countries that cannot give them a boost. But democratic countries in a democratic neighborhood owe a surprising proportion of their democracy level to the support they receive from their neighbors.

However, it also matters which network is operating. Not just any linkages among countries will produce significant effects: it matters which countries are connected. It also matters which region you look at, as the effects are not uniform. This is mostly a function of the average level of democracy in each region, but it also depends on the neighbor network coefficient for the region. Modeling multiple networks reveals more differentiated and sensitive understanding than simply modeling one big global neighbor network. Similarly, it would probably help to disaggregate military alliances: NATO probably has a different effect than the Warsaw Pact; the OAS and OAU may matter while ASEAN may not; British colonization probably had different effects than Spanish or Portuguese or French.

Contiguity is by far the strongest channel of influence. Again, contiguity is best considered a proxy for many channels of influence that are correlated with distance. Alliances help explain why contiguity matters, but there are probably many other kinds of distance-related ties that matter, yet are omitted from these models: communication of ideas and norms through literature, news, television, movies, and social media; trade; migration and other population flows; and so on. We need more research on these specific proximity-based channels of influence.

4.8.2 Dynamic Trends

Figures 4.6 illustrates how shocks from neighbors are predicted to affect selected countries' level of polyarchy over time. The shocks we used in this simulation are the expected levels of polyarchy in each neighbor, in each period, as predicted by domestic variables alone. Unlike Figures 4.2–4.5, which simulate the effect of single shock, Figure 4.6 shows what the model expects to happen when each country contributes a new shock – that is, a domestically predicted level of polyarchy – in each two-year period. Because the shocks are predictions based on domestic variables only, they are roughly the instrumental shocks used in the model to estimate contagion among neighbors, and therefore pre-contagion shocks. The effects shown in the graph are the steady-state expected consequences of these shocks as they develop in each country, period by period.

This facet plot uses the distinct regional neighbor network coefficients from Table 4.2. Clearly, we are no longer dealing with a model whose predicted effects are a simple function of one variable. These effects are functions of the regional network coefficient, the set of neighbors each country has, how many neighbors it has, how democratic the neighbors are, and how much the temporal lags carry over the previous period's increment into the current

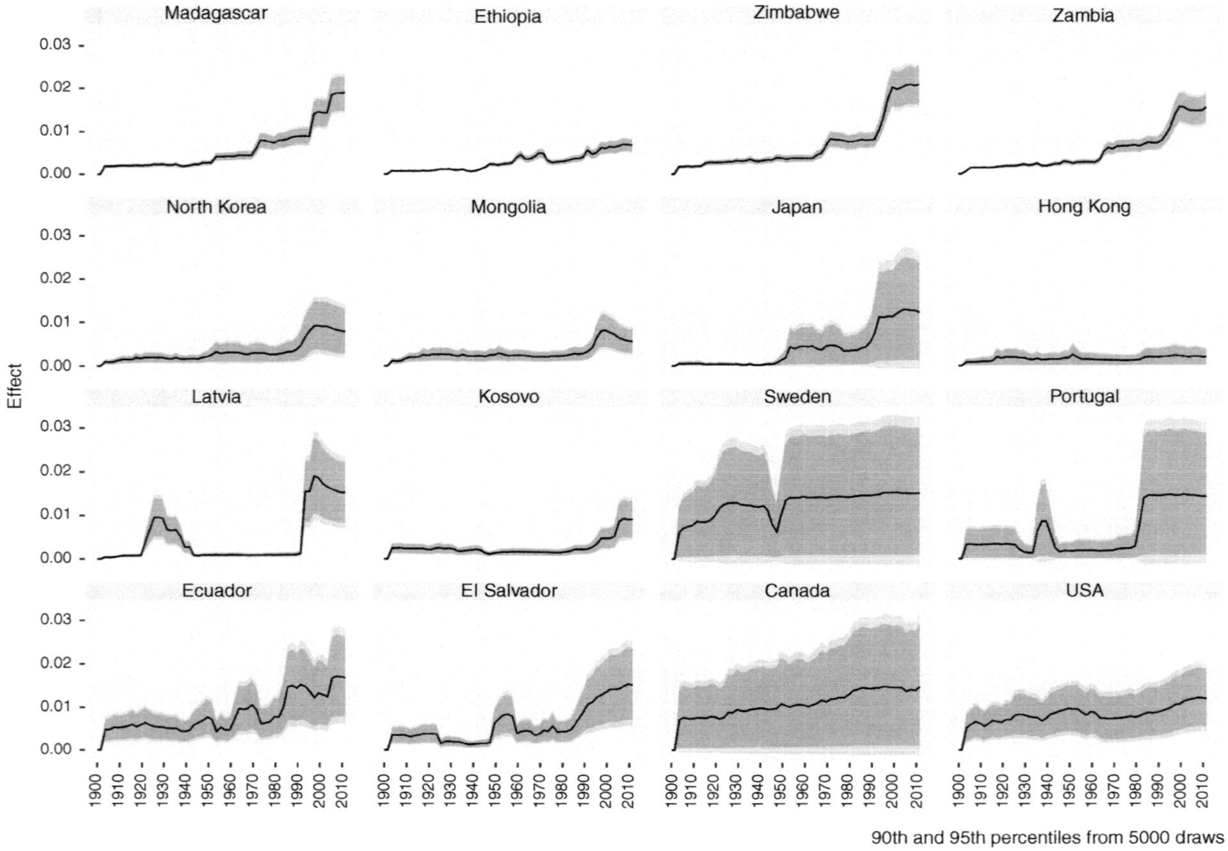

FIGURE 4.6 Simulated effects of neighbors on electoral democracy in selected countries

period. The confidence bounds around each predicted effect reflect the variances and covariances of several of these conditions. The effects and their certainties therefore vary a great deal across regional networks and by country within them:

- The predicted effects are much more certain in some regions, such as sub-Saharan African countries next to South Africa in the 1990s, Latvia, and Kosovo) than in others. The least certain effects are on democratic countries surrounded by other democratic countries, such as Sweden and Canada.
- The effects are much larger in some countries than in others within the same region (Zimbabwe vs. Ethiopia; North Korea vs. Hong Kong; Latvia vs. Kosovo).
- The largest effects are on less-democratic countries bordered by more-democratic ones, such as Zimbabwe next to South Africa in the 1990s. The smallest effects are on nondemocratic countries surrounded by other non-democratic countries (Portugal before the Spanish transition in the 1970s and countries on the Arabian Peninsula, not shown here; but see the map later in the text).

4.8.3 Map of Frontline Contagion Zones

Ultimately, the best way to understand what our model says about spatial relationships is to see the simulated effects on a map such as Figure 4.7. It is important to bear in mind that this is *not* a map of levels of electoral democracy like those many of us have encountered elsewhere; rather, this map shows the neighbor network effect estimates. It does so for just one period, 2009–2010. It cannot show the confidence intervals around the estimates, but it does a good job of showing the geographic locations of the predicted high and low effects. The dark zones are regions where pro-democracy influence from neighbors is absent because most of the countries in that zone are highly undemocratic. The brightest zones are those where neighbors are estimated to exert the strongest influence in favor of electoral democracy. These zones do not necessarily contain the most democratic countries on the map; instead, they are zones receiving the most democratic influence. In this sense, we can call them the front-line zones for contagion.

Two patterns are most striking about Figure 4.7. First is the contrast between the bright frontline zones and the dark zones lacking democratic influence. In 2009–2010 (and beginning in the late 1990s) the frontline zones were located in Latin America, Eastern Europe, and Southern and West Africa. The Arabian Peninsula was a kind of impenetrable bastion of nondemocracy. The other striking patterns are the shaded bands of supranational gradients separating the bright and dark zones. The positive influences received by Eastern Europe and West and Southern Africa fade dramatically as one moves toward the darkness of the Arabian Peninsula. The degree of international influence

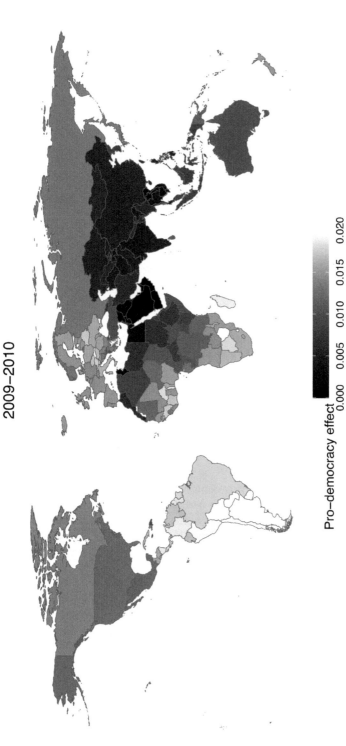

2009–2010

Pro-democracy effect

0.000   0.005   0.010   0.015   0.020

FIGURE 4.7 Front lines of polyarchy-level contagion in 2009–2010
Notes: Higher values (lighter shades) do not reflect levels of electoral democracy. They indicate the frontline of contagion: zones of influence favoring electoral democracy emanating from contiguous countries. Black indicates zones in which influence favoring electoral democracy is absent.

transcends the levels of democracy found in individual countries, which would be more variegated. This map reveals that our STAR model does a good job of extracting an elegant spatial pattern from a mass of noisy data.

Furthermore, although Figure 4.7 is a snapshot that cannot show it, the spatial pattern revealed by the model evolves.[33] Few countries were very democratic in 1900 by V-Dem's criteria, so the whole world was black or dark gray at that time. In the Inter-War Years, lighter gray zones took shape in the Nordic countries and Canada. After World War II, fronts gradually intensified in Western Europe, especially Sweden; then Canada; and briefly in South America. By the mid-1980s, Spain was on the front line as well. In the 1990s, first Latin America, then Eastern Europe, then Southern and West Africa became the leading frontline zones, and the dark areas that had covered most of Asia and Africa from the beginning shrank down to the Arabian Peninsula, flanked by gray bands. These macro-historical and geographic trends could become a useful component of explanations for democratization.

Nevertheless, it is important to remember that these simulated effects do not show what actually happened; rather, they show the implications of our models: what would have happened in each case if the model were correct.[34] The simulated effects are analogous to predicted values from a regression, albeit more complex regressions than we usually see. However, we think they give readers a better sense of the kinds of relationships that our models are designed to estimate.

4.9 CONCLUSIONS

This chapter produces extensive evidence showing that international influences matter for democracy outcomes such as levels of polyarchy and its upturns and downturns. Our estimates suggest that over many decades, contagion from neighbors has boosted the average level of polyarchy in the most democratic region of the world by an amount equivalent to 20 percent of the entire range of the polyarchy scale. The ties among neighbors and allies have tended to double or magnify by 50 percent the sizes of upturns and downturns, respectively, in the first few years after a shock. Colonial networks may also transmit small increments of upturns from colonizers to colonies and back in the first year; however, their long-run impact is uncertain. Exogenous shocks matter, too. Involvement in international wars tends to lower the level of polyarchy and

---

[33] An animated color version of Figure 4.7 is available at https://youtu.be/jz-ilFu42WY.

[34] This is why the map shows simulated effects on the Soviet Socialist Republics and South Sudan even before they became independent: the simulated effects depend only on their neighbors' values. Predictions for these cases should not be taken very seriously, but they are the model's attempt to show what the effects of contagion on them would have been if they had been independent. Note: Because the model did not generate this kind of counterfactual prediction for Kyrgyzstan before 1991, we assigned it the same values as Kazakhstan's for those years.

reduce the size of upturns. Global economic growth, by contrast, tends to increase the size of upturns by a small amount.

These conclusions are based on complex analyses of extensive V-Dem data, including colonies before independence. We are aware of the risks of large-N quantitative analysis, which concern all the other chapters in this book and are discussed in the introductory and concluding chapters. In this chapter we attempt to avoid the worst problems by using the latest tools of spatial econometric modeling. First, we interact our variable of interest – democracy outcomes in other countries – with **W** networks, which are the best way to model dependence among units. They are unusually large, in fact global, networks for this type of analysis. Second, rather than testing these networks in simple cross-sections as much of the literature has, we use a STAR model that can also handle panel data, in this case covering more than 100 years of history for the whole world. Third, this is one of very few analyses of democratization that tests multiple networks against one another in order to learn which kinds of ties most powerfully channel international influence. Fourth, our use of a network-correlated error term helps us distinguish true contagion from domestic influences that happen to be spatially clustered. Fifth, we use domestic variables as instruments for democracy outcomes "there" to prevent the endogeneity inherent in our multidirectional networks from confounding our estimates of the truly international effects. Our use of instrumental variables does a much better job of dealing with this inferential threat than the usual practice of trusting temporal lags (which we also use) to do the job. Finally, rather than limiting our interpretations to tables of regression coefficients, we employ computational simulations of long-run steady-state effects of counterfactual shocks. These simulated effects are necessary for understanding the substantive implications of the models. No analysis of observational data can completely eliminate confounded estimates, but we have improved upon the methods used by other researchers addressing this topic.

Paradoxically, controlling for the endogenous network effects does not substantially modify estimates of the short-term impacts of domestic variables. The evidence so far reassures us that models of democracy outcomes that test domestic variables exclusively, like those in the other chapters of this book, do not yield substantially biased estimates. However, there are so many hypotheses about international influences that have not yet been tested that this conclusion is subject to change.

5

Economic Determinants

Carl Henrik Knutsen and Sirianne Dahlum

5.1 INTRODUCTION

Some of the most prominent theoretical arguments and debates on what causes democracy concern features of the economy, including both short- and long-term economic processes. One notable example is the debate on whether or not long-term economic development enhances democratization, centering on different versions of modernization theory (e.g., Lipset 1959) and criticisms of such theories (see, e.g., Munck 2019). A second example concerns the debate on how income inequality affects democratization, with a number of intriguing theoretical arguments predicting that, respectively, high (Acemoglu and Robinson 2000; Ansell and Samuels 2014), intermediate (Acemoglu and Robinson 2006), or low (Boix 2003) levels of income inequality enhance democratization.

What is common to both of these debates – and many others on the economic determinants of democracy – is the lack of robust empirical evidence in support of any particular conclusion. Sensitivity analyses and other studies suggest that conclusions hinge on model specifications, such as the sample of countries and time period covered in the analysis, and the measurement of democracy (e.g., Boix 2011; Casper and Tufis 2003; Gassebner et al. 2013; Munck 2019; Rød et al. 2020; Teorell 2010). As a result, the question of if and how various economic factors influence democracy is currently far from resolved.

The analysis presented in this chapter informs these, and other, key debates on economic explanations of democracy. We revisit the link between economic factors and democracy drawing on V-Dem's carefully constructed measures of democracy, covering all countries in the world, with extensive time series from 1789–2018. Drawing on the insight that explanations of democratization may differ from explanations of democratic decline (e.g., Teorell 2010), we always distinguish between positive and negative changes in democracy in our analyses, and we always employ estimators that account for potential omitted time-invariant, country-specific factors that may affect democracy as well as economic variables. Key examples of such factors are the geographic determinants of democracy investigated in Chapter 3 in this volume and (fairly) stable political-historical or cultural features that may have persistent effects on political institutions. We mainly rely on the Polyarchy measure of electoral democracy (Teorell et al. 2019) for our analysis, but results drawing on alternative measures, both from V-Dem on different notions of democracy and from other sources, are briefly discussed and reported in Online Appendix 5 (available at: https://chknutsen.com/publications/). The various tests contained in this chapter should contribute to a better understanding of the sources behind the mixed findings in the extant literature on economic determinants of democracy.

First, we consider how economic development influences democracy, with a main focus placed on the most widely studied aspect of development, namely income level as operationalized by GDP per capita. Next, we will consider the role of education and urbanization, both of which can be considered proxies for wider economic development but also as socioeconomic features pertinent for democracy in their own right. When reassessing the "modernization hypothesis," we find robust evidence that GDP per capita is positively linked to levels of democracy. Further analyses suggest that GDP per capita is not, however, positively linked to democratization: Rather, there is some evidence that GDP per capita is *negatively* linked to democratic upturns. But, there is also robust evidence that income level is associated with a lower likelihood of democratic downturns. In other words, GDP per capita could be stabilizing for (all) regimes – being associated with a lower likelihood of *both democratization and democratic declines*. We do not find robust evidence that other aspects of socioeconomic modernization, such as education and urbanization, are systematically linked to democracy or democratization.

Second, we consider structural features of the economy related to the type of production and the types of assets that are predominant, as this can vary greatly even across countries at similar income levels. Important theoretical arguments and extant empirical studies suggest that such factors matter for prospects of democracy, for instance, because production factors differ in terms of how mobile assets are (see, e.g., Boix 2003). Thus, we discuss the role of natural resource production and wealth – engaging with the large literature on the "resource curse" (e.g., Haber and Menaldo 2011; Ross 2012) – as a potential deterrent of democracy. We will also discuss the role of industrialization as well as global financial integration in enhancing democracy. Our findings provide some, though far from unequivocal, support for the resource curse argument: We identify a negative association between income from natural resource dependence and democracy level, as expected from the resource curse theory, but we do not find much evidence that resource dependence is systematically linked to (particular forms of) democratic change. The strongest evidence in favor of structural economic determinants of democracy is the finding that an economy dominated by agricultural production is bad news for democracy.

Reliance on agricultural production is negatively associated with level of democracy as well as with democratization. This could either be because agricultural production proxies for the lack of global financial integration or the immobility or assets, or because it captures more general levels of economic modernization and lack of industrialization. However, we do not find a direct link between level of industrialization and democracy.

Third, we address economic phenomena that are of a more short-term nature. While the literature suggests that (long-run) economic development may promote democracy, several arguments and findings suggest that good economic performance in the short run may *reduce* the likelihood of democratization. Conversely, economic crises are often proposed to be, and are empirically identified as, important predictors of democratization in relatively autocratic regimes as well as democratic reversals (for early arguments and analysis, see, e.g., Gasiorowski 1995; Haggard and Kaufman 1995; Przeworksi and Limongi 1997). We will thus look more closely on how short-term economic growth affects democracy, but we also consider other key macro-economic indicators that may change fairly rapidly, and are typically associated with economic crises, such as inflation and unemployment. In brief, our results suggest that short-term economic performance measures are, indeed, important predictors of democracy. Although we do not find evidence that economic crisis is related to democratization, we find that it is positively associated with declines in democracy (and, conversely, that economic crisis is positively linked to democratic survival). For instance, there is evidence that both economic growth and low inflation is related to lower likelihoods of democratic downturns, but only the former finding is robust. This finding on income growth aligns with arguments suggesting that the occurrence of triggering factors (see also chapter on international determinants), including events such as economic crisis, and not only structural factors of a more long-term nature, influences regime stability and change (see, e.g. Miller 2012; Treisman 2020).

Fourth, we engage with the debate on how income inequality and other types of economic inequalities, notably related to the distribution of land, affect democracy. The link between (various forms of) inequality and democracy has been a very active field of research over the past fifteen years, with several prominent theoretical contributions (e.g., Acemoglu and Robinson 2006). Nonetheless, empirical findings on the role of income inequality are typically non-robust (see Knutsen 2015), especially when it comes to the role it plays in affecting democratization (Houle 2009). Meanwhile, some recent studies have suggested that low *land inequality* enhances democratization (Ansell and Samuels 2010, 2014). When reassessing these empirical findings and debates, we find no robust evidence consistent with the hypothesis that inequality is conducive to democratization, across various ways of measuring income and land inequality. Nor do we find any evidence that inequality is harmful for democratic survival. Hence, our findings add to the body of empirical studies throwing some cold water on theoretical expectations that inequality strongly shape prospects for democracy.

The remainder of the chapter is structured as follows: In Section 5.2 we consider, in sequence, four types of economic determinants, namely (1) economic development, (2) structural features of the economy, (3) short-term economic changes, and (4) inequality. For each of these four types, we provide a literature review, starting with the core theoretical arguments linking these types of determinants to democracy, before we turn to a discussion of existing empirical studies. Directly after each literature review, we present our empirical analyses. For each cluster of economic determinants, we select a subset of relevant indicators and explore how these correlate with (1) level of democracy, (2) changes in democracy (in either direction), (3) democratic "upturns," and (4) democratic downturns. In Section 5.3, we bring these analyses together by selecting the most relevant indicators (weighted based on theoretical considerations and the preliminary results from the previous section) from the four clusters of economic determinants and entering them together in our favored, comprehensive "economic determinants of democracy" specification.

5.2 EXTANT RESEARCH ON ECONOMIC DETERMINANTS OF DEMOCRACY

5.2.1 Economic Development

The most frequently cited explanations of regime change highlight aspects of socioeconomic development. Seymour Martin Lipset (1959) argued that societies experiencing socioeconomic modernization, with growing income levels, more education, industrialization and urbanization, will eventually acquire and maintain democratic political institutions. Although proponents of this argument have generally been more concerned with offering empirical evidence than detailed and coherent theoretical frameworks, three main arguments seem to be at the core of the modernization hypothesis. First, several scholars suggest that populations in highly (economically) developed societies should have access to more resources, including material resources, education and mass media, and hence should be a more effective source of collective action to promote democratization (for an updated review and discussion, see Dahlum 2017). Citizens living in an industrialized and urban society should also benefit from new social networks and physical proximity to other citizens that makes it easier to coordinate and overcome collective action problems.

Second, economically developed countries should have a class structure that facilitates transitions from autocratic to democratic regimes. Socioeconomic development should strengthen the middle class, which according to Lipset is a main force for democracy – through promoting democratic transitions and mitigating democratic backsliding (see also, e.g., Moore 1966). An alternative argument holds that economic development and industrialization lead to a stronger industrial working class, which may serve as an effective force for democratization due to their organizational capacity and strong preferences of economic distribution (e.g., Aidt and Jensen 2014; Rueschemeyer et al. 1992).

Third, modernization may promote democratization because it induces certain shifts in people's attitudes or beliefs. In particular, it has been argued that socioeconomic development – and the material security that arises due to economic development – yields more emphasis on values such as tolerance, trust, and freedom in the general population. Such values – often referred to as "liberal values" – may induce stronger preferences for democracy and eventually regime change, if the regime in power does not offer democratic freedoms that correspond to people's demands (e.g., Inglehart and Welzel 2005; Welzel 2015).

Numerous empirical studies have originated from the "modernization thesis." The main bulk of this literature has focused on GDP per capita, capturing a country's average income (and production) level. Given the vast number of studies on the income – democracy relationship (see, e.g., Munck, 2019 for a review), we highlight only some of the particularly notable studies and results. By doing so, we also frame the discussion around methodological debates that inform our selection of research design in the following sections. These debates notably include discussions on the appropriateness of drawing information from comparing across countries versus controlling for country-fixed effects (e.g., Acemoglu et al. 2008) as well as the appropriateness of distinguishing between effects on democratic "upturns" versus "downturns" (e.g., Przeworski et al. 2000). We spend some additional space discussing these methodological choices for studies on income and democracy, but these choices are also highly relevant for several other economic determinants discussed in this chapter such as natural resource production (see, e.g, Gassebner et al. 2013 and income inequality (see, e.g., Houle 2009).

While it is not the first study on economic development and democracy (see Munck 2019), Lipset's (1959) article titled "Some Social Requisites of Democracy" is often taken as a starting point for the systematic, empirical study of how income (and other features of economic development, as we will discuss later) affects regime type. Studying twenty-eight "European and English-speaking" countries and twenty Latin American countries, Lipset identified clear differences in (average) per capita income and other measures of wealth between "more" and "less" democratic countries within these two regions. In subsequent decades, several statistical studies on cross-country data replicated the correlation between income and democracy, also when expanding the sample to include countries from additional continents, introducing new control variables and employing more refined estimation techniques (see, e.g., Burkhart and Lewis-Beck 1994; Diamond 1992; Londregan and Poole 1996).

The predominant view that income enhances democracy was challenged, or at least nuanced, by the end of the 1990s, with the seminal study of Przeworski and Limongi (1997) and the methodologically more refined study by Przeworski et al. (2000). Drawing on a binary conception and measure of democracy, the key argument and finding is the following: while income enhances democratic survival, it does not clearly enhance democratization. The authors' finding that high GDP per capita levels have a clear stabilizing effect on already existing democracies is very robust and has been replicated in numerous studies (see. e.g., Boix and Stokes 2003; Gassebner et al. 2013, Rød et al. 2020; but see Acemoglu et al. 2009). However, Przeworski and coauthors fail to find a clear (linear) effect of income on democratic transitions. Boix and Stokes (2003), Epstein et al. (2006) and Hadenius and Teorell (2005), among others, subsequently contest this result, suggesting that the relationship is "recovered" if one extends the sample time period back to the nineteenth century, employs alternative measures of democracy, or accounts for natural resources income being different from other types of income. Yet, subsequent sensitivity analysis on binary democracy indicators have shown that the income-democratization link is, indeed, very tenuous and only survives in particular model specifications (Gassebner et al. 2013; Rød et al. 2020). In line with this, Teorell's (2010; chapter 3) analysis on income and democratic upturns/downturns (measured using a continuous democracy measure) only shows clear results for downturns.

More recently, even the link between democratic survival and income has been challenged on methodological grounds. Employing statistical models that control for country-specific effects on political regime type, Acemoglu et al. (2009) claim that this relationship is driven by omitted variable bias. There may be political-historical experiences (e.g., related to the nature of colonization) or particular geographic features – as discussed extensively in Chapter 3 of this volume – that influence both the level of economic development and the conditions for a stable democratic regime. In another study, the authors report that the observed cross-country correlation between income and level of democracy disappears once accounting for country-fixed effects (Acemoglu et al. 2008; see also Alexander et al. 2011; Moral-Benito and Bartolucci 2012). One interpretation is that the correlation stems from unmeasured confounding factors that are (at least fairly) time-invariant, relating, for instance, to particular political-historical experiences or geographic factors (as studied in Chapter 3), that affect both income and democracy in the same direction.

Yet, also these null-results have been challenged, with different studies suggesting that the relationship between income and democracy is recovered – even when accounting for country-fixed effects – once one employs data back to the nineteenth century or more appropriate estimators (Benhabib et al. 2011; Boix 2011; Che et al. 2013; Faria et al. 2014; Gundlach and Paldam 2009;

Heid et al. 2012).[1] In a recent study, Knutsen et al. (2019b), using fixed effects OLS models and V-Dem data, show that also the specific measure of democracy matters, identifying a much clearer relationship between income and democracy measures focused narrowly on the electoral aspects of democracy.

While the specific nature of the income–democracy relationship is far from settled in the literature, there are several methodological points to be drawn from this review, which can inform our model specifications. First, choices of democracy measure, control variables, and time period of the sample may all influence the relationship under study (see also Rød et al. 2020), and we should thus explicitly assess sensitivity to such choices. Second, separating the effect of income on *democratic upturns* – that is, positive changes in democracy score – from the effect on *democratic downturns* – negative changes in democracy score – can be highly informative. Third, controlling for country-fixed effects may influence results, and is key for avoiding omitted variable bias. These methodological issues seem to reoccur when considering the relationships between democracy and other socioeconomic factors, which we now turn to.

Although the majority of existing studies on the modernization-democracy link have looked at GDP per capita, this may not offer the most accurate operationalization of the modernization hypothesis. For instance, some authors propose that a high education level is the relevant trait explaining why modernized countries tend to be more democratic (Murtin and Wacziarg 2014), reflecting Lipset's argument that education is a major determinant of democracy. Theoretically, education can be plausibly tied to democratization, as a resource that may help citizens' to coordinate against authoritarian regimes (Glaeser et al. 2007), as a source of stronger preferences for liberal democracy (Dahlum 2017), and through its positive relationship with middle-class size and strength (Lipset 1959)

Empirically, a number of studies suggest a positive association between education and regime type. Several contributions suggest that education is positively related to *levels of democracy*, but do not distinguish between democratic upturns or downturns (see e.g., Aleman and Kim 2015; Barro 1999; Benavot 1996; Glaeser et al. 2007; Papaioannou and Siourounis 2008). Other studies also identify an effect of education on *transitions to democracy* (Murtin and Wacniarg 2014; Sanborn and Thyne 2014). It is less clear, however, whether the education-democracy link is due to a spurious effect rather a causal effect (see Acemoglu et al. 2006). Acemoglu et al. suggest the former, but this been contested by studies demonstrating that the positive effect holds when using arguably more appropriate estimators for highly persistent variables such as education and

---

[1] A number of recent studies further disaggregating the process of regime change and investigating conditional relationships have come to the conclusion that income typically stabilizes autocracies, but that when autocracies first break down (Kennedy 2010), experience leader deaths (Treisman 2015), or violent leader removals (Miller 2012), the regime change is much more likely to be in a democratic direction in rich countries than in poor.

accounting for endogenous effects (Bobba and Coviello 2007; Castello-Climent 2008).

Other components of modernization that are treated in the literature are urbanization and communication technology, although few direct empirical tests of these variables have been carried out. *Urbanization* has been argued to enhance the prospects for democratization in particular, as an urban population has a higher capacity for protest and coordinated collective action against a dictator (see e.g., Bates 1981; Hobsbawm 1973; Herbst 2009; Wallace 2013). Also pertaining to how economic modernization may facilitate coordination, Teorell (2010) finds that proliferation of the mass media is positively related to democratic survival (see also, e.g., Rød et al. 2020).

We now turn to empirical analysis of how the above-discussed features of economic development relate to democracy, drawing on V-Dem data as well as sources for measures of economic development that allow us to include a large number of countries globally across long time spans. The dependent variables pertaining to democracy used for this analysis were presented in Chapter 1, but let us here quickly sum up the main such variables (alternative measures used for robustness tests are described when they are used in analyses later): Our main democracy measure is V-Dem's Polyarchy index (Teorell et al. 2019), and the four dependent variable specifications, as described in Chapter 1, are as follows:

1. level of democracy (measured in $t+1$),
2. change in democracy (from t to $t+1$),
3. upturns in democracy (from t to $t+1$, with negative changes recoded as 0), and
4. downturns in democracy (from t to $t+1$, with positive changes recoded as 0).

We highlight that we have rescaled Polyarchy, so that it ranges from 0 to 100 instead of 0 to 1, variable for all regressions that we report in tables in this chapter. The core independent variables pertaining to economic development that are tested in this section, and the sources from which they are drawn, are listed in Table 5.1. In order to test different aspects of economic development, we employ five different measures. Two of these measures are similar indicators drawn from different data sources, measuring Ln GDP per capita, to test the robustness of the most widely studied economic determinant of democracy to potential measurement errors and differences in coverage. The three other measures pertain to quite different aspects of development, namely education level, urbanization, and the spread of communications technology (television sets) in the population. In this section, we display parsimonious regression models (that mitigate issues of multicollinearity and posttreatment bias) that only include each indicator of development in isolation. However, this may come at the cost of one variable (e.g., average years of education) picking up relevant effects from other economic factors (e.g., income level or urbanization) that it is strongly correlated with. Thus, we caution against overinterpreting results from any single regression and point forward to tests where we also include multiple covariates simultaneously.

TABLE 5.1 *Indicators of democracy and economic development*

Aspect	Concept	Indicator/measure	Variable tag	Max years in time series	V-Dem polities covered	Source
Outcome measure	Democracy	Electoral Democracy/ Polyarchy	*v2x_polyarchy*	230	199	Varieties of Democracy, v.9. (Coppedge et al. 2018)
Economic development	Income	Ln GDP per capita	*e_migdppc*	228	163	The Maddison Project (2013)
Economic development	Education	Avg years of education for population 15+	*e_peaveduc*	199	137	Morrison and Murtin (2009)
Economic development	Urbanization	Ratio of Urban Population to Population	*e_miurbani*	201	162	Clio Infra (clio-infra.eu)

Our benchmark estimator is – due to the continuous nature of our dependent variables – ordinary least squares (OLS). Country-year is the unit of analysis, and we cluster errors by country to account for panel-specific heteroscedasticity and autocorrelation. Our benchmark specifications always include country- and year-fixed effects, as well as the lagged level of democracy for dependent variables that capture changes in democracy (as, e.g., the room for further democratization depends critically on the preexisting level of democracy).

For our benchmark specifications, we use a one-year lag on all covariates. This is certainly an arbitrary choice, and it is likely that the optimal lag structure will vary across covariates. The problem is that there are few authoritative models that imply exactly how long the appropriate lag should be for most of these indicators. One exception is that the reviewed literature and plausible theoretical arguments (e.g., on crises as focal points) lead us to expect that measures of short-term changes such as GDP per capita growth and inflation should work either instantaneously or with a one-year lag. Although changes in structural factors such as urbanization or inequality may very well affect democracy with a longer lag, we thus opted for a simple one-year lag as a homogeneous specification across models. In Online Appendix 5, we present robustness tests on the main results for alternative lag structures, namely five- and ten-year lags. As anticipated, using such longer lags weakens the results for the short-term economic change variables, but (more surprisingly) also weakens different results for income level, as measured by GDP per capita, both on democratic upturns and downturns.

The inclusion of country-fixed effects helps us to account for time-invariant, country-specific factors that may affect democracy. Key examples of such factors are the geographic factors investigated in the previous chapters and (fairly) stable political-historical or cultural features (e.g., Acemoglu 2008). Regarding the former, John Gerring's Chapter 3 presents evidence that (relatively) stable geographic factors such as average temperature and closeness to a natural harbor is linked to democracy level. When it comes to cultural factors, Chapter 3 finds that European ancestry is associated with higher democracy levels today. Given that these factors may also influence the economic variables considered in our chapter, it is important to account for such time-invariant factors in our models.

The year-fixed effects account for international shocks (such as the end of a world war) or (flexible) global time trends in factors that influence regime type.[2] Notably, democratization and reverse experiences have come clustered together (globally and regionally) in particular time periods, popularized by

---

[2] One concern is that the year-fixed effects, by adding often more than 200 dummies to our regressions and disallowing comparisons across particular years, give inefficient estimates. We thus retested all our model specifications by using decade dummies, thus opening up for comparisons within decades. Results are very similar, at least in terms of sign and significance, when we use these alternative controls for temporal trends, as shown in Online Appendix 5, Tables A2 and A3.

Huntington's (1991) term "waves of democratization," as discussed and illustrated in Chapter 2 of this book. Such waves could reflect, for instance, technological changes, ideological currents, or the geopolitical situation in terms of power balance between various (democratic or autocratic) powers. These may also capture spillover effects from other countries during wave or reverse wave years, although Chapter 4 in this volume highlights that such effects will be highly contingent on the country in question, and how it is located in various international networks, and may thus not be controlled for well by including year dummies. More generally, we warn against interpreting our coefficients as other than controlled correlations, as plausible time-variant, country-specific controls are not accounted for in these early specifications.

We highlight that, despite the controls for country- and year-fixed effects, threats to drawing causal inferences from the controlled relationships discussed later still remain. First, our research design cannot rule out the possibility of *reverse causation* – that is, that any identified association between economic factors and democracy is really driven by democracy influencing economic factors. There is indeed a vast body of literature arguing that democracy is a key driver of economic development (including GDP per capita and education levels) (e.g., Lake and Baum 2001) and economic growth (see, e.g., Knutsen 2012 for a review), and that it reduces economic inequality through redistribution of resources (see, e.g., Boix 2003). Related contributions suggest that democracy and economic development reinforce each other in a positive feedback loop, thereby making it very hard to disentangle the precise causal relationship. Second, although the inclusion of country- and year-fixed effects account for either omitted confounders that are constant over time but varies between countries or confounders that vary over time but not between countries, it does not account for unobserved effects that vary both over time and between countries. For instance, there could be country-specific time trends in certain socioeconomic or cultural factors, which are driving both economic development and democracy. For these reasons, we cannot interpret the estimates in this chapter as causal effects.

We start by investigating how the different indicators of economic development relate to level of democracy, as measured by the Polyarchy index. These specifications are reported in the upper (A) panel. As mentioned, GDP per capita, which measures income level, is the most widely used proxy for economic development, more broadly. In Model A1, we thus employ Ln GDP per capita, using a PPP-adjusted GDP measure with data from the Maddison Project (Bolt and van Zanden 2014). The data being PPP-adjusted means that local price levels are taken into account when measuring income, thus providing a better measure of the living standards and potential consumption that an "average income" provides than, for example, exchange-rate adjusted GDP data that do not account for local price levels. The natural log transformation of the GDP per capita measure comes with both econometric and theoretical/validity benefits: First, this concave transformation of the data gives an income distribution that is closer to the normal and contributes to mitigate the influence of extreme observations. Second, the transformation, which weighs changes at the lower end of the GDP per capita scale more heavily, also comports with plausible theoretical notions of what such an income change reflects in terms of societal and economic transformations different contexts. An increase of, say, 1,000 USD in average income reflects a very large increase in living standards, and likely also in the production structure of the economy and functioning of society, for a country that starts out as dirt poor, where GDP per capita is around the minimum existence level (say, current DRC or China of 1950). In contrast, an increase of 1,000 USD in GDP per capita level would be barely noticeable, and not reflect any larger economic or societal transformation, in current Luxembourg or Norway.

Concerning coverage, the Maddison data includes time series extending back into the nineteenth century. As estimates for income are reported with gaps in the time series for the earlier decades, often ten or twenty year intervals, even for those country that have fairly decent coverage, these data have been interpolated (assuming constant GDP per capita growth rates) between observations. In total, 163 countries are included in Model A1 and the longest time series extend across 228 years, yielding 16,342 country-year observations.

The results reported in Model A1 support the standard "Lipset hypothesis," in that income level as measured by Ln GDP per capita is systematically correlated with democracy level. The point estimate is positive, and the t-value is 3.2. We remind that the benchmark specification includes country-fixed effects, and as such the result from Model A1 is more in line with the findings from Knutsen et al. (2019b), than with the null-results in, for example, Acemoglu et al. (2008), which are based on far shorter time series.[3]

Among the two remaining indicators of economic development, namely average years of education in the (15+) population (Model A2) and urbanization (A3), only the education measure is statistically significant, and then only at the 10 percent level (t = 1.8). Thus, while all coefficients are positive, there is no robust relationship between economic development, broadly speaking, and democracy level when controlling for country- and year-fixed effects.[4]

[3] When running similar specifications that exclude the country-fixed effects, and thus incorporate variation from cross-country comparisons, we find that many results are fairly similar, but that both income and education are more strongly correlated with Polyarchy changes. However, results remain non-robust for urbanization. Also, the results for income on both Polyarchy level and downturns remain robust when omitting the country-fixed effects, but the negative correlation with democratic upturns is no longer statistically significant at conventional levels. These results are reported in Online Appendix 5, Table A6.
[4] Previous studies have highlighted that, given the typically slow-moving nature of GDP per capita and democracy measures, OLS fixed effects regressions may fail to pick up effects of income on democracy, even if they exist (e.g., Heid et al. 2012). This should, however, be a smaller concern for studies such as ours that rely on long time series, and thus ensure ample within-country variation in both economic development and democracy for many countries. Yet, as noted earlier, we do report results from regressions without country-fixed effects in Appendix Table A.6.

This conclusion is further strengthened when considering the specifications in Panel B of Table 5.2 using change in Polyarchy (from t−1 to t) as the dependent variable. The Maddison measure of income is insignificant with a t-value of 1.0. Among the other indicators of development, none are statistically significant even at the 10 percent level, although Urbanization comes the closest with a t-value of 1.6.

As the extensive debates that followed the publication of Przeworski and Limongi's (1997) seminal article have highlighted, however, the lack of a robust relationship between economic development and democracy may simply be due to development having heterogeneous effects on democratization and on processes of autocratization. Notably, economic development may not matter much for democratization, or democratic upturns, but it may be key for avoiding democratic breakdowns (Przeworksi et al. 2000) or downturns more generally (see Teorell 2010). Indeed, the regressions reported in Panels C and D of Table 5.2 support this notion.

No indicator of economic development is positively and significantly related to democratic upturns. In fact, Ln GDP per capita is negatively signed, though only weakly significant at the 10 percent level. Hence, when only focusing on upturns and controlling for the initial level of democracy (Polyarchy level in year t−1), our results resemble those of, for example, some of the dynamic panel models of Acemoglu et al. (2008), which control for the lagged dependent variable. Other studies that have found a negative relationship have also relied on dynamic panel models, including Fayad et al. (2012), although Moral-Benito (2013) carefully show that such negative results are contingent on the particular dynamic panel estimator. Even if this should be the case, our regressions, which extend back to the nineteenth century, at least do not find a clear positive link with democratic upturns (Boix 2011; cf. Boix and Stokes 2003).[5]

In contrast, all the indicators are positive, and both income and average years of education are statistically significant at least at the 5 percent level, in the downturns regressions. The relationship between GDP per capita and democratic downturns, more specifically, is particularly robust (t = 5.8), and it displays a systematic correlation with downturns in the expected direction even when we add average years of education as a control (whereas education turns insignificant at conventional levels). Hence, our results corroborate the already widely believed pattern that higher income levels mitigate democratic downturns (see also, e.g., Rød et al. 2020).

---

[5] One potential explanation for the negative coefficient on income (for upturns) could be that most very rich countries have already democratized and thus exhausted their potential for further upturns, thereby biasing the relationship. However, we remind that we do control for initial level of democracy in these regressions. Further, when we restrict the analysis to countries starting out with Polyarchy levels of, respectively, <0.8 or <0.9, and thus ample room for further upturns in the following year. The results, however, show a negative (though nonsignificant) relationship between Ln GDP p.c. and upturns also for these restricted samples.

TABLE 5.2 *Benchmark regressions including indicators of economic development*

	(1) b/(t)	(2) b/(t)	(3) b/(t)
A: Polyarchy level			
Ln GDP pc (Maddison)	5.930*** (3.209)		
Avg. years education (15+)		1.589* (1.781)	
Urbanization			3.053 (0.566)
N	16359	14325	16978
R^2	0.605	0.588	0.517
B. Polyarchy changes			
Ln GDP pc (Maddison)	0.106 (0.989)		
Avg. years education (15+)		0.030 (0.605)	
Urbanization			0.440 (1.608)
N	16342	14310	16947
R^2	0.065	0.059	0.054
C: Upturns			
Ln GDP pc (Maddison)	−0.197* (−1.829)		
Avg. years education (15+)		−0.044 (−0.780)	
Urbanization			0.299 (1.103)
N	16342	14310	16947
R^2	0.070	0.065	0.066
D: (Avoiding) Downturns			
Ln GDP pc (Maddison)	0.303*** (5.763)		
Avg. years education (15+)		0.075** (2.373)	

(continued)

TABLE 5.2 *(continued)*

	(1) b/(t)	(2) b/(t)	(3) b/(t)
Urbanization			0.141 (0.974)
N	16342	14310	16947
R^2	0.040	0.031	0.031

Notes: All specifications include country- and year-fixed effects. Specifications in B, C, and D also control for (lagged) level of Polyarchy. Dependent variables measured in year t+1 and all covariates in year t. The dependent variable (Polyarchy) has been rescaled so that it ranges from 0–100. We note that positive coefficients in panel D means that a covariate correlates with smaller/fewer democratic downturns. *** p < 0.01, ** p < 0.05, * p < 0.1.

5.2.2 Structural Features of the Economy

Economies differ in many other respects than their level of development, whether broadly defined or (especially) more narrowly defined according to income level. Countries with identical levels of income may derive this income from very different production activities, have very different types of capital assets and ownership structures. Such differences can be relevant for influencing regime type and regime change.

At a general level, the relative propensity of movable versus immovable or specific versus general capital assets have been highlighted as relevant for democratization (see, e.g., Clark et al. 2017), although different authors point to slightly different mechanisms. Boix (2003), for example, highlights the importance of the economic elite – assumed to initially support an incumbent autocratic regime – holding movable assets for chances of democratization. In such an economy, the elite do not deem the redistributive consequences of prospective democratization to be too costly. The reason is that their assets cannot easily be expropriated, and taxes will be kept low even under democratization – where the poor median voter presumably rules – since the economic elites can credible threaten with their "exit option" of moving assets abroad.

A more detailed sociological version of the argument, making finer distinctions between classes and groups of producers, highlights differences between the industrial and large-scale agricultural production. Various scholars have made the point that landowners, due to immovable assets that may be heavily taxed or even expropriated under democracy, have strong incentives to hinder democratization (See, e.g., Albertus 2017; Ansell and Samuels 2014). In contrast, urban, industrial elites, at least in certain instances, have incentives to promote democratization due to the less specific/

movable nature of their assets as well as the presumed compatibility between democratic governance and such modes of production (e.g., Ansell and Samuels 2014; Cervellati et al. 2006).

Adding to this, we discussed previously how urbanization and industrialization create groups of workers who have the requisite capabilities and incentives to pursue democratization "from below." While we will not reiterate this general argument, we note that several theoretical and case study contributions have pointed to workers in certain sectors being especially effective agents in mobilizing for democratization, notably the urban middle classes (e.g., working in the service industries or as educated professionals; see Moore 1966; references) or industrial workers (Collier 1999; Rueschmeyer et al. 1992). Recent quantitative work also finds that opposition mobilization led by these urban groups, in particular by industrial workers, is relatively more effective in terms of engendering democratization (Dahlum et al. 2018). This argument is discussed much more in depth, and retested, in Bernhard and Edgell's Chapter 7 of this book.

A different argument is that autocrats can tax economic elites (and others) higher, without assets being moved abroad or hidden from the autocrat's view, in an economy dominated by immovable assets (such as natural resources or rich agricultural land) than in an economy dominated by movable assets (such as human capital or financial assets). In other words, the production structure of the economy determines the extent to which an autocrat (or regime elites) can monopolize revenue generated in the country's economy. Certain types of natural resource extraction constitute one source of easily controllable wealth that autocrats or regime elites can monopolize, and direct access to vast amounts of (unconditionally provided) foreign aid is another (Bueno de Mesquita and Smith 2009; Clark et al. 2017). Such revenues are key for providing regime actors with ample resources to use for co-optation of threats or for investing in security apparatuses and repressive capacity, which, in turn, prolongs autocratic survival and hinders democratization (e.g., Bueno de Mesquita and Smith, 2009; Cuaresma et al. 2011; Smith, 2004, 2006).

Empirically, the prevalence of natural resource wealth within the country, or more specifically the dependence of the economy on income from natural resources production, has attracted particular interest among the theoretically relevant structural features. Following the wider political-economy literature on "Resource curses" – the observation that a wealth of, and especially an economic dependence on, mineral and fuel resources may induce several bad macroeconomic and political-institutional outcomes (for a recent review, focusing on corruption, see Knutsen et al. 2017a) – several scholars have proposed a link between resource extraction and autocracy. In a seminal study, Ross (2001) explores whether or not oil has anti-democratic effects and, if so, whether the effect is present in different regions of the world. Drawing on cross-section time series data from 113 countries, measured between 1971 and 1997, Ross answers both questions in the positive. He attributes the relationship to three likely mechanisms. These are, first, a "rentier effect" where rulers employ resource windfalls to mitigate pressures for increased accountability; second, a "repression effect" related to increased government resources for buying repressive capacity; and, third, a "modernization effect" as oil income fails to generate the social changes anticipated (by modernization theory) to follow economic development.

In subsequent work (e.g., Ross 2012), Ross has nuanced some of these claims, for instance, finding stronger support for the "rentier" mechanism than alternative mechanisms and highlighting the time-variant effects of oil on democracy, with particularly strong negative effects in recent decades following large-scale nationalization of oil companies in the 1970s. Several other recent and careful empirical studies have replicated the finding that natural resource abundance, or related measures, mitigate level of democracy (Aslaksen 2010; Tsui 2010), hinders democratization (Boix 2003; Gassebner et al. 2013) or increases the durability of existing authoritarian regimes (Andersen and Aslaksen 2013; Cuaresma et al. 2011).

Yet, these findings have been challenged by recent contributions employing alternative designs and strategies for inference. Liou and Musgrave (2014) use the price spike following the 1973 OPEC oil embargo as an exogenous source of information and relies on a synthetic control strategy for studying seven "treated" (becoming oil-reliant) countries. They find little evidence of any effect on regime type. The time series results in Haber and Menaldo (2011), drawing on data all the way from the beginning of the nineteenth century onward, also sow doubt about the causal link between natural resources and autocracy (for a critical review of this study and alternative specification suggesting a "resource curse," in recent decades, see Andersen and Ross (2014)).

While less intensively scrutinized, empirical studies have also tested for relationships between other theoretically relevant structural features of the economy and regime type/regime change. Results are typically mixed between studies, or contingent on particular conditions being in place for the relationship to operate. For instance, while some find that trade openness is positively linked to democratization (e.g., Lopez-Cordova and Messiner 2008), others find no clear link between economic openness and democratization (e.g., Milner and Mukherjee 2009). Concerning the international mobility of key capital assets, studies have found that increased exposure to international export and financial markets is linked to democracy, but only in the presence of social spending and welfare policies that provide safety nets for those who lose out from globalization (Rudra 2005). The effect of financial capital integration may also be a complex function of the initial level of income inequality (Freeman and Quinn 2012).

Regarding agricultural production versus industrial production, political scientists have proposed that the predominant type of production – not the least because this indirectly matters for the incentives of elites to democratize (e.g., Moore 1966) or for the incentives and organizational capacity of citizens to work for democracy (e.g., Rueschemeyer et al. 1992) – has implications for regime type and stability. An economy focused on agricultural production (see review in Albertus 2017), and then more specifically if the sector has high land inequality (e.g., Ansell and Samuels 2014) or labor-intensive agricultural production (Albertus 2017), is widely considered to be detrimental to democratization. Also, when mobilized regime opposition is dominated by peasants, the chances of subsequent democratization are far smaller than when opposition is dominated by urban middle classes or, especially, industrial workers (Dahlum et al. 2019). Yet, in a recent sensitivity analysis, Rød et al. (2020) find little robust evidence of a negative relationship between broader measures such as employment share in agriculture or agriculture's share of the economy, on the one hand, and democratization or democratic survival on the other. Instead, Rød et al. find that a higher industrial share of the economy is correlated with lower chances of democratization.

Table 5.3 reports describe the measures used in our analysis of how structural features of the economy relate to democracy. We follow the same template as in the subsection 5.2.1, and run OLS models with errors clustered by country and country- and year-fixed effects. We also here test different dependent variable specifications measuring changes in or level of Polyarchy.

Our literature review and discussion of production structures and asset types focused heavily on the prevalence of natural resources, income stemming from such resources, and the economy's dependence on such income. Thus, the first two measures that we regress against level of democracy, in Panel A Table 5.4 capture, respectively, natural resource wealth (from Haber and Menaldo 2011) and natural resource dependence (from Miller 2015), and both data sources allow us to include data extending back into the nineteenth century. Only the latter measure is negatively and systematically correlated with Polyarchy level ($t = -2.0$ in Model 5). Thus, our results follow the previously detected pattern that measures capturing resource dependence are more strongly linked to autocratic outcomes than measures capturing resource income.

Yet, for Polyarchy change in Panel B, or when we split up the changes to Polyarchy into upturns and downturns in Panels C and D, respectively, none of the natural resource coefficients are statistically significant. These results are robust to controlling for income level (see Appendix Table A7). In sum, whereas there is no robust link between natural resource income and dependence with either democratic upturns or downturns, there is evidence suggesting that natural resource dependence is linked to lower levels of democracy.

When it comes to the two remaining measures – capturing, respectively, the shares of manufacturing income and agricultural income of total income – there are also statistically significant and noteworthy relationships with the different dependent variables. More specifically, agricultural income is clearly linked both to democracy level (Model A7) and change (B7). However, we note that agricultural income share of GDP is negatively correlated with several of the "modernization" variables tested in the previous section (income, education,

TABLE 5.3 *Indicators of structural features of the economy*

Aspect	Concept	Indicator/measure	Variable tag	Time series	V-Dem polities covered	Source
Structural features of the economy	Natural resources wealth	Petrol, coal, natural gas, and metals production per capita	e_total_resources_income_pc	107	163	Haber and Menaldo (2011)
Structural features of the economy	Natural resources dependence	Percent government revenues from oil, natural gas, and minerals	s_mil_resdep2	207	161	Miller (2015)
Structural features of the economy	Industrialization	Share of GDP from manufacturing	wdi_manufacturing_pctgdp	58	170	World Bank (2016)
Structural features of the economy	Resource mobility	Share of GDP from agriculture	s_mil_agro	192	160	Miller (2015)

TABLE 5.4 *Benchmark regressions including indicators of structural features of the economy*

	(4) b/(t)	(5) b/(t)	(6) b/(t)	(7) b/(t)
A: Polyarchy level				
Natural resource income per capita	0.000			
	(0.079)			
Natural resource income/GDP		−0.120**		
		(−1.992)		
Manufacturing income/GDP			−0.191	
			(−1.050)	
Agricultural income/GDP				−0.244***
				(−3.138)
N	10529	13067	6150	11060
R^2	0.408	0.505	0.354	0.503
B: Polyarchy change				
Natural resource income per capita	0.000			
	(0.077)			
Natural resource income/GDP		−0.004		
		(−0.653)		
Manufacturing income/GDP			−0.008	
			(−0.283)	
Agricultural income/GDP				−0.023***
				(−3.874)
N	10524	13046	6034	11048
R^2	0.065	0.065	0.105	0.070
C: Upturns				
Natural resource income per capita	0.000			
	(0.463)			
Natural resource income/GDP		−0.002		
		(0.287)		
Manufacturing income/GDP			0.029	
			(1.355)	
Agricultural income/GDP				−0.023***
				(−4.004)
N	10524	13046	6034	11048
R^2	0.068	0.072	0.087	0.078

(continued)

TABLE 5.4 *(continued)*

	(4) b/(t)	(5) b/(t)	(6) b/(t)	(7) b/(t)
D: (Avoiding) Downturns				
Natural resource income per capita	−0.000 (−0.599)			
Natural resource income/GDP		−0.002 (−0.699)		
Manufacturing income/GDP			−0.037** (−2.322)	
Agricultural income/GDP				−0.001 (−0.181)
N	10524	13046	6034	11048
R^2	0.026	0.032	0.051	0.030

Notes: All specifications include country- and year-fixed effects. Specifications in B, C, and D also control for (lagged) level of Polyarchy. Dependent variables measured in year t+1 and all covariates in year t. The dependent variable (Polyarchy) has been rescaled so that it ranges from 0–100. We note that positive coefficients in panel D means that a covariate correlates with smaller/fewer democratic downturns. *** $p < 0.01$, ** $p < 0.05$, * $p < 0.1$.

and urbanization), and we thus highlight the importance of considering the robustness of the agricultural income variable to controlling for such features. We will present such models toward the end of this chapter.

Further, when splitting up the types of change, however, agricultural income is only clearly liked to upturns. This result, however, is very strong and clear, with the agricultural income/GDP coefficient being negative and with a t-value of −4.0. This corroborates existing findings in the literature suggesting that an economy dominated by agricultural production may severely mitigate the chances of democratization (see, e.g., Ansell and Samuels 2010, 2014). In contrast, manufacturing income as share of total income systematically mitigates downturns (t = −2.3 in Model D8), but is not clearly linked neither to Polyarchy level, change nor upturns. It should, however, be noted that these results draw on far fewer country-year observations (around 6,000) and time series that do not extend back to the nineteenth century.

5.2.3 Short-Term Economic Changes

We have so far discussed economic determinants that may be considered structural factors that influence the baseline risks of regime change (in one or more particular directions). But, numerous contributions on regime change, as well as related processes such as mass protests, revolutions, and coups d'état, often point to the importance of "triggering factors" for explaining regime change. One underlying theoretical notion pertains to the importance of clearly demarcated and publicly observable "signals" that allow actors in opposition to the regime to resolve their "collective action problems" (Olson 1965). Various individuals may have personal preferences for regime change, but remain incapable of realizing these preferences unless coordinating their actions (in space and time) with others. Protesting in the streets or otherwise challenging an incumbent regime alone is likely to be ineffective and may carry high costs – rational individuals are therefore likely to avoid challenging the regime unless they know that others will join their efforts (see, e.g., Tullock 2005). Once a sufficient number of individuals are protesting (or otherwise challenging the regime), the protests are likely to rapidly expand due to "cascading" or "snowballing" effects (see, e.g., Lohmann 1994).[6]

Events of various kinds may function as signals that alleviate collective action, and thus trigger regime change, including leader deaths (e.g., Treisman 2015) or elections (e.g., Knutsen et al. 2017b). Yet, economic crisis is one prominent such event/signal that may allow regime opponents to coordinate and mobilize (see, e.g., Acemoglu and Robinson 2006). Economic crises take different forms, but sharp drops in income levels or the stock market, the bursting of property bubbles, cutbacks in public expenditure, rapid exchange rate fluctuations, hyperinflation, crop failures and price hikes on key subsistence goods, and so on, can all happen over relatively limited time intervals and provide natural focal points for opposition against the regime. Such dynamics are recognized both by in-depth historical accounts from different time periods and regions (see, for instance, Rapport 2008) as well as suggested by various large-N studies on different types of crises (Hendrix and Haggard 2015; Hendrix and Salehyan 2012; Ponticelli and Voth 2011).

In addition to serving as a focal point for collective action (for actors *already* desiring regime change), economic crises can alter regime preferences in key parts of the population by spurring "grievances" against the regime. The regime may (rightly or wrongly) be attributed blame for the economic crisis, and citizens may experience negative emotional responses that lead them to pursue regime change (see, e.g., Davies 1962; Gurr 1970). Regime actions responding to reduced public revenue during crises, for instance, in the form of cutbacks in social expenditure (Ponticelli and Voth 2011) or patronage payments (e.g., Bratton and van de Walle 1997), could further escalate grievances. An alternative (rationalist) mechanism pointing in the same

[6] This insight is particularly relevant for regime-challenging efforts in autocracies, where an additional layer of uncertainty about the behavior of others is that citizens engage in "preference falsification" (Kuran 1995); individuals keep their discontent with the regime private, until observing that others are actually also dissatisfied with the regime, and it is safer to express their own true opinions.

direction is that crises lead to reduced personal incomes in the present and/or future. This, in turn, reduces the opportunity costs of participating in a rebellion against the regime, as indicated by studies on opportunity costs and civil war (e.g., Collier and Hoeffler 2004), and this logic can be generalized to other forms of (risky) regime-challenging activities, such as participating in drawn-out anti-regime protests, or coup attempts.

Finally, short-term economic performance such as economic growth may strengthen an incumbent regime through offering financial resources that may be used to prevent regime change. Although there are reasons and prior evidence suggesting that the effect of short-term performance on regime stability and change may depend on the initial set of institutions (see, e.g., Bernhard et al. 2001), we anticipate effects both for initially democratic and autocratic regimes. While an authoritarian leader may be able to mitigate regime change by buying off its "support coalition" or investing in repression, a democratic leader can use it to invest in public services and goods that will promote popular support. Thus, negative short-term economic developments may increase the prospects of regime change due to collective action, grievance, and/or opportunity cost mechanisms. Conversely, high economic growth and other short-term developments, suggesting the absence of an economic crisis, should expectedly correlate positively with regime stability.

When it comes to democratizing regime changes as well as autocratization processes, most empirical studies have used short-term GDP per capita growth as an indicator of short-term economic change. Different studies have, indeed, found that slow or negative economic growth is strongly correlated with regime changes of various kinds, including the breakdown of both democratic and autocratic regimes.[7] In their classic study, Przeworski and Limongi (1997), using a binary measure of democracy, found that slow short-term economic growth increases the likelihood of democratization (i.e., a transition from autocracy to democracy) and democratic breakdown (transition from democracy to autocracy).[8] Teorell (2010: chapter 3) finds analogous results when employing a continuous measure of democracy and separately investigating democratic upturns and downturns. In their sensitivity analysis of fifty-nine proposed determinants of democratization and democratic breakdown, Gassebner et al. (2013) find that GDP per capita growth is among the few very robust determinants of democratization, suggesting that slow short-term growth substantially increases the chances of transition from autocracy to democracy. Yet, other studies have also reported regime-destabilizing effects of slow GDP per

---

[7] Also a host of more specific processes tightly associated with regime change such as civil wars (Hegre and Sambanis 2006), riots and protests (Ponticelli and Voth 2011), revolutions (Knutsen 2014), and coups d'état (Gassebner et al. 2016) are also negatively correlated with short-term GDP per capita growth.

[8] Nuancing the latter relationship, Przeworski and Limongi (1997) also report that relatively wealthy democracies are quite resistant to economic crises whereas poor democracies are particularly vulnerable.

capita growth (e.g., Aidt and Leon 2016; Ciccone 2011; Haggard and Kaufman 1995; Kennedy 2010). While the overall impact of growth on level of democracy is unclear, and depends on the degree of democracy of the incumbent regime in place, extant studies do thus suggest that high economic growth should mitigate both democratic upturns and democratic downturns.

There is also some evidence that high levels of unemployment may trigger regime change. Campante and Chor (2012) find that unemployment is associated with irregular turnovers of the executive leader, in both democratic and autocratic regimes.[9] They also find that this effect is particularly pronounced when education levels are high, suggesting that education coupled with macroeconomic weakness may induce regime change, as high expectations generated by education are not met by economic opportunities. Others have suggested that accelerated levels of inflation are linked to instances of democratic breakdown (Haggard and Kaufmann 1995, see also Gasiorowski and Power 1998). Concerning democratization, Gasiorowski (1995) finds evidence that crisis characterized by high inflation actually inhibit such regime change, although the relationship seems heterogeneous across time and especially strong from the 1950s through the early 1970s.

Table 5.5 reports the measures used in our analysis of how short-term economic factors relate to democracy. Once again, we employ the same template in terms of model specification and choice of dependent variable. Table 5.6 reports the results.

Column 8 reports regressions including GDP per capita growth during the last year as a regressor, with data drawn from the Maddison dataset used earlier for measuring income level. While there is a positive, but no statistically significant, correlation with Polyarchy level (t = 1.5 in A8), there is a clear relationship between GDP per capita growth and change in Polyarchy in Model B8; higher short-term growth is related to increases in democracy.

There is thus some, but not robust, evidence that high GDP per capita growth correlates with changes in democracy when we include both upturns and downturns in Panel B, Panel C shows no evidence. However, independent of choice of measure, that high growth relates to democratic upturns. In fact, this result follows what one may expect from the thorough existing studies such as Kennedy (2010). To reiterate, Kennedy (2010) finds that high growth reduces the chances of regime change in autocracies, but that – conditional on change actually happening – high growth increases the share of changes being democratizing ones. When taken together, these two different mechanisms may wash each other out when considering the aggregate relationship between growth and upturns.

Such mixed mechanisms do not pertain to the relationship between economic growth and democratic downturns – the clear expectation is that high growth should stabilize existing democracies and, more generally, help countries avoid

---

[9] Although leadership change does not necessarily entail regime change, the majority of leadership changes do also culminate in regime change.

TABLE 5.5 *Indicators of short-term economic changes*

Aspect	Concept	Indicator/measure	Variable tag	Time series	V-Dem polities covered	Source
Short-term economic changes	Economic growth	Percent growth in GDP per capita from t–1 to t	gdppcgrowth_mad	227	163	The Maddison Project (2013)
Short-term economic changes	Inflation	Annual inflation rate (i), log transformed by taking $\ln(i_{min} + 1 + i)$	lninfl	222	160	Clio Infra (clio-infra.eu)
Short-term economic changes	Unemployment	Unemployed as percentage share of work force	wb_unemp_pct	26	146	World Bank (2013)

TABLE 5.6 *Benchmark regressions including indicators of short-term economic changes*

	(8) b/(t)	(9) b/(t)	(10) b/(t)
A: Polyarchy level			
GDP p.c. growth (Maddison)	0.033		
	(1.486)		
Unemployment rate		0.322**	
		(2.335)	
Inflation rate (log-transformed)			−0.478
			(−0.420)
N	16199	3786	12387
R^2	0.612	0.112	0.592
B: Polyarchy change			
GDP p.c. growth (Maddison)	0.024***		
	(2.970)		
Unemployment rate		0.034	
		(1.145)	
Inflation rate (log-transformed)			0.130
			(0.527)
N	16186	3785	12375
R^2	0.067	0.130	0.064
C: Upturns			
GDP p.c. growth (Maddison)	0.011		
	(1.633)		
Unemployment rate		0.009	
		(0.380)	
Inflation rate (log-transformed)			0.342
			(1.375)
N	16186	3785	12375
R^2	0.070	0.114	0.072
D: (Avoiding) Downturns			
GDP p.c. growth (Maddison)	0.013***		
	(4.063)		

(continued)

TABLE 5.6 (*continued*)

	(8) b/(t)	(9) b/(t)	(10) b/(t)
Unemployment rate		0.025* (1.699)	
Inflation rate (log-transformed)			−0.212* (−1.749)
N	16186	3785	12375
R^2	0.039	0.055	0.035

Notes: All specifications include country- and year-fixed effects. Specifications in B, C, and D also control for (lagged) level of Polyarchy. Dependent variables measured in year t+1 and all covariates in year t. The dependent variable (Polyarchy) has been rescaled so that it ranges from 0–100. We note that positive coefficients in panel D means that a covariate correlates with smaller/fewer democratic downturns. *** p < 0.01, ** p < 0.05, * p < 0.1.

regime changes in a more autocratic direction. Indeed, this is what the results in Panel D reveal; independent of source of GDP data, high economic growth is strongly correlated with mitigating democratic downturns, and the relationship is statistically significant at all conventional levels.

As for the two other measures of short-term economic changes, unemployment and inflation, results are also mixed. The unemployment rate data (from the World Bank) are restricted only to more recent decades, leaving us with fewer than 4,000 country-year observations to draw inferences from. The level regression (A9), somewhat surprisingly, shows that a higher unemployment rate predicts a higher level of democracy. However, unemployment is not systematically correlated to change in democracy level, and we also find null-results both for democratic upturns and downturns if we employ the conventional 5 percent level of significance. However, when relaxing the significance threshold to 10 percent, we find that countries with higher unemployment rates observe smaller/fewer downturns in democracy.[10]

In contrast, inflation data has more extensive coverage, yielding regressions with about 12,000 country-year observations in Column 10. There is no correlation between inflation and democracy level, change, or upturns. However, high inflation rates are, as expected, correlated with stronger democratic downturns, although the coefficient in Model D10 is statistically significant only at the 10 percent level. Yet, as for GDP per capita growth, there

---

[10] The coefficient is, however, sensitive, as it is weakened and no longer significant at the 10 percent level once we add Ln GDP per capita as a control to Model D9.

146	Carl Henrik Knutsen and Sirianne Dahlum

are indications that poor short-term economic performance predicts regime change in a more autocratic direction.[11]

5.2.4 Inequality

Theoretical arguments proposing that the distribution of income (and other economic assets) affect the makeup of political regimes have a long history, with lineages back to Aristotle's Politics and nineteenth-century social scientists such as Marx and de Tocqueville. The theorized link between income inequality and democracy appears in numerous more recent accounts as well, although the proposed mechanisms linking inequality with regime type vary quite a lot – and so does the predicted *direction* of the relationship. Lipset (1959), for example, argues that low inequality is conducive to democracy since this reduces the extent of social conflict, which presumably undercuts democratic regimes. In contrast, Acemoglu and Robinson (2000) argue that high inequality brings about democratization because it increases the demand for democracy by the (relatively poor) masses. Let us expand on three alternative types of accounts linking inequality to democracy.

First, the so-called redistributionist models of democracy building on Meltzer and Richard (1981) – including the widely cited models in Acemoglu and Robinson (2000, 2006) and Boix (2003) – predict a relationship between income inequality and electoral aspects of democracy related to the presence of contested multiparty elections and the extension of the franchise. In brief, the poor median voter presumably determines policy under democracy, preferring high tax rates and extensive redistribution. In autocracies, rich elites are in power and prefer low taxes and the absence of progressive redistribution. For the rich elites and the poor masses alike, income inequality affects the willingness (and possibly also the capabilities) to fight for their favored regime. Thereby, inequality should affect the likelihood of having multiparty elections and the extension of voting rights. Despite these core assumptions being common across redistributionist models, other differences between them generate quite different hypotheses on the direction (and shape) of the inequality – democracy relationship:

To simplify, Boix's model (2003) predicts that higher income inequality (in most contexts) will reduce the probability of democratization. The rich have more to lose from the

---

[11] We also tested alternative specifications focusing more specifically on episodes of very high inflation, thus disregarding variation at lower levels of inflation. We anticipate that such episodes are particularly likely to be disruptive to the economy, social relations, and politics, and thus conducive to regime change. Specifically, we operationalize a high-inflation episode as a year in which prices increased by more than 100 percent (i.e., more than doubled), and construct a dummy variable that we use instead of log-transformed inflation rate that takes the value 1 for each year a country experiences such high inflation (about 2.4 percent of all 12,632 recorded observations). The results, which are reported in Appendix Table A8, suggest that high-inflation episodes are correlated with lower democracy levels, but they are also correlated with larger subsequent upturns in democracy.

poor setting (redistributive) policies in inegalitarian societies, and the rich will therefore be less susceptible to yield to demands for introducing multi-party elections or expanding the franchise to poorer groups. Acemoglu and Robinson (2000), however, predict that higher inequality actually increases chances of democratization: The rich cannot credibly commit to future redistribution in inegalitarian societies – where redistribution will be extremely expensive to the rich – under dictatorship. In a later, more comprehensive argument, Acemoglu and Robinson (2006) suggest that the probability of democratization is actually a hump-shaped function of inequality. The probability is relatively low in very egalitarian societies (with low mass demand for democracy), but also in very inegalitarian ones (with low willingness by elites to supply democracy).

Second, Ansell and Samuels (2014) recently launched a well-founded criticism of the validity of redistributionist theories of democratization, questioning both core assumptions and key predictions from such theories. We will not detail these criticisms in length here, but rather draw attention to Ansell and Samuels' own "elite competition" theory of democratization. These authors highlight that industrialization, urbanization, economic development, and the related growth of an urban middle class, is associated with increasing rather than decreasing income inequality. Hence, increased income inequality – at least in developing countries – is related to growing power resources for a new urban elite, which is expectedly supportive of democracy. Under dictatorship, elite groups in power do not only have strong incentives to avoid progressive redistribution to the masses, but they also have the means and incentives to expropriate resources from other relatively wealthy groups (see also, e.g., North 1990).[12] Hence, dictatorships typically have worse protection of property rights than democracies (Knutsen 2011). Up-and-coming urban, economic elites, as Ansell and Samuels (2014) highlight, have more to lose economically, in absolute terms, from such expropriation than the masses and should have better capacities to organize against the current regime than the poor masses. If high income inequality signals that these groups are resourceful, it is likely to correlate positively with democratization. Ansell and Samuels (2014) propose that high land inequality should display the inverse relationship with democratization, given that this signals that agrarian elites and large-scale landowners are resourceful (see also Ansell and Samuels 2010). Historically, agrarian elites have often served as entrenched supporters of autocratic regimes (see also our discussion earlier on structural features of the economy).

Third, yet other scholars, such as Dahl (1989) or Przeworski (2010), have focused on how high levels of income inequality may undermine the quality and functioning of electoral and other democratic institutions, by concentrating economic resources in the hands of the few. Such resources can be used to lobby, bribe, or otherwise influence decision makers in the political system, be it legislators, bureaucrats, media members, or members of the judiciary. Money in

---

[12] Further, as Albertus and Menaldo (2012) highlight, there may be particularly strong political incentives (in addition to the economic) for elites associated with the regime to expropriate other elites.

politics is widely regarded as a potential problem, especially if the money is concentrated in few hands. Conversely, having equal opportunities for political influence among citizens is widely considered as central for the realization of a well-functioning democracy (see, e.g., Dahl 1998). Along these lines, high levels of income inequality can be expected to contribute to democratic downturns, even when we take for given the presence of formal-democratic institutions.

Economic inequality thus figures among the central determinants in many prominent theories of democratization. Against this backdrop, the results from empirical studies on the net relationship between inequality and democracy have been strikingly mixed or non-robust (see, e.g., Teorell 2010):

First, there are comparatively few recent empirical studies published in top journals on this vital topic, which could indicate a "file drawer problem" (i.e., null-findings and non-robust findings are not published, or not even sent in to journals). Second, the findings that are published are mixed. Some studies find non-robust results (or mainly null result) on links between inequality and democracy (e.g., Knutsen 2015; Przeworski et al. 2000; Teorell 2010). Studies reporting positive results using a particular specification are often contested in later studies using slightly different specifications or sets of observations (cf. Muller 1988, 1995 and Bollen and Jackman 1985, 1995; Boix 2003 and Ansell and Samuels 2010, 2014; Haggard and Kaufman 2016). Third, the studies that do find results often fail to account for very plausible threats to inference, such as country-specific effects on regime type, a reverse causal effect from democracy on income inequality driving the correlations, or that very small and systematically selected samples of countries induce sample selection biases. When trying to correct for such omitted variable-, endogeneity- and sample-selection biases, Knutsen (2015) finds no robust evidence of any effect of income inequality on democracy – results hinge on the specific inequality measure used and other specification choices. Fourth, some of the published studies that do report clear relationships often report very particular nonlinear effect patterns (e.g., Burkhart 1997, 2007), which – when taken in combination with relatively few observations – might stem from overfitting to the data. In sum, there is little robust evidence that income inequality, measured for society as a whole, matter for regime type (in a straightforward, context-independent manner).

One potential explanation of the mixed results (for models on level of or net changes in democracy) may stem from inequality having quite different effects on transitions to/upturns in democracy and on breakdowns of/downturns in democracy. Making such a distinction, Houle (2009) explicitly argues that inequality should not be expected to affect transitions to democracy. The main reason is that redistributionist models (e.g., Acemoglu and Robinson 2000, 2006; Boix 2003) predicting such a link make unrealistic assumptions about the relatively poor masses' capabilities in overcoming collective action problems and organizing threats against incumbent autocrats. In contrast, Houle (2009) argues, high inequality should increase the chances of breakdown for existing democracies.[13] Drawing on a minimalist (DD/ACLP)

---

[13] The argument is that elites have stronger incentives to get rid of democracy – in order to cut down on redistribution – in inegalitarian countries, and elites do not face the type of collective action

measure of democracy, and using the share of income going to capital owners in the industrial sector as a proxy for inequality, Houle reports clear evidence of the latter relationship. Still, this relationship is not robust to using more conventional measures of inequality, such as Gini coefficients on market income inequality for the population as a whole (Knutsen 2015). Also other studies separating between effects on upturns and downturns in democracy fail to find a clear, robust effect of inequality, also on democratic downturns (e.g., Teorell 2010). Altogether, the empirical literature thus suggests that there may not be any clear net effect of inequality on regime type that holds for conventional (Gini and other) measures of income inequality within the wider population.[14]

Recently, empirical researchers have therefore increasingly focused on testing more elaborate hypotheses, such as investigating whether the income inequality – democratization link appears only in certain contexts, such as during economic crises (Doorsch and Maarek 2014) or in open economies (Freeman and Quinn 2012). Further, scholars have started dissecting the "economic inequality" concept, showing that, for instance, land inequality (Ansell and Samuels 2010, 2014; see also Ziblatt 2008) have a clearer relationship with democratization than measures of overall income inequality. More generally, choice of measure of income inequality can dramatically affect the estimated relationship with democracy (e.g., Knutsen 2015; Przeworski et al. 2000). We therefore experiment with different measures of inequality, in our investigation later, thus assessing theoretically relevant differences on how, for example, overall income inequality and interclass inequality relate to certain political regime features.

Table 5.7 describes the inequality measures that we draw on for our empirical analysis. Table 5.8 presents the different results from our benchmark specifications, following the template laid out in previous subsections.

We start out, in Column 11, using data from Solt 2009), with conventional Gini coefficients on market income. These are conventional measures of inequality in the pre-tax and pre-redistribution income distribution for the entire population (see, e.g., Lambert 2001 for discussions on inequality measures). Replicating null-results from recent studies on such measures of income inequality and democracy (e.g., Knutsen 2015), the Gini coefficient is far from statistically significant at the 5 percent level for any of the four

---

issues that the masses face when trying to organize successful coups d'etat against incumbent democratic regimes.

[14] We note that this lack of any robust net effect on a "composite democracy measure" – such as Polity or the Freedom House index – is still consistent with at least some of the theoretical arguments in the literature being true. These arguments often (at least implicitly) suggest we should expect links between inequality and only some "parts" of the democracy concept. If inequality affects some aspects of democracy, but not others, regressions run on composite democracy measures mixing such aspects would lead to causal heterogeneity, masking the more specific causal links that might exist. We probe this conjecture by running robustness tests on different V-Dem indices capturing distinct such aspects of democracy later.

TABLE 5.7 *Indicators of economic inequality*

Aspect	Concept	Indicator/measure	Variable tag	Time series	V-Dem polities covered	Source
Inequality	Land inequality	Family farms as share of cultivated land	s_mil_van_familyf	149	160	Vanhanen (2003) via Miller (2015)
Inequality	Market income inequality	Gini coefficient on income before taxes and redistributoin	gini_market	53	148	Solt (2014), SWIID
Inequality	Wage share of income	Percentage share of manufacturing income going to wages	wageshare1	50	134	UNIDO INDSTAT

TABLE 5.8 *Benchmark regressions including indicators of economic inequality*

	(11) b/(t)	(12) b/(t)	(13) b/(t)
A: Polyarchy level			
Gini market income (Solt)	0.108 (0.558)		
Wage share		0.278 (1.505)	
Family farms			0.142*** (2.622)
N	4164	3696	11209
R^2	0.328	0.284	0.492
B: Polyarchy change			
Gini market income (Solt)	0.004 (0.151)		
Wage share		−0.004 (−0.121)	
Family farms			0.005 (0.826)
N	4162	3693	11198
R^2	0.082	0.114	0.067
C: Upturns			
Gini market income (Solt)	−0.003 (−0.148)		
Wage share		0.035 (1.549)	
Family farms			0.004 (0.815)
N	4162	3693	11198
R^2	0.089	0.106	0.075
D: (Avoiding) Downturns			
Gini market income (Solt)	0.007 (0.605)		
Wage share		−0.039** (−2.152)	

(continued)

TABLE 5.8 (continued)

| | (11) | (12) | (13) |
	b/(t)	b/(t)	b/(t)
Family farms			0.001
			(0.348)
N	4162	3693	11198
R^2	0.025	0.045	0.030

Notes: *** p < 0.01, ** p < 0.05, * p < 0.1. All specifications include country-and year-fixed effects. Specifications in B, C, and D also control for (lagged) level of Polyarchy. Dependent variables measured in year t+1 and all covariates in year t. The dependent variable (Polyarchy) has been rescaled so that it ranges from 0–100. We note that positive coefficients in panel D means that a covariate correlates with smaller/fewer democratic downturns.

dependent variable specifications. We also tested an alternative income inequality Gini coefficients (an interpolated Gini measure from UNU-WIDER, contained in V-Dem v.8), and results were similar. Income inequality within the population, at least as operationalized by Gini coefficients, is not systematically related to democracy.

As Knutsen (2015) discusses at some length, there are several alternative interpretations of such null-results on measures of income inequality and regime change. The first and most obvious one is that there is no strong and clear effect of income inequality on regime change. The second one is that there may be non-monotonic or highly context-dependent effects that are hard to detect by using aggregated regression coefficients in a setup such as in Table 5.8.[15]

Yet other explanations are methodological; there are measurement errors in the inequality data – where Gini coefficients in different countries are collected using surveys of widely varying quality, and where even the concept measured varies across countries and time (see, e.g., Knutsen 2015: 7–8) – and measurement error issues are further exacerbated by the amount of imputation needed to construct full time series (see Solt 2009). Moreover, inequality is very slow-moving, making it harder to clearly identify any true effect (especially given that we control for country-fixed effects). Hence, there is a possibility that we are failing to capture a real effect for methodological

---

[15] Several theoretical studies suggest that the relationship between inequality and regime change may be non-monotonic, and one prominent hypothesis is that the link between income inequality and democratization prospects is inversely u-shaped. Thus, we also tested versions of Model 11 that includes a squared Gini coefficient term, in additional to the linear one. The results are reported in Appendix Table A9, and they do indeed suggest a nonlinear, and even hump-shaped, correlation between the market income Gini and democracy level. However, there is no evidence of any such pattern – or indeed any systematic correlational pattern even when including both the linear and squared Gini terms – when assessing any of the three change-specifications of Polyarchy.

reasons. However, the lack of any sizeable or robust relationship, given the numerous specifications tested in previous studies as well as here, at least make clear that, at present, "there is little evidence that income inequality causally affects democracy in any simple and systematic manner" (Knutsen 2015: 29). However, previous studies (e.g., Houle 2009; Rød et al. 2020) have found clearer relationships when rather employing wage income (or capital income) as share of total income as a measure of (between-class/group) income inequality. Yet, the wage share measure is not significantly related to neither democracy level (A12), democracy change (B12), nor democratic upturns (C12). Somewhat surprisingly, however, high wage share is negatively related to the downturns measure, which contrasts with the seminal results in Houle (2009), who relied on a dichotomous democracy measure. While Houle's results suggested that lower interclass inequality mitigated democratic breakdown, the results reported in D16 suggest that lower such inequality spurs democratic downturns. However, the results in Houle and here are limited to data from after 1960, and the regressions in Column 12 only include about 3,700 country-year observations.[16] Further, the results reported in Model D12 may be driven by omitted variable bias; the wage share coefficient is reduced in size and no longer significant (t = -1.6) once we include a control for Ln GDP per capita.

Finally, Vanhanen's measure on land of family farms as share of total farmland is commonly used as a measure of land inequality (e.g., Ansell and Samuels 2014; Boix 2003), with a high score indicating low such inequality. Thus, the positive and significant (t = 2.6) coefficient in A13 imply that lower land inequality predicts higher democracy levels. However, in contrast with the findings and argument in Ansell and Samuels (2010, 2014), we find no systematic relationship with democratic upturns (C13). Neither do we find a clear relationship to democratic change (B13) nor to democratic downturns (D13).

5.3 COMPREHENSIVE ANALYSIS AND DISCUSSION

The previous section was divided into four subsections, corresponding to four clusters of economic determinants. So far, we have thus considered the relationship between the different types of economic determinants and democracy in isolation. This section brings the discussions from the previous one together in a more comprehensive analysis that simultaneously involves different types of economic determinants.

We employ a simple selection rule to bring together the presumably most relevant predictors, based on the initial analysis, for each of the dependent variable specifications. Specifically, for each of the four specifications, we

---

[16] When we rerun models using the alternative inequality measure from Solt on the limited number of observations that also have data on wage share. These results are reported in Appendix Table A10, and show no systematic correlation between the Gini and any of the outcomes in this limited sample either.

include all covariates that passed the 10 percent statistical significance threshold. However, a few of the variables have limited time series, resulting in listwise deletion of a substantial number of country-year observations in the regressions on Polyarchy level (where unemployment rate is included) and downturns (where both unemployment rate and wage share are included). These regressions contain less than 2,000 country-year observations, and most time series are shorter than twenty years, making it hard to draw inferences from fixed effects models Thus, we also run separate specifications only including those (statistically significant) covariates that have time series extending back into the nineteenth century. The results are presented in Table 5.9 as well as in Online Appendix 5, Table A1 in the online appendix. In Table 5.9, we focus on results for the more powerful and reliable specifications including covariates with long time series, whereas Table A1 also includes the full models with the short time series covariates. None of the covariates included in these latter specifications are statistically significant at the 5 percent level.

For the Polyarchy level regressions, the rules set out in the previous paragraph pick out Ln GDP per capita, average years of education, natural resource income per capita, agricultural income/GDP, and family farms as the only relevant covariates in the regression drawing on long time series back to the nineteenth century (Model 14).[17]

Indeed, this long time series specification replicates most of the results from the earlier partial specifications. More specifically, GDP per capita is positively correlated to democracy level, with a highly significant coefficient (t = 4.8). Likewise, natural resources dependence (t = –2.6), agricultural income (t = –2.7), and family farms (t = 3.5) retain their coefficients and are highly significant even in this extensive specification. The only exception among the covariates is average years of education, which loses significance and even changes sign when controlling for all the other relevant economic determinants. Hence, the clear result from the partial specification in Table 5.2 for education seems to be due to education correlating highly with other economic factors that are linked to democracy level. Education is, as discussed, one proxy of economic development and thus correlates highly with GDP per capita. While the education coefficient may be attenuated partly due to posttreatment bias in Model 14, insofar as higher education levels affect, for instance, long-term economic development (e.g., Mankiw et al. 1992), there is at least no robust evidence supporting a direct relationship between education and democracy level (see also Dahlum 2017).

In contrast, there is clear evidence of a direct link between income and democracy level. We note that this results holds up not only to the control for country-and year-fixed effects (cf. Acemoglu et al. 2008), but also key structural features of the economy as a natural resource income and agricultural income as well as land inequality. Thus, this seems to be a pretty strong result.

---

[17] Unemployment rate is added as a relevant covariate with short time series in Appendix Table A1.

TABLE 5.9 *Extensive regression specifications combining statistically significant covariates (with long time series) from parsimonious regressions*

DV: Polyarchy level	DV: Pol. change (14) b/t	DV: Polyarchy upturns (15) b/t	DV: (Avoiding) (16) b/t	Polyarchy downturns (17) b/t
Ln GDP p.c.	9.561*** (4.833)		−0.313** (−2.030)	0.296*** (3.384)
Avg. years education (15+)	−0.359 (−0.234)			0.008 (0.159)
Natural resource income p.c.	−0.169* (−2.555)			
Agricultural income/GDP	−0.207*** (−2.696)	−0.023*** (−3.489)	−0.026*** (−4.382)	
GDP p.c. growth		0.023*** (2.708)		0.011** (2.472)
Inflation				−0.169 (−1.405)
Family farms	0.170*** (3.547)			
N	8661	9959	9987	9462
R²	0.548	0.077	0.084	0.039

Notes: *** p < 0.01, ** p < 0.05, * p < 0.1. All specifications include country- and year-fixed effects. Specifications in B, C, and D also control for (lagged) level of Polyarchy. Dependent variables measured in year t+1 and all covariates in year t. The dependent variable (Polyarchy) has been rescaled so that it ranges from 0–100. We note that positive coefficients in the rightmost column means that a covariate correlates with smaller/fewer democratic downturns.

Nonetheless, we remind that this relationship is sensitive to the choice of data source for GDP measurement, but also – as we display in the online appendix – to which aspects of democracy that are measured. The clear correlation with Polyarchy, which is the measure used in Table 5.9, is in line with the results from Knutsen et al. (2019) that income is more strongly related to the electoral aspects of democracy than other aspects.

There is also clear evidence that high natural resource dependence is negatively related to democracy level, further bolstering existing findings on a "resource curse" operating on political regime type (see, e.g., Ross 2001, 2012). Again, we highlight that this analysis accounts for potential confounding stemming from country-specific factors, which have previously been argued to be responsible for the correlation between resource variables and democracy (Haber and Menaldo 2011). Finally, the analysis corroborates existing studies highlighting the importance of the agricultural sector for the development, or lack of such, of democracy (e.g., Ansell and Samuels 2014; Boix 2003; Albertus 2017). A sizeable agricultural sector and high degrees of land inequality are clearly detrimental to democracy level according to this analysis. In other words, whereas a sizeable agricultural sector, on average, seems to mitigate democracy, the effects of agricultural production may be heterogeneous. More specifically, it seems that the distribution of farmland matters. Insofar as land is mainly occupied by family farmers, our estimations suggest that this feature (implying an egalitarian distribution of land) may counterbalance the negative effect on democracy from having a high share of economic production in the agricultural sector.

We note that the tests conducted in Model 14 are conservative tests; country- and year-fixed effects, alongside other relevant features of the economy are held constant. We noted, for example, the correlation between features such as (low) income levels and (high) shares of agricultural production in income, and that for previous models where these variables were entered alone, one variable could pick up and effect of the omitted correlated variable. In the model with multiple relevant controls, we have a different concern, pertaining to collinearity. Give the correlation between covariates, and resulting multicollinearity, we might get high standard errors and sensitive results. Indeed, variance inflation (VIF) tests on Model 14 suggest that income level, education, and agricultural share of income obtain VIF values above the standard threshold of 5. To further assess sensitivity, we thus ran reduced versions of Model 14 dropping each of these three problematic covariates from the model, seriatim. However, results show that the income coefficient is consistently positive and significant, agricultural income share is consistently negative and significant, and education is consistently insignificant. Hence, the main results from Model 14 are robust.

There are far fewer variables included, when we follow the rules laid out earlier on including previously significant covariates, for the specification with changes in Polyarchy as dependent variable. In fact, the only economic variable included on the right-hand side of this regression is Agricultural income and GDP per capita growth. The regression covers 9,959 country-year observations, and once again we control for country- and year-fixed effects, as well as the initial level of Polyarchy. The two included determinants remain robust, as GDP per capita growth remains positively signed ($t = 2.7$) and agricultural income/GDP negatively signed ($t = -3.5$). A fast-growing economy and an economy where agricultural income makes up a smaller share tend to display larger net increases in Polyarchy. However, as our reviews of the literature suggested, even these results may not be too informative. The reason is that the effect from a particular economic determinant on changes in democracy may vary substantially depending on whether we consider the propensity to induce positive changes or to induce (or mitigate) negative changes (e.g., Houle 2009; Przeworski et al. 2000). We thus turn to the arguably more informative change-specifications that consider democratic upturns and downturns separately, which are displayed in the rightmost columns of Table 5.9.

Model 16 is the Upturns regressions. The first thing to note is the relatively few economic variables included as covariates, with only Ln GDP p.c. and agricultural income/GDP turning up (weakly) significant in the partial analysis. The long time series specification including both covariates at the same time replicates the results from the partial models discussed in the previous section. Higher income levels are associated with lower expected upturns, and this result is even stronger in Model 16 than in the partial model, and the share of income coming from agriculture is also negatively related to downturns.

Whereas the latter result is easy to triangulate with results reported for the level models and existing work – a strong agricultural sector hinders democratization – the clear and negative income result may seem counterintuitive both in light of the level results as well as predominant theories of democratization (e.g., Boix 2003; Lipset 1959; Przeworski and Limongi 1997). Still, as already discussed, it is consistent with some previous (dynamic panel) specifications accounting for country-specific effects and initial level of democracy. Interestingly, one plausible explanation is proposed by Kennedy (2010) who highlights that a higher GDP per capita may stabilize all kinds of regimes, both democratic and autocratic, whereas the probability of a change being in a democratic direction, if it first occurs, may still increase in income level. The result in Model 21 may simply stem from the first of these mechanisms dominating the second one on aggregate in this extensive sample with 9,987 country-year observations.

Finally, we consider how the relevant economic determinants, selected from the partial models following the rules laid out earlier, related to democratic downturns. In contrast to the Upturns regressions, the Downturns regressions include multiple relevant economic determinants. More specifically, Model 18 includes Ln GDP per capita, Average years of education, GDP per capita growth, and Ln Inflation. Indeed, the short time series specification reported in Appendix 5, Table A.1 (with few observations and no significant covariates), further adds manufacturing income as share of GDP, unemployment rate, and wage share of total income

Two of the statistically significant covariates from the partial downturns specifications, namely average years of education and Ln inflation, turn insignificant when entered simultaneously with the other relevant covariates. Thus, there is no robust evidence of a direct relationship between high education or low inflation, on the one hand, and the avoidance of democratic downturns on the other, once conditioning on other relevant factors. One main reason for this may be the inclusion of yet another measure of economic development in addition to education, namely Ln GDP per capita, and another measure of short-term change in addition to Ln Inflation, namely GDP per capita growth. Both of these measures drawing on GDP data remain positive and clearly associated with democratic downturns.

The result for Ln GDP per capita thus corroborates the large body of evidence already establishing the relationship between high income level and the avoidance of democratic breakdowns/downturns. In fact, our results are in line with those from the sensitivity analysis by Rød et al. (2020) using binary democracy measures: Income is a robust determinant, whereas the robustness of the relationships between other measures of economic development and democratic breakdown depends critically on the inclusion or exclusion of income as a control.

Regarding GDP per capita growth, the positive sign of the coefficient indicates that high short-term growth helps countries avoid democratic downturns, corroborating results presented, for instance, by Przeworski and Limongi (1997) on a binary democracy variable. Conversely, these results corroborate the widespread notion discussed earlier that sluggish short-term growth or economic crises spur democratic downturns.[18]

5.4   CONCLUSION

What are the implications of the many empirical tests that we have presented for the merits of economic theories of democracy? We round off this chapter by highlighting four key insights from our empirical exercise as well as their implications for the literature on economic determinants of democracy.

First, there is generally a lack of robust evidence that (various aspects of) economic development are positively linked to democratization (i.e., positive changes in democracy score). This finding adds to a considerable literature challenging modernization theory in its purest form (e.g., Acemoglu et al. 2008; Munck 2019; Przeworski et al. 2000), the latter stipulating that economic development should promote not only democratic survival but also democratization. Indeed, some of our findings show that the most widely used indicator of economic development, GDP per capita, is actually *negatively* linked to democratization. Other indicators of economic modernization, namely education and urbanization, are not statistically significant predictors of positive changes in democracy score. The only result that is somewhat consistent with the hypothesis that economic development promotes democratization is the finding that agricultural income (as share of GDP) is negatively linked to democratization. This measure could be considered a proxy for the lack of economic modernization, given the strong reliance on agricultural production in traditional economies, but, as discussed, it could

---

[18] As for the other results in Table 9, the GDP per capita growth results are replicated if we substitute Polyarchy, that is, V-Dem's measure of electoral democracy with V-Dem's Liberal Democracy Index (see Appendix Table A.11. However, we fail to replicate any of the results when rather using Polity2 than measures from V-Dem. We add that results are also weaker for natural resource dependence and income level in the level regression, whereas no results from Table 9 are clearly strengthened when replacing Polyarchy with Polity2. While there may be several patterns contributing to these differences in results, one potential factor may be higher measurement error in Polity2 than in Polyarchy, especially for the pre-1900 period (see Knutsen et al. 2019), which should contribute to weaker correlations relevant predictors.

also be a proxy for lack of resource mobility, thereby tapping into other theoretical arguments than modernization theory. It should be noted that the former interpretation is not supported by other tests – for instance, we do not find that income from manufacturing (as share of GDP) is positively related to democratization. Hence, apart from the agricultural finding, our analysis offers another nail in the coffin for the merits of modernization theory.

Second, there is evidence that a high income level stabilizes all political regimes, by lowering the likelihood of both positive *and* negative changes in democracy. This finding is consistent with modernization theory's proposition that economically developed democracies should be more likely to survive, for instance, due to the democratic norms presumably held by citizens in economically developed societies. Yet, the finding that income reduces the likelihood of both democratic decline *and* democratization suggests that a high income level has a stabilizing effect more generally (see also Kennedy 2010; Treisman 2015). This is inconsistent with the expectation from modernization theory that economic development should make autocratic regimes more prone to transitioning to democracy. While the question of why income stabilizes (all) regimes deserves much more attention in future research, different promising explanations can be found in literature on the role of economic development and income as a tool for political survival, indicating that the ability of both dictators and democratic leaders to remain in power is boosted by access to economic resources (e.g., Bueno de Mesquita and Smith 2009; Kennedy 2010).

Third, our analysis reiterates the widely documented finding that strong short-term economic performance is good news for democracy, in the sense that it is associated with a lower likelihood of democratic declines. The flip side of this argument is, of course, that economic crisis (in the sense of low or negative GDP growth) is associated with a higher likelihood of democratic decline. While supporting existing studies on the association between economic crisis and democratization breakdown (e.g., Haggard and Kaufmann 1995), this finding demonstrates the importance of "triggers" also when it comes to explaining democratic backsliding.

Finally, although a large body of theoretical arguments, including several well-known formal models, has linked economic inequality to democratic transitions through various mechanisms, we do not find robust evidence that various indicators of economic inequality are systematic predictors of democracy. Our finding aligns with recent empirical studies presenting evidence contradicting theoretical expectations about the link between economic inequality and democracy (e.g., Haggard and Kaufmann 2016; Houle 2009). Notably, in addition to *not* identifying a robust link between economic inequality and democratic upturns, we also fail to identify a link between inequality and democratic downturns. The latter finding goes against expectations that rising economic inequality is a threat to the survival of existing democracies. As much as one would intuitively expect good things to go together (here, economic equality and democracy), our evidence does not provide evidence that economic equality is a necessary, or even a strongly facilitating, condition for democratic survival.

In sum, drawing on the carefully constructed V-Dem measures on democracy, covering all countries across an extensive time series, this chapter corroborates several long-standing insights regarding the economic determinants of democracy. For instance, we offer additional support for the widely documented finding that economic performance promotes regime stability – among both democracies and autocracies. We also corroborate results suggesting that economic inequality is not systematically related to changes in democracy. However, our analysis also draws attention to other, less acknowledged ways in which democracy is shaped by economic factors. In particular, we find that a high income level is associated with a reduced likelihood of democratic upturns. Although this finding is far from robust and associated with much uncertainty, it is neither new nor very surprising in light of several recent and important contributions (e.g., Kennedy (2010) and Treisman (2015) find evidence consistent with the notion that income mitigates autocratic breakdown), it challenges widely held assumptions suggesting that economic development is a force for democratic transitions. This notion has continued to remain popular among both political scientists and policymakers. Our results indicate that development *might* on the contrary harm prospects of democratization.

6

Political Institutions and Democracy

Allen Hicken, Samuel Baltz, and Fabricio Vasselai

The study of political institutions is one of the core parts of comparative politics. We describe and analyze political institutions not (just) because they are intrinsically interesting as objects of scientific inquiry. We study institutions because we believe that they matter for other things we care about – accountability, responsiveness, good governance, quality of life, and so on. They do so by shaping the incentives and capabilities of economic and political actors, and by influencing which of those actors have a seat at the decision-making table. Among the outcomes of chief interest to political scientists and institutional engineers is democracy. Do certain kinds of political institutions make democracy more or less durable? Are some configurations of institutions more or less conducive to democracy? To what extent do political institutions influence the degree or quality of democracy? Generations of scholars and practitioners have grappled with these questions, from Weber and Madison, to Dahl and Lijphart.

The result of this rich literature is an abundance of theorizing, accompanied by a less than abundant and often inconsistent empirical record. Many studies of the effects of institutions analyze the role that institutions played in a small number of cases of democratic breakdown or maintenance. See, for example, work on the contribution of political institutions to the breakdown of democracy under the Weimar Republic,[1] or the failure of presidential democracy in Latin America (Linz and Valenzuela 1994). When scholars have attempted to look at the effect of institutions in a broader, comparative context, using quantitative data, the results have often been inconsistent and inconclusive.

The challenge with empirically connecting political institutions to democratic outcomes led one well-known political scientist to conclude that

[1] See Shugart and Carey (1992) for a summary.

162 *Allen Hicken, Samuel Baltz, Fabricio Vasselai*

institutions may be endogenous and epiphenomenal (Przeworski 2004, 528–529). In fact, a large literature on democratization and democratic durability assigns most of the causal weight to noninstitutional factors such as economic development and (in)equality (Acemoglu and Robinson 2006; Ansell and Samuels 2014; Boix 2003; Przeworski 2004; Svolik 2008). However, some scholars in this camp acknowledge that institutions might play a role in facilitating collective action to deter would-be democratic defectors (Acemoglu and Robinson 2006; Boix 2003) or facilitate democracy-sustaining cooperation and coordination between key actors (Svolik 2012).

In this chapter we review some of the prominent arguments regarding the relationship between political institutions and democracy. In keeping with the theme of this volume we use data from the Varieties of Democracy Project to (re)evaluate these arguments. Specifically, we focus on two primary outcomes of interest – the durability of the democracy/likelihood of breakdown, and the quality or level of democracy. Using V-Dem data has at least two chief advantages. First, V-Dem provides a much longer time series with which we can evaluate our theories. Many of the most prominent institutionalist theories were derived from studies of particular eras – for example, the breakdown of the democracies in interwar Europe, or the collapse of second wave democracies in Latin America. And, out of necessity, most quantitative work on the topic has focused on a limited period of time (post-WWII, post-1970, post-1990, etc.). As a result, there is uncertainty about the degree to which the literature's findings (or lack thereof) depend on the time period they examine.

Second, V-Dem supplies multiple continuous measures of democracy. All studies of democratic durability/breakdown, whether they are quantitative or qualitative, have to pick a cut off or threshold for what they consider democratic and nondemocratic. One has to decide where the line between democracy and non-democracy lies, and, by extension, which countries are on either side of that line. Decisions about where to locate that cut off (a Polity score of 5, or 6, or 7?) are somewhat arbitrary, but very few studies consider whether results are sensitive to where we draw the line. Does the answer we get depend on our choice of cut off? The continuous nature of the V-Dem data allows us to selection multiple cut offs and observe whether the results we get are sensitive to where we draw the line.

If V-Dem data allow us to better evaluate the effects of political institutions, the obvious question is: which institutions? The list of potential institutions is lengthy, from rule of law to the judiciary. Were we more ambitious, we could also examine institutions that have an indirect effect on democracy through their influence on things like economic growth and development – for example, property rights, or an independent central bank. However, in the interests of tractability, we have chosen to focus on three broad categories of institutions: state capacity, executive regime type (i.e., presidential v. parliamentary), and the party system. For each of these categories there is a developed theoretical and empirical literature on which we can draw, with clear (though not uncontroversial) predictions about how these institutions should shape democratic outcomes.

We acknowledge that our focus on these three broad categories of institutions excludes some institutions that many scholars deem important. The clearest example of this is the rich literature on consensus/powersharing versus centripetal/majoritarian institutions (Graham et al. 2017; Lijphart 1977, 1984, 1999; Reilly 2012; Selway and Templeman 2012), a careful review of which could easily fill an additional chapter in this volume. Other institutions we exclude because the literature on these institutions and their relationship to democratic outcomes is less abundant (but by no means, nonexistent). This includes federalism (Boix 2003; Myerson 2006), judicial independence (Reenock et al. 2013), and legislative institutions (Fish 2006; Sing 2010). We also ignore institutions for which the main effect is theorized to be an indirect one – for example, electoral institutions, property rights, and rule of law.[2]

In the remainder of this chapter we first review the theoretical reasoning connecting state capacity, executive regime type, and the party system to democratic outcomes. For each category, we also review the relevant empirical literature and discuss the state of the field as we see it. Finally, we reevaluate the strength of these theories based on data from V-Dem. We find strong support for the role of state capacity, but mixed or no support for executive regime type or party system variables. Finally, we conclude by discussing the important role of electoral experience in many of our models.

6.1 INSTITUTIONS AND DEMOCRACY

At a fundamental level it is impossible to think of democracy without thinking about political institutions. To a large extent, political institutions *define* what we consider a democracy, and what we do not. Most definitions hold free and fair elections to be a minimal requirement for democracy (Dahl 1971). Liberal conceptions of democracy add to the electoral criterion a requirement that there also be constraints on executive power in the form of checks and balances. Beyond this definitional role, what is the relationship between political institutions and democratic quality and stability? Do certain institutions lead to a greater risk of democratic breakdown? Is the level or quality of democracy in part a function of the kinds of institutions a state adopts? We consider three categories of institutional theories that examine these questions: state capacity, executive regime type, and party systems.

---

[2] We also leave aside work on the effect of institutions in non-democracies. For work on the role of legislatures and/or elections see: Boix and Svolik (2013); Gandhi (2008); Gandhi and Przeworski (2007). For work on authoritarian regime type see: Geddes et al. (2014); Hadenius and Teorell (2007); Knutsen and Nygard (2015); Teorell (2010). For work on institutionalized parties see: Brownlee (2007); Magaloni (2006); Magaloni and Kricheli (2010).

6.1.1   State Capacity

Modern democratic consolidation requires a functioning state and "useful" state bureaucracy (Linz and Stepan 1996, 11). Without a functioning state it becomes more difficult to detect and deter potential defectors from the democratic bargain. A dysfunctional state bureaucracy is also associated with poor governance, less provision of public goods, and higher levels of grievance among both citizens and elites. The link between state capacity and the stability and quality of democracy has been drawn again and again by scholars (e.g., Anderson et al. 2014b; Bäck and Hadenius 2008; Bratton and Chang 2006; Cornell and Lapuente 2014; Fortin 2012; Mansfield and Snyder 2007; Møller and Skanning 2011).[3] Scholars differ, however, in how they conceptualize state capacity, and in how they choose to operationalize their concepts.[4]

In general, scholars have conceptualized state capacity as consisting of a number of dimensions: *coercive capacity, administrative capacity,* and *legitimacy.*[5] Rooted in Weber (1965) and Tilly (1975) one approach is to conceptualize state capacity as *coercive capacity,* or the state's monopoly on the legitimate use of force within its territory (Anderson et al. 2014a). Where states lack coercive capacity, destabilizing irredentist movements will be more common, and "conflicts are more likely to spin out of control and undermine democratic regimes" (Anderson et al. 2014b, 1307). In addition, where states lack coercive capacity, *administrative capacity* and *state legitimacy* are likely to be threatened as well.

A second way to conceptualize state capacity is as *administrative capacity,* also referred to as administrative effectiveness. Administrative capacity concerns the capacity of the bureaucracy to design and effectively implement public services and regulations across a country's territory (Anderson et al. 20014a, 1209). The idea that a well-functioning state bureaucracy is a necessary condition for a stable and well-functioning democracy can be traced to Weber and Schumpeter. Weber famously argued that bureaucracies were crucial institutions in the modern state (democratic or autocratic) (Weber 1968). Schumpeter tied the state bureaucracy to the viability of democracy itself, including a professional bureaucracy as one of his five conditions for democratic order (Schumpeter 1942, 206). Taking their cue from Schumpeter,

---

[3] A related line of work reverses the causal arrows and examines how democratization shapes state capacity (Bäck and Hadenius 2008; Carbone and Memoli 2015), or considers how the two interact or coevolve or (Bratton and Chang 2006; Fortin 2012; Fukuyama 2014; Mazzuca and Munck 2014).
[4] See Anderson et al. 2014a for a review.
[5] Many authors, including Linz and Stepan (1996) and Anderson et al. (2014a) refer to "stateness" rather than state capacity. Anderson et al. (2014a) consider *coercive capacity, administrative capacity,* and *legitimacy* to be dimensions of stateness. Some scholars also treat *fiscal capacity* as its own separate dimension (others consider it a part or consequence of administrative capacity) while recent work by Brambor et al. identifies *information capacity* as a possible additional dimension (2020).

most scholars consider meritocratic recruitment as the sine qua non of administrative capacity.[6]

There are at least three separate arguments connecting administrative capacity to democratic outcomes. First, administrative capacity is positively correlated with information – where capacity is high the government is able to gather better information about public needs, brewing conflicts, and threats to peace and order. Second, high capacity states perform better at the tasks related to democratic governance, including providing public goods, running free and fair elections, and maintaining order. Third, a professional bureaucracy serves as a constraint on opportunistic actions by incumbents, including attempts to centralize power, and thus, also serves as a reassurance to wary opponents who might otherwise be tempted to launch preemptive actions, such as a military coup (Cornell and Lapuente 2014).

Finally, some scholars introduce a third dimension of stateness or state capacity – *legitimacy*. Legitimacy refers to agreement by the citizenry about the boundaries of the state and the rules for inclusion and exclusion. Given the difficulty in operationalizing legitimacy most empirical studies focus on administrative or coercive capacity, and we do the same in this chapter.[7]

Regardless of which dimension of state capacity we focus on, the argument is that high levels of state capacity should be positively correlated with better, more stable democracies. The empirical work largely bears this out. Using both quantitative and qualitative methods scholars have found that state capacity is positively associated with stronger, more durable democracies (e.g., Bäck and Hadenius 2008; Bratton and Chang 2006; Cornell and Lapuente 2014; Fortin 2012; Møller and Skanning 2011). Scholars disagree about which dimension of state capacity is most important, and how to best measure the concept, but there is a strong consensus that state capacity increases regime durability, whether that regime is democratic or autocratic (Anderson et al. 2014b; Slater and Fenner 2011; van Ham and Seim 2018).

6.1.2 Executive Regime Type

When it comes to democratic stability, perhaps no institution has received greater attention than executive regime type. Juan Linz, based on his analysis

---

[6] There is a disagreement about whether bureaucratic autonomy increases or decrease administrative capacity.

[7] Rustow, for example, argues that a precondition of democracy is that "the vast majority of citizens in a democracy-to-be must have no doubt or mental reservations as to which political community they belong to." (1970, 350) Anderson et al. set as a minimal condition that "people within the territory accept the supremacy of the state and communion with fellow citizens." (2014a, 1209). Where such consensus about the legitimacy of the state is lacking, any government, whether democratic or authoritarian, will be imperiled. However, this may be especially true for democracies (Mazzuca and Munck 2014), where competitive elections can spark violence and social division (Bates 1983).

of democratic collapse in Latin America, forcefully argued that presidentialism was inimical to democratic stability (Linz 1990). Two features of presidential systems were to blame. First, the popular election of both president and the legislature produces a system of dual, and sometimes competing, democratic legitimacy. Second, the fact that both the president and legislature sit for fixed terms, with the survival of each independent of the other, means that presidential systems are inherently rigid.

These two features combine to imperil presidential regimes through three related logics. First, while the requirement for legislative majorities exists in parliamentary system, this same imperative is lacking in presidential regimes. As a result, presidential regimes are more likely to have presidents with minority cabinets, leading to a greater risk of deadlock between the president and legislature. Second, because of separate survival there are weaker incentives for cooperation and party discipline in presidential regimes, compared to their parliamentary counterparts. Finally, the fact that decision-making is more decentralized under presidential systems means that there is more conflict and a greater likelihood of deadlock/paralysis.

While many found Linz's argument persuasive, there was strong pushback from other comparative scholars. As Elgie notes in his review of the literature, the counterarguments can be grouped into two different types of critiques (Elgie 2005).[8] The first wave of responses to Linz argued that the effect of regime type is contingent on other institutions.[9] Specifically, the likelihood of breakdown is greatest when presidential systems are paired with a highly fragmented party system, undisciplined parties, or where the president is extremely powerful (Mainwaring 1993; Mainwaring and Shugart 1997; Shugart and Carey 1992). Outside of these configurations, however, presidential regimes are no more likely to break down. A second wave of critiques focused on the variation within parliamentary and presidential regimes, noting that the actual institutional and operational details within each regime type are varied and complex (Chaisty et al. 2014; Cheibub and Limongi 2002). Some of these scholars attempted to move beyond the dichotomous categorization of regime type and build more general theories that could apply across regime types – for example, veto players (Tsebelis 1995) or chains of delegation (Strøm 2000).

Efforts to test Linz's argument have yielded mixed results. In Table 6.1 we catalogue attempts to test the effect of presidentialism on democratic quality or longevity in the literature. We found twenty-four separate studies that attempt to empirically evaluate the effect of presidentialism on democracy (though in

---

[8] While we agree with Elgie's general classification scheme, we differ somewhat on where we assign individual scholars.

[9] Critics also question Linz on case selection grounds, arguing both that Linz relied too heavily on the Latin American experience, and that presidential systems tend to be the institution of choice by countries facing severe governance challenges (Horowitz 1990; Mainwaring and Shugart 1997).

TABLE 6.1 *Empirical evaluations of executive regime type*

Authors	Relationship between presidentialism and democracy
Shugart and Carey 1992	Contingent
Riggs 1993	Negative
Stepan and Skach 1993	Negative
Mainwaring 1993	Contingent
Mainwaring and Shugart 1997	Contingent
Power and Gasiorowski 1997	No relationship
Alvarez 1998	Negative
Przeworski et. al. 2000	Negative
Bernhard et. al. 2001	Contingent
Cheibub and Limongi 2002	Negative
Saideman et al. 2002	No relationship
Boix 2003	Contingent
Bernard et al. 2003	No relationship
Bernard et al. 2004	No relationship
Cheibub 2007	No relationship
Svolik 2008	Contingent
Hiroi and Omori 2009	Contingent
Maeda 2010	Negative
Sing 2010	No relationship
Alemán and Young 2011	No relationship
Chaisty et. al. 2014	Contingent
Svolik 2015	Negative
Cornell et al. 2016	No relationship
Bernard et al. 2020	No relationship

some cases, executive regime type was not the main variable of interest). In 70 percent of these studies (17/24) authors found either no effect for executive regime type, or found that the effect of presidentialism was contingent.[10] Only

[10] The nature of contingency is varied. For example, Boix (2003) finds that the effect of presidentialism on democratic survival depends on an unfavorable type and distribution of economic assets, but finds no independent, negative effect of presidentialism. Svolik (2008) finds that presidentialism reduces the odds of survival only in the presence of low levels of economic development, but that the overall effect is small compared to economic indicators. Bernhard et al. (2001) look into the relationship between economic shocks and democratic breakdown and consider whether institutions mediate the effect of such shocks. They find that the effect of regime type depends on the nature of the party system. Parliamentary regimes with few parties are more resilient to shocks than presidential regimes with lots of parties. However, when times are good, presidential regimes with lots of parties are more robust.

seven of the twenty-four studies found a negative effect of presidentialism that was consistent with Linz's argument. In general, those studies that pay closer attention to selection effects and confounding variables tend to find null or contingent effects. Even when the empirical findings are broadly supportive of Linz, the conclusions that authors draw are often quite nuanced. For example, both Maeda (2010) and Svolik (2015) find that presidentialism has no effect on the risk of a coup, but it does raise the risk that elected incumbents will try and end democracy from the inside. Cheibub and Limongi also find a negative association, but then cast doubt on the most popular causal mechanisms and suggest that the relationship may in fact not be causal at all (2002).

In short, the relationship between executive regime type and democracy remains a contested one, both theoretically and empirically. As we will discuss in more detail later, with V-Dem data we can address one of the most common critiques in this literature – that is, that Linz's argument and subsequent empirical findings are driven by Latin American cases in a particular period of history. Reanalyzing this question using different data allows us to supplement these summaries of past results with something in the spirit of a meta-analysis.

6.1.3 Parties and Party Systems

In many ways political parties are *the* key institutions in modern democracies (Schattschneider 1942). As such, it is no surprise that parties and party systems have received their fair share of scrutiny for their contribution to democratic stability and breakdown. Two particular variables have received the bulk of attention: *party system fragmentation* and *party/party system institutionalization*.

A common refrain from early scholars of democracy and democratic breakdown was that party system fragmentation increased the risk of democratic breakdown. Linz was among the first to make the argument that a high degree of party system fragmentation contributed to the failure of democracy in Latin American (1978). Sartori expanded on this idea, arguing that while party system fragmentation is problematic for democratic stability, the most acute threat comes from the combination of party system fragmentation and political polarization. The resulting polarized multipartism is associated with centrifugal politics and a corresponding tendency toward extremism, all of which raise the risk of instability. As discussed in the prior section, other scholars argued that fragmentation was particularly problematic when combined with presidentialism (Mainwaring 1993).

As persuasive as these arguments are, the empirical support has been mixed at best. Careful case studies have traced the contribution of high levels of fragmentation to democratic breakdown in specific historical cases – for example, see Lepsius (2017) on the collapse of democracy in interwar Germany. Furthermore, in cross-national quantitative analyses some scholars have found a negative relationship between fragmentation and democratic survival under presidentialism (Bernhard et al. 2001; Mainwaring 1993; Negretto 2006). However, most cross-national quantitative studies find no robust relationship between fragmentation and breakdown, either on its own, or in interaction with other institutional variables (Bernhard et al. 2003, 2004; Gasiorowski and Power 1998; Maeda 2010; Power and Gasiorowski 1997; Reenock et al. 2013; Sing 2010).

A second dimension of the party system that may bear on democratic quality and stability is party/party system institutionalization.[11] Political parties are the symbolic face and workhorses of democracy. Political parties help articulate, aggregate, and channel public demands and social pressures. They help voters hold governments accountable and raise the costs of democratic defection for would-be autocrats (Bernhard et al. 2020). They can also serve as mechanisms for balancing short-term/narrow interests and longer-term/broader interests. If they work well, voters are more likely to be content. If they do not, then the legitimacy of democracy itself can be a casualty (Mainwaring and Torcal 2006; Ufen 2008). Political parties are also the main organizational alternatives to the military in many democracies. When they are healthy and robust, the military is more likely to remain in the barracks. When there are weak and dysfunctional, the resulting vacuum can prove an irresistible temptation to would-be autocrats.[12]

There is less empirical work evaluating the connection between party/party system institutionalization and democratization than there is on fragmentation, but a few studies have addressed the question. In their response to Linz, Mainwaring and Shugart (1997) argue that presidential regimes are more likely to breakdown when combined with weak, undisciplined parties. Lai and Melkonian-Hoover (2005) note the failure of most studies to consider the role of political parties in democratic transition and consolidation. They find that party competition increases the probability of a transition to democracy, and that democracies are more likely to survive where parties play a major role in the political system and there is robust party competition (Lai and Melkonian-Hoover 2005). Looking specifically at party institutionalization, Cornell et al. (2016) find that party institutionalization does not moderate the positive effects of an active civil society. Bernhard et al. (2020) also find that

---

[11] Institutionalized parties have stable bases of support, robust organizations, and distinct party labels that are meaningful to both voters and candidates (Bernard et al. 2020; Levitsky 1998; Mainwaring and Scully 1995). Party *system* institutionalization refers to the degree to which the parties in the system are themselves are institutionalized, as well as the degree to which there is stability in the pattern of interparty competition (Mainwaring and Scully 1995). In more recent work, Mainwairng (2018) narrows the definition of party system to only the stability of inter-party competition, and treats party institutionalization as a factor that contributes to party system institutionalization, rather than a defining feature (Mainwaring 2018, 4)).

[12] Scholars generally argue for a positive linear relationship between institutionalization and democracy, though some argue too much institutionalization can threaten democracy (Coppedge 1994, Roberts 1998; Stockton 2001).

there is no interactive relationship between party institutionalization and civil society strength, but they do find that each variable independently lowers the risk of a democratic breakdown.

In summary, we have reviewed three sets of institutions that are believed to have some effect on the longevity and quality of democracy. The existing literature generally finds strong support for the positive influence of state capacity on democratic strength and stability. The findings on executive regime type are decidedly more mixed, but with most studies finding no strong independent effect for presidentialism on the probability of breakdown. The results for party systems are similarly inconsistent. Most studies find no independent effect for party system fragmentation, but some studies have found evidence that party institutionalization helps improve and stabilize democracy. We turn now to our tests of some of these theories using V-Dem data.

6.2 DATA AND METHODS

To evaluate the effect of institutions we rely on two types of models. Most of the theories about the effect of institutions on democracy are concerned with democratic durability, which suggests a survival analysis is the most appropriate model. This is consistent with the approach in most of the recent literature on institutions and democracy. As a robustness test we also conduct a secondary analysis using linear panel regression models to investigate the conditional partial correlations between institutional factors and the level of democratization of a country. Finally, in the interests of comparability with other chapters, we also examine the effects of institutions on the change in the level of democracy, as well as on upturns and downturns.

6.2.1 Dependent Variable

Our primary dependent variable is the *polyarchy* variable from V-Dem version 9. Polyarchy ranges from 0 to 1, with 1 being the highest level of democracy. When estimating the survival models, we use various cut points within polyarchy to divide countries into democratic and nondemocratic in a given year. When estimating panel models for the level of democratization, the full interval polyarchy is our outcome variable of interest.

6.2.2 Independent Variables

6.2.2.1 State Capacity

As we discussed, scholars of state capacity and democracy have focused on three types of state capacity: *coercive capacity, administrative capacity*, and *legitimacy*. Most empirical studies focus on coercive or administrative capacity, given the difficulty of assessing legitimacy absent survey data. We follow suit in this analysis. The next question is how to operationalize coercive and administrative capacity. The literature has employed a wide variety of measures, including taxes as a percentage of GDP, military expenditures, rule of law, bureaucratic quality, infrastructure capacity, political stability, government effectiveness, regulatory quality, and control of corruption. In selecting our measure we place a premium on country-year coverage and on the fit between concept and measure. For these reasons we select two proxies for state capacity. For coercive capacity we use a measure of the percentage of territory over which a state has effective control (*territory*). For administrative capacity, following the approach of Gjerlow et al. (2018) we use a measure of the level of bureaucratic professionalization (*state capacity*). Both of these measures come from V-Dem. In the end, because the variable for state control over territory is never significant and including it does not alter the remaining results, we report only *state capacity* in the analyses later. For robustness we also include a measure of *information capacity* as developed by Brambor et al. (2020).

6.2.2.2 Executive Regime Type

Most existing datasets of executive regime type are limited in scope – either by country coverage or by time period. As a result, we constructed our own unique dataset of executive regime type. The dataset offers a yearly assessment of executive regime type for all sovereign countries since the French Revolution (16,910 country-years), matching the coverage in V-Dem. For each country-year we identify whether a country had a president, prime minister, or both, and whether or not those positions were elected (see Baltz et al. n.d. for more details). This flexible measure of presidentialism and parliamentarism allows us to compare various dimensions of Linz's (1990) hypothesis: throughout the analysis we will focus on comparing systems with elected presidents to systems without elected presidents, systems with elected prime ministers to systems without elected prime ministers, and systems that elect both to systems that do not elect their head of government.

The resulting dataset gives us information about whether or not an elected president served during that country-year, but by itself the dataset does not contain information about the powers of that president. Because the power of the presidency is a key mechanism in Linz's (1990) hypothesis, we also use V-Dem data to construct a composite variable that distinguishes regimes with figurehead presidents (e.g., Ireland) from true presidential regimes. To do this, we classify as presidential any country-year where the president is also the head of government, as measured in V-Dem (*Strict President*). As a further check, we also consider the various actions that the head of government is able to undertake in that country-year, such as the ability to appoint or dismiss officials or dissolve legislative bodies.

6.2.2.3 Party Fragmentation

Ideally, we would measure party system fragmentation directly through a weighted or unweighted count of the number of parties in the system.

Existing datasets have only partial coverage, leaving us with a lot of missing data. As an alternative, we use two proxies for party system fragmentation: the lower chamber seat share held by the largest party (*largest seat share*), which we obtain from V-Dem, and a measure of the electoral system, where 1 equals majoritarian, which we get from V-Dem and the Contestation dataset (Gerring et al. 2018) (*majorit. electoral system*). For both variables high values should be associated with less fragmentation, ceteris paribus.

6.2.2.4 Party Institutionalization
To measure the average institutionalization of parties within a given country-year, we use the Party Institutionalization Index (PI) from V-Dem (*party institutionalization*) (Bizzarro et al., 2017). PI is an index created from five party-related components: the nature of party organization, the extent to which parties have permanent branches, the nature of party linkages with voters, whether parties have distinct party platforms, and the degree of legislative party cohesion.

6.2.2.5 Control Variables
We match several existing datasets onto these country-years in order to control for other important historical variables. We include the country-year's GDP/capita (logged) and the GDP growth rate from the Maddison Project Database (Bolt et al. 2018), ethnic fractionalization from the Ethnic Power Relations dataset (Wimmer et al. 2009), and each observation's history of colonization from the Issue Correlates of War (ICOW) Colonial History Data (Hensel 2018). We also use the colonial history dataset to build a variable that records the number of years since a country become independent. A full list of variables used in the paper is available in Appendix 1 Table 1A.

6.3 RESULTS AND ANALYSIS

6.3.1 Survival Analysis

We first examine the results of the survival analysis. We estimate a series of parametric models with a Cox specification of the baseline hazards. The resulting coefficients represent the hazard rate, which is the risk of that a country ceases being a democracy at any given point in time. Positive numbers mean an increased risk of democratic breakdown; negative numbers represent a reduced risk of breakdown.

Because polyarchy is a continuous measure, there is no one correct way to translate it into a dichotomous measure of democracy. What cut point should we choose to determine the lowest polyarchy score that can still be considered a democracy? This complication, however, is also an opportunity: it allows us to test whether our results vary depending on which threshold we choose. We therefore look at the risk of breakdown over every value of polyarchy,[13] categorizing every country-year with a polyarchy value above that threshold as a democracy and every country-year below that threshold as a non-democracy. Thus, for every polyarchy value we produce a binary classification in the same format as previous classifications of democracies in the literature. Then, we conduct a survival analysis using every one of these alternative classification schemes and examine how results change (or do not change) as we move the cut point.

Our specific test is a democratic survival model that yields the hazard rate connected to different types of institutional variables. The core question of the survival model is whether or not democracies with certain configurations of state capacity, presidential regime type, party system fragmentation, and party institutionalization are more or less likely to become autocracies. Of course, the structure of the survival analysis also means that we can just as easily run the survival model with the classification reversed, and ask the opposite question: are autocracies that have certain institutional characteristics (e.g., electing a head of government) more or less likely to become democracies than countries that do not have those characteristics (e.g., no elections for the head of government).

All of our results are therefore split into the probability of a democratic "step-up," in which the polyarchy value of an autocracy rises above the arbitrary cut point in that model, and a "step-down," in which the polyarchy value of a democracy falls below the arbitrary cut point in that model. We use this terminology to call attention to the possibility that transitions from above the polyarchy threshold to below the polyarchy threshold can represent quite small changes in the value of polyarchy, since the value might be just barely above the polyarchy cut point in one year and then just barely below that cut point in the next (and vice versa for cases that begin below the cut point in one year and rise above the cut point in the next year).

Having picked a threshold and classified countries according to whether or not their polyarchy level is greater than that threshold, we can identify step-downs and step-ups. If a country-year has a polyarchy level below the threshold one year after it had a polyarchy level above the threshold, then we consider a step-down to have happened in that year. Conversely, if a country-year has a polyarchy level above the threshold one year after it had a polyarchy level below the threshold, then we consider a step-up to have happened in that year. Note that our approach is similar to the upturns and downturns analyses in other chapters in this volume, except that rather than looking at whether a country experiences a year-on-year positive or negative change, we are looking at whether or not a country crosses one of our cut points (in a positive or negative direction). Our approach allows us to incorporate survival analysis.

---

[13] Up to 1 decimal place, and omitting values that are either so large or so small that there are not enough cases above or below them.

Before presenting results for all of the possible cut points, we can first focus on a few focal cut points. In Table 6.2 we present results for both a cut point of 0.5, which is the middle of the polyarchy measure, and 0.7, which we take to be a reasonable representation of the approximate polyarchy value for a stable democracy.[14] We also use the cut point developed by V-Dem as part of the Regimes of the World (RoW) project (Lührmann et al. 2018). The cut point divides liberal and electoral democracies, from electoral and closed autocracies. Finally, we identify the cut point in the polyarchy measure, which optimally mimics the binary measure of democracy or autocracy used by Svolik (2008). First, we match Svolik's (2008) dataset onto the V-Dem country-years. Svolik's (2008) dataset includes 3,402 country-year observations. We are able to match 2,902 observations onto our dataset of 10,875 observations. We then run through every possible binary version of the polyarchy measure, searching for the cut point that most closely matches Svolik's classification scheme. The polyarchy cut point that most closely mimics Svolik's (2008) classification is either 0.422 or 0.423, which both classify 2,492 country-years identically to Svolik's (2008) classification, and classify 410 country-years differently from Svolik's (2008) classification. We apply that cut point to our full dataset, to as closely as possible represent what a test of our hypotheses might look like using Svolik's (2008) classification scheme on V-Dem data.

Consistent with most of the existing literature we find that high state capacity, measured as the degree to which the bureaucracy is professionalized, lowers the risk of a democratic breakdown. This is the case across all four of our models in Table 6.2.[15] By contrast, we find no support for the presidentialism hypothesis. In fact, in two of our models, presidentialism is associated with a small but significant *decrease* in the risk of a democratic decline. We also find no support for the party system hypotheses. The coefficients for party institutionalization and the electoral system are not significant in any of the models, and, counter our hypothesis, the seat share of the largest party is associated with a *greater* risk of a step-down. The latter likely reflects the fact that the greater danger to democracy is too much power in the hands of one party, rather than too much fragmentation.[16]

---

[14] In our dataset, the 75 percent quantile is 0.622. If we arbitrarily subset this to only postwar democracies by checking the 75 percent quantile from 1945 onward, we find a value of 0.726. So, we arbitrarily run the model with 0.7, the simple round number that lies between these values.

[15] We also ran models that include state control over territory and state information capacity as robustness tests (Appendix 2). As mentioned previously, state control of territory has no significant effect. The effect of information capacity is inconsistent, with a negative effect in some models, a positive effect in some models, and no effect in others.

[16] We also tried interacting presidentialism and party fragmentation in an effort to test whether the combination of presidentialism and high fragmentation is particularly hazardous, but found no support for that hypothesis.

TABLE 6.2 Cox Hazard models of step-down

	V-Dem's regimes of the World		polyarchy cut point: 0.5		polyarchy cut point: 0.7		polyarchy approx. Svolik's: 0.422	
	beta	s.e.	beta	s.e.	beta	s.e.	beta	s.e.
Strictly presidential system:	**−0.81**	**0.33**	**−0.68**	**0.29**	−0.02	0.35	−0.56	0.30
Majoritarian electoral system:	−0.82	0.46	−0.30	0.37	**−0.91**	**0.48**	0.31	0.32
State capacity:	**−11.61**	**1.57**	**−8.33**	**1.36**	**−6.98**	**1.83**	**−8.83**	**1.40**
Largest seat share:	**2.00**	**0.82**	**2.09**	**0.72**	**3.49**	**0.94**	**1.80**	**0.70**
Party institutionalization	−0.59	0.96	−0.80	0.89	1.90	1.37	−1.38	0.86
Log of GDP per capita	**−1.16**	**0.21**	−0.20	0.19	−0.23	0.24	−0.11	0.20
GDP growth	**−4.92**	**1.82**	**−5.10**	**1.71**	−0.76	3.21	**−4.63**	**1.93**
Ethnic fractionalization	**1.15**	**0.57**	0.46	0.49	**1.78**	**0.72**	−0.35	0.47
Former UK colony	0.14	0.51	−0.36	0.45	−0.60	0.52	**−0.99**	**0.48**
Likelihood ratio test:	104.8		90.2		57.7		95.0	
N	3378		3424		2229		388	
Events	58		70		56		62	

Notes: Results in bold are statistically significant at a p-value level of 0.05.

In Figure 6.1 we show the effects of four of our main independent variables across a range of possible cut points. The first panel shows the effect of electing a (powerful) president compared to electing a prime minister on the probability that the country will experience a step-down – a decline in its polyarchy score. For most of the possible values of polyarchy, the effect of presidentialism on the probability of a step-down is indistinguishable from no effect, with a small range in which the effect is slightly negative. For the entire range of polyarchy below the cut point 0.32, and for nearly the entire range of polyarchy above the cut point 0.60, almost no cut point has a significant effect, with the exception of a few at the very top of the testable range. But of the twenty-nine cut points between 0.32 and 0.60, all but eight have a significant and negative effect on the probability of a step-down; the others are not significantly different from zero. So, for most democratic cut points, presidentialism has no effect on the probability of a step-down, but for most of the cut points in the middle of the range presidentialism has small a negative effect. Neither outcome is consistent with the perils of presidentialism as described by Linz and others.

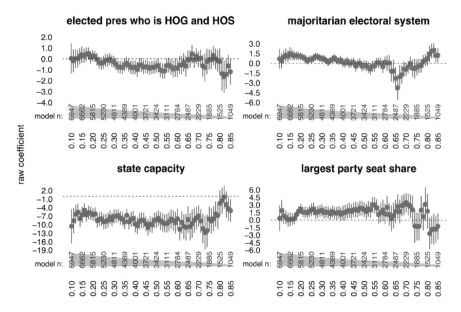

Polyarchy thresholds (below: non–democracy, above or same: democracy)

FIGURE 6.1 The effect on the probability of a step-down

Turning to our other institutional variables, the strongest and most consistent effects are for state capacity. State capacity dramatically reduces the probability of a step-down for almost every possible cut point. By contrast, the effect of the electoral system is indistinguishable from zero for most cut points, with two exceptions. At very low cut points, majoritarian electoral systems are associated with an increased risk of a step-down. At cut points between 0.65 and 0.68 majoritarian institutions have the hypothesized negative effect, but at the highest several cut points they have a positive effect. Finally, for most cut points the seat share of the largest party is positively associated with the risk of backsliding.

In Figure 6.2, we take a short detour to look at whether our set of institutional variables has any effect on the probability that a country experiences a "step-up" – moving from nondemocratic to democratic across any given cut point. State capacity has a consistent positive impact on the probability of a step-up, and the coefficient size is increasing as the polyarchy value increases (for models using four of these thresholds see Table 6.2). The only case in which the coefficient for state capacity is indistinguishable from 0 is for extremely low polyarchy cut points, where nearly every country is classified as a democracy, so the only cases that could experience a step-up are the most extreme autocracies. In terms of party system fragmentation, our two measures

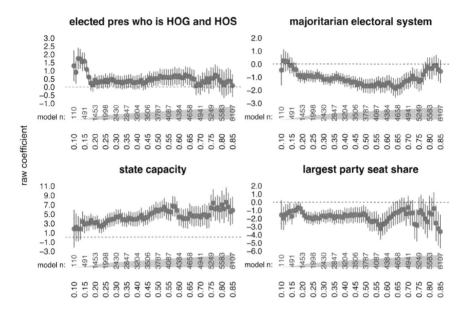

Polyarchy thresholds (below: non–democracy, above or same: democracy)

FIGURE 6.2 The effect on the probability of a step-up

reveal the same pattern. More (less) fragmentation, whether measured through the electoral system or by the largest party's seat share, is associated with a higher (lower) probability of a step-up across most cut points.

What about the effect of presidentialism on step-up? For most polyarchy cut points below the value 0.45, the coefficient is indistinguishable from 0, and the same is true for almost every cut point above a polyarchy value of 0.66. For most of the values inside of this range, the presence of an elected president has a very slightly positive effect on the probability of a step-up. The one major exception to this pattern is, again, several extremely low cut points. These cases, which are the few hundred most extremely autocratic country-years in the dataset, show a strongly positive relationship between having a president and the probability of a step-up, compared to cases in which a prime minister is elected. Each of these coefficient estimates corresponds to a sample size of a few hundred country-years that are on the extreme low end of the polyarchy measure.

So far, we have investigated the relevance of having a president that is both head of government and head of state to the probability of a step-up or of a step-down. This has meant using a binary variable whose reference case is *"not* having a president that is both HOG and HOS." Another interesting possibility opened by our dataset is that of comparing the election of different types of Head of Government against the presence of a nonelected head of government. This is what we do next. Specifically, we rerun the previous models now including three binary variables related to system of government. One indicates whether the country-year had an elected president. Another indicates whether the country-year had an elected prime minister. The third indicates whether the country-year had both an elected president and an elected prime minister. The reference case for this categorical analysis, therefore, is having neither an elected president nor an elected prime minister.

The result is shown in Figure 6.3, where we reestimate the previous models for the probability of a step-down using this new frame of analysis. When

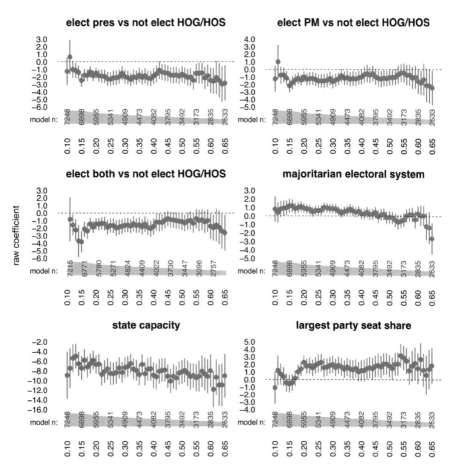

FIGURE 6.3 The effect on the probability of a step-down

comparing having just an elected president to not electing a head of government, we see that for all polyarchy cut points from 0.14 up to the maximum testable cut point, 0.65 – with the exception of just the two polyarchy cut points 0.42 and 0.62 – the presence of an elected president significantly decreases the probability of a step-down compared to not electing and head of government. In the case of elected prime ministers, many fewer cut points are distinguishable from zero. However, electing a prime minister significantly decreases the probability of a step-down for every cut point from 0.14 to 0.40 except for 0.33, as well as for the cut points between 0.46 and 0.51, and for the cut points 0.61 and 0.65. Electing a prime minister never significantly increases the probability of a step-down. And electing both significantly decreases the probability of a step-down for every cut point from 0.12 to 0.43, as well as six more cut points toward the top of the range. The presence of a majoritarian electoral system has mixed effects, slightly increasing the probability of a step-down for some low cut points while increasing the probability for some high cut points. State capacity always substantially decreases the probability of a step-down, while the centralization of seats in the largest party increases the probability of a step-down for most of the range of cut points between 0.18 and 0.56.

These coefficient estimates for step-down probabilities are mirrored by the coefficients for step-up probabilities when electing a president, electing a prime minister, or electing both compared to not electing any head of government (Figure 6.4). Electing a president consistently increases the probability of a step-up for most values of polyarchy compared to not electing any head of government, but the effect declines as the cut point increases, crossing 0 at values greater than 0.40. Electing a prime minister slightly increases the probability of a step-up compared to not electing any head of government at low levels of the polyarchy, but above 0.20 it does not make a difference. Finally, electing both increases the probability of a step-up for most cases where the polyarchy cut point is below 0.35.

So, quite a surprising finding emerges from this analysis – one that we were not explicitly looking for. We find that electing presidents, prime ministers, or both similarly impact the probability of a step-up or of a step-down. That is, we found strong support for the idea that the very act of holding elections increases the chance of an improvement in democracy in future periods, and lowers the risk of a democratic decline. For most cut points, countries that hold elections for their head of state and/or head of government are more likely to experience a step-up in their democracy score, and less likely to see a decline in subsequent years. In short, in authoritarian, semi-authoritarian, semi-democratic, and nonconsolidated democracies, electing a president and/or prime minister makes a difference: it decreases the likelihood of a step-down and increases the likelihood of a step-up. However, executive regime type does make a difference. Compared to holding no election, electing a president is more likely to prevent a step-down or induce

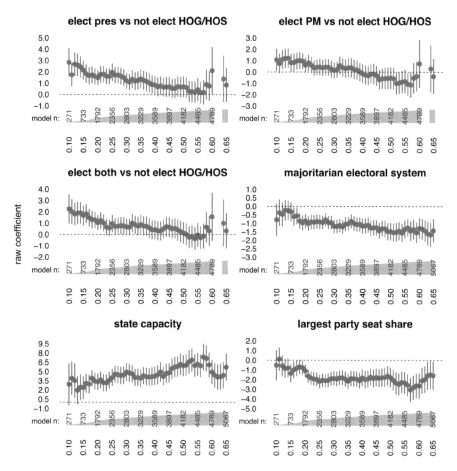

Polyarchy thresholds (below: non–democracy, above or same: democracy)

FIGURE 6.4   The effect on the probability of a step-up

a step-up than electing a prime minister is, consistent with arguments by Templeman (2012) and Roberts (2015).

Naturally, there might be some endogeneity at play since there could exist third factors that commonly affect both democratization in general and the occurrence of elections in particular. Yet, we think it is unlikely that those would account for all the eventual impact of holding elections. While further investigation is still needed, this idea is consistent with arguments in the literature about the democratizing effects of elections, even if those elections are not initially free and fair (Bratton and van de Walle 1997; Lindberg 2006a, 2006b, 2009; Teorell and Hadenius 2009).

6.3.2 Pooled Time Series Results

In an effort to check the robustness of the results from our survival analysis, we keep the same independent variables but look at how they affect the level of democracy in a given country. In order to do this, we estimate panel linear models where V-Dem's polyarchy variable is the outcome variable. The explanatory variables of interest and the controls will be the same as those used in the survival analysis – with the only difference being that we also include the variables with a one-year lag. All models estimated here are either fixed or random effects time-varying models, and all use Cribari-Neto (2004)'s heteroskedasticity-consistent robust standard errors (popularly known as HC4). We also repeat the models three times, once for the whole dataset, once for country-years with polyarchy lower than 0.5 (roughly representing less democratic countries), and once for country-years with polyarchy greater or equal than 0.5 (roughly representing more democratic countries).

Table 6.3 displays the results for all models, giving us estimates of the conditional partial correlation between each independent variable and the level of polyarchy in a given country-year. Consistent with the survival analysis we find no effect for presidentialism when we use fixed or random effects and when the model includes the whole sample or only less democratic countries, and a small positive effect for non-lagged variable in more democratic countries, again, inconsistent with a peril of presidentialism argument.

On the other hand, the coefficients for state capacity are always statistically significant and have the expected sign and substantial magnitude. This is also consistent with what we found previously in the survival models–state capacity is positively correlated to the level of democratization in a country. Unlike in our survival models, party institutionalization is positively and significantly associated with higher levels of democratization when using the panel data, as hypothesized.

Turning finally to our proxies for party system fragmentation, our results depend on the sample we use. When we use the entire dataset, majoritarian electoral institutions and largest party seat share are negatively associated with the level of democracy. Yet, notice that the coefficients of these two variables are not consistently statistically significant when less democratic countries are dropped from the dataset. This would suggest that the partial correlation between our two fragmentation proxies and polyarchy is only relevant for lower levels of democracy. This makes sense. At low levels of polyarchy the greatest risk to democracy is not too much fragmentation, it is too much concentration in the hands of the ruling party/ruling elite. A higher concentration of seats in the hands of a single party (as well as majoritarian electoral rules that help facilitate such a concentration) should be negatively correlated with levels of democracy.

TABLE 6.3 *Pooled time series*

	All cases				Polyarchy < 0.5				Polyarchy >= 0.5			
	fixed effects		random effects		fixed effects		random effects		fixed effects		random effects	
	coef.	s.e.	coef.	s.e.	coef.	s.e.	coef.	s.e.	coef.	s.e.	coef.	s.e.
Strictly presidential system:	**0.01**	0.01	**0.01**	0.01	-0.01	0.01	-0.01	0.01	**0.10**	**0.04**	**0.11**	**0.04**
Lagged 1 year:	0.02	0.01	0.02	0.01	0.00	0.01	0.01	0.01	-0.07	0.04	-0.06	0.03
Majoritarian electoral system:	**-0.07**	**0.01**	**-0.07**	**0.01**	**-0.03**	**0.01**	**-0.04**	**0.01**	**-0.03**	**0.01**	**-0.03**	**0.01**
Lagged 1 year:	-0.04	0.01	-0.04	0.01	-0.01	0.01	-0.01	0.01	-0.00	0.01	-0.00	0.01
State capacity:	**0.46**	**0.04**	**0.46**	**0.04**	**0.33**	**0.04**	**0.33**	**0.04**	**0.37**	**0.05**	**0.37**	**0.05**
Lagged 1 year:	**0.28**	**0.04**	**0.28**	**0.04**	0.07	0.04	0.07	0.04	**0.14**	**0.05**	**-0.13**	**0.05**
Largest seat share:	**-0.10**	**.01**	**-0.10**	**0.01**	**-0.08**	**0.01**	**-0.08**	**0.01**	**-0.04**	**0.02**	**-0.04**	**0.02**
Lagged 1 year:	**-0.10**	**0.01**	**-0.10**	**0.01**	**-0.07**	**0.01**	**-0.06**	**0.01**	-0.02	0.02	-0.02	0.02
Party institutionalization	**0.26**	**0.01**	**0.26**	**0.01**	**0.11**	**0.01**	**0.11**	**0.01**	**0.24**	**0.02**	**0.20**	**0.02**
Log of GDP per capita	**0.07**	**0.00**	**0.07**	**0.00**	0.01	0.00	0.00	0.00	**0.05**	**0.00**	**0.05**	**0.00**
GDP growth	-0.02	0.02	-0.03	0.02	0.01	0.01	0.01	0.01	-0.04	0.02	-0.04	0.03
Ethnic fractionalization			**0.13**	**0.03**			**0.06**	**0.02**			**0.07**	**0.03**
Former UK colony			**0.05**	**0.02**			**0.06**	**0.02**			-0.01	0.02
Intercept			**-0.55**	**0.02**			**0.12**	**0.02**			**-0.20**	**0.02**
Adjusted R^2:	0.77		0.77		0.41		0.46		0.66		0.70	
N countries:	132		132		112		112		93		93	
N time points:	4–182		4–182		1–107		1–107		1–151		1–151	
N cases:	6,825		6,825		3,452		3,452		3,195		3,195	

Notes: Results in bold are statistically significant at a p-value level of 0.05

6.4 CONCLUSION

In this chapter, we used V-Dem data to re-examine the effect of some of the most well-studied political institutions on democratic stability and quality. We focused on how three categories of institutions shape democracy: state capacity, executive regime type such as presidential or parliamentary systems, and features of party systems such as fragmentation and institutionalization. Because there is no single true method for dividing V-Dem's many-valued polyarchy measure into "democracy" and "autocracy" bins, we considered every possible definition, so that readers can interpret our results based on whatever their own preferred polyarchy cut point is. For each of these cut points, we estimated how different arrangements of the institutions of interest affect the probability that a democracy survives as a democracy, or the reverse probability, that an autocracy survives as an autocracy. We supplemented these survival analyses with panel linear models, checking the results of the survival models using a pooled time series analysis, and the two analyses agreed on nearly every substantive detail.

Regarding state capacity, the results of our analyses confirm the main results of previous studies. The prevailing theoretical argument about the role of state capacity in democratic quality is that democracies with higher state capacity should typically experience better and more stable democratic governance. Past empirical work has reinforced this expectation. And our analysis resoundingly agrees: we found that state capacity, operationalized as administrative capacity, dramatically lowers the risk that a democracy will experience a democratic breakdown. It is almost irrelevant how values of polyarchy are translated into a definition of democracies and autocracies: for nearly every possible cut point, high state capacity is an important predictor of continued democracy.

Contra Linz, we did not find any evidence to support the peril of presidentialism. In fact, for countries that are neither fully autocratic nor fully democratic, we found that presidentialism increases the chances of a step-up to fuller democracy. So, for countries that we might not consider to be democratic, presidential regimes actually have a higher probability of becoming democratic enough to meet our definition of a democratic regime. The direction of these substantive results is consistent with the bulk of recent research on how executive regime types affect the level of democracy, but the use of V-Dem data enables us to uncover intriguing details about how these institutional arrangements affect many different levels of democracy.

Regarding party systems, we find no support for the claim that party system fragmentation decreases the level of democracy. Rather, our results suggest that the centralization of power is a greater threat to overall democratic stability. We find that centralization of power in the hands of one party is an obstacle to democratic improvement for countries at lower levels of polyarchy. In the pooled time series analysis, we found some support for the positive role of party institutionalization in supporting democracy.

Allen Hicken, Samuel Baltz, Fabricio Vasselai

Our results – on the benefits of state capacity, the unimportance of executive regime type, and the risk of centralization of power rather than party system fragmentation for democratic stability – largely agree with recent empirical and theoretical findings. However, by considering how institutional arrangements affect the probability of a democratic step-up or a democratic step-down when democracies are defined in hundreds of different ways, we are able to make much more precise claims about how different institutional arrangements matter for countries that have different levels of democracy.

7

Democracy and Social Forces

Michael Bernhard and Amanda B. Edgell

7.1 INTRODUCTION

Popular contention occupies a prominent place in the understanding of democratization processes for those who attribute an important role to agency.[1] Further, the role of an active citizenry after the installation of democracy has been posed as one of the factors that leads to democratic stability and greater responsiveness. This chapter begins with a discussion of three different meta-approaches that problematize the role of social forces as central to the origins of democracy and its maintenance. These are the literatures on social force incorporation, the role of contentious civil society in transitions to and from democracy, and civil society as the realm of interest articulation in established democracy. The three approaches overlap to some extent with major figures in these debates crossing boundaries and making contributions to multiple literatures.

After this discussion of the three approaches, we explore new possibilities in measuring the impact of social forces on democracy using the Varieties of Democracy (V-Dem) civil society data and resistance campaign data available through the Nonviolent and Violent Campaigns and Outcomes (NAVCO) project. Based on a sample of 156 countries from 1900 to 2014, including 10,205 observations, we find that both civil society organizational capacity (operationalized as a lagged stock variable) and nonviolent protest campaigns have positive effects on annual changes to democracy across a range of democracy indicators. We also find that right-wing anti-system movements constitute the largest tangible threat to democracy.

[1] This research is supported by the Riksbankens Jubileumsfond (M13–0559:1, PI: Staffan I. Lindberg), the Knut and Alice Wallenberg Foundation (PI: Staffan I. Lindberg), the University of Gothenburg (E 2013/43), and the University of Florida Foundation in support of the Raymond and Miriam Ehrlich Chair.

7.2 SOCIAL FORCES, INCORPORATION, AND DEMOCRACY

The foundational work on social forces and their incorporation focuses on class-based struggles. In the *Social Origins of Democracy and Dictatorship*, Barrington Moore (1964) concentrates on the strength of the early modern bourgeoisie and how this affected the ways in which the extant rural classes (peasants and landlords) adapted to the commercialization of agriculture. Where the nobility adopted modern commercial methods of farming, as in the United Kingdom, France, and the United States, democracy prevailed. Where feudal methods transformed into labor repressive capitalist practices, the paths of development depended on the strength of the bourgeoisie. Where it was moderate, as in Germany or Japan, fascism emerged. Where it was minimal, as in Russia or China, this resulted in peasant rebellion and communism.

Building on these Moorean foundations, the second generation of comparative historical analysis placed greater emphasis on the integration of working-class formations into competitive oligarchic systems. Capitalist development made it dangerous for rulers to ignore concentrated urban populations with shared grievances and low collective action costs. In these accounts, the timing of incorporation and the potential for alliances between social formations are key conditioning variables that determine regime outcomes. O'Donnell (1973) showed how import substitution industrialization provided a conducive material basis for incorporating the middle and working classes into electoral systems with new welfare protections. The subsequent saturation of domestic market demand undermined the material basis of this settlement and led to subsequent bureaucratic authoritarian episodes where state repression reduced consumption to boost investment and exports. Expanding on O'Donnell, Collier and Collier (1991) also look at the timing of working-class incorporation as the prime determinant of regime outcomes across eight Latin American cases.

In Western Europe, Luebbert (1991) concentrates on the outcomes of late nineteenth-century struggles over working-class incorporation to explain interwar regime outcomes. In the case of early incorporation under liberal hegemony, the logic of the market contained interwar class antagonisms, whereas those who missed this earlier incorporation juncture needed to rely on political containment strategies (social democracy or fascism) during the interwar era. Working-class incorporation and the ability of conservative parties to compete electorally are also critical for determining whether the ruling class decides to play by the rules of democracy or subvert them (Ahmed 2014; Ziblatt 2017).

In the most comprehensive geographic treatment using comparative historical analysis, Rueschemeyer et al. (1992) explore the links between socioeconomic modernization and democracy. They see democracy as an epiphenomenon of capitalist development, wherein capitalism produces new classes, both working and middle, with new interests that are better served by a democratic environment in which to pursue them. In their account they pay attention to these so-called middle sectors, their changing commitments to democracy by time and place, and their capacity to organize.

More recently, distributionist accounts of democratization have carried on in the spirit of the comparative historical school by creating a stylized model of class distributional conflict. In the model, the rich are a potential threat to democracy out of fear of expropriation by lower-class revolutionaries (Acemoglu and Robinson 2006; Boix 2003). Using the median voter tipping point of the Meltzer–Richard model (1981), they theorize that situations of low threat to expropriation of the rich (equality, high capital mobility) promote democracy. By contrast, the overthrow of democracy is likely when the poor can use their numerical advantage to take democratic political control, making threats to expropriate the rich seem credible. Despite the theoretical sophistication of this argument, there is a substantial body of empirical evidence that fails to confirm the theory (Karakoç 2017; Haggard and Kaufmann 2016; Reenock etal. 2007; Slater et al. 2014). The chapter in this volume on economic determinants by Knutsen and Dahlum also fails to find strong evidence of distributionist theories. On the contrary, the most comprehensive test to date finds that income inequality makes transitions to democracy *more likely*, due to the desire of those who have recently gained wealth to create legal safeguards against expropriation and establish legislative control over taxation (Ansell and Samuels 2014).

While class incorporation dominates discussions, the literature also documents other important incorporation struggles. Paxton (2000) contends that the prevailing operationalizations of democracy disregard the incorporation of women, ignoring one of the principal struggles for equality under the law, and anachronistically pushing the realization of full-blown democracy further back in time. Since her critique, several rich studies documenting women's suffrage struggles or other struggles to put women's concerns on the agenda through movements and protests have found their way into the literature (e.g., Banaszak 1996; McConnaughy 2014; Murdie and Peksen 2014; Paxton et al. 2006). Evidence suggests that women's mobilization has helped to initiate political protests and subsequent transitions in a range of cases (Tripp 2001; Waylen 2007). Using novel sequence analysis methods, Wang et al. (2017) show that the extension of civil liberties to women is essential for democratization.

Others have looked at the incorporation of the ethnic, religious, and racial minorities as a component in the struggle for democracy. Kopstein and Wittenburg (2010) directly challenge the class incorporation framework used to conceptualize West European and Latin American democratization by showing that ethnic exclusion remained the greatest barrier to democratization in Eastern Europe. Recent work on subnational authoritarianism provides evidence that pockets of ethnic exclusion in the

United States delayed the full realization of democracy (Mickey 2015). Yashar (2005) shows that discrimination against indigenous populations has been a durable barrier to democracy in Latin America. Finally, Kalyvas (1996) and Gould (1999) show that the integration of religious populations who saw democracy initially as an assault on tradition is also a crucial step in social incorporation.

Unfortunately, the data to test for other incorporation struggles, like gender, ethnicity, and religion, are still not complete enough for the kinds of tests we perform here; nevertheless, we include them in the literature review, both so as not to minimize their importance as part of the narrative of democratic incorporation and to mark them as important items for efforts in improving the data environment for understanding the historical emergence of democracy.

7.3   CIVIL SOCIETY AND DEMOCRACY

Rueschemeyer et al. (1992) represent a bridge between the older social forces incorporation literature and a newer literature on civil society. In their discussion of class mobilization, they draw attention to the expression of class interests through organizations in an autonomous civil society, which provides new social actors the space and organizational capacity to press their claims vis-à-vis anti-democratic ruling-class actors and the coercive capacities of the state. Their approach is characteristic of the neo-Gramscian approach to the relationship between democracy and civil society. It shares with Gramsci the notion of civil society as a site of contestation between different organized interests and state actors, whether autonomous or captured by particular social forces (Migdal 1988). This approach highlights the effect of contentious politics between social forces on democratic progress and regress.

7.3.1   Contentious Politics as a Catalyst

The concept of civil society reemerged in the study of the enfeeblement of the authoritarian regimes in Latin America and Eastern Europe in the late 1970s and early 1980s. Alfred Stepan (1985) and Andrew Arato (1993 [1981]) pioneered its redeployment to make sense of the reemergence of oppositional political organization and challenges to the limits of expression in the public sphere. With the onset of the third wave of democratization, the role of civil society was conceptualized as essential to defeating incumbent efforts to shore up authoritarianism by pushing for democracy and the convoking of free and fair founding elections. In cases where civil society remained passive, authoritarian incumbents were able to maintain themselves in power. Where civil society actors pressed for further change, democratization became possible (Linz and Stepan 1996; O'Donnell and Schmitter 1986; Przeworski 1991).

The neo-Gramscian school echoes those who have stressed the role of contentious politics as an essential component of successful transitions to democracy. Some observers find a strong connection between protest movement strength and successful democratization of authoritarian regimes (Brancati 2016; Della Porta 2014; Haggard and Kaufman 2016). Others look at the coincidence of protest movements and international pressures as essential to democratic breakthroughs in the developing countries and in late-democratizers in the postcommunist world (Beaulieu 2014; Beissinger 2007; Bunce and Wolchik 2011; Levitsky and Way 2006). Others using a more historical institutionalist framework stress the timing of contentious mobilization, arguing that protest and pressure by democratic opposition movements during critical junctures have a decisive impact on democratic outcomes and the quality of democracy that follows (Bernhard 2016; Bernhard and Jung 2017; Fernandes and Branco 2017; Fishman 2017). Other important work focused on postcommunist politics suggests that civil society can compensate for weaknesses in other democratic arenas such as party systems, thus overcoming democratic deficits (Ekiert and Kubik 1999).

An insurgent civil society can also have a dark side. Kopstein and Chambers (2001) show that authoritarian movements emerge and can persist on the margins of the democratic public space. This constitutes a threat when these anti-democratic movements become more mainstream. Substantial case-based empirical work investigates this phenomenon in the interwar period. Berman (1997) and Riley (2010) find that the capture of civil society organizations (CSOs) by fascist and reactionary movements was an essential pattern of democratic breakdown in several prominent cases like Weimar Germany, Italy, Spain, and Romania.

Despite the rich casework on which these accounts are based, it would be wrong to generally conclude that civil society is a threat to democracy. Studies from the V-Dem project provide ample large-N evidence that an active civil society is a strong predictor of democratic survival in both the interwar period (Cornell et al. 2020) and for the whole of the twentieth century (Bernhard et al. 2020). The latter argue that civil society helps to cement democratic settlements by imposing costs on would-be authoritarian defectors.

7.3.2 Civil Society and Organized Interests

Another influential stream of research that connects civil society with democracy grows out of the literature on political culture. When one digs deeply into the theoretical side of culture-centered arguments, it becomes clear the attitudes underlying this notion of culture grow out of behavioral interactions with other citizens in organizations and with the state. Drawing inspiration from Tocqueville's views on how civic activism kept democracy in America from turning into mobocracy (de Tocqueville 1838), this literature treats the behavioral consequences of participation in civic organizations as crucial for healthy democracy. This neo-Tocquevillian school of thought is more focused on the organizational life of existing democracies and how civil society is able to convey its interests to a responsive state. It is a theory of what makes democracy stable rather than embedded in a dynamic theory of regime change.

Beginning with The Civic Culture by Almond and Verba (1963), political scientists have concerned themselves with the political behaviors that create good democratic citizens. The civic culture includes a plurality of citizens who were actively and effectively engaged in politics. Because the notion of culture used here is expansive and includes behavior, it encompasses activism, and thus is akin to theories that explicitly model civil society in terms of citizen organization or activism. The civic culture in turn gave rise to a host of kindred neo-Tocquevillian studies that come to similar conclusions, that the activist model of citizen engagement has salutary effects for democracy.

Putnam et al. (1994), beginning with *Making Democracy Work*, argue that civic participation creates social capital and stimulates generalized social trust. A healthy civil society leads to better government and in turn greater support for democracy. Inglehart and Welzel (2005) in *Modernization, Cultural Change and Democracy* find that economic modernization leads to systematic shifts in values and culture toward autonomy and equality that makes the spread of democracy globally more likely.

One can read subtle differences within the prominent literature on this subject on how a participatory culture or civil society bolsters democracy. The cultural arguments are more about how the values and attitudes of citizens are congruent with democracy. The greater the proportion of citizens that hold those values the easier it is for democracy to function and persist. The social capital argument is more indirect in its causal pathways. Organizational behavior in civil society creates trust that enhances the performance of government institutions, making democracy more effective, in turn inspiring the loyalty of the citizenry.

7.4   THEORETICAL EXPECTATIONS

The impact of different social forces on democracy and democratization is difficult to study in a large-N framework. Comparable cross-national data for large numbers of countries over time has, until now, been quite hard to come by. In addition, the literature on social forces and democratization operates according to a radically different ontology than most large-N research. Classical comparative historical analysis looks at the process of regime change as slow-accruing and marked by major punctuated events that challenge and change long-term regime equilibria. More recent work relying on the historical institutional variant sees the definitive impact of social forces as highly time dependent. They emerge as important players when the structural constraints posed by path dependence are weakened and purposive action by organized political and social actors has sufficient autonomy to remake institutional arrangements to transform existing structures. Social forces affect democratization by either demanding incorporation into the system of contestation (e.g., struggles for enfranchisement) or by organizing to remove constraints on competition (multipartism, free and fair electoral practices, secret ballot, one person-one vote, other forms of unequal representation like rotten boroughs or gerrymandering) or its prerequisites (e.g., free of speech and association) (Capoccia and Ziblatt 2010).

In the literature highlighted earlier, the preponderance of theory suggests that the impact of the mobilization and incorporation of popular social forces has a salutary effect on democracy. First, the activation of social forces and their struggles for incorporation is one of the motive forces behind democratization, both in comparative historical accounts and actor-centered process models of transition. We can also gauge the importance of different patterns of class alliance that emerge in the mobilization of social groups as highlighted in the second generation of comparative historical analysis, particularly the political choices of working-class and middle-class actors. In Latin America, scholars highlight whether middle- and working-class interests can find common ground in democracy (O'Donnell 1973; Rueschemeyer et al. 1992) and in Europe, Luebbert (1991) finds that the choices of family farmers to make alliances with labor or urban middle-class parties had critical ramifications for whether the second wave of industrializing states took a fascist or social democratic turn in the interwar period. Recent coding of the NAVCO data by Dahlum, Knutsen, and Wig (2019) allow us to examine the generalizability of such pathways.

Second, the implication of the behavioral research that argues that social activism promotes either political cultures more congruent with democracy or higher levels of generalized social trust that lead to more effective government is that such activist democracies should be more insulated from the negative effects of poor performance on legitimacy (Linz 1978; Lipset 1959). Therefore, we expect higher levels of social engagement to be correlated with higher democracy scores.

However, there are two threads in the literature that highlight risks for democracy in social activism. Distributionist accounts make the assumption that high levels of lower-class, especially left wing, agitation for political or economic equality will unsettle the upper classes and provoke hard-line responses to prevent democratic transition, and reactionary backlash in existing democracies, producing breakdowns. The distributionists in their quest for parsimony perhaps go too far and see all lower-class mobilization as revolutionary, whereas those who have read extensively in the history of working-class organizations know that not all movements that challenge upper-class privilege are revolutionary, and in fact, most are reformist and peaceful in nature, especially early in their organizational life (Bartolini 2000, 78–86). Radicalization has often been a product of state repression or the experience of war. Historical work on interwar Europe points out that in terms of threats to order, the contemporary right is more likely to use violence under democratic rule than their counterparts on the left (Mann 2004, 16–17).

The bad civil society argument follows a logic of equilibrium similar to Huntington (1968). He argues that when popular participation outstrips the institutional capacity of the political system to process demands, the result will be disorder and even regime failure. Whereas some anti-democrats may well fear democracy will replace an orderly society with mob rule, or that some sets of institutions are less suited to respond to an organized citizenry, it hardly seems fair to blame democratic movements for the actions of reactionaries protecting their privileged political status. Despite a few conspicuous examples of mass unrest leading to dictatorship, notably through revolution, greater organizational capacity for excluded social forces tends to promote democracy not only in the long term, but on balance, even in the short term.

Still, the case evidence presented by authors like Berman (1997) and Riley (2010) and the specification of distributionist models serve as a cautionary tale that the nature of mobilization can be very important. Despite thinking that the nature of the threat is overstated compared to the salutary effect of most forms of social mobilization, it may not be trivial, and certainly ignoring it if it has some basis in reality will not make our models perform better. Thus, we think it is important to think about when mobilization could constitute an authoritarian revolutionary threat. To capture this dimension of debate, we will try to model our regressions in such a way as to capture those cases where mass mobilization is more likely to threaten democracy. Utilizing new data resources, a small literature, inspired by the literature on how violent state birth makes new states more bellicose, has examined how violent and nonviolent social mobilization affect long-term democratic prospects. Overall, it finds that violent forms of social activism have negative impacts on democracy compared to nonviolent forms of action (Bayer et al. 2016; Bethke and Pinckney 2021; Celestino and Gleditsch 2013; Teorell 2010).

7.5 RESEARCH DESIGN

Our theory in this chapter is predicated on a huge literature in comparative historical analysis and historical institutionalism that has investigated the historical emergence of democracy using both Millian comparative methods and process tracing. It is based on a body of evidence of literally hundreds if not thousands of causal process observations. The aim in this chapter is to extend the external validity of this rich body of findings using large-N correlational methods with a broad sample of 156 countries from 1900 to 2014. While we cannot track and measure social forces like small-N researchers, Rueschemeyer et al. (1992) present us with a proxy – civil society. Social forces organize for change and to do so they create CSOs, make demands, and organize protests. Thus, reiterating the approach used by Bernhard and Karakoç (2007), we can roughly gauge the impact of social forces by looking both at civil society organizational capacity and whether civil society mobilizes for change. We make use of distinct measures of civil society organizational capacity, anti-system movements, and protest campaigns to gauge the extent to which the emergence and actions of social forces are correlated with enhanced levels of democracy. These are summarized in Table 7.1.

Three new datasets provide the opportunity to test for the effects of civil society mobilization and organization on democratization by affording researchers substantial time series cross-sectional observations. The first of these, produced by the Varieties of Democracy (V-Dem) Project, provides country-year level measures of a variety of factors affecting democratic regime outcomes utilizing expert coded surveys (Coppedge et al. 2019a). We draw on indicators from its civil society battery to gauge different aspects of its development over extended periods of time. Therefore, our models are unique in their assessment of the effects of civil society both on the basis of mobilization and more routine political action through organization. The second dataset, the NAVCO provides multilevel data on major violent and nonviolent resistance campaigns (Chenoweth 2011; Chenoweth and Stephan 2011).[2] The data are based on expert opinion, and code the origin and end dates of resistance campaigns, as well as characteristics of the campaign itself. We use these data to assess the effects of distinct episodes of resistance activity. We supplement these data using the coding by Dahlum et al. (2019), which captures the class character of the NAVCO campaigns. This newest dataset provides us with the most explicit class coding to date and this allows us to more directly test some of the contentions of the comparative historical literature, especially those concerned with alliances between different social forces.

7.5.1 Measuring Civil Society Organizational Capacity

The operation and persistence of CSOs represents an accumulation of experience, expertise, tactical knowledge, and social bonds that are enhanced over time in ways that are not captured by short-term observations like country-year snapshots. Theoretically, past experience should accumulate over time and embed itself organizationally, but older experiences will become less relevant as cadres are replaced by the march of time. Therefore, we begin our analysis by treating the organizational capacity of civil society as a stock that fluctuates throughout the history of a polity. We use this measure to test arguments about associational capacity (de Tocqueville 1838), the civic culture (Almond and Verba 1963), and social capital (Putnam et al. 1994).

---

[2] We utilize version 1.1 because it provides greatest coverage (1900–2006).

TABLE 7.1 *Summary of social forces indicators used in the main analyses*

Aspect	Concept	Indicator/measure	Variable tag	Max years in time series	V-Dem polities covered	Source
Social mobilization	CSO capacity	Civil society participatory environment stock	*csstockn*	119	174	V-Dem (v9)
Social movements	Anti-system movement strength	CSO anti-system movements	*v2csantimv*	119	175	V-Dem (v9)
Social movements	Left-wing movements	Leftist, socialist, communist anti-system movements	*v2csanmvch_6*	119	175	V-Dem (v9)
Social movements	Right-wing movements	Rightist, conservative, party of order anti-system movements	*v2csanmvch_7*	119	175	V-Dem (v9)
Social movements	Violent campaign	Violent anti-system campaign	*navco_viol_lag*	108	174	NAVCO (v1.0)
Social movements	Nonviolent campaign	Nonviolent anti-system campaign	*navco_nviol_lag*	108	174	NAVCO (v1.0)
Social movements	Luebbert's thesis	Industrial workers/peasants (ended t−1)	*luebbert_end*	108	174	Dahlum, Knutsen, and Wig (2019)
Social movements	Middle sectors thesis	Industrial workers/middle class (ended t−1)	*midsect_end*	108	174	Dahlum, Knutsen, and Wig (2019)

Notes: Max years in time series and V-Dem polities covered are limited to sovereign years only (using the variable *v2svindep* from V-Dem v9).

We measure civil society organizational capacity as a stock using the following formula:

$$CivStock_{i,t} = \sum_{\tau=0}^{\tau=t-t_1} \delta^{\tau}(v2csprtcpt)$$

where δ is one minus the annual depreciation rate and $v2csprtcpt$ is the V-Dem indicator for the civil society participatory environment. Thus, we treat the annual depreciation rate as a weight on the accumulated civil society stock up to the previous year (t_{-1}). For interpretation purposes, we normalize the stock measure to fall within a zero to one interval, where zeros represent no experience with associational life and ones represent the fullest possible extent of experience.[3]

As a baseline, we assume that the effects of civil society stock for the first year of one generation are likely to depreciate by the time the next generation attains maturity (i.e., approximately thirty years). To do so, we apply a 10 percent annual depreciation rate. This assumption is theoretically informed by the literature linking generational shifts to changes in civil society mobilization (e.g., Bernhard and Karakoç 2007; Howard, 2002; Putnam 2000). It also reflects our empirical observation that the indicator for civil society participatory environment is less persistent than levels of democracy, which are typically given a 1–6 percent annual depreciation rate when measured as a stock (e.g., Gerring et al. 2005; Gerring et al. 2012; Persson and Tabellini 2009).[4]

It is quite possible that the depreciation rate for civil society organizational capacity is not constant across all country-years but varies based on other contextual factors. The erosion of social capital and norms of civic culture may occur outside the bounds of inter-generational changes. If this is the case, our generation-based depreciation rates will overestimate civil society stock during periods when other factors promote *intra*-generational declines in associational capacity. In particular, we hypothesize that periods of heightened government repression of CSOs will have such an effect. In Appendix B, we provide robustness checks of our main models using an alternative measure of civil society organizational capacity that adjusts the baseline 10 percent annual depreciation rate upward as government repression of CSOs increases. To do so, we draw on the V-Dem indicator for government repression of CSOs (v2csreprss).[5]

We draw on the Historical V-Dem data to extend measurement of civil society stock as far back in time as possible but constrain the estimation sample to sovereign country-years from 1900 to 2014. For countries without Historical V-Dem data, we assume that they enter the V-Dem

[3] We do so using the min–max method, where the maximum is based on the upper bound of the uncertainty measure from the V-Dem measurement model. See Appendix 7A for more details.
[4] See Appendix 7A, Figure 7.A1. [5] For more details, see Appendix 7A.

dataset with a tabula rasa, scoring zero on the civil society stock measure during their first year of observation. This is less than ideal but is limited to just eight countries.[6] Because countries in the V-Dem data sometimes experience a gap in coding due to occupation or federation with another state, we measure civil society stock based on values for the V-Dem country-unit that acts as the governing power (see Coppedge et al. 2019c). This applies to some cases entering the dataset later (e.g., Croatia as Yugoslavia up to 1990) and cases with gaps in coding (e.g., Austria during German annexation from 1938–1944). In Appendix 7A, we provide a list of cases we have assigned in this way (Table 7.A1) and an illustration of how this measure works with empirical examples.

7.5.2 Measuring Civil Society Mobilization

We also consider distinct episodes of civil society mobilization. To do so, we begin with the V-Dem data on anti-system opposition movements, defined as "any movement – peaceful or armed – that is based in the country (not abroad) and is organized in opposition to the current political system" (Coppedge et al. 2019b,182). We measure the strength of anti-system movements based on their general relationship with the regime ($v2csantimv$). This variable is calculated using point estimates from the V-Dem measurement model that behaves similarly to z-scores. The original survey scale ranges from zero (no or very minimal) to four (a high level of anti-system movement activity that poses a real threat to the regime). For our largest sample of cases, the measure of anti-system movement strength ranges from –3.14 to 4.02 with an average score of –0.49.[7]

We also take into account the disposition of anti-system movements drawing on the V-Dem variable for anti-system movement character ($v2csanmvch$) and more fine-grained data collected by the NAVCO project (Chenoweth and Stephan 2011). The V-Dem data identifies the ideological nature of anti-system movements, specifically whether any could be characterized as "leftist, socialist, communist" or "rightist, conservative, party of order" (Coppedge et al. 2019b, p.183). These variables are based on the proportion of experts who indicated the presence of such movements within the country-year. Because more experts will be aware of and code the presence of these movements as their visibility increases, we treat these variables as proxies for left-wing and right-wing anti-system *salience*. In our sample, the average value for left-wing movements is 0.34 and right-wing movements is 0.16. In Appendix 7B, we also provide additional models testing

---

[6] We provide details on which countries enter the models with fewer than a generation (thirty years) of accumulated stock and present robustness checks omitting these country-years from the analysis (see Table 7.A2, Figure 7.A5, Figure 7.A6, and Table 7.B5).

[7] For reference, the linearized original scale ($v2csantimv\_osp$) ranges from 0.03 to 3.98, with an average 1.27.

for the relationship between democracy and ethnic- and religious-based anti-system movements (see Table 7.B13).

The NAVCO dataset allows us to explore the relationship between democracy and violent and nonviolent resistance campaigns (Chenoweth 2011).[8] The NAVCO project defines a resistance campaign as "a series of observable, continual tactics in pursuit of a political objective" (Chenoweth and Stephan 2011, p.14). These campaigns are classified based on their resistance methods, where (non)violence is coded by an expert consensus on whether the primary tactics physically threatened their targets.[9] Because the NAVCO project provides rich details on the start and end dates of these campaigns, we are able to not only estimate the relationship between democracy and ongoing resistance campaigns, but also the long-term trends in democracy after a campaign has ended. To do so, we measure the time since entry or since the last campaign ended, taking the natural logarithm to allow for a return to some equilibrium state. This time variable is then interacted with indicators capturing whether the campaign that most recently ended was violent or nonviolent.[10] Finally, we also use recent data collected by Dahlum et al. (2019) that identifies the social character of NAVCO campaigns. These data differentiate the dominant actors and participants of the NAVCO campaigns, including industrial workers, the middle-class, peasants, and others. This extension of the NAVCO data allows us to test prominent theories of class-based coalitions and historical democratization.

7.5.3 Measuring Democracy

Similar to other chapters in this volume, we often rely on the V-Dem electoral democracy index (EDI, *v2x_polyarchy*) for our main dependent variable. This index provides for a middle-range definition of democracy capturing many of the elements of participation and contestation outlined by Dahl's (1971) concept of polyarchy. The EDI is a composite measure of freedom of association (v2x_frassoc_thick), clean elections (v2xel_frefair), freedom of expression (v2x_freexp_thick), elected officials (v2x_elecoff), and suffrage (v2x_suffr).[11] We primarily focus on annual changes in democracy scores. Following the procedure outlined in the introduction to this volume (adapted from Teorell 2010), we model total annual change, as well as upward and downward movements. Total change is the net difference in democracy score between t and t_{-1}. Upward movements include all positive changes, with

---

[8] This strategy matches closely with models of violent and nonviolent protest found elsewhere in the literature (e.g., Teorell 2010).

[9] The term consensus comes directly from the NAVCO project, see Chenoweth and Stephan (2011).

[10] Admittedly, this approach sacrifices information for simplicity. However, the number of ongoing anti-system movements in a given year remains small – with a maximum of three for violent anti-system campaigns and two for nonviolent campaigns.

[11] These indicators are aggregated using a combination of weighted averaging and five-way multiplicative interactions (Coppedge et al. 2019b; Teorell et al. 2019).

negative and no change coded as zeros. Similarly, downward movements include all negative changes, with positive and no change coded as zeros. Because freedom of association is included in the EDI, we also estimate models using thinner measures of "procedural democracy." The Munck procedural democracy index (*v2x_munck*) accounts for electoral accountability based on (1) an elected executive (*v2x_accex*), (2) clean elections (*v2x_elfrefair*), (3) multiparty elections (*v2x_multiparty*), and (4) universal suffrage (*v2x_suffr*). The thinner Schumpeter procedural democracy index (*v2x_schump*) only accounts for the first three components.[12] For models using the civil society stock measure, we only report results for the procedural democracy outcome variables because of the large potential for endogeneity with the electoral democracy index.[13] Table 7.2 reports summary statistics for the three outcome variables. Because a country's level of democracy is likely to influence the rate at which it experiences changes, we also control for the lagged level of democracy in all change models.[14]

7.5.4 Control Variables

We balance the desire to avoid omitted variable bias while maintaining a large number of countries for a long time period. The literature shows that regime type tends to co-vary with level of economic development (Boix and Stokes 2003; Lipset 1959; Przeworski and Limongi 1997; Knutsen and Dahlum, this volume). We control for wealth using the natural log of gross domestic product (GDP) per capita. Because changes to regimes may occur during moments of economic crisis (Gasiorowski 1995), we also control for annual percent change in GDP per capita. Both GDP and GDP growth are measured using the Maddison Project (Bolt and van Zanden 2014). Evidence suggests that regimes with access to material rents are less likely to experience change (Smith 2004). We control for this using oil production per capita (Ross and Madhavi 2015; Wimmer et al. 2009).

---

[12] Derived from Munck (2009) and Schumpeter (1942), using methods developed by Hegre et al. 2020).

[13] We are particularly concerned about the freedom of association index, which includes variables for CSO entry and exit and government repression of CSOs. Appendix 7B provides a full set of models estimating the relationship between our other predictors of interest and the procedural democracy indexes.

[14] Where the lagged level is the same measure of democracy as the change outcome. Our expectation is that countries with higher levels of democracy will be more stable and thus less prone to change generally, not unlike the way in which economists have expected the rate of growth to slow as economic development proceeds (Barro 1998).

TABLE 7.2 *Summary statistics for outcome variables*

	Level				Change			
	Mean	Std. Dev.	Min	Max	Mean	Std. Dev.	Min	Max
Electoral democracy	0.415	0.282	0.009	0.948	0.004	0.046	−0.519	0.702
Munck procedural democracy	0.321	0.345	0.000	0.947	0.005	0.069	−0.831	0.860
Schumpeter procedural democracy	0.341	0.348	0.000	0.947	0.005	0.073	−0.831	0.868

7.5.5 Estimation Strategy

The full sample covers 156 sovereign countries from 1900 to 2014, a maximum of 10,205 observations. With country-year data, ordinary least squares regression often produces biased and inconsistent estimates. To mitigate against such potential bias, we include country fixed effects. We are unable to include a full battery of control variables for the entire time span under analysis. Rather than sacrificing earlier time periods and reducing our sample due to missing data that are systematically based on geopolitical placement and developmental levels, we opt to control for all within-country factors using fixed intercepts. In addition, because fixed effects models estimate the within-country effects, we can be more confident that our results are not driven by endogenous selection effects between countries.[15] In all models, the main predictors and control variables are lagged by one year to help mitigate against reverse causality. Finally, we include country-clustered robust standard errors to account for heteroskedasticity and year fixed effects to account for temporal dependence. We begin with an initial set of models estimating the level of democracy based on civil society organizational capacity. Thereafter, we focus on annual changes in democracy to better assess the *potential* causal effects of civil society, anti-system movements, and resistance campaigns.

---

[15] This contrasts with population averaged models that estimate the anticipated outcome based on differences between countries with different values on a covariate. With this approach, if some unobserved factor that makes countries more prone to social mobilization also makes those countries more likely to democratize (or autocratize), our comparisons between countries would be biased.

7.6   RESULTS

7.6.1   Civil Society Organizational Capacity

Table 7.3 reports the main results for our stock measure of civil society organizational capacity. In general, the models support the neo-Tocquevillian conclusion that active citizen engagement has salutary effects for democracy. There is a significant positive relationship between civil society organizational capacity and the level of procedural democracy. All else equal, as a country moves from the twenty-fifth percentile (0.41) to the seventy-fifth percentile (0.69) on the civil society stock measure, we see an estimated improvement of 0.18 (out of 1.0) on the Munck procedural democracy index. This is illustrated in Figure 7.1 using predicted margins and 95 percent confidence intervals.

TABLE 7.3   *Civil society organizational capacity and procedural democracy*

	(1) Level	(2) Change	(3) Upturns	(4) Downturns
Civil society	0.651***	0.035**	0.033**	0.002
	(0.079)	(0.012)	(0.010)	(0.006)
GDP per capita (ln)	0.079***	0.007**	0.001	0.006***
	(0.019)	(0.003)	(0.003)	(0.001)
GDP growth (%)	0.045	0.040*	0.006	0.035***
	(0.040)	(0.020)	(0.015)	(0.008)
Oil production (per capita)	−0.003*	−0.000	−0.000	−0.000
	(0.001)	(0.000)	(0.000)	(0.000)
Regional diffusion	0.604***	0.065***	0.035**	0.029***
	(0.093)	(0.015)	(0.012)	(0.008)
Lagged democracy		−0.109***	−0.076***	−0.033***
		(0.011)	(0.008)	(0.005)
Constant	−0.972***	−0.073**	−0.018	−0.055***
	(0.148)	(0.026)	(0.023)	(0.013)
R^2 Overall	0.659	0.040	0.033	0.030
R^2 Within	0.588	0.080	0.070	0.038
R^2 Between	0.635	0.144	0.041	0.082
AIC	−10580.467	−26228.42	−30752.015	−37554.577
BIC	−9720.022	−25367.975	−29891.57	−36694.132

Notes: Estimated coefficients and country-clustered robust standard errors from country and year fixed effects models. Dependent variable is the level and annual change in the Munck procedural democracy index (see Hegre, Bernhard, and Teorrell, 2020). All independent variables are lagged by one year (t_{-1}). N = 10,205; Countries = 156; ^ p < 0.10; * p < 0.05; ** p < 0.01; *** p < 0.001.

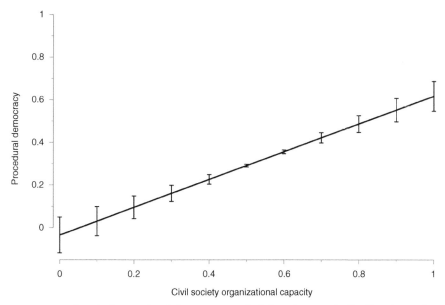

FIGURE 7.1 Level of procedural democracy and civil society stock. Predicted margins and 95 percent confidence intervals based on results from Model 1

The results for annual changes in procedural democracy also support theories about the importance of citizen engagement for democratization. Net annual changes in procedural democracy are associated with higher values on the civil society stock measure. All else equal, as a country moves from the twenty-fifth to the seventy-fifth percentile on civil society organizational capacity, estimated annual changes on the Munck procedural democracy index increase from nearly zero to 0.01. This finding holds when upturns are analyzed as separate phenomena and when procedural democracy is measured using a thinner Schumpeterian conceptualization that does not account for suffrage (see Table 7.B2). It also holds when we employ a country-year specific depreciation rate for the civil society stock measure based on government repression of civil society (see Tables 7.B1 and 7.B2). In addition, the repression-based depreciation measure provides some contingent evidence that higher levels of civil society organizational capacity reinforce against autocratization or democratic downturns. As shown in Figure 7.2, this is not the case for when civil society stock is measured with a constant generational depreciation rate.[16]

---

[16] While this raises greater endogeneity concerns, we also run models testing the short-run effects of the civil society participatory environment using one- and three-year lags. The results are similar but with smaller effect sizes and, as expected, decreasing estimated effects as the lag increases. We report these results in Table 7.B6.

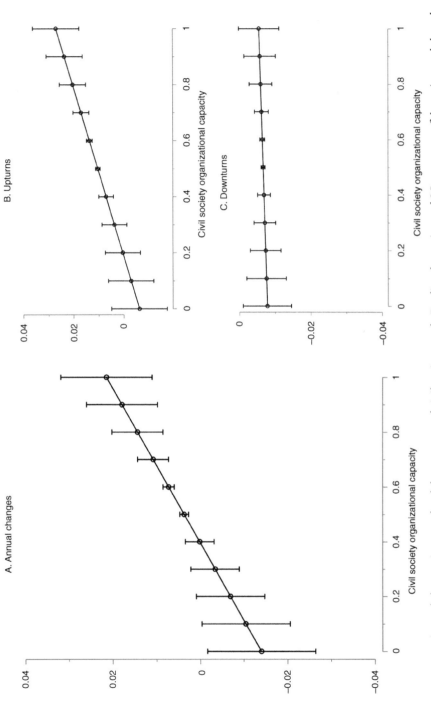

FIGURE 7.2 Annual changes in procedural democracy and civil society stock. Predicted margins and 95 percent confidence intervals based on results from Model 2–4

7.6.2 Civil Society Anti-System Mobilization Using V-Dem

Table 7.4 reports the results from models estimating the relationship between the V-Dem measure of anti-system movement strength and annual changes in electoral democracy using the EDI. The results in Models 6 and 7 suggest that as anti-system movements gather strength, regimes are generally more prone to experience annual changes in electoral democracy *in either direction*. All else equal, countries are expected to experience roughly equal increases in annual upturns and decreases in annual downturns ($\sim$0.01 in either direction) on the EDI as anti-system movement strength increases from the twenty-fifth (–1.42) to the seventy-fifth percentile (0.44). This results in nearly zero correlation between anti-system movements and net overall annual changes democracy

TABLE 7.4 *Strength of anti-system movements and electoral democracy*

	(5) Change	(6) Upturns	(7) Downturns
Anti-system movement strength	–0.000	0.003***	–0.004***
	(0.001)	(0.001)	(0.000)
GDP per capita (ln)	0.003^	0.001	0.002*
	(0.002)	(0.002)	(0.001)
GDP growth (%)	0.033***	0.008	0.024***
	(0.010)	(0.007)	(0.005)
Oil production (per capita)	–0.000	–0.000	–0.000
	(0.000)	(0.000)	(0.000)
Regional diffusion	0.054***	0.028**	0.027***
	(0.013)	(0.011)	(0.007)
Lagged democracy	–0.069***	–0.043***	–0.026***
	(0.007)	(0.006)	(0.003)
Constant	–0.030^	0.003	–0.033**
	(0.017)	(0.014)	(0.011)
R^2 Overall	0.044	0.045	0.044
R^2 Within	0.079	0.08	0.058
R^2 Between	0.121	0.019	0.096
AIC	–34591.618	–39578.921	–46913.818
BIC	–33723.942	–38711.245	–46053.373

Notes: Estimated coefficients and country-clustered robust standard errors from country and year fixed effects models. Dependent variable is the annual change in the electoral democracy index *(v2x_polyarchy)*. All independent variables are lagged by one year (t_{-1}). N = 10,205; Countries = 156; ^ $p < 0.10$; * $p < 0.05$; ** $p < 0.01$; *** $p < 0.001$.

reported in Model 5.[17] In other words, both democratization and autocratization seem to intensify when stronger anti-system movements are in play. This suggests that the regime context and the character of these movements affect how they influence democratic (and autocratic) regime change.

To better understand how the regime context moderates the relationship between anti-system campaigns and levels of democracy, we interact anti-system movement strength with lagged scores on the EDI. This interaction should tell us whether the relationship between anti-system mobilization and annual changes in democracy depends on the existing regime conditions. The results presented in Figure 7.3 suggest that this is the case.[18] This graph plots the estimated slopes and 95 percent confidence intervals for anti-system movement strength at different levels of lagged democracy. Each of the points and confidence intervals represents the estimated effect of a one-unit increase in anti-system movement strength on annual changes, upturns, or downturns in democracy.

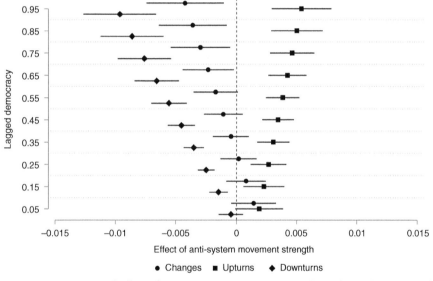

FIGURE 7.3 Estimated effect of anti-system movement strength moderated by levels of electoral democracy (t–1). Predicted effect and 95 percent confidence intervals for a one-unit change in anti-system movement strength on annual changes, upturns, and downturns in electoral democracy given the level of democracy in the year prior (t–1). Based on results from Table 7.B8 (Models 1–3).

[17] This result is similar for procedural democracy reported in Table 7.B7.
[18] For full results using the EDI and the Munck procedural democracy index, see Table 7.B8.

Figure 7.3 suggests that anti-system movement strength has a significant, negative association with annual changes in democracy in countries that already score 0.58 or higher on the EDI. For example, for a country scoring 0.15 on the EDI (or within the nineteenth percentile for our sample, such as Portugal in 1973 and Rwanda in 1994), changes in anti-system movement strength have no significant correlation with annual changes on the EDI. By contrast, for a country scoring 0.65 (the seventy-third percentile, such as Armenia in 1991 and Bolivia in 2014), we see a one-unit increase in anti-system movement strength is associated with 0.002 decline in annual changes on the EDI.[19] While this might seem small, recall that annual changes within our sample average just 0.004 (Table 7.2).

Figure 7.3 also illustrates divergent results for upturns and downturns. At higher levels of democracy, increases in anti-system movement strength are associated with significantly more severe annual downturns in democracy. We also see larger upturns as anti-system movements intensify and the existing levels of democracy are higher; however, this moderating effect is only significant at the 94 percent level (chi^2 = 3.68). These results, combined with the overall negative moderating effects shown for annual changes and downturns, suggest that stronger anti-system movements may present pathways for democratic deterioration rather than democratization in authoritarian regimes.

The relationship between anti-system movements and democratization may also vary by the character of the movement. To test whether this is the case, we incorporate additional information from V-Dem expert-coded indicators on anti-system movements. We focus primarily on their ideological orientation. The results for Model 8 presented in Table 7.5 suggest that left-wing and right-wing anti-system movements do not generally explain annual changes in democracy.[20] However, right-wing movements are associated with significantly more severe downturns when these are treated separately in Model 10. All else equal, as the salience of right-wing mobilization increases from zero to 0.25 (i.e., from the fiftieth to the seventy-fifth percentile), annual downturns in democracy are predicted to grow from −0.005 to −0.008. Again, while these changes seem quite small, they are nevertheless substantial given that the average annual downturn observed in our models is −0.004 (Table 7.2). This finding also holds for our measure of procedural democracy at the 94 percent confidence level (p = 0.059), suggesting that right-wing anti-system movements may have more of a negative association with attacks on the liberal

---

[19] For reference, Figure 7.B1 plots predicted annual changes in the EDI for the twenty-fifth, fiftieth (median), and seventy-fifth percentiles.

[20] We run additional tests to see whether there are interactive effects between the strength of anti-system movements and the salience of right- and left-wing mobilization (Table 7.B10). Among these tests, the interactive effect of anti-system movement strength and right-wing movements is significant for downturns. All others are nonsignificant at the 95 percent level. This suggests that right-wing movements may enhance downturns and that this becomes more severe as the overall strength of anti-system movements increases.

TABLE 7.5 *Anti-system movement character and electoral democracy*

	(8) Change	(9) Upturns	(10) Downturns
Anti-system movement strength	0.000	0.003***	−0.004***
	(0.001)	(0.001)	(0.000)
Left-wing movements	0.000	−0.003	0.003
	(0.004)	(0.004)	(0.002)
Right-wing movements	−0.007	0.004	−0.011**
	(0.006)	(0.005)	(0.004)
GDP per capita (ln)	0.003^	0.001	0.002*
	(0.002)	(0.002)	(0.001)
GDP growth (%)	0.032***	0.009	0.024***
	(0.009)	(0.007)	(0.005)
Oil production (per capita)	−0.000	−0.000	−0.000
	(0.000)	(0.000)	(0.000)
Regional diffusion	0.054***	0.028*	0.026***
	(0.013)	(0.011)	(0.006)
Lagged democracy	−0.068***	−0.044***	−0.024***
	(0.008)	(0.006)	(0.004)
Constant	−0.030^	0.004	−0.034**
	(0.017)	(0.014)	(0.011)
R^2 Overall	0.044	0.045	0.045
R^2 Within	0.079	0.08	0.061
R^2 Between	0.118	0.016	0.095
AIC	−34592.049	−39579.396	−46947.894
BIC	−33709.912	−38697.259	−46072.987

Notes: Estimated coefficients and country-clustered robust standard errors from country and year fixed effects models. Dependent variable is the annual change in the electoral democracy index (*v2x_polyarchy*). All independent variables are lagged by one year (t_{-1}). N = 10,205; Countries = 156; ^ p < 0.10; * p < 0.05; ** p < 0.01; *** p < 0.001.

components of democracy like freedom of association and expression, rather than procedural ones directly related to the function of elections.[21]

We also tested for the effects of ethnic- and religious-based anti-system movements from the V-Dem dataset (Table 7.B13). The tests detected no relationship between ethnic-based anti-system movements and democratization. However, we do find a negative association between religious-based anti-system

---

[21] For full results, see Table 7.B9.

groups and annual changes in democracy. They also seemed to be associated with weaker upturns in democracy but had no statistically significant effect on downturns.

In Tables 7.B11 and 7.B12, we check for any moderating effects of existing levels of democracy and civil society organizational capacity on the relationship between ideological anti-system movements and democratization. These results suggest that as existing levels of democracy increase, left-wing mobilization is associated with significantly higher annual changes in democracy. This is driven by less severe annual downturns, with no significant relationship to annual upturns. In other words, left-wing movements tend to protect against democratic backsliding in more advanced democracies but may not be as successful at encouraging autocratic regimes to democratize (see Figure 7.B2). We do not find similar results for civil society organizational capacity as a moderator for left-wing mobilization. By contrast, the results show little evidence that the impact of right-wing mobilization is moderated by civil society organizational capacity or existing levels of democracy. The one exception to this is change in level of procedural democracy, where right-wing anti-system movements are associated with larger decreases in the level of democracy at higher levels of civil society organizational capacity. This finding is consistent with the casework of Berman (1997) and Riley (2010) on how right-wing capture of civil society mobilization has been used to undermine democracy. This provides some support for the logic of the bad civil society argument.

7.6.3 Civil Society Mobilization Using NAVCO

To further explore how the nature of civil society mobilization correlates with annual changes in electoral democracy, we run models accounting for resistance campaigns and their primary tactics as found in the NAVCO dataset. Table 7.6 estimates the relationship for ongoing violent and nonviolent campaigns. As shown in Model 11, nonviolent mobilization during the previous year is associated with significantly higher annual growth in democracy. This finding holds when we consider annual upturns separately in Model 12. Meanwhile, annual downturns in electoral democracy appear to be more severe when the country experienced a violent resistance campaign during the previous year as shown in Model 13. The correlation between violent campaigns and democratic downturns falls below standard significance levels (p = 0.09) when using the Munck procedural democracy index.[22] This suggests that violent resistance campaigns may have a greater negative effect on downturns in liberal components of democracy like freedom of expression or association, rather than electoral procedures.[23]

[22] See Figure 7.B14 for estimates using the Munck measure of procedural democracy.
[23] These results are generally reflective of those found in the literature using other measures of violent and nonviolent resistance (Teorell 2010). We also provide estimates using the cross-national time series dataset, originally developed by Arthur S. Banks (1971) and currently maintained by

TABLE 7.6 *Violent and nonviolent resistance campaigns*

	(11) Change	(12) Upturns	(13) Downturns
Violent campaign	−0.003	0.003	−0.005***
	(0.002)	(0.002)	(0.002)
Nonviolent campaign	0.036***	0.037***	−0.001
	(0.008)	(0.008)	(0.002)
GDP per capita (ln)	0.003	0.000	0.003***
	(0.002)	(0.002)	(0.001)
GDP growth (%)	0.034**	0.008	0.026***
	(0.011)	(0.008)	(0.005)
Oil production (per capita)	−0.000	0.000	−0.000^
	(0.000)	(0.000)	(0.000)
Regional diffusion	0.056***	0.033**	0.024***
	(0.013)	(0.011)	(0.006)
Lagged democracy	−0.060***	−0.040***	−0.021***
	(0.007)	(0.006)	(0.003)
Constant	−0.031^	0.009	−0.040***
	(0.018)	(0.014)	(0.010)
R^2 Overall	0.062	0.069	0.031
R^2 Within	0.093	0.102	0.043
R^2 Between	0.053	0.028	0.031
AIC	−31445.879	−35968.841	−42377.699
BIC	−30632.603	−35155.565	−41571.557

Notes: Estimated coefficients and country-clustered robust standard errors from country and year fixed effects models. Dependent variable is the annual change in the electoral democracy index *(v2x_polyarchy)*. All independent variables are lagged by one year (t_{-1}). N = 9,265; Countries = 157; ^ p < 0.10; * p < 0.05; ** p < 0.01; *** p < 0.001.

The NAVCO data also allow us to test for the immediate and long-term relationship between resistance campaigns and democratization after these campaigns have ended. At the campaign level, Chenoweth and Stephan (2011) show that nonviolent resistance produces significantly greater democratization five

Databanks International (Banks and Wilson, 2018). While the number of peaceful demonstrations during the previous year are generally associated with democratization (as shown in Table 7.B20) the effect is quite small (0.001) and not robust to estimation limited to democratic upturns. Unlike Teorell (2010), we also see some evidence that the number of riots (i.e., violent protests) during the previous year promote annual movement in either direction for electoral democracy (and procedural democracy at the 90 percent confidence level). We also replicate the null finding for labor strikes. Given the results from Dahlum et al. (2019), this suggests that the effects of general labor strike activity differ markedly from sustained organized labor mobilization against the regime.

years later. However, their models are limited to the set of cases that experienced a resistance campaign, and thus might be prone to selection effects. Specifically, the reason for cessation of a nonviolent campaign on balance is likely to be success. Suppression by force could well be met with counterviolence and thus change the nature of the campaign. Likewise, their models are limited to the effects five years later. Instead, we introduce a series of models in Table 7.B15 that account for long-term effects by interacting indicators for the campaign type and years since the most recent campaign ended (or entry if no previous campaign has occurred). We present predicted margins and 95 percent confidence intervals from these models in Figure 7.4. All else equal, the year after a violent campaign ends, the estimated annual change in electoral democracy is 0.011. By contrast, if that same campaign had been nonviolent, electoral democracy would have increased by about 0.060, a significant difference. These effects appear to persist for some time (around fifteen years) with diminishing magnitude. Starting at about twelve years after the campaign ended, similar estimated annual changes in democracy are observed for violent and nonviolent campaigns.

In the appendix, we report the additional models estimating the relationship between other types of resistance campaigns found in the NAVCO dataset and democratization. Drawing on extensive data collection efforts by Dahlum, Knutsen, and Wig (2019), we estimate the associated rates of democratization when social mobilization is dominated by industrial workers, the middle class, peasants, and other sectors of society. The results presented in Table 7.B17 largely replicate these authors' earlier work, suggesting that when resistance campaigns are dominated by industrial workers, they have a robust positive relationship with rates of democratization.[24]

We also use the Dahlum, Knutsen, and Wig coding to test the general validity of time- and space-bound theories of class-based coalitions in the promotion of democratic outcomes. Specifically, we address Luebbert's theory (1991) of social democracy as a product of a working class and farmer alliance in interwar Europe, as well as, theories of a middle-sector (working and middle class) alliances as a path to democracy in Latin America (O'Donnell 1973; Rueschemeyer et al. 1992).[25] Our tests presented in Table 7.7 provide support for the idea that both of these campaign configurations, when concluded, are associated with positive changes in the EDI and enhanced democratic upturns. The results show similar effects while these campaigns are ongoing, except for

---

[24] The middle class may also contribute to democratic upturns, but with less robust results. Annual downturns in electoral democracy appear to be more severe when peasants dominate resistance movements; however, this finding does not hold for procedural definitions of democracy.

[25] To qualify for Luebbert's working class and farmer coalition, the resistance campaign must include industrial workers and peasants, with one of these two groups dominating. To qualify for the middle-sectors thesis, the resistance campaign must include industrial workers and the middle class, with one of these two groups dominating. We also report results using the Munck procedural democracy index in Table 7.B16.

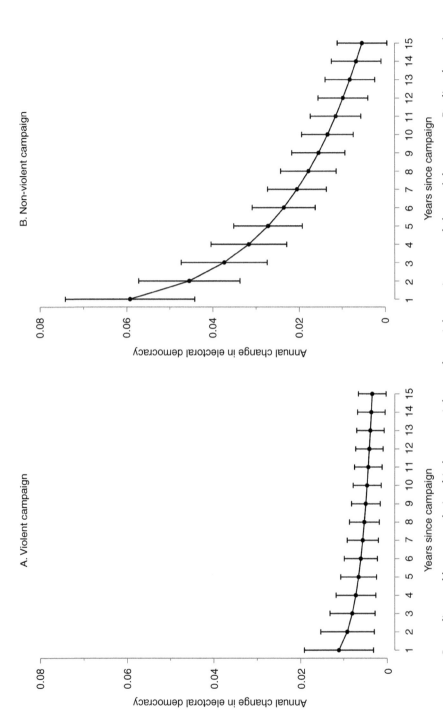

FIGURE 7.4 Immediate and long-run relationship between violent and nonviolent resistance and electoral democracy. Predicted margins and 95 percent confidence intervals based on results from Table 7.B15 (Models 1–3).

TABLE 7.7 *Resistance campaigns by class-based coalitions and subsequent electoral democracy*

	(14) Change	(15) Upturns	(16) Downturns	(17) Change	(18) Upturns	(19) Downturns
Luebbert campaign ended	0.076**	0.086***	-0.010			
	(0.023)	(0.022)	(0.010)			
Middle sector campaign ended				0.094***	0.099***	-0.005
				(0.019)	(0.018)	(0.007)
Other campaign ended	0.030***	0.033***	-0.004	0.020**	0.024***	-0.005^
	(0.007)	(0.006)	(0.002)	(0.007)	(0.006)	(0.003)
Campaign ongoing	-0.003	0.004^	-0.007***	-0.003	0.004^	-0.007***
	(0.002)	(0.002)	(0.002)	(0.002)	(0.002)	(0.002)
GDP per capita (ln)	0.004^	0.001	0.003***	0.004^	0.001	0.003***
	(0.002)	(0.002)	(0.001)	(0.002)	(0.002)	(0.001)
GDP growth (%)	0.031**	0.007	0.025***	0.032**	0.008	0.025***
	(0.010)	(0.008)	(0.005)	(0.010)	(0.008)	(0.005)
Oil production (per capita)	-0.000	-0.000	-0.000	-0.000	-0.000	-0.000
	(0.000)	(0.000)	(0.000)	(0.000)	(0.000)	(0.000)
Regional diffusion	0.055***	0.034**	0.022***	0.056***	0.034**	0.022***
	(0.013)	(0.011)	(0.006)	(0.013)	(0.011)	(0.006)
Lagged democracy	-0.063***	-0.042***	-0.02***	-0.062***	-0.041***	-0.021***
	(0.007)	(0.006)	(0.003)	(0.007)	(0.006)	(0.003)

(*continued*)

TABLE 7.7 (*continued*)

	(14) Change	(15) Upturns	(16) Downturns	(17) Change	(18) Upturns	(19) Downturns
Constant	-0.034^	0.003	-0.037***	-0.033^	0.004	-0.037***
	(0.018)	(0.014)	(0.010)	(0.018)	(0.014)	(0.010)
R^2 Overall	0.063	0.076	0.035	0.069	0.087	0.035
R^2 Within	0.096	0.111	0.046	0.102	0.121	0.045
R^2 Between	0.074	0.06	0.022	0.067	0.046	0.022
AIC	-31472.141	-36069.996	-42398.275	-31538.087	-36166.569	-42396.52
BIC	-30651.732	-35249.587	-41577.865	-30717.677	-35346.159	-41576.11

Notes: Estimated coefficients and country-clustered robust standard errors from country and year fixed effects models. Dependent variable is the annual change in the electoral democracy index (*v2x_polyarchy*). All independent variables are lagged by one year (t_{-1}). $N = 9,265$; Countries = 157; $\wedge p < 0.10$; $* p < 0.05$; $** p < 0.01$; $*** p < 0.001$.

some evidence of short-term contractions in the level of electoral democracy (undoubtedly from short-term repression).[26]

7.7 DISCUSSION AND CONCLUSIONS

A rich literature contends that social forces play important roles in effecting regime change. The neo-Tocquevillian school contends that civic organization enhances (and is perhaps even essential) to the functioning of democracy. This approach focuses on how associational life fosters positive citizen engagement and bonds of social trust, developing an underlying level of social capital within a society. Meanwhile, neo-Gramscian theories address distinct episodes of political mobilization as crucial elements within episodes of democratization. Periods of mass mobilization pressure regimes to introduce democratic reforms that reduce limits on competition or include previously excluded groups in the system of competition. Nevertheless, the picture is not always so positive. Scholars have also contended that civil society can sometimes take on an *uncivil* nature, fomenting violence and triggering episodes of autocratization. In this chapter, our approach was to explore whether support exists for these dynamics within a large sample of countries across several generations.

The neo-Tocquevillian argument is perhaps the most challenging to model in such a context. While case-based evidence supports the argument that countries with higher levels of civic engagement tend to have more stable democracies (Putnam et al. 1994), it is also highly likely that the development of social capital is contingent upon associational guarantees that are often embedded within definitions of liberal democracy. Thus, to avoid engaging in tautology, we limited our analysis of the neo-Tocquevillian argument to minimalistic and highly procedural measures of democracy. To proxy social capital, we developed a novel measure of CSO capacity conceptualized as a stock that accumulates within a polity but depreciates over time. Here we find robust empirical support for the idea that civil society organizational capacity promotes democratic development.

To assess the role of contentious politics, we modeled the effects of anti-system movements as operationalized in the V-Dem data, as well as resistance campaigns measured by the NAVCO project. Consistent with actor-centered accounts of regime change we find that anti-system movements and campaigns for change are ever-present actors in many forms of regime change and depending on the context and the nature of the actor, important to processes of both democratization and autocratization. Therefore, both the strength and nature of mobilization are important for establishing explanations about how social forces affect democratization. We also find that the nature of the existing regime affects the impact of anti-system movements. In more democratic

---

[26] These models are reported in Table 7.B18. The downturn finding is not robust when the Munck procedural measure of democracy is used in Table 7.B19.

polities the presence of anti-system actors tends to be associated with autocratization, whereas in highly authoritarian regimes they are more likely to be associated with democratizing change.

When we turn to the ideological motivations behind anti-system movements, the results indicate that democratic downturns are exacerbated in the face of salient right-wing anti-system movements. This is congruent with the upsurge in far-right extremism and populism, and the current backlash against liberal democracy (Plattner 2019). It is also congruent with an older established line of research that explored the rise of interwar fascist regimes in Europe or bureaucratic authoritarianism in Latin America (Linz 1978). We find some limited evidence for variants of theories of bad civil society (Berman 1997; Riley 2010). Generally speaking, right-wing anti-system movements, but not left wing, constitute an enduring threat to democracy. Furthermore, when civil society is strong, it contributes to stronger deteriorations in cases of downturn. This also provides limited support for the assumptions of the distributionist school of regime change. Right-wing backlash seems to exacerbate crises of democracy, though we find little evidence that left-wing mobilization provokes it.

This study confirms previous findings about violent and nonviolent mobilization. Violent resistance campaigns are associated with more severe democratic declines, and their net negative effects continue to accrue over time for several years. By contrast, nonviolent campaigns are associated with immediate and long-term positive changes in democracy. Finally, this study provides the first statistical evidence that confirms the findings on specific patterns of class coalition derived from the comparative historical work on regime trajectories in twentieth-century Latin America by Rueschemeyer, Stephens and Stephens (1992) and interwar Western Europe by Luebbert (1991). Moreover, the predicted association is significant for a global sample, and thus exhibits patterns of generalizability.

8

Causal Sequences in Long-Term Democratic Development and Decline

Michael Coppedge, Amanda B. Edgell, Carl Henrik Knutsen, and Staffan I. Lindberg

The goal of this book has been to review and retest many of the major hypotheses about democratization and democratic decline by using Varieties of Democracy data. In this chapter, we use "punctuated equilibrium" as a framework to understand why democratization tends to happen in spurts and setbacks that interrupt periods of relative stability. Stability, we argue, is the norm because several deep-historical static or slowly changing conditions, such as geography and demography, set the stage for the possibility of democratization. Furthermore, these distal conditions give rise to gradually evolving intermediate forces, some associated with modernization, that tend to reinforce one another while they contribute to democracy. These forces promote institutional development in the form of institutionalized political parties and impartial state bureaucracies, which also reinforce each other and form a "protective belt" that tends to stabilize both democratic and undemocratic regimes. Nevertheless, other intermediate and proximate variables such as civil society activity and short-term economic performance can upset the stable equilibrium, producing sudden upturns and downturns.

Because retesting so many hypotheses is a daunting challenge requiring deep mastery of diverse literatures, ready access to additional evidence from outside the V-Dem dataset, and considerable research time, the collaborators on this volume agreed on a division of labor, with specialized chapters on geography and demography, international influences, economic conditions, civil society, and institutions. Since existing theories and empirical studies suggest that several of the proposed causal factors may have very different effects on different types of regime outcomes, most chapters distinguish among the possible causes of levels of democracy, change in democracy, and upturns (positive annual changes) and downturns (negative annual changes). As a consequence of these choices, each chapter's conclusions are rich and complex; the conclusions of all the chapters combined are even richer and more complex. Collectively, the foregoing chapters have nevertheless ruled out some common explanations of democratic development. They have also found empirical support for some explanations that have hitherto received less attention and developed theory about how, why, and under what conditions each explanation holds true.

In Chapter 3, Gerring focuses on static or slowly changing determinants of average levels of polyarchy (a term we use interchangeably with "electoral democracy" and, often, simply "democracy") across countries. He finds that distance from natural harbors and a warm climate are unfavorable to democracy, while Protestant and European-descended populations are favorable factors. Moreover, ethnic heterogeneity may help and religious heterogeneity may hurt democracy, but these relationships are not robust. Gerring is finally agnostic about the negative empirical relationship of democracy with Islam.

Gerring's study of the most exogenous factors sets the stage for the study of various other determinants of democratic development. In Chapter 4, Coppedge, Denison, Friesen, Tiscornia, and Xu find that when countries experience an upturn or a downturn in electoral democracy, their neighbors tend to change in the same direction, albeit to a much smaller degree. Similarly, countries surrounded by democratic neighbors tend to become more democratic down the road. Although this effect is initially small, positive feedback over several decades among groups of democratic neighbors amplifies the gap between them and groups of undemocratic neighbors. This effect is larger in more democratic regions (Western Europe, North America, Australia, and New Zealand; Eastern Europe; and Latin America) than in less democratic regions (Asia, Africa, and the Middle East). Furthermore, other kinds of international networks such as alliances and colonial relationships influence selected regime outcomes as well. Specifically, upturns tend to spread among alliance members, while alliances appear to inhibit the spread of downturns; and upturns tend to spread to and from current and former colonies and their colonizers. Exogenous shocks sometimes matter as well: international war tends to harm democracy in the short term, while global economic expansions are beneficial.

In Chapter 5, Knutsen and Dahlum reassess several major economic hypotheses concerning per capita income, industrialization, economic growth, inequality, and their relationships with democracy levels and changes, as well as democratization and democratic decline. Contrary to recent claims that the relationship between income and democracy is spurious, they find that per capita GDP tends to raise the level of democracy and temper the severity of downturns; but that it does not systematically contribute to upturns. Another robust finding is that the more the economy relies on agricultural production, the smaller upturns tend to be. Moreover, the authors find that strong short-term economic growth renders downturns less severe.

In Chapter 6 on institutions, Hicken, Baltz, and Vasselai produce strong evidence that state capacity (measured as professionalized bureaucracy) aids electoral democracy. However, they find that, whether one wishes to explain levels of or changes in democracy, the empirical evidence regarding the presidentialism versus parliamentarism debate and various hypotheses about the relevance of party systems is inconclusive.

Finally, in Chapter 7, Bernhard and Edgell present the hitherto most comprehensive demonstration that democracy benefits from a civil society with high organizational capacity, vibrant social movement campaigns, and nonviolent protest. They also show the converse, that right-wing anti-system movements pose a serious threat to democracy.

In this concluding chapter, our task is to fit these partial explanations together into a more comprehensive model and suggest a theoretical story that is consistent with the abovementioned empirical relationships. To some degree, this is necessarily an exploratory exercise, subject to the well-known risk of capitalizing on chance. We did not start with a comprehensive overarching theory and derive from it a series of hypotheses to be tested with our data. Instead, we begin with empirical relationships (most of which are consistent with existing theories laid out in previous chapters), which we attempt to knit together into a compelling overarching theory.[1]

Two empirical relationships that underlie all the preceding chapters demand attention. First, more of the global variation in democracy happens between countries than within countries. Simply and concretely, in OLS regressions, time (year dummies) accounts for 24 percent of the variance in the Electoral Democracy Index (EDI) from 1900 to 2017, whereas place (country dummies) accounts for 55 percent. This suggests that we could explain more than half of the variance in democracy if we could explain the large, long-lasting differences between countries, also known as country fixed effects. Every student of democratization knows about this pattern, but in recent years few have focused on it as a research question. Given that so much of the variation stems from differences between countries, we think it important to pay attention to these "big drivers" of democracy. Gerring does so in Chapter 3, and we build on his efforts in this chapter.

Second, changes in electoral democracy consist of many small, incremental shifts, interrupted by very few large upturns or downturns. Half of the annual upturn observations in the EDI are between zero and 0.10 (on a scale of 0 to 1), while only 10 percent are between 0.64 and 1. Likewise, half of the downturns are between zero and −0.08, while only 10 percent are between −0.46 and −1.[2] In studies of evolution, earthquakes, policy change (Baumgartner et al. 2009; Jensen et al. 2019), and war, this pattern of relative stability is called punctuated

---

[1] A few variables tested in preceding chapters are not retested here.
[2] The upturns calculation excludes the downturn observations, which are coded zero, and the downturns calculation excludes the upturn observations, which are coded zero.

equilibrium. This concept applies to democratization as well (Capoccia and Ziblatt 2010). The models that we develop here explain this pattern, first by explaining how equilibria arise and persist, then by explaining the forces that can disrupt those equilibria.

This chapter includes additional data analysis that provides more guidance about how to combine hypotheses from different theories into a more comprehensive whole. One of the thorniest challenges in this enterprise is deciding which variables to include and which ways to point the causal arrows that connect them. Several of the factors explored in this volume are also likely to exhibit two-way or reverse causality. For example, theories about social capital (Putnam 1994) and civic culture (Almond and Verba 1963) suggest that experiences with democracy foster civil society, which, in turn, insulates democracy from downturns. In addition, past experiences of civil society participation may build upon one another, meaning that variables capturing social mobilization contain considerable inertia. Combining hypotheses from different chapters multiplies such questions, not least because there are presumably causal relationships between factors treated as controls in other chapters. Do national-level institutions give rise to and constrain civil society organizations, or do those organizations get laws passed that shape the institutions? In this chapter, we face these challenges by restricting our models to the variables identified as important by previous chapters, allowing them to influence one another in every possible way that makes theoretical sense, and using path analysis – a type of structural equation modeling – to reveal which theorized causal paths are most consistent with the empirical patterns in the data.

As noted in the introduction, all of our empirical work consists of analysis of observational data, so ultimately, we cannot claim to have run truly decisive tests of causal hypotheses. Experiments, whether lab, natural, or field, provide the least-confounded inferences about causal relationships. However, by design they avoid examining complex multicausal processes that unfold over time (Bisbee et al. 2017). They also lack external validity: they simply cannot test hypotheses that cover nearly all countries in the entire modern democratic era. Causal identification from experiments is only one of the strategies for learning about the world, and it is rarely a feasible strategy for assessing the questions asked in this book. One cannot run experiments on countries' geography, neighborhood, alliances, economic development, institutions, or civil society. All of the preceding chapters were informed by large literatures that included case studies and small-N comparisons, as well as large-N analysis of observational data. Each methodological approach brings its own insights and blind spots (Coppedge 2012; Coppedge and Kuehn 2019). Case studies benefit from nuanced concepts, evidence, and careful process-tracing but say little about generalization and invariant causes. Small-N comparisons advance toward conceptual and empirical generalization and incorporate variation in a larger number of potential explanations but multiply confounders and sacrifice some nuance without generalizing very far.

Our large-N quantitative analysis has weaknesses as well. It leads us to overlook causal heterogeneity by region or historical period, it leaves us to speculate about multiple mechanisms that might account for the empirical relationships we report, it forces us to omit variables that have not been measured in our large sample, it increases specification uncertainty, and so on. Nonetheless, we consider it the best practical way to evaluate the general truth of beliefs about causes of democracy and its dynamics.[3] However, we stress that the building blocks for the synthesizing exercise in this chapter are not merely empirical correlations. Every hypothesis is backed by a plausible story. As the extensive literature reviews attest, existing theories of democratization guide Chapters 3–7 in the selection of variables from the start. We begin, therefore, with explanations that other scholars have developed into theory and that many scholars consider relevant for explaining democracy levels, upturns, or downturns.[4] Many of these theories have gained traction and some are widely believed in the community of democracy scholars. The fact that previous chapters performed empirical testing that winnowed many theoretically grounded and widely accepted hypotheses into a smaller set of hypotheses that are not only consistent with some evidence, but in fact more consistent with the best available evidence than many competing hypotheses, should only burnish their credibility. This next stage of theory building therefore stands on unusually solid ground.

Thus, readers should approach this chapter as a theory development exercise informed by a lot of prior theory and new empirical evidence. That is the gap we seek to fill, for the benefit of the many people who need reasonable conclusions about processes on this scale – teachers, students, policymakers, journalists, and even experimentalists who need to know which ideas are worth their attention. In that sense, it is an invitation for others to test our conclusions in other ways.

8.1 OVERVIEW OF ARGUMENTS

In this section we summarize our main conclusions. Most fundamentally, we believe that understanding a process as complex and long-term as democratization over more than a century requires distinguishing distal causes from proximate ones. Each kind of cause must play a different role in

---

[3] We use causal language in this book because we deal with theories and hypotheses about causal relationships, which we understand as possessing constant conjunction, proximity, temporal priority, and theoretical reasons to expect that such relationships are true. We believe that using causal language does not require us to employ the best methods for ruling out confounders, which are inapplicable to the scale of the phenomenon we seek to understand. Alternative terms, such as "descriptive relationships" or "empirical regularities," do not reflect the serious efforts we have made to meet the criteria for causal inference, however imperfect our tests may be.

[4] Unlike the preceding chapters, this one does not model change (irrespective of direction) in electoral democracy because we observed that in most of the previous chapters, coefficients of change were very close to the sum of the coefficients for upturns and downturns.

a comprehensive theory. The distal causes are distant in the sense that they came into being long ago, often before the modern democratic era. They are static or change slowly, and it is therefore usually safe to treat them as exogenous variables. They include features of geography (such as climate zone and distance from natural harbors), ethnic fractionalization, Protestant population, and the proportion of the population descended from Europeans. In contrast, proximate causes developed more recently through human activity and tend to change frequently or radically. Many of these variables must be assumed to be endogenous. Examples include short-term economic performance (growth, inflation, the value of mineral exports[5]) and social movement campaigns.

Between the distal and proximate causes lie intermediate causes of two kinds: "distinct" and "similar" intermediate causes. The first are conceptually distinct from "democracy" but are too dynamic and recent in origin to be treated as exogenous. In fact, they tend to be endogenous to more distal and other intermediate causes. At the same time, they help shape the proximate causes of democracy. Therefore, they provide some potential causal linkages between the distal and proximate causes. This set of causes includes some of the most widely studied socioeconomic determinants of democracy: per capita GDP, literacy, and the development of industry versus agriculture.

The second kind of intermediate causes consists of institutions and organizations that lie on the conceptual periphery of democracy: things that are almost, but not quite, part of democracy itself, at least when employing a somewhat narrow conception of democracy, such as the one underlying our Electoral Democracy index. Similar intermediate causes, therefore are more likely to be empirically associated with democracy. They also tend to be somewhat dynamic, although change is often episodic. Our examples are the rule of law, institutionalized political parties, and a vibrant civil society.[6]

Astute readers will have noticed that none of these explanatory factors is new; other scholars added them to the list of likely causes of democracy long ago. Our contribution, therefore, is not to add new hypotheses to the list; it is to show where each explanatory factor belongs in a new, more comprehensive causal sequence. Getting the causal sequence right could help resolve some long-running

---

[5] The presence of oil or other exportable minerals in a country's territory could be treated as a distal variable, as it was determined by geology before the evolution of Homo sapiens. However, the variable we use is the value of exports of such minerals as a percentage of GDP, which also depends on the development of an oil industry and fluctuates dramatically depending on world commodity prices. This variable therefore plays a hybrid role as a proximate factor that is largely exogenous.

[6] Our rule of law variable is the same variable, V-Dem's *v2clrspct*, or "Transparent laws with predictable enforcement," that the authors of Chapter 6 label "state capacity." We think it makes as much, if not more, sense to interpret this variable as measuring a thin concept of the rule of law. We must also make it clear that this variable is only one of the variables used in V-Dem's index *v2xcl_rol*, which captures a thicker concept of the rule of law despite its label, "Equality before the law and individual liberty index." We apologize for confusing our readers. Instances in which substituting the thicker index for the thin measure makes a difference are noted in the empirical sections.

debates in the empirical democratization literature, such as the debate about whether per capita GDP causes transitions, merely sustains democracy, or has only a spurious relationship to democracy (Acemoglu et al. 2008; Gassebner et al. 2013; Jackman 1973; Przeworki and Limongi 1997; Rød et al. 2020). Another example pertains to debates about whether climate, "cool water," and historical inequality are useful for explaining democratization in the present day (Acemoglu et al. 2001; Ansell and Samuels 2014; Mellinger et al. 2000; Welzel 2013). Causally distant or historical "upstream" causes are likely to have insignificant effects if proximate "downstream" causes are included as covariates in the same additive model. Consequently, researchers who specify their models differently tend to disagree about which variables matter. They would be more likely to agree, or at least have more fruitful discussions, if they would specify the causal sequences appropriately. An important specific example: In our causal sequence models, the most frequently tested predictor in the literature, the log of per capita GDP, has no direct effect on levels, upturns, or downturns. However, it is a significant indirect predictor of all three. All of its contributions are mediated by other variables.

Strictly speaking, our sequential claims concern causal rather than temporal sequences, although the two types of sequences can be related. This way of thinking is similar to reasoning about causal mechanisms and mediation analysis or the Michigan School's "funnel of causality" (Campbell et al. 1980), although our analysis is on a grand scale. Such relationships are best depicted in path diagrams. The key question is whether X → Y and W → Y, rather than X → W → Y or W → X → Y. In other words, do X and W both have an independent effect on Y, or is the influence of one of these variables channeled through (mediated by) the other? Both possibilities could be true to some degree, but the more completely one variable channels the contributions of another, the more useful it is to treat them as steps in a sequence.

We believe that the fourfold distinction among distal, distinct-intermediate, similar-intermediate, and proximate causes is a useful heuristic, but we do not use it rigidly. Other explanatory variables may not fit neatly in any of these categories or even the exogenous-to-endogenous continuum on which they lie. For example, economic growth rates and international shocks such as wars and pandemics are dynamic and temporally proximate, but conceptually completely distinct from democracy. Other international influences such as geographic proximity and colonial ties are hybrids: networks with deep historical roots that serve as conduits for short-term dynamic stimuli. Table 8.B1 in Appendix 8B describes all variables used in this chapter.

Figure 8.1 provides some empirical justification for our distinctions among types of causes. The horizontal axis shows how well values on each variable are explained by their value a decade prior.[7] The distal variables display very strong

---

[7] "Dependence" here is the coefficient of each variable at time t-10 in a panel regression that uses it to explain the same variable at time t, controlling for year dummies, with errors clustered by

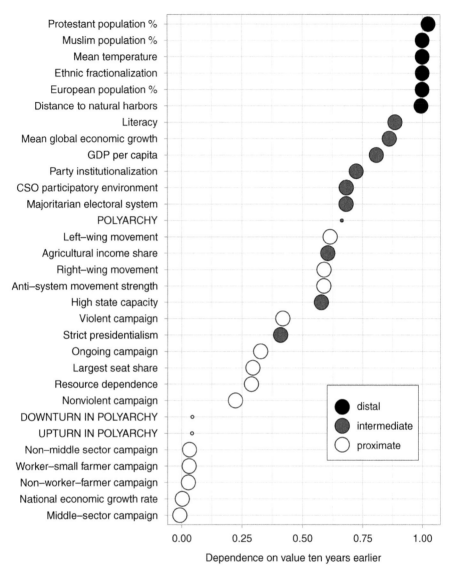

FIGURE 8.1 A rough criterion for causal proximity

time dependence. For most of the proximate variables, the ten-year lag explains less than half of the variance. For most of the intermediate variables, the lag explains

country. The sample is from 1900 to 2017. Some variables, such as literacy, would show less time dependence if the nineteenth Century were included. Time dependence may be exaggerated for variables that were interpolated from sparse data.

more than half, but less than all, of the variance. The correspondence is not perfect because some social movement campaigns are long-lasting and "strict presidentialism" changes with every suspension of elections. Nevertheless, the distinction is still useful in a loose sense. The EDI – our dependent variable – lies near the center of the distribution, which helps explain why both static and dynamic variables are correlated with it. Upturns and downturns are much more dynamic, and therefore likely to be better explained by the proximate variables ranked close to it.

It is important to understand these differences and model them appropriately so that the more proximate causes do not "eclipse" – render invisible – the more distal ones. The intermediate causes can eclipse the distal causes, in the sense that if both kinds of causes are treated as exogenous explanations of electoral democracy, several of the distal causes lose statistical significance. In effect, the distal causes do help explain levels of democracy, but the contributions of many of them are channeled completely through the intermediate causes. In a similar way, the proximate causes may eclipse the distal and intermediate ones. The more proximate a cause is, the greater the risk that it is a "post-treatment confounder" relative to the more distal causes.

The latter observation does not mean that one should never include both distal and proximate variables in a model. Whether it is appropriate to do so depends on where one's focus lies. If the variables of interest are proximate, as in most short-term case studies, they must be included, even if they make it appear that distal variables do not matter. If the variables of interest are distal, as in macro-historical analyses, proximate variables may well obscure their contributions, but this is most likely when the model ignores the possibility that the proximate variables are endogenous to the distal ones. Further in the text we explain how path analysis helps specify these endogenous relationships appropriately and can make it possible to include distal and proximate variables in the same model without favoring one or the other as the primary focus of the analysis.

We find the distinction among distal, intermediate, and proximate causes is useful for explaining levels of democracy. Concretely, if a country enjoys the rule of law, institutionalized parties, and vibrant civil society, the level of electoral democracy can be high in the short term even if the level of socioeconomic development is low. (In the longer term, however, poor socioeconomic conditions may well erode the proximate features.) We then show that the same distinction also clarifies the different roles played by geography, demography, modernization, economic growth, institutions, and social movements in both upturns and downturns in democracy, as measured by our EDI.

Another key part of our argument is that the similar intermediate institutions and actors – institutionalized parties, the rule of law, and especially civil society – tend to reinforce one another. This is not only a plausible theoretical proposition, but something we find clear empirical support for in the analysis later. If the contributions of these features are all favorable to democracy, they tend to remain in equilibrium, providing a stable favorable environment for democracy; if they are all harmful to democracy, they provide a stable unfavorable environment, so it is hard for democracy to emerge, both now and in the future. If one feature is out of sync, the others tend to bring it up (or down) to their level. We find that these intermediate features form an important self-reinforcing protective belt around the democratic (or nondemocratic) regime. This belt helps explain why levels of democracy tend to be incremental and dramatic changes are rare. Democracy – and non-democracy – tends to exist in a punctuated equilibrium (Eldredge and Gould 1972; Goertz 2003). Most states vary only slightly from some stable position on the democracy–non-democracy continuum for years, but then suddenly experience a more dramatic transition or breakdown. The historical norm is that few states change slowly and gradually over decades, although the most recent and current "wave" of autocratization is characterized by such incremental changes leading to "slow deaths" of democracy (e.g., Lührmann and Lindberg 2019).

Another important finding from our analysis is that levels, upturns, and downturns in democracy are not only different phenomena, but also have quite different sets of causal factors. Not only are the sets distinct, but they also vary in magnitude; most notably, we find more predictors of democratic upturns than downturns. This pattern resembles those found in sensitivity analysis performed on dichotomized democracy measures, capturing democratic transitions and democratic breakdowns (Gassebner et al. 2013; Rød et al. 2020). These differences could stem from different processes. As noted by Rød et al. this could partly reflect "less variation and, thus, greater uncertainty in estimates associated with the fewer transitions to dictatorship from democracy than vice versa … The large difference could [also] reflect that previous theoretical efforts and empirical studies, which have informed our variable selection, are more attuned to explaining democratization … But, democratic breakdowns also could be processes that inherently are harder to explain than democratization episodes" (Rød et al. 2020: 102–104). However, it is also possible that the hypotheses entertained in this volume favor understanding upturns over downturns and that we have overlooked some factors that would account for downturns better.

Table 8.1 summarizes the best proximate, intermediate, and distal determinants of levels, upturns, and downturns according to the more detailed models presented later in this chapter.[8] Predictors that affect the democracy

---

[8] This chapter does not retest many of the variables that appear in preceding chapters for various reasons. First, we excluded many variables from Chapter 3 because they do not vary much, or at all, over time and we therefore could not include them in our many models that use fixed-effects estimation. This decision excluded Early democracy, Muslim population, Agricultural suitability, Desert share of territory, Irrigation potential, Island, Land area, Landlocked, Precipitation, Region, River distance, Ruggedness, Small state, Fertile soil, Tropical share of territory, Islamic conquest, Arabic language, State history to 1500, Gender equality, Frost days, Caloric suitability, Caloric variability, Fish, and Mountains. Although we were able to include some relatively invariant variables in the random-effects estimates found in Table 8.2, we decided to favor the few distal variables that performed most robustly in the summary tests reported in Tables 3.3 and 3.4. Second, we similarly excluded some variables that did not perform as well as other variables in the same chapter. These

TABLE 8.1 *Summary of findings*

Outcome	Direct causes other than controls			Indirect effects other than controls (net effects)		
	Levels	Upturns	Downturns	Levels	Upturns	Downturns
Proximate Determinants						
Polyarchy level, lagged	+	−	−		−	mixed
Dependence on oil/other natural resources					mixed	−
Ongoing campaigns					+	
Nonviolent campaign		+			+	
Non-worker-farmer campaign		+			+	
Non-middle sector campaign		+			+	
Mean global economic growth		+			+	
Middle sector campaign		+				
National economic growth			+		−	
Left-wing movement				−	−	
Right-wing movement						
Anti-system movement		−			+	
Worker-farmer campaign		+				
Intermediate Determinants						
Agricultural income/GDP	−	−	−	−	−	
CSO participatory environment	+	+		+		
High state capacity	+					+
Institutionalized parties				+		

(continued)

included Education, Urbanization, and Inflation from Chapter 5; and Former UK colony from Chapter 6. Third, high rates of missingness made it too costly to include Market income inequality and Wage share of income from Chapter 5. Fourth, several variables that had significant coefficients in preceding chapters became insignificant when tested against the more diverse set of variables in this chapter. This phenomenon led us to drop Election year and Internal war (from Chapter 4) and Family farms and Unemployment rate (from Chapter 5). Fifth, knowing that tests involving a large number of variables tend to turn up a few false positives, we decided to drop a few variables whose significant apparent affects made little theoretical sense. Specifically, we felt uncomfortable arguing that episodes of hyperinflation positively affect levels and upturns (Chapter 4); and that a majoritarian electoral system and the seat share of the largest party are causes rather than effects of the level of democracy (Chapter 6). Finally, our civil society measure is CSO participatory environment rather than the civil society stock measure used in Chapter 7 so that our models do not credit civil society for the influence of other long-term institutional developments that could be correlated with the stock measure.

TABLE 8.1 (*continued*)

Outcome	Direct causes other than controls			Indirect effects other than controls (net effects)		
	Levels	Upturns	Downturns	Levels	Upturns	Downturns
GDP per capita, logged				+	+	mixed
Strict presidentialism		+				
Literacy				+	+	+
Distal Determinants						
Protestant population	+				mixed	
Ethnic fractionalization						
Mean temperature						
Natural harbor distance						
European-descended population						

Notes: Direct causes are lagged one year relative to the dependent variable. Indirect causes are lagged two years. Only first- and second-order causes (causes and causes of causes) are included here, as third-order causes tend to be very small.

outcome directly, indicated by a single arrow pointing from the variable to the democracy outcome in Figures 8.2 to 8.4, have "direct" effects. Some predictors also or only have "indirect" effects, indicated in the figures by two or more arrows linking the variable to the outcome through one or more mediating variables. In this sense, these figures are causal mediation diagrams. A plus sign means that positive values of the variable tend to raise the level of polyarchy, increase the magnitude of an upturn, or decrease the magnitude of a downturn. A minus sign means that positive values of the variable tend to lower the level of polyarchy, decrease the magnitude of an upturn, or increase the magnitude of a downturn. In brief, plus signs are good for democracy and minus signs are bad for it. "Mixed" means that effects on some outcomes are positive and whereas effects on other outcomes are negative.

Most of the causes of democracy levels are intermediate variables, most of the causes of upturns are proximate variables, and the causes of downturns are evenly divided between intermediate and proximate variables. Overall, there is surprisingly little overlap among the causes of the different outcomes.

For the most part, the empirical results in this chapter are consistent with those in the preceding chapters. Table 8.1 reports findings about twenty-four hypothesized direct causes of polyarchy levels, upturns, and downturns.[9] Fifty-

---

[9] We exclude Table 8.1's net indirect effects from this tally because net effects are products of two or more coefficients and are therefore not comparable to the direct effects tested in other chapters.

five of the sixty-three test results were consistent with the conclusions of earlier chapters. (We consider our finding that strict presidentialism makes downturns smaller to be consistent with Chapter 6's finding that it makes downturns less likely.) All but one of the differences in the findings concerned variables that lost statistical significance when tested in this chapter's more fully specified models. They include export dependence, global and national economic growth, ethnic fractionalization, mean temperature, natural harbor distance, and European-descended population as predictors of the level of polyarchy; national economic growth as a predictor of upturns; and right-wing movements and ethnic fractionalization as predictors of downturns. There is only one instance in which a contradictory finding appeared: Chapter 5 found no significant impact of agricultural income as a share of GDP on downturns; we find that agriculture's income share worsens downturns.

Finally, although we cannot test this claim here, various international networks linking countries together, such as geographic proximity and membership in international organizations, also matter for levels of democracy and upturns and downturns, as discussed in Chapter 4.[10] Countries that are embedded in networks of democracies tend to become and remain more democratic; those linked with undemocratic countries tend to become or remain less democratic. Therefore, the striking spatial clustering of democracy and non-democracy tends to be self-reinforcing. There may also be spatial dependence among many of the other intermediate and proximate causes studied in this chapter, including the institutions and actors forming the "protective belt" – opposition campaigns in a country may spur similar campaigns in neighboring countries and there could be cross-border diffusion in political party characteristics, to take two examples. If so, this could both contribute to the spatial clustering of regimes that we observe in the data and serve as a further self-reinforcing mechanism for the protective belts of countries situated in networks with largely similar countries.

8.2   EMPIRICAL MODELS OF SEQUENCES

The case for treating distal, distinct-intermediate, and similar-intermediate variables as stages in a causal sequence is easy to make. First, there are plausible theoretical reasons to expect that these variables fit into a causal sequence. Gerring cites abundant research in Chapter 3 arguing that malaria

---

We also exclude lagged polyarchy level as a predictor, as not all chapters included it their specifications; and four of the distal variables that were not previously tested as predictors of upturns or downturns.

[10] The analyses in Chapters 4 and 8 depend on different variants of regression. Most of the analysis in this chapter consists of path analysis, a special case of structural equations models. The analysis in Chapter 4 is a special type of spatial econometrics model that interacts variables with spatial weight matrices. It also includes a structural equation for its instrumental variables feature, but not multiple equations to deal with endogeneity. It is not clear how these techniques could be combined.

is endemic to hot climates and discourages economic development. Distance from natural harbors makes long-distance trade costly, depriving large areas of opportunities for economic growth. Protestant and European-descended population are largely legacies of European migration which, alongside exploitation of local populations and resources, diffused technology, human capital, and norms that planted seeds of development and democracy. The existence of oil and other mining deposits eventually increased income in many countries, but in ways that tended to concentrate resources in the state, undermining the autonomy of private firms and citizens. Thus, distal variables make sense as primarily indirect causes of democracy that act through economic development and the diffusion of ideas and norms.

The distinct-intermediate variables, in turn, probably affect democracy through similar-intermediate variables. The transformation of agricultural societies into industrial economies and later service and information economies increased income and expanded access to education. To be sure, these "modernization" processes have wrought environmental catastrophe, loss of community, population displacement, inequality, and technologies of repression. However, these processes also diversified interests, and urbanization made it easier for like-minded people to find one another and band together in social movements, forming a vibrant civil society. Political parties formed, where allowed; and some states, at least, established effective legal systems. These achievements do not constitute democracy, the way we define it here, but they are building blocks of democracy. Thus institutional development links economic and social development to democracy.

Second, it is easy to show empirically that the more proximate variables tend to eclipse the more distal ones. Building on the ranking of variables by temporal dependence in Figure 8.1, in Table 8.2 we run relatively simple random effects panel models that use the most promising variables from each chapter to explain levels of polyarchy from 1900 to 2010. Model 1 tests six distal variables that emerged as relevant determinants of democracy level in Chapter 3. Percentage of Protestants, mean temperature, and European-descended population are all statistically significant.

Model 2 in this table adds three distinct-intermediate variables from Chapters 3–5: literacy, agricultural income, and the log of per capita GDP. Per capita GDP is estimated to be significant but mean temperature loses significance and dependence on oil or other natural resource exports becomes significant. A likely reason for the loss of significance is that all of the effects of mean temperature on electoral democracy are channeled through per capita GDP.[11] The other three distal variables may retain their significance because

---

[11] There are other possible reasons for the loss of significance, such as collinearity, correlated errors, or omitted variables. Hence, we do not conclude that this simple analysis proves causal sequencing, only that this evidence is consistent with that hypothesis. However, the path models to follow provide better evidence of sequencing, although there are some exceptions.

TABLE 8.2 *Intermediate and distal determinants of levels of Polyarchy assuming exogeneity*

Model Predictors	1 coeff./s.e.	2 coeff./s.e.	3 coeff./s.e.
Distal			
Percentage of Protestants	0.0046***	0.0046***	0.0048
	0.0009	0.0008	0.0078
Mean temperature	−0.0051*	−0.0001	0.0015
	0.0023	0.0026	0.0180
Ethnic fractionalization	−0.0710	−0.0168	−0.1430
	0.0581	0.0560	0.3616
Natural harbor distance	−0.0001	0.0000	−0.0003
	0.0001	0.0001	0.0003
Dependence on oil/other nat. res.	−0.0008	−0.0016*	−0.0007
	0.0008	0.0008	0.0050
European-descended population	0.0024**	0.0020*	0.0031
	0.0009	0.0009	0.0060
Distinct Intermediate			
Literacy		−0.0004	0.0006
		0.0008	0.0054
Agricultural income/GDP		−0.0010	−0.0045
		0.0007	0.0057
ln(GDP per capita)		0.0780***	0.1932
		0.0229	0.1550
Similar Intermediate			
Institutionalized parties			1.9847***
			0.6713
CSO participatory environment			0.6477***
			0.0630
Majoritarian electoral system			−0.4717***
			0.1441
High state capacity			0.6301***
			0.0804
intercept	2.0242**	−0.0609	1.8384
	0.6868	0.8852	6.1152
Decade dummies	*not shown*		
R^2 within	0.490	0.511	0.751

(*continued*)

TABLE 8.2 (*continued*)

Model	1	2	3
Predictors	coeff./s.e.	coeff./s.e.	coeff./s.e.
R^2 between	0.498	0.557	0.822
R^2 overall	0.527	0.579	0.830
Observations	5,127	5,127	5,127
N countries	127	127	127

Notes: Dependent variable: EDI (Polyarchy). The estimator uses random effects with standard errors clustered by countries. All intermediate variables are lagged one year. The only distal variable that is lagged is Dependence on oil. *** $p < 0.01$, ** $p < 0.05$, * $p < 0.1$.

they have an impact on electoral democracy that is not fully mediated by any of the intermediate variables.

Model 3 adds four similar-intermediate predictors to Model 2: institutionalized parties, CSO participatory environment, majoritarian electoral system, and high state capacity. Their inclusion in the model washes out the significance of all the distal and distinct-intermediate variables. Again, a plausible interpretation of this change is that one or more of the four similar-proximate variables channel all of the variance from the distal and intermediate variables that is useful for explaining the variance of electoral democracy.

However, these panel models assume that all these variables are exogenous, that is, they may be intercorrelated but they cause only the outcome variable, not one another. This assumption is inconsistent with the causal sequencing we just described. If there are causal sequences, then some variables are endogenous to others. Throwing all the variables into a simple additive model is likely to give us the wrong answers. It favors the contributions of the variables that have direct effects on democracy and falsely diminishes the contributions of those that have only indirect effects. It may even make it appear that the more distal variables do not matter at all, if their contributions flow entirely through more proximate variables.

Therefore, in the rest of this chapter we use path analysis to test the sequential hypotheses appropriately. Path-analytic models enable us to learn more about which variables have only direct effects on the outcome and can therefore be treated as exogenous and which have indirect effects that are mediated by other variables. The great challenge of path analysis is that it increases specification uncertainty, that is, doubt about which variables to include in a model and where to place the causal pathways that link them. We cope with this uncertainty by estimating what could be called "reasonably" saturated models. A saturated model would include all possible paths, testing the hypothesis that every variable depends on every other variable. Even if it were possible to estimate such a model (it is not), it would not be reasonable, as there is no theoretical justification for assuming a causal relationship between some pairs of variables. For example, a country's economic growth rate cannot affect the location of natural harbors and the present cannot affect the past. We take this a bit farther by stipulating that (a) all the distal variables are exogenous (causes but not effects); (b) each endogenous variable (one that is an effect and may also be a cause) has a one-year lag of itself as an exogenous predictor; and (c) in the models of upturns and downturns, distal variables are not allowed to be direct causes of the outcome. We do allow distal variables to be direct causes of polyarchy levels, however, as Chapter 3 demonstrated that several distal variables are good predictors of countries' average levels of polyarchy. Aside from these restrictions, the models are saturated: distal variables can cause distant-intermediate and similar-intermediate variables, both types of intermediate variables can cause each other and the outcome, and the outcome can have feedback effects on any of the intermediate variables.

Admittedly, this setup has a rather exploratory spirit, which we think appropriate given that our goal is theory-building rather than mounting the most rigorous test possible. Nevertheless, the way we estimate these models includes severe precautions to reduce the risk of capitalizing on chance. With time series data, major threats to inference are spurious correlation and serial autocorrelation. If there are secular time trends in two variables, they will be correlated whether there is a causal relationship or not; and if past values strongly predict present values, models tend to overstate statistical significance. One correction for these issues is to use a lagged outcome variable as a predictor, which helps purge time trends from the estimates of effects. As in the rest of this book, all of our models after Table 8.1 do this. Also, every predictor of an endogenous variable is lagged one year behind it except for invariant distal predictors. In addition, we control for period effects by using dummy variables for each decade of the twentieth century. Differencing the dependent variable is another correction for autocorrelation, and this is one thing that our upturns and downturns variables accomplish. Because we are working with panel data, we also take two measures to address any correlation between countries and the error term: using country-fixed-effect estimation and clustering errors by countries.[12]

A remaining challenge is the risk that the effects of the endogenous variables may be, in a sense, contaminated by their own predictors, especially if the model is misspecified. A common solution is to include an instrumental variable that is a good predictor of the endogenous variable and probably has no direct effect on other variables that are directly linked to the outcome (once controlling for the covariates included in the model). Such instrumental variables allow us to predict what the value of the endogenous variable would have been if it were not contaminated by other variables in the model, which helps produce a less biased

---

[12] We use Stata 15's SEM command to estimate our path models. Because this command lacks a fixed effects option, we run the model using variables that have already been centered around their country means.

estimate of its effects. In our models, every endogenous variable is instrumented by a lag of itself. In most cases, these lags are very strong predictors.[13]

We represent the estimates of these reasonably saturated models in path diagrams that map only the significant paths. We do not trim the models first. In this way, what we present are conservative estimates of the significant causal paths. After using lagged dependent variables, first differences, country and decade fixed effects, lagged predictors, clustered errors, and instrumental variables, it is a bit surprising that any significant relationships survive even with our large sample and extensive time series; yet many do. In fact, because lagged versions of each variable are used in each endogenous equation, one could also view our models as analogous to large, interlocking Granger causality or mediation tests, with Figures 8.2 through 8.4 and Figures 8C.1 to 8C.3 as causal mediation diagrams. Structural equations for these models are written out in Appendix 8A.

Some specification uncertainty inevitably remains. We do not have measures of all the factors we would like to include. Collinearity among some variables, such as literacy and GDP per capita, probably influences some estimates. The controls we adopted tend to favor short-term over long-term effects. Moreover, we have barely begun to examine the possibility that the models would be different for shorter historical periods, or for regions of the world, than they are when we estimate effects for all country-years at once. Nevertheless, the models that emerge from this gauntlet of checks provide reasonable starting points for sketching an integrated theory about causal sequences that, on average in a very large sample, determine levels, upturns, and downturns in electoral democracy.

We present three models later in the text – one for levels of polyarchy, one for upturns, and one for downturns. Appendix 8C also contains three alternative models of upturns. In the body of the chapter, we represent the models only as path diagrams; tables with full estimates appear at the end.

8.3 MODELING LEVELS OF ELECTORAL DEMOCRACY

Figure 8.2 translates the estimates from Table 8.3 into a path diagram in which each arrow shows the influence of a predictor on an endogenous variable. In all of these diagrams, the outcome variable (level, upturns, or downturns) is at the right edge, distal variables are near the left edge, and intermediate variables are in between. Variables that appear in multiple models are located in approximately the same place in each figure. Solid lines represent positive effects; dashed lines represent negative effects. Line widths are proportional to

---

[13] Whether our instruments also satisfy the exclusion restriction is harder to know, especially in models with so many endogenous variables. However, it seems reasonable to assume that the lagged instrument predicts its own later values much better than it predicts the effects of those later values.

the standardized coefficients.[14] Therefore, thick lines indicate effects that are relatively strong and significant; thin lines indicate effects that are either relatively weak or less certain, or a mixture of both. As noted, paths that failed to meet the threshold of significance at the conventional 0.05 level do not appear in the figure. Further, each endogenous variable has a gray circular arrow representing the coefficient of its own lag.[15] All models include an intercept and error term for each endogenous variable. The tables of estimates in Appendix 8C report this information, but we have omitted these elements, as well as the nonsignificant paths, from the path diagrams to make them easier to read.

Figure 8.2 tells an interesting story that we recount in reverse order, starting with the outcome. Polyarchy is the product of four direct and one indirect factors that include a mix of institutions, organizations and behavior, economic development, and cultural factors. Our story explains how these variables work together as a causal sequence.

The three closest causes are similar-intermediate variables that form what could be called a "protective belt" for polyarchy: a self-reinforcing inner ring of variables that to some degree shield polyarchy from more distant influences and tend to keep it close to its recent past levels. What is labeled "CSO participatory environment" in Figure 8.2 could also be called a "vibrant civil society," as the description of the top category of this V-Dem indicator reads, "There are many diverse CSOs and it is considered normal for people to be at least occasionally active in at least one of them." What is labeled "High state capacity" could just as well be called "the rule of law": "The law is generally fully respected by the public officials. Arbitrary or biased administration of the law is very limited." "Institutionalized parties" is an index that measures "level and depth of organization, links to civil society, cadres of party activists, party supporters within the electorate, coherence of party platforms and ideologies, party-line voting among representatives within the legislature" (Coppedge et al. 2019b). The first two variables have a direct additive impact on polyarchy and Institutionalized parties reinforces both of them, so they are compensatory: strength in one can partially compensate for weakness in another's contribution to polyarchy. Civil society plays the most central role. A vibrant civil society reinforces the rule of law both directly and indirectly, through institutionalized parties. If polyarchy weakens, civil society and the rule of law tend to support it. If the rule of law is challenged, a vibrant civil society

---

[14] All of our tables of path model estimates report both standardized and unstandardized coefficients.

[15] Their widths are not comparable to the widths of the other pathways because the lags of the endogenous variables usually have coefficients close to 1, while other paths tend to be much smaller. Using different scales make it possible to discern some differences among the contributions of these other paths. We have disregarded the SEM convention of using curved arrows to represent covariances among errors so that the diagrams are more legible. None of our models includes error covariances; both curved and straight arrows represent regression coefficients.

TABLE 8.3 *Path models of levels of Polyarchy*

Endogenous variable	Predictors	coef.	unstd. coef.	std. s.e.	z	p
Polyarchy						
	Institutionalized parties$_{t-1}$	0.0969	0.0063	0.0773	1.25	0.210
	CSO participatory environment$_{t-1}$	0.0515***	0.0278	0.0112	4.58	0.000
	High state capacity$_{t-1}$	0.0483***	0.0174	0.0152	3.17	0.002
	Agricultural income$_{t-1}$	−0.0014*	−0.0115	0.0007	−2.13	0.033
	GDP per capita$_{t-1}$	0.0137	0.0046	0.0184	0.75	0.455
	Literacy$_{t-1}$	0.0002	0.0022	0.0006	0.38	0.706
	Polyarchy$_{t-1}$	0.9277***	0.9121	0.0092	101.05	0.000
	Protestant population	0.0044**	0.0108	0.0015	2.98	0.003
	Natural harbor distance	−0.0622	−0.0005	0.4377	−0.14	0.887
	Resource dependence$_{t-1}$/1000	−0.3312	−0.0011	0.7250	−0.46	0.648
	European population$_{t-1}$/100	−0.0577	−0.0009	0.1442	−0.40	0.689
	1900s	−0.1018*	−0.0096	0.0451	−2.26	0.024
	1910s	−0.0862	−0.0071	0.0446	−1.93	0.053
	1920s	−0.0654	−0.0081	0.0396	−1.65	0.098
	1930s	−0.1254**	−0.0163	0.0404	-3.10	0.002
	1940s	−0.1833**	−0.0138	0.0623	−2.94	0.003
	1950s	−0.0157	−0.0025	0.0345	−0.45	0.650
	1960s	−0.0702*	−0.0118	0.0300	−2.34	0.019
	1970s	−0.0523	−0.0091	0.0312	−1.68	0.094

(continued)

1980s	-0.0042	-0.0008	0.0243	-0.17	0.864
1990s	0.0839***	0.0174	0.0198	4.23	0.000
intercept	0.0556*	0.0300	0.0223	2.49	0.013

Institutionalized parties$_{t-1}$

Protestant population	0.0000	0.0005	0.0001	0.15	0.879
Natural harbor distance	0.0145	0.0018	0.0191	0.76	0.447
Resource dependence$_{t-2}$/1000	-0.0223	-0.0012	0.0487	-0.46	0.647
European population$_{t-1}$/100	-0.0040	-0.0009	0.0123	-0.33	0.744
Institutionalized parties$_{t-2}$	0.9601***	0.9596	0.0056	172.16	0.000
CSO participatory environment$_{t-2}$	0.0016*	0.0133	0.0007	2.26	0.024
Polyarchy$_{t-2}$	-0.0012**	-0.0180	0.0005	-2.60	0.009
High state capacity$_{t-2}$	0.0012	0.0067	0.0008	1.62	0.105
Agricultural income$_{t-2}$	0.0000	-0.0019	0.0001	-0.26	0.794
GDP per capita$_{t-2}$	0.0018	0.0092	0.0011	1.69	0.090
Literacy$_{t-2}$	0.0002***	0.0234	0.0000	4.63	0.000
intercept	0.0010**	0.0083	0.0004	2.68	0.007

CSO participatory environment$_{t-1}$

Protestant population	0.0025***	0.0116	0.0008	3.34	0.001
Natural harbor distance	-0.0154	-0.0002	0.1958	-0.08	0.937
Resource dependence$_{t-2}$/1000	0.0567	0.0004	0.4381	0.13	0.897
European population$_{t-1}$/100	-0.1021	-0.0029	0.0901	-1.13	0.258
Institutionalized parties$_{t-2}$	0.0011	0.0001	0.0395	0.03	0.979
CSO participatory environment$_{t-2}$	0.9683***	0.9603	0.0051	191.10	0.000

(*continued*)

Endogenous variable	Predictors	coef.	unstd. coef.	std. s.e.	z	p
	$Polyarchy_{t-2}$	-0.0039	-0.0071	0.0031	-1.27	0.205
	High state capacity$_{t-2}$	0.0005	0.0003	0.0069	0.07	0.946
	Agricultural income$_{t-2}$	-0.0007*	-0.0103	0.0003	-2.01	0.044
	GDP per capita$_{t-2}$	0.0155*	0.0096	0.0078	2.00	0.046
	Literacy$_{t-2}$	0.0010***	0.0182	0.0003	3.77	0.000
	intercept	0.0149***	0.0149	0.0028	5.35	0.000
High state capacity$_{t-1}$						
	Protestant population	0.0016	0.0112	0.0010	1.71	0.087
	Natural harbor distance	-0.0909	-0.0021	0.1509	-0.60	0.547
	Resource dependence$_{t-2}$/1000	-0.0211	-0.0002	0.3318	-0.06	0.949
	European population$_{t-1}$/100	-0.1634	-0.0069	0.1160	-1.41	0.159
	Institutionalized parties$_{t-2}$	0.1028**	0.0186	0.0391	2.63	0.009
	CSO participatory environment$_{t-2}$	0.0118	0.0175	0.0046	2.55	0.011
	Polyarchy$_{t-2}$	-0.0058	-0.0156	0.0038	-1.52	0.128
	High state capacity$_{t-2}$	0.9360***	0.9302	0.0086	109.26	0.000
	Agricultural income$_{t-2}$	-0.0012**	-0.0273	0.0004	-3.11	0.002
	GDP per capita$_{t-2}$	0.0116	0.0107	0.0078	1.49	0.136
	Literacy$_{t-2}$	-0.0003	-0.0088	0.0003	-1.21	0.227
	intercept	0.0053	0.0079	0.0028	1.86	0.062
Agricultural income$_{t-1}$						
	Protestant population	0.0391**	0.0118	0.0150	2.61	0.009

(*continued*)

Natural harbor distance	-2.5553	-0.0026	2.4784	-1.03	0.303
Resource dependence$_{t-2}$/1000	13.2641	0.0055	7.7862	1.70	0.088
European population$_{t-1}$/100	-3.0864	-0.0057	1.7032	-1.81	0.070
Institutionalized parties$_{t-2}$	-1.4780**	-0.0118	0.5324	-2.78	0.005
CSO participatory environment$_{t-2}$	0.0755	0.0049	0.0638	1.18	0.237
Polyarchy$_{t-2}$	0.0452	0.0054	0.0414	1.09	0.275
High state capacity$_{t-2}$	-0.0755	-0.0033	0.0893	-0.85	0.398
Agricultural income$_{t-2}$	0.9229***	0.9272	0.0095	97.04	0.000
GDP per capita$_{t-2}$	-0.8119***	-0.0332	0.1639	-4.95	0.000
Literacy$_{t-2}$	-0.0256***	-0.0301	0.0047	-5.38	0.000
intercept	-0.5010***	-0.0330	0.0425	-11.79	0.000

GDP per capita$_{t-1}$

Protestant population	-0.0005*	-0.0037	0.0002	-2.08	0.038
Natural harbor distance	-0.1151	-0.0028	0.0751	-1.53	0.125
Resource dependence$_{t-2}$/1000	0.7839*	0.0079	0.3212	2.44	0.015
European population$_{t-1}$/100	-0.0893***	-0.0040	0.0268	-3.34	0.001
Institutionalized parties$_{t-2}$	0.0419**	0.0082	0.0154	2.72	0.007
CSO participatory environment$_{t-2}$	0.0017	0.0027	0.0025	0.67	0.502
Polyarchy$_{t-2}$	0.0010	0.0030	0.0014	0.76	0.445
High state capacity$_{t-2}$	0.0000	0.0000	0.0025	0.00	1.000
Agricultural income$_{t-2}$	-0.0002	-0.0054	0.0001	-1.51	0.131
GDP per capita$_{t-2}$	0.9804***	0.9780	0.0038	255.50	0.000
Literacy$_{t-2}$	0.0001	0.0032	0.0001	0.77	0.441
intercept	0.0209***	0.0337	0.0013	16.01	0.000

(continued)

TABLE 8.3 (*continued*)

Endogenous variable	Predictors	coef.	unstd. coef.	std. s.e.	z	p
Literacy$_{t-1}$						
	Protestant population	0.0160**	0.0041	0.0053	3.03	0.002
	Natural harbor distance	2.9580	0.0025	1.7385	1.70	0.089
	Resource dependence$_{t-2}$/1000	8.0458	0.0028	6.4027	1.26	0.209
	European population$_{t-1}$/100	-2.0612**	-0.0032	0.7801	-2.64	0.008
	Institutionalized parties$_{t-2}$	-0.2498	-0.0017	0.3093	-0.81	0.419
	CSO participatory environment$_{t-2}$	0.0269	0.0015	0.0495	0.54	0.587
	Polyarchy$_{t-2}$	-0.0085	-0.0009	0.0371	-0.23	0.819
	High state capacity$_{t-2}$	-0.0903	-0.0033	0.0534	-1.69	0.091
	Agricultural income$_{t-2}$	0.0047	0.0040	0.0031	1.51	0.130
	GDP per capita$_{t-2}$	-0.0655	-0.0023	0.0820	-0.80	0.425
	Literacy$_{t-2}$	1.0069***	1.0012	0.0023	441.79	0.000
	intercept	0.6169***	0.0343	0.0440	14.01	0.000
Error variances						
	Polyarchy	0.1640	0.0476	0.0159		
	Institutionalized parties	0.0008	0.0513	0.0001		
	CSO participatory environment	0.0564	0.0563	0.0064		
	High state capacity	0.0422	0.0945	0.0050		
	Agricultural income	12.5117	0.0543	2.1743		
	GDP per capita	0.0055	0.0142	0.0007		
	Literacy	1.1779	0.0037	0.1931		

Notes: Log pseudolikelihood = -37363.499. N = 6,191. Number of countries: 136. * $p < 0.05$, ** $p < 0.01$, *** $p < 0.001$.

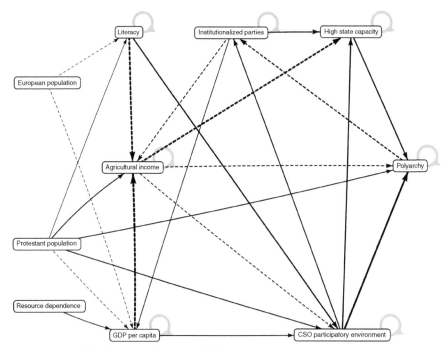

FIGURE 8.2 Path diagram of causes of Polyarchy levels

and institutionalized parties support it.[16] If parties are challenged, an active civil society supports them. For many years, many researchers struggled to demonstrate that social movements have significant effects on policy or regime change. Consequently, much of this literature focused on describing what movements do and how they arise rather than assessing their impact. Our model strongly suggests that the general health of civil society plays the most central role in sustaining polyarchy in the medium term. This finding is in line with Chapter 7, which concludes that civil society actors can be very important for spurring and sustaining transitions to democracy.

An equilibrium sustained by mutually reinforcing variables is called "homeostasis." It is important to remember, however, that the homeostatic equilibrium can be undemocratic, too. If civil society, parties, and the enforcement of the law are respectively weak, inchoate, and arbitrary, then

[16] If we substitute "V-Dem's Equality under the law and individual liberties" index for the Rule of Law/High State Capacity measure, the rule of law also strengthens civil society. In that model, literacy and the Protestant population variable also support the rule of law, while the level of polyarchy affects it negatively.

the level of polyarchy is predicted to be low and each link in the belt is likely to keep the others weak as well.

Moving leftward in Figure 8.2, we see that the elements of the protective belt are not entirely self-contained. These variables depend importantly on several aspects of socioeconomic development: industrialization and urbanization (a reasonable interpretation of low values of the agricultural share of GDP), GDP per capita, and literacy. Other aspects of development, such as high education and a large service sector, probably also matter, but these are the ones that we could measure extensively and thus include in our model without cutting the time series or number of countries in the sample short. Agricultural income is negatively associated with every element in the protective belt as well as with polyarchy directly. Literacy and GDP per capita both lessen dependence on agriculture and help strengthen civil society. They have no direct impact on the level of polyarchy, which qualifies the finding in Chapter 5. This provides a corrective to modernization theory (Inglehart and Welzel 2005; Lipset 1959; Welzel 2013). Modernization does favor democracy, but mostly indirectly. Previous work has focused on a varied set of mediating variables, including the presence of particular values and attitudes in the population (e.g., Inglehart and Welzel 2005). This model suggests what the causal mechanisms are for modernization: first, a healthy civil society; then institutionalized parties and the rule of law.

Homeostasis combined with the possibility of change implies that democratization is characterized by punctuated equilibrium: long patterns of stability interrupted by sudden dramatic changes. Homeostasis resists change, and because it works at the end of the causal sequences, it usually succeeds. Regime changes are rare and stability or small changes are the norm. However, when the socioeconomic factors that support a democratic civil society fail, civil society can deteriorate to the point where it can no longer sustain parties or the rule of law, and democracy can fail. By the same logic, in an undemocratic system, socioeconomic development may strengthen civil society, which in turn becomes able to strengthen parties and the state. If they encourage a transition to democracy, or if a transition happens for other reasons, then the protective belt may now be strong enough to sustain it.

In Figure 8.2, the "Protestant population" variable is the fifth direct cause of polyarchy. It also appears as an indirect cause that works by strengthening civil society. There seems to be a general rule that the distal causes tested in Chapter 3 affect democracy only indirectly (European population, natural harbor distance) or are not significant at all (Muslim population, ethnic fractionalization). Protestant population seems to be an exception. However, these distal variables must be interpreted with caution, as they are relatively invariant and in many cases are based on interpolations of sparse data. A one-year lag is probably not meaningful. Furthermore, the Protestant and European population variables are probably little more than proxies for many kinds of European influence, such as state-building, the rule of law, Christianity, and the diffusion of political norms through colonial domination, education, and trade. A multilevel model would be better for examining the distal causes such as Protestant population and these other variables that are nearly invariant.[17]

8.4 MODELING UPTURNS IN ELECTORAL DEMOCRACY

The short-term aspects of democratization, which this volume operationalizes as annual upturns and downturns in levels of democracy, are the processes that punctuate the existing equilibrium. (That is, they do when they are large enough; most changes are very small.) Both upturns and downturns are much more dynamic than levels, as shown in Figure 8.1. We therefore expected that upturns and downturns would have more proximate direct causes than democracy levels do.[18]

To select a satisfactory model of upturns, we began with the variables from earlier chapters that best explained this outcome – which tended to be proximate variables – and added all the intermediate and distal variables that could plausibly help cause them. We actually specified four different models of upturns because of overlaps among many of the social forces variables that would have made them difficult to interpret if they had all been combined into a single model. The model we present here focuses on the role of violent and nonviolent resistance campaigns; the other three models are shown in Appendix 8.C. The upturns model presented in the main text has fifty-four possible causal paths, not counting decade dummies and intercepts, but only thirty of them attained significance. As with the model of levels of polyarchy depicted in Figure 8.2, we mapped the statistically significant coefficients as arrows in the path diagram shown in Figure 8.3.

One powerful direct cause of upturns is the lagged level of polyarchy. This is less of an explanatory variable and more of an essential control. Its negative coefficient means that undemocratic countries have more room for improvement and therefore tend to experience larger upturns than countries that are already democratic and have less room for improvement. Controlling for the difficulty of making large gains in democratic political systems enables us to estimate the other effects better.

As expected, two of the other direct causes of upturns are proximate. First, a strong civil society, and in particular nonviolent campaigns that arise from

---

[17] Figure 8.2 contains some surprising feedback effects. This model says, for example, that polyarchy weakens the institutionalization of political parties. This is surprising because overall these two variables are positively correlated. It is perhaps less surprising that institutionalized parties decrease agricultural income, insofar as they are linked to processes of economic development (Bizzarro et al. 2018). However, we did not expect to find that Protestant population improves agricultural income and decreases GDP per capita.

[18] As in previous chapters, upturns are measured as positive changes in the EDI since the previous year and downturns are negative changes. All other non-missing observations are coded zero.

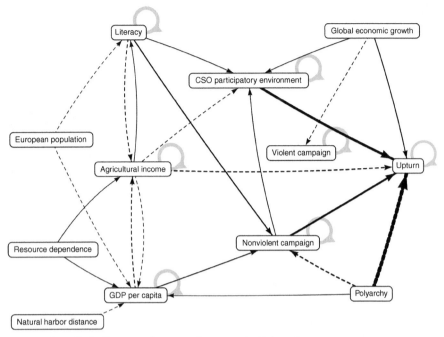

FIGURE 8.3 Path diagram of causes of upturns in Polyarchy

civil society, favor larger upturns in polyarchy.[19] Another civil society variable, "CSO participatory environment," also strengthens upturns in this model.[20] Our findings are consistent with other research (Chenoweth and Stephan 2011) and the advocacy of nonviolence by, for instance, Mahatma Gandhi and Martin Luther King, Jr. The models reported in the appendix add that opposition campaigns dominated by coalitions of workers-small farmers and non-worker-farmers make upturns larger, as do both middle-sector and non-middle-sector campaigns. These findings are generally consistent with arguments by Luebbert (1991) and Rueschemeyer et al. (1992), respectively. It is not clear to us why our model does not confirm the Chapter 7 finding that violent campaigns weaken upturns. However, Figure 8.C.3 suggests that left-wing movements weaken upturns indirectly, by weakening civil society.

The second proximate direct cause of upturns is the mean expansion rate of the global economy. We can only speculate about the causal mechanisms that

[19] The "non-violent campaign" variable, as explained in Chapter 7, marks the year after a nonviolent campaign ended, in most cases because the campaign was successful (see Chenoweth and Stephan 2011). Our model indicates that upturns tend to be larger in the aftermath of nonviolent campaigns.

[20] Here we use the level variable rather than the stock variable the Chapter 7 authors created from it, but these two paths are roughly consistent with Chapter 7.

TABLE 8.4 *Path model of upturns in Polyarchy using violent and nonviolent campaigns*

Endogenous variable	Predictors	unstd. coef.	std. coef.	s.e.	z	p
Upturn						
	Agricultural income$_{t-1}$	-0.0002***	-0.0682	0.0000	-3.49	0.000
	GDP per capita$_{t-1}$	-0.0003	-0.0049	0.0011	-0.26	0.798
	Literacy$_{t-1}$	0.0000	0.0173	0.0000	0.83	0.405
	CSO participatory environment$_{t-1}$	0.0072***	0.2043	0.0008	8.96	0.000
	Nonviolent campaign$_{t-1}$	0.0339***	0.1467	0.0074	4.60	0.000
	Violent campaign$_{t-1}$	0.0009	0.0064	0.0017	0.50	0.615
	Polyarchy$_{t-1}$	-0.0065***	-0.3381	0.0006	-10.71	0.000
	Upturn$_{t-1}$	0.2433***	0.2459	0.0195	12.45	0.000
	Global economic growth$_{t-1}$	0.2281*	0.0410	0.0937	2.43	0.015
	1900s	-0.0150***	-0.0705	0.0032	-4.74	0.000
	1910s	-0.0102***	-0.0567	0.0027	-3.75	0.000
	1920s	-0.0078**	-0.0484	0.0026	-3.01	0.003
	1930s	-0.0098***	-0.0629	0.0026	-3.76	0.000
	1940s	-0.0018	-0.0112	0.0025	-0.69	0.490
	1950s	0.0006	0.0045	0.0025	0.23	0.816
	1960s	-0.0031	-0.0260	0.0019	-1.64	0.100
	1970s	-0.0018	-0.0167	0.0020	-0.88	0.379
	1980s	-0.0017	-0.0160	0.0018	-0.93	0.352

(continued)

TABLE 8.4 (*continued*)

Endogenous variable	Predictors	unstd. coef.	std. coef.	s.e.	z	p
	1990s	0.0042***	0.0429	0.0012	3.46	0.001
	intercept	0.0029	0.0791	0.0015	1.87	0.062
Agricultural income$_{t-1}$						
	GDP per capita$_{t-2}$	-0.9067***	-0.0370	0.1440	-6.30	0.000
	Literacy$_{t-2}$	-0.0230***	-0.0282	0.0043	-5.36	0.000
	Agricultural income$_{t-2}$	0.9238***	0.9278	0.0089	103.85	0.000
	Natural harbor distance/1000	-1.2712	-0.0015	2.3063	-0.55	0.581
	Resource dependence$_{t-1}$/1000	13.5804*	0.0060	6.2731	2.16	0.030
	European population$_{t-1}$/1000	-1.8042	-0.0031	1.5341	-1.18	0.240
	Polyarchy$_{t-2}$	0.0366	0.0046	0.0257	1.42	0.154
	intercept	-0.4645***	-0.0311	0.0295	-15.77	0.000
GDP per capita$_{t-1}$						
	GDP per capita$_{t-2}$	0.9832***	0.9767	0.0031	317.16	0.000
	Literacy$_{t-2}$	0.0001	0.0035	0.0001	1.04	0.300
	Agricultural income$_{t-2}$	-0.0003*	-0.0071	0.0001	-2.21	0.027
	Natural harbor distance/1000	-0.1317*	-0.0037	0.0583	-2.26	0.024
	Resource dependence$_{t-1}$/1000	0.9880***	0.0106	0.2863	3.45	0.001
	European population$_{t-1}$/100	-0.0707**	-0.0030	0.0245	-2.88	0.004
	Polyarchy$_{t-2}$	0.0032***	0.0097	0.0008	3.86	0.000
	intercept	0.0173***	0.0282	0.0012	14.63	0.000
Literacy$_{t-1}$						
	GDP per capita$_{t-2}$	-0.0240	-0.0008	0.0688	-0.35	0.727
	Literacy$_{t-2}$	1.0078***	1.0029	0.0018	547.39	0.000

(*continued*)

Agricultural income$_{t-2}$	0.0080*	0.0065	0.0031	2.55	0.011
Natural harbor distance/1000	1.0629	0.0010	1.4164	0.75	0.453
Resource dependence$_{t-1}$/1000	10.0473	0.0036	5.4253	1.85	0.064
European population$_{t-1}$/100	-1.5660*	-0.0022	0.7634	-2.05	0.040
Polyarchy$_{t-2}$	-0.0070	-0.0007	0.0164	-0.43	0.670
intercept	0.6385***	0.0347	0.0366	17.43	0.000

CSO participatory environment$_{t-1}$

Nonviolent campaign$_{t-2}$	0.1127**	0.0171	0.0398	2.83	0.005
Violent campaign$_{t-2}$	0.0016	0.0004	0.0136	0.12	0.904
Global economic growth$_{t-1}$	2.4009**	0.0152	0.8523	2.82	0.005
GDP per capita$_{t-2}$	-0.0032	-0.0019	0.0080	-0.40	0.689
Literacy$_{t-2}$	0.0011***	0.0190	0.0003	4.12	0.000
Agricultural income$_{t-2}$	-0.0010**	-0.0141	0.0003	-2.82	0.005
Polyarchy$_{t-2}$	0.0025	0.0045	0.0028	0.90	0.371
CSO participatory environment$_{t-2}$	0.9550***	0.9480	0.0051	188.58	0.000
intercept	0.0150***	0.0146	0.0023	6.57	0.000

Nonviolent campaign$_{t-1}$

Global economic growth$_{t-1}$	-0.0805	-0.0033	0.1371	-0.59	0.557
GDP per capita$_{t-2}$	0.0091***	0.0355	0.0023	3.89	0.000
Literacy$_{t-2}$	0.0005***	0.0594	0.0001	3.42	0.001
Agricultural income$_{t-2}$	-0.0002	-0.0213	0.0002	-1.23	0.220
Polyarchy$_{t-2}$	-0.0068***	-0.0818	0.0016	-4.28	0.000
CSO participatory environment$_{t-2}$	-0.0014	-0.0090	0.0025	-0.54	0.587
Nonviolent campaign$_{t-2}$	0.6101***	0.6033	0.0480	12.71	0.000

(continued)

TABLE 8.4 (*continued*)

Endogenous variable	Predictors	unstd. coef.	std. coef.	s.e.	z	p
	Violent campaign$_{t-2}$	-0.0032	-0.0056	0.0067	-0.48	0.632
	intercept	0.0028**	0.0178	0.0010	2.84	0.004
Violent campaign$_{t-1}$						
	Global economic growth$_{t-1}$	-0.6327**	-0.0152	0.2304	-2.75	0.006
	GDP per capita$_{t-2}$	0.0022	0.0050	0.0047	0.48	0.634
	Literacy$_{t-2}$	0.0000	0.0003	0.0001	0.04	0.970
	Agricultural income$_{t-2}$	-0.0001	-0.0064	0.0002	-0.59	0.553
	Polyarchy$_{t-2}$	0.0012	0.0086	0.0017	0.73	0.463
	CSO participatory environment$_{t-2}$	-0.0010	-0.0036	0.0028	-0.34	0.731
	Nonviolent campaign$_{t-2}$	-0.0009	-0.0005	0.0132	-0.07	0.947
	Violent campaign$_{t-2}$	0.8303***	0.8331	0.0155	53.70	0.000
	intercept	0.0047***	0.0174	0.0012	3.85	0.000
Error variances						
	Upturn	0.0011	0.8524	0.0001		
	Agricultural income	12.9790	0.0583	1.9953		
	GDP per capita	0.0062	0.0164	0.0006		
	Literacy	1.1807	0.0035	0.1724		
	CSO participatory environment	0.0801	0.0759	0.0075		
	Nonviolent campaign	0.0148	0.6067	0.0018		
	Violent campaign	0.0224	0.3040	0.0026		

Notes: Log pseudolikelihood = 28,085. N = 8,301. Number of countries: 150. * p < 0.05, ** p < 0.01, *** p < 0.001.

appear to connect economic expansion with upturns in democracy. One possibility is that economic expansion around the world creates a positive-sum environment in which citizens are more optimistic and governments can afford to be more tolerant. Global economic expansion also strengthens upturns indirectly, by bolstering civil society participation, according to our model. Still, there is a large gap between cause and effect for these paths, which invites more thorough investigation.

One distinct-intermediate variable in Figure 8.3 has a direct effect on upturns – namely the share of GDP produced in the agricultural sector. Its negative sign means that societies where agriculture has been displaced by industry and the service sector tend to experience larger upturns in democracy. The displacement of agriculture also strengthens civil society, but according to this model the direct effect does not operate through that channel. However, we recommend caution in interpreting the contributions of the socioeconomic variables, as they are so intercorrelated that their contributions to other variables that it can be difficult to tease them apart. More conservatively, we can say that there is something about the process of economic and social development that tends to strengthen upturns directly even though the exact mechanisms are unclear. We refer readers to Chapter 5 for a more in-depth discussion of these questions.

The indirect effects in Figure 8.3 deserve some attention as well. First, since nonviolent campaigns play a prominent role, a key question is: what brings them about? Our model says that they are less likely to occur in more democratic regimes, perhaps because when there are competitive elections, there is less need for the opposition to organize large-scale and persistent collective action demanding political change. However, they are more likely to occur in high-income, educated societies. Thus, we confirm the Chapter 5 finding that GDP per capita has no direct effect on upturns, but add the amendment that it does favor upturns indirectly, through its positive influence on nonviolent campaigns. Second, what conditions foster a healthy civil society? Our model says that the participatory environment is healthier when campaigns are nonviolent, literacy is high, the economy relies less on agriculture, and the global economy is expanding more. This evidence can be construed as qualified support for the linkage between "modernization" and democracy: socioeconomic development helps, but mostly indirectly, with a vibrant civil society and nonviolent resistance campaigns as two of the intervening variables.

This model also shows the lagged level of polyarchy having a positive effect on per capita income. In fact, in this model, reverse causation is most directly responsible for the association between democracy levels and GDP per capita (although income affects upturns indirectly through five other circuitous paths). If correct, this model therefore challenges the interpretation of one of the most robust empirical relationships from modernization theory, in a way that is consistent with several other recent studies finding potentially large, positive long-term developmental dividends of democracy (e.g., Acemoglu et al. 2019; Bollyky et al. 2019; Colagrossi et al. 2020; Knutsen 2021; Murshed et al. 2020; Wang et al. 2019).

We expect that many readers will find this rough causal sequencing of geography, socioeconomic development, short-term growth, and social movements to be plausible. Our contribution is not so much the general idea as the demonstration that this overall sequence is consistent with sophisticated models backed by a tremendous amount of quantitative evidence.

8.5 MODELING DOWNTURNS IN ELECTORAL DEMOCRACY

As in previous chapters of this book, our analysis confirms the belief, which we can find expressed back as far as Rustow (1970), that downturns are not simply the opposite of upturns. To be sure, if we compare the path diagram for downturns (Figure 8.4) with the model of upturns in Figure 8.3, there are some shared elements. Resource dependence, literacy, agricultural income, GDP per capita, CSO participatory environment, and lagged polyarchy appear in both figures. However, there are new variables in the downturns model: High state capacity (rule of law), national (rather than global) economic growth, and strict presidentialism. Also, European population and natural harbor distance are indirectly relevant for upturns but not downturns. The alternative upturns model of Figure 8.C.3 in Appendix 8C is a bit more comparable to this downturns model because they both include anti-system and left- and right-wing movements. Nevertheless, even when the same elements are significant, the pathways connect them in different ways. For example, a vibrant civil society strengthens upturns but has no effect on downturns, and anti-system movements directly affect downturns but not upturns. The stories that our upturns and downturns models tell are thus substantially different.

Before getting into a detailed interpretation, it is important to clarify what negative and positive effects mean. Because all of the values of the downturns variable are negative or zero, higher values of a variable worsen the downturn when its coefficient is negative and dampen the downturn (shift it in a positive direction, toward zero) when its coefficient is positive. Lower values of a variable have the opposite effects. For example, negative national economic growth, multiplied by its positive coefficient, is estimated to worsen downturns in polyarchy while positive growth times the positive coefficient tends to dampen them. In contrast, the lagged polyarchy score is always positive. Its negative coefficient and dashed arrow mean that downturns are more severe in the most democratic cases and less severe in the least democratic cases. In other words, this term adjusts for the fact that democracies have farther to fall on the polyarchy scale than non-democracies.

The most important finding in the downturns model is that anti-system movements contribute to downturns.[21] Although this definition counts both

[21] The codebook definition of a high value on this variable reads, "There is a very high level of anti-system movement activity, posing a real and present threat to the regime." Further clarification from the codebook: "An anti-system opposition movement is any movement – peaceful or

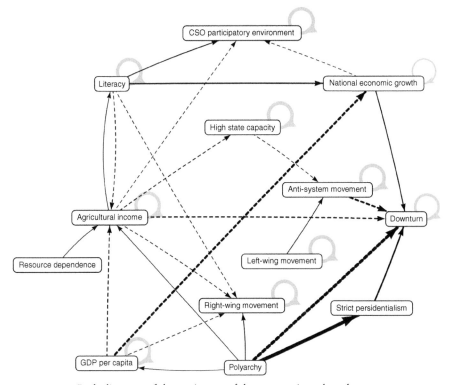

FIGURE 8.4 Path diagram of determinants of downturns in polyarchy

left-and right-wing (and other) movements, in Figure 8.4 only left-wing movements help produce anti-system movements. Right-wing movements are effects, not causes, in this model. This result runs contrary to Chapter 7, which reports that right-wing movements contribute to downturns. However, the path analysis is consistent with a familiar Cold War story in which left-wing movements, such as communist insurgencies, pose a threat to democracy and the right-wing anti-system forces are reactionary elite conspiracies that lack a mass movement but succeed with the backing of the military and, often during this period, the United States. Certainly, there are many exceptions to this account, but it may be the most common one, and therefore the one that best characterizes average tendencies in our very large sample.

armed – that is based in the country (not abroad) and is organized in opposition to the current political system. That is, it aims to change the polity in fundamental ways, *e.g.*, from democratic to autocratic (or vice versa), from capitalist to communist (or vice versa), from secular to fundamentalist (or vice versa). This movement may be linked to a political party that competes in elections but it must also have a 'movement' character, which is to say a mass base and an existence separate from normal electoral competition." (Coppedge et al. 2019b)

TABLE 8.5 *Path model of downturns*

Endogenous variable	Predictors	unstd.coef.	std. coef.	s.e.	z	p
Downturn$_t$						
	Agricultural income$_{t-1}$	-0.0001**	-0.0536	0.0000	-2.96	0.003
	GDP per capita$_{t-1}$	0.0012	0.0291	0.0008	1.40	0.162
	Literacy$_{t-1}$	0.0000	-0.0269	0.0000	-1.20	0.230
	Strict presidentialism	0.0074***	0.0775	0.0021	3.55	0.000
	High state capacity$_{t-1}$	0.0003	0.0097	0.0008	0.44	0.657
	CSO participatory environment$_{t-1}$	0.0005	0.0201	0.0006	0.80	0.422
	National economic growth$_{t-1}$	0.0111*	0.0357	0.0048	2.32	0.021
	Anti-system movement$_{t-1}$	-0.0027***	-0.1061	0.0005	-5.48	0.000
	Left-wing movement$_{t-1}$	0.0011	0.0081	0.0022	0.48	0.629
	Right-wing movement$_{t-1}$	-0.0059	-0.0342	0.0034	-1.72	0.085
	Polyarchy$_{t-1}$	-0.0026***	-0.2026	0.0005	-5.66	0.000
	Downturn$_{t-1}$	1.9101***	0.1920	0.2325	8.21	0.000
	Resource dependence$_{t-1}$/1000	-0.0256	-0.0072	0.0250	-1.02	0.306
	1900s	-0.0016	-0.0115	0.0019	-0.83	0.407
	1910s	-0.0023	-0.0126	0.0019	-1.21	0.227
	1920s	-0.0036*	-0.0337	0.0018	-1.96	0.050
	1930s	-0.0055*	-0.0553	0.0021	-2.55	0.011
	1940s	-0.0091*	-0.0436	0.0043	-2.15	0.032

(continued)

	Coefficient	Std. Error	Std. Coef.	t	p
1950s	-0.0024	0.0016	-0.0283	-1.50	0.133
1960s	-0.0046**	0.0017	-0.0605	-2.74	0.006
1970s	-0.0032*	0.0016	-0.0461	-2.06	0.040
1980s	-0.0007	0.0012	-0.0104	-0.61	0.542
1990s	0.0004	0.0008	0.0070	0.56	0.573
intercept	0.0027**	0.0010	0.1122	2.57	0.010

Agricultural income$_{t-1}$

	Coefficient	Std. Error	Std. Coef.	t	p
Polyarchy$_{t-2}$	0.0666*	0.0304	0.0082	2.19	0.028
Agricultural income$_{t-2}$	0.9253***	0.0082	0.9282	112.17	0.000
GDP per capita$_{t-2}$	-0.9842***	0.1502	-0.0398	-6.55	0.000
Literacy$_{t-2}$	-0.0232***	0.0042	-0.0277	-5.48	0.000
Resource dependence$_{t-1}$/1000	0.0164**	0.0063	0.0073	2.59	0.010
intercept	-0.4707***	0.0325	-0.0317	-14.50	0.000

GDP per capita$_{t-1}$

	Coefficient	Std. Error	Std. Coef.	t	p
Polyarchy$_{t-2}$	0.0018*	0.0008	0.0054	2.24	0.025
Agricultural income$_{t-2}$	-0.0001	0.0001	-0.0024	-0.69	0.488
GDP per capita$_{t-2}$	0.9908***	0.0032	0.9873	312.35	0.000
Literacy$_{t-2}$	0.0001	0.0001	0.0034	0.96	0.335
Resource dependence$_{t-1}$/1000	-0.0006	0.0003	-0.0067	-1.84	0.066
intercept	0.0198***	0.0013	0.0328	15.09	0.000

(continued)

TABLE 8.5 (continued)

Endogenous variable	Predictors	unstd.coef.	std. coef.	s.e.	z	p
Literacy$_{t-1}$						
	Polyarchy$_{t-2}$	-0.0214	-0.0022	0.0188	-1.14	0.254
	Agricultural income$_{t-2}$	0.0070*	0.0059	0.0029	2.44	0.015
	GDP per capita$_{t-2}$	-0.0763	-0.0026	0.0706	-1.08	0.280
	Literacy$_{t-2}$	1.0100***	1.0043	0.0018	557.05	0.000
	Resource dependence$_{t-1}$/1000	0.0063	0.0024	0.0048	1.33	0.184
	intercept	0.6474***	0.0364	0.0398	16.27	0.000
Strict presidentialism						
	Polyarchy$_{t-2}$	0.0331***	0.2407	0.0090	3.68	0.000
	Agricultural income$_{t-2}$	-0.0007	-0.0407	0.0009	-0.77	0.444
	GDP per capita$_{t-2}$	-0.0402	-0.0961	0.0242	-1.67	0.096
	Literacy$_{t-2}$	-0.0008	-0.0566	0.0008	-1.03	0.301
	intercept	-0.0052	-0.0207	0.0068	-0.77	0.442
High state capacity$_{t-1}$						
	Polyarchy$_{t-2}$	0.0031	0.0081	0.0023	1.34	0.181
	Agricultural income$_{t-2}$	-0.0012***	-0.0262	0.0003	-3.82	0.000
	GDP per capita$_{t-2}$	0.0084	0.0072	0.0064	1.31	0.190
	Literacy$_{t-2}$	0.0000	0.0000	0.0002	0.00	0.997
	High state capacity$_{t-2}$	0.9354***	0.9343	0.0062	150.12	0.000
	intercept	0.0016	0.0023	0.0020	0.77	0.441

(continued)

CSO participatory environment$_{t-1}$

Polyarchy$_{t-2}$	0.0004	0.0008	0.0032	0.13	0.898
Agricultural income$_{t-2}$	-0.0007*	-0.0106	0.0004	-2.03	0.042
GDP per capita$_{t-2}$	0.0009	0.0006	0.0089	0.11	0.915
Literacy$_{t-2}$	0.0015***	0.0261	0.0003	5.46	0.000
High state capacity$_{t-2}$	0.0033	0.0023	0.0063	0.52	0.600
National economic growth$_{t-2}$	-0.1030*	-0.0081	0.0486	-2.12	0.034
Anti-system movement$_{t-2}$	0.0071	0.0066	0.0057	1.23	0.218
Right-wing movement$_{t-2}$	-0.0312	-0.0043	0.0353	-0.88	0.378
Left-wing movement$_{t-2}$	-0.0205	-0.0038	0.0184	-1.12	0.263
CSO participatory environment$_{t-2}$	0.9626***	0.9523	0.0054	177.36	0.000
intercept	0.0144***	0.0143	0.0028	5.14	0.000

National economic growth$_{t-1}$

Polyarchy$_{t-2}$	0.0017	0.0409	0.0009	1.85	0.064
Agricultural income$_{t-2}$	-0.0001	-0.0272	0.0001	-1.16	0.245
GDP per capita$_{t-2}$	-0.0173***	-0.1345	0.0037	-4.68	0.000
Literacy$_{t-2}$	0.0002*	0.0549	0.0001	2.19	0.029
High state capacity$_{t-2}$	0.0025	0.0226	0.0018	1.42	0.156
National economic growth$_{t-2}$	0.0941***	0.0962	0.0274	3.43	0.001
intercept	0.0005	0.0060	0.0008	0.58	0.561

Anti-system movement$_{t-1}$

Polyarchy$_{t-2}$	-0.0003	-0.0006	0.0034	-0.09	0.931
Agricultural income$_{t-2}$	-0.0003	-0.0040	0.0004	-0.62	0.537

(continued)

TABLE 8.5 (*continued*)

Endogenous variable	Predictors	unstd.coef.	std. coef.	s.e.	z	p
	GDP per capita$_{t-2}$	0.0003	0.0002	0.0106	0.03	0.975
	Literacy$_{t-2}$	-0.0005	-0.0098	0.0003	-1.52	0.128
	High state capacity$_{t-2}$	-0.0187*	-0.0138	0.0085	-2.20	0.028
	National economic growth$_{t-2}$	0.1503	0.0126	0.0793	1.90	0.058
	Anti-system movement$_{t-2}$	0.9303***	0.9266	0.0066	141.30	0.000
	Right-wing movement$_{t-2}$	0.0224	0.0033	0.0355	0.63	0.527
	Left-wing movement$_{t-2}$	0.0722**	0.0142	0.0258	2.80	0.005
	intercept	-0.0065*	-0.0069	0.0032	-2.01	0.044
Left-wing movement$_{t-1}$						
	Polyarchy$_{t-2}$	0.0005	0.0047	0.0005	0.88	0.377
	Agricultural income$_{t-2}$	0.0000	0.0007	0.0001	0.14	0.889
	GDP per capita$_{t-2}$	-0.0035	-0.0114	0.0019	-1.88	0.060
	Literacy$_{t-2}$	-0.0001	-0.0068	0.0001	-1.28	0.202
	High state capacity$_{t-2}$	-0.0005	-0.0018	0.0018	-0.28	0.782
	National economic growth$_{t-2}$	0.0044	0.0019	0.0089	0.49	0.624
	Anti-system movement$_{t-2}$	0.0004	0.0018	0.0012	0.28	0.776
	Right-wing movement$_{t-2}$	-0.0019	-0.0014	0.0061	-0.31	0.755
	Left-wing movement$_{t-2}$	0.9428***	0.9413	0.0064	146.81	0.000
	intercept	0.0005	0.0025	0.0007	0.66	0.511
Right-wing movement$_{t-1}$						
	Polyarchy$_{t-2}$	0.0019***	0.0251	0.0005	3.57	0.000
	Agricultural income$_{t-2}$	-0.0002**	-0.0196	0.0001	-2.77	0.006

(*continued*)

GDP per capita$_{t-2}$	−0.0032*	−0.0135	0.0015	−2.09	0.037
Literacy$_{t-2}$	−0.0001**	−0.0157	0.0000	−2.79	0.005
High state capacity$_{t-2}$	−0.0030	−0.0148	0.0016	−1.84	0.065
National economic growth$_{t-2}$	−0.0024	−0.0013	0.0067	−0.36	0.722
Anti-system movement$_{t-2}$	−0.0008	−0.0054	0.0009	−0.87	0.382
Right-wing movement$_{t-2}$	0.9258***	0.9207	0.0091	101.72	0.000
Left-wing movement$_{t-2}$	0.0046	0.0061	0.0052	0.90	0.371
intercept	0.0004	0.0025	0.0004	0.87	0.384

Error variances

Downturn	0.0005	0.9274	0.0001
Agricultural income	13.0000	0.0590	2.2067
GDP per capita	0.0057	0.0157	0.0007
Literacy	1.1352	0.0036	0.1769
Strict presidentialism	0.0606	0.9587	0.0078
High state capacity	0.0463	0.0955	0.0053
CSO participatory environment	0.0665	0.0659	0.0069
National economic growth	0.0059	0.9814	0.0009
Anti-system movement	0.1134	0.1282	0.0097
Left-wing movement	0.0038	0.1104	0.0004
Right-wing movement	0.0029	0.1472	0.0004

Notes: Log pseudolikelihood = −11,553. N = 6,753. Number of countries: 137. * $p < 0.05$, ** $p < 0.01$, *** $p < 0.001$.

Another surprising conclusion is that downturns tend to be smaller in presidential systems, that is, those in which the same person is head of state and head of government, whether they are democratic or not. This estimate appears contrary to Linz (1994), which argued that presidential democracies are more prone to breakdown. Our estimate is hardly the first challenge to Linz's argument (e.g., Cheibub 2007), but we still find it surprising and difficult to explain. If we wanted to explain the probability of downturns rather than their magnitude, we would want to see whether influential leaders who wish to subvert democracy tend to succeed, and under what conditions. Mainwaring and Pérez-Liñán (2013) find support for this idea.

One similarity with the upturns model is that downturns tend to be larger in more agriculture-dependent economies. Thus, economic development, in the sense that the sectoral composition of the economy changes away from agricultural production, amplifies upturns and moderates downturns. The latter result contrasts with the nonsignificant findings in Chapter 5 on agricultural income share and downturns, although agricultural income was found to mitigate democratic outcomes in all other specifications in that chapter as well. It should be noted, however, that the specifications in Chapter 5 did not account for potential indirect effects of agricultural income on downturns, for instance, its negative effects on state capacity or civil society.

Several indirect effects identified in Figure 8.4 merit comments. First, high state capacity/rule of law makes anti-system movements less prevalent.[22] It makes sense that movements that seek to overturn the political system tend to arise where the system enforces the law arbitrarily or delivers public services unfairly. This finding does not go as far as Rothstein's emphasis on impartial public administration and Fukuyama's claim that state-building should be a higher priority than democracy promotion (Fukuyama 2004; Rothstein 1998). Our conclusion is also different from Norris's argument that the combination of democracy and capable governance deliver better socioeconomic outcomes than either democracy or capable governance alone, as we are not trying to explain outcomes other than changes in democracy (Norris 2012). All we claim is that an impartial, strong state can help prevent movements that tend to undermine democracy.

Second, growth tends to be slower in high-income or less literate countries but faster in lower-income or more literate countries. These tendencies are well known and have strong theoretical underpinnings in economic growth theory (e.g., Barro and Sala-i-Martin 2004), although the net effect on downturns contradicts the Chapter 5 argument that income reduces the magnitude of downturns. Here, the indirect effect of GDP per capita on downturns is to reduce national economic growth, thereby making downturns larger than

---

[22] This effect disappears if we substitute V-Dem's thicker rule of law index for the thinner measure. In that model, literacy also tends to strengthen the rule of law while the level of polyarchy tends to weaken it; and the rule of law strengthens civil society.

they would otherwise be. However, a higher income does reduce the share of agricultural production in GDP, and this reduction, in turn, enhances state capacity and the participatory environment for civil society organizations.

Third, right-wing movements tend to be found in poor, illiterate societies; but also in less agricultural societies that are relatively democratic. In other words, right-wing movements are stronger in societies that are rather democratic and industrialized, but without sharing the benefits equitably. This tension raises the intriguing possibility that the gap between expectations raised by a modicum of democracy and industrialization and the reality of low incomes and lack of education creates resentments that breed mobilization on the right. This could also be a backlash against minoritarian policies of democracy in societies where the majority of voters are rural, poor, and less educated. Farmers, as blue-collar workers, may see minority protections as a form of "line skipping" that undermines their hard work and threatens their values (Claassen 2020; Hochschild 2018). Perhaps right-wing movements are less of a problem where economic and social development evolve in a more even and egalitarian fashion.

8.6 CAVEATS

Although we believe there are novel, interesting, and plausible lessons that can be learned from the preceding analysis, we are aware of several weaknesses and advise readers to interpret the results cautiously. Most obviously, it is hard to be certain that we have specified our models correctly. There are many variables in play and the number of ways to combine them in path diagrams increases combinatorially with the number of variables. Theoretical reasoning and selection based on empirical fit can help mitigate some of the issues with these daunting numbers. Theoretical reasoning provides some guidance about ruling out some possibilities but never enough to narrow the possibilities down to one certain model. We have relied heavily on model fit to lead us to the best specification, but perhaps too heavily. The best-fitting and most robust model is not necessarily the correct one. It is always possible that the "true" model requires some surprising choices that yield estimates that are far from robust.

Second, path analysis assumes that the explanatory variables are measured without error. We have not attempted to incorporate measurement models to deal with systematic error, and we have not taken advantage of the method of composition using the posteriors from V-Dem's measurement model to factor in more random measurement error.

Third, we have not yet found a way to combine the path models with the spatial models estimated in Chapter 4. It seems likely that the same international influences reported there would be replicated in path models, but it is difficult to be sure of that at this point. It is also difficult to know how the inclusion of these influences would alter the estimates for other variables.

Fourth, in our path models, but even in this book more generally, we have not attempted to examine the endogeneity of components of democracy itself. How does judicial independence affect executive accountability? How important is freedom of the press for the fairness of elections? We have not addressed such questions, and not accounting for them could influence the estimates presented earlier.

Fifth, aside from some revealing descriptive analysis in Chapter 2, we have mainly limited our focus to electoral democracy/polyarchy in this book. This may seem like a strange omission coming from participants in a project that calls itself Varieties of Democracy, but there is only so much that we can do in one book if we aim for thorough analysis.

Sixth, it is all but certain that we have omitted some relevant variables in our analysis, both in this concluding chapter and in the book, overall. None of our models include measures of public opinion, as survey data do not exist for most of our historical sample and would be impossible to obtain without a time machine. Our models mostly ignore influential theorizing about elites, leadership, alliances, and pacts. We incorporate new data on various kinds of social movements, the timing of their campaigns, the groups they represent, and how violent they are; but we have no data that could capture elite attitudes about democracy. Neither do we account for political inclusion and equality with respect to gender, race, ethnicity, religion, class, or sexual orientation. In the downturns model, polarization would be a promising explanatory variable. Some V-Dem variables could begin to address these issues.

Finally, we have barely attempted (only in some other chapters, not in this one) to check for causal heterogeneity by historical period or region. We have controlled for year or decade dummies in our analysis, but we have not assessed whether the influence of different determinants of democracy vary systematically by time and place.

In response to some of these doubts, we can say we have done all that is feasible at present even if it less than perfect. In response to others, we have to admit that more could be done, but not within the limits of this book. We will continue working on these questions and also encourage others to pick up where we have left off. In response to still others, we really have no adequate answer except to remind everyone that scientific conclusions are always partial, uncertain, and provisional. We learn what we can from the methods we have chosen and offer our lessons modestly to the ongoing scholarly conversation.

8.7   A REVISED UNDERSTANDING OF DEMOCRATIZATION

If we could for a moment set aside our own caution and take our findings at face value, they would have several important implications for our understanding of the development and decline of democracy. First, the best direct explanations for upturns in the short term are nonviolent resistance campaigns in the context of low democracy, a healthy and active civil society, an expanding global economy, and a domestic economy that is not very dependent on agriculture. In the longer term, a dozen other factors can indirectly either strengthen or weaken upturns, and they include civil society variables, modernization variables, and distal variables, interacting in complex ways.

Second, in the short term, downturns tend to be larger in democratic countries with a large anti-system movement and a shrinking domestic economy. Downturns may, surprisingly to us, also be smaller in presidential systems. In the long term, weak rule of law and illiteracy can contribute to conditions that are favorable for a large downturn. We have fewer explanations for downturns, which are the rarest events in this study. As noted, this observation corresponds well with earlier sensitivity analysis of determinants of regime transitions using binary democracy measures, which find fewer robust determinants of democratic breakdowns than democratization episodes (Gassebner et al. 2013; Rød et al. 2020). Polarization and anti-democratic leadership would be good candidates for an explanation (e.g., Lührmann 2021).

In general, these conclusions about upturns and downturns place greater emphasis on dynamic, proximate variables such as social mobilization and economic growth than on the slowly evolving variables of modernization theory or geographic or cultural determinants. Our third implication is therefore that it is crucially important for scholars to pay attention to the sequencing of causes. When we estimate relationships, we should be aware of any posttreatment/downstream variables in the model and not be too quick to dismiss upstream variables that are not statistically significant. By the same token, when a model contains only distal or intermediate variables, we should remain alert to the possibility that proximate variables are likely to mediate their effects. We encourage the use of path analysis or other types of analysis that are able to model complex, endogenous relationships appropriately.

Fourth, we have explained why punctuated equilibrium characterizes democratization. One reason that long periods of stasis set in is that nearly invariant distal variables such as European population and Protestant population (understood as proxies for various kinds of European influence) and distance from natural harbors put states on an initial trajectory that favors or discourages (but by no means rigidly determines) later democratization. A second reason is that socioeconomic development variables such as industrialization, income levels, and literacy, which are caused partly by the distal conditions, themselves change slowly and incrementally and are mutually reinforcing. The third reason is that a few similar-intermediate causes – the rule of law, a healthy civil society, and institutionalized parties – form a protective belt around the level of polyarchy, pushing the political system toward homeostasis. These characteristics are also very stable, so they usually exert consistent influence on the level of democracy, helping to stabilize it at whatever level it has attained. In addition, the causes in this belt reinforce one another in a way that tends to stabilize the belt's influence on polyarchy as long as there are no shocks from variables that lie outside this system. All of these processes tend to make the level of democracy sticky.

Nevertheless, conditions downstream from the protective belt can upset the equilibrium, resulting in large upturns or downturns. A powerful anti-system movement and/or a deep and probably sustained economic downturn can override the equilibrium and cause a breakdown of democracy. It is also possible that upstream conditions, especially the erosion of the standard of living, can weaken civil society, parties, and the rule of law to the point where polyarchy begins a death spiral from which it is difficult to recover. Alternatively, nonviolent resistance movements can erode the stability of nondemocratic regimes, especially where civil society participation is protected and global economic prospects seem promising. In the longer run, even if civil society and party and state institutions are weak, socioeconomic development can strengthen them so that they can generate and sustain upturns. While democracy levels are typically persistent, the last two centuries have witnessed numerous examples of countries in different regions of the world that have broken out of an undemocratic equilibrium and experienced substantial democratization.

If these models are correct, then they suggest what the most likely drivers of trends circa 2020 may be. We dare not make predictions about the future, but we can offer some evaluation of the fit of our models to reality in recent years. As has long been true, the most democratic countries tend to be socioeconomically developed countries that possess a healthy civil society, strong rule of law, and institutionalized political parties. However, since about 2009, a number of large countries have experienced some serious erosion. Our downturns model predicts larger erosion in relatively democratic countries with a weak economy in which an anti-system movement has arisen and a downturn happened in the previous year. Although our models explain general tendencies rather than specific cases, it is hard not to see an affinity between these tendencies and the rise of authoritarian anti-pluralists in countries like Brazil, Greece, Hungary, India, Philippines, Poland, Serbia, Turkey, and the United States since the financial crisis of 2008–2009 and during the global economic downturn of the novel coronavirus pandemic (Lührmann 2021). Our model "postdicts" downturns in all of these countries in 2017 (the most recent year with nearly complete data). However, because our model takes many variables into account, the countries with the ten largest predicted downturns for 2017 were Brazil, Niger, Poland, Croatia, Kyrgyzstan, Burundi, Cape Verde, Mauritania, Tanzania, and Bhutan. Of these, all but Kyrgyzstan and Bhutan actually did experience a downturn that year.

The upturns model suggests where to look for signs of the renewal of democratization. Upturns have tended to be stronger in the less democratic countries that nevertheless have a less agricultural economy and a healthy civil society; and especially those with a growing economy and nonviolent opposition campaigns. The countries with the ten largest predicted upturns for 2007 (the most recent year with complete data on the variables in this model) were Liberia, Iraq, Nepal, Thailand, Belarus, Ukraine, Haiti, Democratic Republic of the Congo, Lebanon, and the Maldives. Of these, all but Thailand, Lebanon, and Maldives actually experienced an upturn in 2007.

We began this section with the conditional clause: "If we could for a moment set aside our own caution and take our findings at face value..." so that we could highlight what the most interesting implications of this chapter would be if the analysis is correct. In the Section 8.6, we acknowledged many reasons to remember to be cautious, and we do not ask readers to disregard them. Nevertheless, we have learned much more than nothing. Statistical analysis of observational data always contains uncertainties, but it also reveals a lot, within bounds. At a minimum, we have found some robust empirical tendencies. In addition, this is not barefoot empiricism. The earlier chapters distilled decades of evidence and theoretical debate about why these variables may matter, so our empirical tests are backed by well-known theories that gave us reasons to include them in our models. Furthermore, we have taken many precautions to rule out some of the most common obstacles to causal inference. Others remain, but we think this is about the best anyone can do at this point. We see no other way to test complex ideas about relationships that are generalizable to most of the world and more than a century of history. We hope that others will take our conclusions as the starting line for the next waves of investigation on these questions.

Appendix 3 Variable Definitions

Agricultural suitability. Geographic endowments favoring agricultural production including climate, soil, and terrain. *Source:* Agro-Ecological Zones system (GAEZ), developed by the Food and Agriculture Organization of the United Nations (FAO), downloaded (October 2017) from http://gaez.fao.org/Main.html#. *Scale:* logarithmic. *suita_GAEZ_ln*

Desert. Share of territory classified as desert. *Source:* Tollefsen, Strand, Buhaug (2012). *Scale:* interval. *desert*

GDP per cap. Gross domestic product per capita in constant 1990 dollars, based on data from the Maddison Project (Bolt and van Zanden 2014), supplemented by estimates from Bairoch (1976), Broadberry (2013), Broadberry and Klein (2012), Gleditsch (2002), and the WDI (World Bank 2016), which are combined in a dynamic, three-dimensional latent trait model. *Source:* Fariss et al. (2017). *Scale:* logarithmic. *Maddison_gdppc_1990_estimate_ln*

Harbor distance. Distance from nearest natural harbor (1,000 km), averaged across all grid-cells in a country. *Source:* Gerring et al. (2022). *Scale:* interval. *portdist_natural_1000 km*

Irrigation potential. Areas where irrigation could make a big impact on agricultural productivity, as measured by statistics gathered by the FAO Global Agro-Ecological Zones (GAEZ) 2002 database. *Source:* Bentzen et al. (2016). *Scale:* interval. *irri_impact5*

Island. Indicates whether a country is attached to a continental land mass or not. *Source:* authors. *Scale:* binary. *Island*

Land area. Land area of country. *Source:* Agro-Ecological Zones system (GAEZ), developed by the Food and Agriculture Organization of the United Nations (FAO), downloaded (October 2017) from http://gaez .fao.org/Main.html#. Extra data linearly imputed with data from WDI (World Bank 2016). *Scale:* logarithmic. *area_GAEZ_ln_imp*

Landlock. Coded 1 for landlock, 0 otherwise. *Source:* authors. *Scale:* binary. *landlock*

Latitude. Distance from equator. *Source:* QoG (Teorell et al. 2019). *Scale:* logarithmic. *Latitude_ln*

Muslim. Share of population with Muslim heritage (%). *Source:* La Porta et al. (1999), obtained from QoG (Teorell et al. 2013). *Scale:* interval. *Muslim*

Oil wealth. The total income from mineral resources, per capita. *Source:* Haber and Menaldo (2011). *Scale:* interval. *e_Total_Resources_Income_PC*

Polyarchy. Electoral democracy index. *Source:* V-Dem (Coppedge et al. 2017; Teorell et al. 2019). *Scale:* interval. *v2x_polyarchy*

Population. Official population of a country, counting only those acknowledged as citizens. This is based on the data from the Maddison Project (Bolt, van Zanden 2014), supplemented by estimates from Broadberry and Klein (2012), Gleditsch (2002), Singer et al. (1972), and WDI (World Bank 2016), which are combined in a dynamic, three-dimensional latent trait model. *Source:* Fariss et al. (2017). *Scale:* logarithmic. *Maddison_pop_estimate_ln*

Precipitation. Average annual rainfall. *Source:* Tollefsen, Strand and Buhaug (2012). *Scale:* interval. *prec_gpcc*

Protestant. Share of population with Protestant heritage (%). *Source:* La Porta et al. (1999), obtained from QoG (Teorell et al. 2013). *Scale:* interval. *lp_protmg80*

Regions. A vector of dummies: Eastern Europe and Central Asia (including Mongolia), Latin America, Middle East, North Africa, sub-Saharan Africa, Western Europe and North America, East Asia, South-East Asia, South Asia, the Pacific, and the Caribbean. *Source:* QoG (Teorell et al. 2013). *Scale:* nominal. *e_regionpol*

River distance. Distance from nearest navigable river (km), averaged across all grid-cells in a country. *Source:* Gerring et al. (2022). *Scale:* interval. *rivdist_abs_new*

Ruggedness. Terrain Ruggedness Index, 100 m. *Source:* Nunn and Puga (2012). *Scale:* interval. *rugged*

Small state. Indicates whether a country's population is less than one million. *Source:* authors, calculated from Population (above). *Scale:* binary. *small_state*

Soil. Share of territory with fertile soil. *Source:* Nunn and Puga (2012). *Scale:* interval. *Soil*

Temperature. Mean temperature. *Source:* Taken from PRIO-GRID (Tollefsen et al., 2012) and interpolated to cover the time series: "gives the yearly mean temperature (in degrees Celsius) in the cell, based on monthly meteorological statistics from GHCN/CAMS, developed at the Climate Prediction Center, NOAA/National Weather Service. This indicator contains data for the years 1948-2014." (Tollefsen et al. 2012. *Scale:* interval. *tmean*

Tropical. Share of territory classified as tropical. *Source:* Nunn and Puga (2012). *Scale:* interval. *Tropical*

Urbanization. Share of population living in urban areas (%). *Source:* V-Dem (Coppedge et al. 2017). *Scale:* interval. *e_miurbani*

Appendix 4.A Modeling Spatial Dependence

In spatial econometrics, the standard way to model network relationships is to construct a $\mathbf{W}$ matrix, which is simply a square matrix with one column and one row for each observation in the dataset (Neumayer and Plümper 2016). To analyze a panel dataset with N countries and T time periods, the $\mathbf{W}$ matrix has dimensions NTxNT. In a spatial regression, all spatially dependent terms in the equation are interacted with $\mathbf{W}$ in order to estimate spatial relationships correctly. The cells (denoted w_{ij}) of the matrix contain zeroes for countries (or country-time periods) that are not linked, and nonzero weights to indicate the weight of each column country relative to each row country. For unweighted relationships, the cells contain only zeroes and ones. The weights indicate only direct (first-order) linkages, such as a country's own contiguous neighbors, which constitute the first spatial lag. However, they also imply indirect (second- and higher-order) linkages, or longer spatial lags, such as neighbors of neighbors, neighbors of neighbors of neighbors, and so on. Spatial lags are different from temporal lags because a country tends to have more than one country in its first spatial lag, while a temporal lag always refers to the same country. Weirdly, every country is one of its own second-order spatial lags, as it is always a neighbor of its neighbors unless the linkage is unidirectional. This is another difference with temporal lags, as time flows in only one direction and therefore does not circle back on itself. In spatially lagged relationships, impacts reverberate among countries at a diminishing rate until they die out.

The spatial lag coefficient, ρ, captures only the direct impact of a spatially lagged variable. The full spatial effect, usually called the "steady-state" effect, is the sum of all of the exponentially diminishing spatial lags. This is somewhat analogous to the long-run effect, φ, of a temporal lag. In both cases, one divides the reported coefficient by one minus the lag coefficient (times $\mathbf{W}$, for spatial lags) to obtain the long-run or steady-state (or in the presence of both temporal and spatial lags, long-run steady-state) coefficient. If ρ is large, the spatial dependence diminishes slowly and the cumulative effect is large. If ρ is small, the spatial dependence may die out almost immediately. If so, it may not be useful to model more than the first lag, as Leeson and Dean (2009) did despite using a **W** matrix. Of course, it is always possible that a spatial lag is not significant at all.

In nonspatial regression, we interpret coefficients as the average effect of a unit change in the independent variable, other things being equal. In spatial regression, the effects depend on multiple source countries, and each target country is often linked to a different set of source countries. For this reason, the "effect" is not a single number, but an NTxNT matrix of observation-specific effects. In the Delta Method, one interprets the effects as the propagation of a hypothetical shock through the network. The effect is the sum of the diminishing spatial lag coefficients multiplied by a unit change in the spatially lagged variable for every linked observation.

A final difference between our approach and those used in the existing literature is that we test multiple **W** networks head-to-head: what is known as a multiplex model. It is important to do this because network memberships can overlap: countries tend to ally with neighbors, trade with allies, share a language with their former colonial power, be contiguous with other former colonies of the same power, and so on. When modeled separately, each network is likely to claim some of the credit that properly belongs to overlapping networks. Modeling them together helps sort out which networks matter the most. Although we do not report this, it is also possible to calculate and report a total effect of all networks working together as a way of assessing the relative importance of domestic and international variables. Conveniently, the average indirect effect for multiple networks and a temporally lagged dependent variable is rho divided by one minus each of the first-order spatial and temporal lag coefficients (Franzese and Hays 2008b, 24):

$$1 - \rho_1 \mathbf{W}_1 - \rho_2 \mathbf{W}_2 - \dots - \rho_k \mathbf{W}_k - \varphi \tag{1}$$

In the section on Interpretation, we defend basing our long-run steady-state simulations on rhos estimated in a multiplex model rather than in separate models for each network. The main defense is that our focus on the marginal effects of one network, holding other networks constant, pertains to a hypothetical scenario in with the controlled networks did not exist. But a secondary defense is that the empirical estimates do not differ very much. We offer evidence of that here. Table 4.A.1 compares the rhos for the neighbors, alliances, current colonies, and former colonies networks in models of polyarchy levels, upturns, and downturns, depending on whether the estimates come from multiplex or separate models.

There are some differences, but where they exist, we prefer the multiplex estimates because they appear to do a better job of apportioning credit among networks that overlap to some extent. In models of levels, it makes sense that the one significant network, neighbors, has a larger effect when all networks are

TABLE 4.A.1 *Comparison of multiplex and separate estimates of* ρ

outcome	model	neighbors	alliances	current colonies	former colonies
level	multiplex	0.02496***	0.00316	0.00175	0.00035
	separate	0.01886***	0.00188	0.00284	0.00262
upturns	multiplex	0.35027***	0.19186***	0.07465*	0.05365*
	separate	0.43848***	0.22795***	0.00156	0.03969
downturns	multiplex	0.33475***	0.13947**	0.01451	-0.00747
	separate	0.24356***	0.28891***	-0.61593	-0.12012**

* p < 0.05, ** p < 0.01, *** p < 0.001

included. In models of upturns, it makes sense that neighbors have a smaller effect when three other significant networks are in the same model. And in models of downturns, it makes no sense at all that the former colonial network has a significant negative coefficient when it is estimated separately. That would mean that a downturn in one country leads to upturns in other former colonies. In the multiplex estimate, former colonies have no significant effect.

Appendix 4.B Other Networks

We expect that military alliances matter in a few distinct ways. First, the prospect of enhancing security is a powerful incentive for joining a defensive alliance. Some important alliances, formally or informally, make a certain type of regime a prerequisite for membership, so countries may evolve toward that kind of regime before joining. For example, NATO expects prospective member countries to move toward democracy (although Portugal, Greece, and Turkey have not always conformed to this expectation). This expectation turned into a formal requirement following the Cold War (Schimmelfennig 2007). In the Warsaw Pact, it was the opposite, as both the eastern alliance structure and the nondemocratic regimes were imposed by the Soviet Union. In both cases, influential groups were comfortable with these international alignments and would have resisted promising to defend a country with a very different regime (Siverson and Emmons 1991). Second, once in the alliance, alliance members often exert pressure on other member countries to bring their political regimes into conformity with their own, whether democratic or nondemocratic, through means ranging from quiet diplomacy, to public admonishments, to sanctions, to invasion (as in East Germany, Hungary, and Czechoslovakia). In general, alliance networks can exert pressure ranging from subtle, informational linkages that encourage convergence to forceful, coercive convergence. These theoretical expectations are in line with recent findings casting doubts on the democratic peace literature, specifically that democracies do not make war against other democracies precisely because they tend to be allies and under a powerful ally's protection (McDonald 2015).

Several different causal mechanisms could be relevant in colonial networks. If there is convergence between colonizers and (former) settlement colonies, then the settlers themselves and their ties to the mother country presumably play the main role of transmitting ideas, institutions, and norms, as well as a common language and sometimes religion to the colony. Even beyond the colonies of settlement, however, colonizers and colonies are often linked by language and religion and with them, easy access to literature, news, and entertainment.

These cultural ties could also encourage trade and investment. Colonial elites have often been educated in the colonizing country. In some empires, institutions such as courts, elections, and legislatures were transplanted to the colonies before independence. The most dramatic forms of influence have been economic sanctions and military intervention in former colonies. Such actions reached their peak before independence, with the British in India, the Portuguese in Africa, and the French in North Africa; but France continues to intervene militarily in its former West African colonies, most recently in Mali.

There are, however, other possible mechanisms that would lead colonizers and colonies to diverge in their levels of democracy. Much of the literature on colonialism emphasizes the exploitative nature of these relationships (Acemoglu et al. 2001; Cardoso and Faletto 1979; Lange et al. 2006, Mahoney 2010; Wallerstein 1974). The motivation for colonization was not to spread democracy, but to bring economic benefits to the colonial powers. They, or private firms chartered by them, extracted immense mineral wealth from some colonies and purchased agricultural products from others at artificially low prices. In order to maintain control over colonial territories and populations, colonizers appointed governors who ruled in authoritarian and sometimes violently brutal ways. In the colonies of occupation, colonizers ruled indirectly through local elites, who thereby became less accountable to their own communities. Although France and Portugal considered their colonies overseas territories in a unified empire and even granted them representation in the national parliament (when there was an elected parliament), both states created a second-class "indigenous" citizenship for colonial peoples who were not descended from settlers (Owolabi 2010, 2012). In the most extreme instances, colonizers imported enslaved Africans to provide a workforce for the most difficult and dangerous labor. In sum, at a time when Europe was moving slowly and with fits and starts from absolute monarchy toward proto-democratic systems, its colonial populations were being subjected to profound economic, social, and political inequalities. There are good reasons to expect that the net impact of colonial rule may have caused political development in Europe and its colonies to diverge.

Appendix 4.C Estimation

The spatiotemporal autoregressive (STAR) model is expressed as:

$$y = \rho \mathbf{W}y + \varphi \mathbf{M}y + \boldsymbol{\beta}\mathbf{X} + \varepsilon \qquad (2)$$

(Franzese and Hays 2008a; Lesage and Pace 2009, 27). In equation (2), $\mathbf{W}$ is a matrix of spatial lags and $\mathbf{M}$ is a matrix of temporal lags. Therefore, ρ is the coefficient of spatial dependence and φ the coefficient of temporal dependence. $\mathbf{X}$ is a matrix of domestic independent variables, $\boldsymbol{\beta}$ is a vector of their coefficients, and ε is the error term. Specifically, because we use instrumental variables to address spatial endogeneity, we use generalized spatial two-stage least squares (GS2SLS), which is very similar to feasible generalized least squares and the spatial generalized method of moments (Franzese and Hays 2008a; Land and Deane 1992). As instruments we use the spatial lags of the nonspatial regressors $\mathbf{X}$, which are the "ideal instruments" in many situations because the domestic determinants of democracy in source countries is not likely to directly affect democracy in the target country except through democracy in the source countries.[1] Thus, if there is spatial dependence on polyarchy, then democracy at home is a function of both covariates at home and those same covariates abroad.

This setup also makes it possible, if desired, to model spatial dependence in the errors $(\rho \varepsilon_{jt})$. We choose to include this term in order to correct for spatially dependent bias in omitted variables. For example, many domestic conditions help create and preserve high levels of democracy in Western Europe. We control only for literacy, an imperfect proxy for multifaceted economic and social development, and a few other variables. Still others are certainly omitted, and we do not wish to falsely attribute their influence to spatial dependence: European democracies propping one another up. The spatial

---

[1] Spatial lags of the nonspatial regressors would be problematic instruments if democracy in the target country affected domestic determinants of democracy in source countries (e.g., if democratic neighbors raised literacy in a source country but nondemocratic neighbors did not), or if there is reverse causality in the target country combined with spatial dependence in democracy.

autocorrelation term helps isolate the effects of such omitted domestic variables so that we get a better estimate of the international processes that interest us.

One of our innovations is to test multiple networks of spatial dependence: neighbors, allies, current colonies, and former colonies. Each additional network requires adding another matrix multiplication to the equation. This is computationally costly, but it has a simple impact on the multiplier, which becomes, for the whole sample and k networks (Franzese and Hays 2008b),

$$[I - \rho_1 W_1 - \rho_2 W_2 - \ldots - \rho_k W_k - \varphi My]^{-1}. \tag{3}$$

There is room for improvement in this model. It assumes, for instance, that past polyarchy in country j is exogenous: it influences present polyarchy in country i only through the instrument for present polyarchy in country j. We treat it, in other words, as an instrument, which may or may not be reasonable. Latitude and distance to ports are excellent instruments, as they are obviously exogenous; literacy seems to be a good choice as well, although there is a possibility of reverse causation. But should the time-invariant variables latitude, distance to ports, and the two correction factors be treated as instruments? We did not use them as second-level regressors simply because we do not know how to combine a mixed model with GS2SLS. One could also question whether the time-varying but country-invariant *expand* and *contract* economic shock measures belong in the list of instruments. There are also all the specifications we have not been able to implement yet – weighting, more disaggregated networks, interactions with crisis, and so on. These models simply mark some significant progress on an ongoing journey.

Appendix 4.D Descriptive Information

TABLE 4.D.1 *Descriptive information*

Variable label	Variable name	Source	N	Mean	S.D.	Min	Max
Polyarchy/Electoral Democracy Index	v2x_polyarchy	V-Dem (v9)	8,914	0.3136	0.28	0.007	0.9365
Upturn	Dpolyup	Calculated from V-Dem (v9) v2_polyarchy	9,064	0.0148	0.043	0	0.694
Downturn	Dpolydn	Calculated from V-Dem (v9) v2_polyarchy	9,065	−0.0079	0.029	−0.603	0
Colonizer selection/1,000	lambda_colonizer	Coppedge et al. (2016)	9,738	0.0051	0.003	0.0002	0.0167
Colony selection/1,000	lambda_colony	Coppedge et al. (2016)	9,738	0.0009	0.001	0	0.0044
Election year	Elyear	Calculated from V-Dem (v9) v2xel_elecparl & v2xel_elecpres	8,976	0.2063	0.276	0	1
European population/100	eur_pct_est_smooth	Chapter 3	10,090	0.1766	0.336	0	1
GDP per capita	s_far_Maddison_gdppc_1990_estima	Fariss et al. (2017)	7,306	7.7996	1.101	4.6613	11.353
Global economic growth	Expand	Calculated from logged and imputed version of e_migdpgro, used in Chapter 5, based on the Maddison Project (Bolt and van Zanden 2013)	8,806	0.0038	0.006	0	0.0273
Global GDP contraction	Contract	Calculated from logged and imputed version of e_migdpgro, used in Chapter 5, based on the Maddison Project (2013)	8,806	−0.0039	0.005	−0.0256	0

(continued)

TABLE 4.D.1 (*continued*)

Variable label	Variable name	Source	N	Mean	S.D.	Min	Max
Hyperinflation	Crisis	Dummy based on inflation measure from Clio-Infra (2016)	8,976	0.0284	0.158	0	1
Internal war	internal_war	Recoded from Pettersson (2019) & Sarkees and Wayman (2010)	9,319	0.1192	0.3	0	1
International war	international_war	Recoded from Pettersson (2019) & Sarkees (2010)	9,319	0.0332	0.16	0	1
Latitude	lp_lat_abst	Chapter 3	10,090	0.2892	0.19	0	0.7222
Literacy/1,000	litcyxtend	Imputed from Vanhanen (2003) & World Bank (2016)	9,115	0.0530	0.035	0.0002	0.1
Natural harbor distance/1,000	portdist_natural_km	Chapter 3	10,034	0.3754	0.352	0.0041	1.7652
Protestant population	chrstprotpct	Chapter 3	9,181	11.1921	20.75	0	99.009

Appendix 6.A Details on Variables and Analysis

These plots are histograms of each variable that is explicitly used in the analysis, with a vertical line representing the mean. The sources for these variables are identified in Table 1A. In the Electoral system variable, 1 is any majoritarian electoral system and 0 is otherwise. To obtain the GDP variable, we use the Maddison Project Database's "rgdpnapc," divide it by 1,000, multiply it by the population, and then take the log of one plus that value. In the Pure presidential variable, 1 means only a president is elected, 0 means no Head of State or Head of Government is elected. In the Pure prime ministerial variable, 1 means only a prime minister is elected, 0 means no Head of State or Head of Government is elected. In the Both president and PM variable, 1 means both a president and a prime minister are elected, 0 means no Head of State or Head of Government is elected. Strict president is any case in which the president is (1) the Head of Government, and (2) the Head of Government is also the Head of State.

TABLE 6.A.1 *List of variables*

Variable	Source	Count	Span
Country	Varieties of democracy version 9	10,848	1815–2015
Year	Varieties of democracy version 9	10,848	1815–2015
Polyarchy	Varieties of democracy version 9	10,730	1815–2015
Country ID	Varieties of democracy version 9	10,848	1815–2015
Geographic region	Varieties of democracy version 9	10,848	1815–2015
Majorit. electoral system	Varieties of democracy version 9	9,454	1815–2015
HOG elected directly	Varieties of democracy version 9	6,189	1815–2015
Relative power of HOG	Varieties of democracy version 9	10,733	1815–2015
Regime type	Varieties of democracy version 9	9,101	1900–2015

(*continued*)

TABLE 6.A.1 *(continued)*

Variable	Source	Count	Span
State capacity	Varieties of democracy version 9	10,776	1815–2015
Independent	Varieties of democracy version 9	10,848	1815–2015
Democratic transition	Varieties of democracy version 9	10,657	1815–2015
HOS elected directly	Varieties of democracy version 9	10847	1815–2015
Strict president	Varieties of democracy version 9	10,848	1815–2015
Legislature can remove HOG	Varieties of democracy version 9	6,127	1815–2015
Legislature can remove HOS	Varieties of democracy version 9	10,776	1815–2015
HOG can dissolve legislature	Varieties of democracy version 9	6,119	1815–2015
HOS can dissolve legislature	Varieties of democracy version 9	10,687	1815–2015
Largest seat share	Varieties of democracy version 9	1,671	1815–2015
State authority over territory	Varieties of democracy version 9	10,641	1815–2015
Party institutionalization	Varieties of democracy version 9	9,709	1815–2015
HOG appoints cabinet	Varieties of democracy version 9	6,054	1815–2015
HOG dismisses ministers	Varieties of democracy version 9	6,085	1815–2015
HOG veto power	Varieties of democracy version 9	6,085	1815–2015
HOG proposes legislation	Varieties of democracy version 9	5,498	1820–2015
HOS appoints cabinet	Varieties of democracy version 9	10,715	1815–2015
HOS appoints cabinet (diff categories)	Varieties of democracy version 9	10,715	1815–2015
HOS veto power	Varieties of democracy version 9	10,698	1815–2015
HOS dismisses ministers	Varieties of democracy version 9	10,775	1815–2015
HOS proposes legislation	Varieties of democracy version 9	10,776	1815–2015
Elected PM	Presidentialism-parliamentarianism	10,745	1815–2015
Elected Pres	Presidentialism-parliamentarianism	10,660	1815–2015
Unelected PM	Presidentialism-parliamentarianism	10,745	1815–2015
Unelected Pres	Presidentialism-parliamentarianism	10,660	1815–2015
GDP/capita	Maddison project database	10,261	1815–2015
GDP growth	Maddison project database	10,304	1815–2015
Total population	Maddison project database	10,553	1820–2015
Ethnic Fractionalization	Ethnic power relations	10,848	1815–2015
Urbanization	Cross-national time series data archive	8,677	1815–2002
Historical electoral systems	Contestation dataset	8,903	1815–2015
Independence date	Colonial history data	10,446	1815–2015
Colonial ruler	Colonial history data	10,446	1815–2015

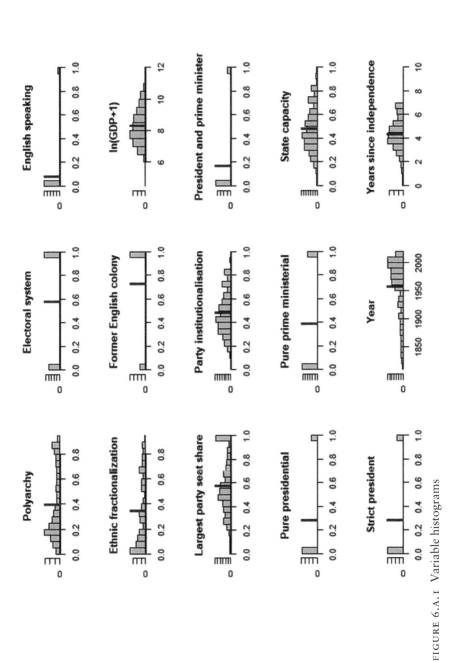

FIGURE 6.A.1 Variable histograms

277

Appendix 6.B Cox Hazard Models

TABLE 6.B.1 *Cox hazard models of democratic step-down*

	V-Dem's regimes of the world		polyarchy cut point: 0.5		polyarchy cut point: 0.7		polyarchy approx. Svolik's	
	beta	s.e.	beta	s.e.	beta	s.e.	beta	s.e.
Strict presidentialism	**–0.79**	0.33	**–0.68**	0.29	–0.01	0.35	–0.53	0.30
Majoritarian electoral system	–0.76	0.47	–0.27	0.37	–0.87	0.49	0.27	0.32
State capacity	**–11.49**	1.60	**–8.27**	1.39	**-6.98**	1.84	**–8.70**	1.39
Largest seat share	**2.07**	0.83	**2.12**	0.72	**3.58**	0.94	**1.98**	0.71
Party institutionalization	–0.43	1.00	–0.67	0.93	2.27	1.39	–1.39	0.89
Log of GDP per capita	–0.10	0.21	–0.18	0.19	–0.18	0.25	–0.10	0.20
GDP growth	**–4.48**	1.96	**–4.88**	1.75	–0.97	3.27	**–4.57**	2.00
Ethnic fractionalization	1.09	0.57	0.43	0.49	1.67	0.73	–0.43	0.47
Former UK colony	0.14	0.51	–0.35	0.45	–0.57	0.53	**–0.85**	0.47
State capacity over territory	–0.02	0.02	–0.01	0.02	–0.04	0.03	–0.01	0.01
Likelihood ratio test		105.8		90.9		58.7		97.0
N		3,379		3,425		2,229		3,873
Events		58		70		56		63

Results in bold are statistically significant at a p-value level of 0.05

TABLE 6.B.2 *Cox hazard models of democratic step-down*

	V-Dem's regimes of the world		polyarchy cut point: 0.5		polyarchy cut point: 0.7		polyarchy approx. Svolik's	
	beta	s.e.	beta	s.e.	beta	s.e.	beta	s.e.
Strict presidentialism	-1.13	0.54	-0.63	0.47	-0.08	0.53	-0.46	0.45
Majoritarian electoral system	-0.21	0.78	-0.33	0.60	-1.13	0.79	-0.40	0.57
State capacity	-13.65	2.66	-12.21	2.39	-7.85	2.34	-7.45	1.93
Largest seat share	4.36	1.64	3.90	1.48	2.27	1.41	2.78	1.20
Party institutionalization	-0.53	1.77	-0.11	1.58	2.56	2.15	-0.45	1.18
Log of GDP per capita	-0.24	0.46	-0.16	0.40	-0.30	0.35	-0.37	0.37
GDP growth	-14.33	4.03	-17.02	3.71	-12.27	4.47	-11.22	3.26
Ethnic fractionalization	0.58	1.11	0.05	0.98	1.14	1.12	-0.20	0.91
Former UK colony	-1.79	1.34	-2.35	1.32	0.62	1.03	-1.86	54.7
State information capacity	-7.74	3.05	-6.08	2.43	4.16	1.90	-2.11	2.38
Likelihood ratio test	79.3		79.2		47.3		60.8	
N	2425		2423		1706		2688	
Events	25		30		34		31	

Results in bold are statistically significant at a p-value level of 0.05

TABLE 6.B.3 *Cox Hazard models of democratic step-down*

	V-Dem's regimes of the world		polyarchy cut point: 0.5		polyarchy cut point: 0.7		polyarchy approx. Svolik's	
	beta	s.e.	beta	s.e.	beta	s.e.	beta	s.e.
Strict presidentialism	-1.43	0.60	-0.91	0.50	-0.11	0.58	-0.52	0.47
Majoritarian electoral system	-0.10	0.80	-0.68	0.62	-1.127	0.79	-0.28	0.59
State capacity	-13.31	2.67	-12.11	2.43	-7.80	2.35	-7.33	1.95
Largest seat share	4.38	1.67	3.61	1.48	2.29	1.41	2.67	1.21
Party institutionalization	-0.03	1.77	-1.01	1.61	2.53	2.15	-0.14	1.26
Log of GDP per capita	-0.05	0.47	0.18	0.41	-0.28	0.37	-0.29	0.40
GDP growth	-13.96	4.00	-16.52	3.80	-12.34	4.49	-10.94	3.27
Ethnic fractionalization	0.39	1.12	-0.39	1.02	1.10	1.14	-0.10	0.93
Former UK colony	-1.68	1.32	-2.11	1.29	0.60	1.04	-18.58	57.4
State capacity over territory	-0.07	0.04	-0.09	0.04	-0.01	0.06	-0.02	0.03
State information capacity	-8.79	3.19	-7.75	2.61	4.064	1.99	-2.54	2.51
Likelihood ratio test	81.82		84.6		47.3		60.8	
N	2425		2423		1706		2681	
Events	25		30		34		31	

Results in bold are statistically significant at a p-value level of 0.05

Appendix 7 A Details of Measurement and Analysis

To assess how organizational life (de Tocqueville 1838), the civic culture (Almond and Verba 1963), and social capital (Putnam 1994) correlates with processes of democratization, we measure civil society organizational capacity as a stock variable that accumulates annually depending on the nature of participation in civil society organizations (CSOs).

We start with the V-Dem indicator measuring the civil society participatory environment (v2csprtcpt). Country experts answer the following question, "Which of these best describes the involvement of people in civil society organizations (CSOs)?" using the following ordinal scale:

0: Most associations are state-sponsored, and although a large number of people may be active in them, their participation is not purely voluntary.
1: Voluntary CSOs exist but few people are active in them.
2: There are many diverse CSOs but popular involvement is minimal.
3: There are many diverse CSOs, and it is considered normal for people to be at least occasionally active in at least one of them.

These responses are aggregated into point estimates taking into account the reliability of the expert's coding decisions using the V-Dem measurement model (see Coppedge et al. 2019b; Pemstein et al. 2019).

The effects of civil society are unlikely to persist forever into the future. Therefore, we also incorporate an annual depreciation rate. The literature provides few clues as to how much we should theoretically expect civil society stock to depreciate annually. Prior measures of democratic stock tend to assume a constant 1 percent depreciation rate, allowing the effects of democracy in a given year to persist for a century (e.g. Gerring et al. 2005; Gerring et al. 2012). The exception is Persson and Tabellini (2009) who estimate their depreciation rates empirically using maximum likelihood estimates and conclude that annual depreciation falls between 1 percent and 6 percent. Still, this work provides little theoretical guidance on whether stocks of social phenomena depreciate at a constant rate or vary across countries and time

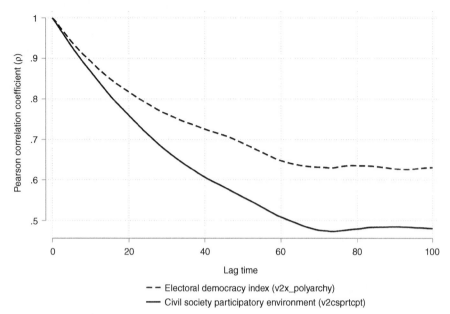

FIGURE 7.A.1 Pairwise autocorrelation coefficients for democracy and civil society participatory environment with up to 100 years lag

periods. It seems reasonable to assume the latter, especially for less persistent phenomena like civil society participation. For example, Figure 7.A1 plots the estimated Pearson correlation coefficients (ρ) when democracy and civil society participatory environment at time (t) are correlated with their lagged values up to 100 years prior. While the pairwise correlation coefficients remain quite high over the course of a century, this association is much higher for levels of democracy than civil society participation.

Based on the observation that the civil society participatory environment is less persistent than democracy, for our main models we apply a 10 percent annual depreciation rate to the civil society stock measure. In other words, we assume that the effects of civil society stock for the first year of one generation are likely to depreciate by the time the next generation attains maturity (i.e., approximately thirty years). Thus, our baseline depreciation rate is also theoretically informed by the literature linking generational shifts to changes in civil society mobilization (e.g., Bernhard and Karakoç 2007; Howard 2002; Putnam 2000).

It is likely, however, that depreciation rates for civil society organizational capacity vary depending on other conditions within a given country-year. In Appendix 7B, we provide robustness checks of our main models using an alternative measure of civil society organizational capacity that adjusts the baseline 10 percent annual depreciation rate as government repression of

CSOs increases. To do so, we draw on the V-Dem indicator for government repression of CSOs (v2csreprss). This variable asks V-Dem country experts "Does the government attempt to repress civil society organizations?" responding on the following ordinal scale: 0 – Severely; 1 – Substantively; 2 – Moderately; 3 – Weakly; 4 – No. As with the civil society participatory environment indicator, expert responses are aggregated using the V-Dem measurement model that also accounts for expert uncertainty. We assume that under conditions where government repression of CSOs is minimal, the generational change argument holds, applying a 10 percent depreciation rate annually during years where countries score highest on government repression of CSOs. We increase the depreciation rate gradually to a maximum of 30 percent during severely repressive years.[1]

Because the government repression of CSOs indicator is also included in the electoral democracy index, we report results using a thin measure of procedural democracy derived from Schumpeter (1942) and a slightly thicker version that incorporates suffrage criteria based on Munck (2009) as the outcome variables for models using the repression-based depreciation rate (see Hegre et al. 2020). We also provide robustness checks of the 10 percent constant

To calculate the stock measures, we use the following formula:

$$CivStock_{i,t} = \sum_{\tau=0}^{\tau=t-t_1} \delta^\tau(v2csprtcpt)$$

where δ is one minus the annual depreciation rate (e.g., 0.90 for the baseline). Thus, we treat the annual depreciation rate as a weight on the accumulated civil society stock up to the previous year (t_{-1}).[2] We then normalize the stock measure using the min–max method to obtain a range of 0 to 1.[3]

We assume that all countries begin with a tabula rasa, scoring zero on the civil society stock measure the year they enter the dataset. Ideally, we would begin measuring the stock of civil society from the beginning of the case. While some countries in the Historical V-Dem data begin as early as 1789, most countries are observed from 1900 or later (regular V-Dem). Yet we know that these polities potentially began accumulating stock earlier. For cases that show no

---

[1] Empirically we do this by assigning the highest values on the estimated upper uncertainty bounds (v2csreprss_codehigh) a 10 percent depreciation rate and the lowest values of the estimated lower uncertainty bounds (v2csreprss_codelow) a 30 percent depreciation. Other values are then assigned their relative values within the 10 percent to 30 percent depreciation interval.

[2] The V-Dem measurement model point estimates take on a scale similar to a normal Z-score. Therefore, these values typically range from –5 to 5. To calculate our stock measure, we rescaled the measurement model estimates to strictly positive values (by adding to absolute value of the observed minimum on the estimated lower uncertainty bound, v2csprtcpt_codelow) to ensure that the raw stock measure is always positive.

[3] We divide by the maximum observed value on the estimated upper uncertainty bound of the stock measure (calculated using v2csprtcpt_codehigh).

evidence of an established polity prior to entering the V-Dem dataset, we code the stock measure as starting from zero on the year of entry (e.g., 1902 for Senegal). Another problem arises because countries in the V-Dem dataset sometimes experience a gap in coding. For cases where an established polity existed under the occupation or governance of another state coded in the V-Dem dataset, we code values based upon the occupying or governing power. This applies to cases entering the dataset later (e.g., Estonia as part of the Russian Empire until 1918) and cases with gaps in coding (e.g., Estonia as part of the Soviet Union from 1940 to 1990). Cases we have assigned this way are shown in Table 7.A.1.

TABLE 7.A.1 *Countries recoded based on occupying power*

Country (id)	Years	Coded as (id) …
Albania (12)	1789–1911	Turkey (99)
Armenia (105)	1826–1989	Russia (11)
Austria (144)	1939–1944	Germany (77)
Azerbaijan (106)	1813–1989	Russia (11)
Bangladesh (24)	1858–1946	India (39)
Bangladesh (24)	1947–1970	Pakistan (29)
Belarus (107)	1789–1989	Russia (11)
Bolivia (25)	1789–1824	Argentina (37)
Bosnia and Herzegovina (150)	1918–1991	Serbia (198)
Bulgaria (152)	1789–1877	Turkey (99)
Burkina Faso (54)	1932–1946	Ivory Coast (64), Mali (28), Niger (60)
Central African Republic (71)	1903–1919	Republic of Congo (112)
Chad (109)	1903–1919	Republic of Congo (112)
Comoros (153)	1914–1945	Madagascar (125)
Costa Rica (73)	1789–1837	Guatemala (78)
Croatia (154)	1867–1918	Hungary (210)
Croatia (154)	1919–1940	Serbia (198)
Croatia (154)	1945–1990	Serbia (198)
Czech Republic (157)	1789–1917	Austria (144)
Dominican Republic (114)	1823–1843	Haiti (26)
Ecuador (75)	1789–1829	Colombia (15)
El Salvador (22)	1789–1837	Guatemala (78)
Estonia (161)	1789–1917	Russia (11)
Estonia (161)	1940–1989	Russia (11)
Finland (163)	1789–1808	Sweden (5)

(continued)

TABLE 7.A.1 *(continued)*

Country (id)	Years	Coded as (id) ...
Georgia (118)	1800–1989	Russia (11)
German Democratic Republic (137)	1789–1944	Germany (77)
Germany (77) (77)	1945–1948	Austria (144)
Greece (164)	1789–1821	Turkey (99)
Honduras (27)	1789–1837	Guatemala (78)
Iceland (168)	1843–1899	Denmark (158)
Iraq (80)	1831–1919	Turkey (99)
Ireland (81)	1789–1918	United Kingdom (101)
Italy (82)	1789–1860	Piedmont-Sardinia (373)
Jordan (83)	1789–1802	Turkey (99)
Jordan (83)	1803–1818	Saudi Arabia (197)
Jordan (83)	1819–1832	Turkey (99)
Jordan (83)	1833–1841	Egypt (13)
Jordan (83)	1842–1918	Turkey (99)
Jordan (83)	1919–1921	Syria (97)
Kazakhstan (121)	1789–1989	Russia (11)
Kyrgyzstan (122)	1876–1989	Russia (11)
Latvia (84)	1789–1919	Russia (11)
Latvia (84)	1940–1989	Russia (11)
Lebanon (44)	1789–1830	Turkey (99)
Lebanon (44)	1831–1841	Egypt (13)
Lebanon (44)	1842–1917	Turkey (99)
Lithuania (173)	1789–1794	Poland (17)
Lithuania (173)	1795–1917	Russia (11)
Lithuania (173)	1940–1989	Russia (11)
Luxembourg (174)	1795–1814	France (76)
Macedonia (176)	1789–1911	Turkey (99)
Macedonia (176)	1912–1990	Yugoslavia
Moldova (126)	1789–1811	Turkey (99)
Moldova (126)	1812–1917	Russia (11)
Moldova (126)	1918–1939	Romania (190)
Moldova (126)	1940–1941	Russia (11)
Moldova (126)	1942–1944	Romania (190)
Moldova (126)	1945–1989	Russia (11)
Mongolia (89)	1789–1910	China (110)

(continued)

Country (id)	Years	Coded as (id) ...
Montenegro (183)	1918–1997	Serbia (198)
Netherlands (91)	1811–1812	France (76)
North Korea (41)	1790–1944	South Korea (42)
Pakistan (29) (29)	1858–1946	India (39)
Panama (92)	1789–1902	Colombia (15)
Paraguay (189)	1789–1810	Argentina (37)
Poland (17)	1796–1806	Russia (11)
Poland (17)	1868–1917	Russia (11)
Poland (17)	1939–1943	Germany (77)
Qatar (94)	1871–1899	Turkey (99)
Saudi Arabia (197)	1819–1821	Egypt (13)
Slovakia (201)	1789–1918	Hungary (210)
Slovakia (201)	1919–1938	Czech Republic (157)
Slovakia (201)	1945–1992	Czech Republic (157)
Slovenia (202)	1789–1918	Austria (144)
Slovenia (202)	1919–1988	Serbia (198)
South Sudan (32)	1789–1899	Egypt (13)
South Sudan (32)	1900–2010	Sudan (33)
Sudan (33)	1789–1899	Egypt (13)
Syria (97)	1789–1830	Turkey (99)
Syria (97)	1831–1841	Egypt (13)
Syria (97)	1842–1917	Turkey (99)
Tajikistan (133)	1864–1989	Russia (11)
Turkmenistan (136)	1864–1989	Russia (11)
Ukraine (100)	1789–1989	Russia (11)
Uruguay (102)	1789–1820	Argentina (37)
Uruguay (102)	1821–1824	Brazil (19)
Uzbekistan (140)	1921–1989	Russia (11)
Venezuela (51)	1820–1829	Colombia (15)
Vietnam (34)	1802–1944	Republic of Vietnam (35)
Yemen (14)	1851–1917	Turkey (99)

To illustrate how the stock measure works, first imagine a country where the accumulated stock of civil society is 100 at t_1. For the next thirty years, the state sponsors most associations, sometimes making membership nonvoluntary. As a result, it consistently scores zero (0) on civil society participatory environment. In other words, during this time period it does not gain any stock. Meanwhile, its existing stock depreciates at an annual rate, either 10 percent or based on government repression of CSOs. Figure 7.A2 predicts the trend for this country's civil society stock over this thirty-year period given the different levels of government repression.

Next, we address whether our stock measure has face validity. Figure 7.A3 plots the global average of civil society stock from 1900 to 2018 using the baseline 10 percent depreciation rate. Throughout most of this period, global averages on civil society organizational capacity have remained between 0.4 and 0.6 out of one. Prior to the end of World War I, we see a monotonic increase in global civil society stock from 0.46 in 1900 to 0.55 in 1917. The immediate aftermath of WWI saw a slight decline in global civil society stock, reaching a low point of 0.54 in 1920 before it increased again to about 0.56 in 1930. Leading into and during World War II, global civil society stock again depreciated to about 0.49, where it remained throughout most of the Cold War period. As expected, in the post-Cold War era, we see an upturn in civil society stock globally, increasing from 0.51 in 1989 to 0.64 in 2018.

Figure 7.A4 plots the values over time for four familiar cases – China, France, Kenya, and the United States. After a bumpy round throughout the first half of the 1800s, France shows an upward trend in its civil society stock from the late

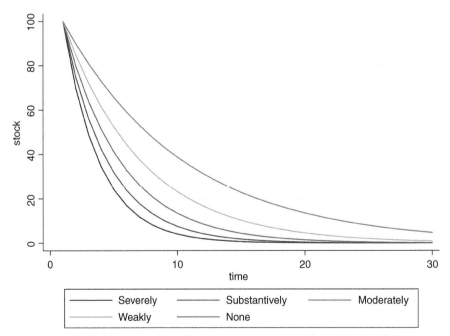

FIGURE 7.A.2 Depreciation of a stagnant civil society stock (100) over thirty years, based on level of government repression. Values for None also show estimates using the baseline 10% rate.

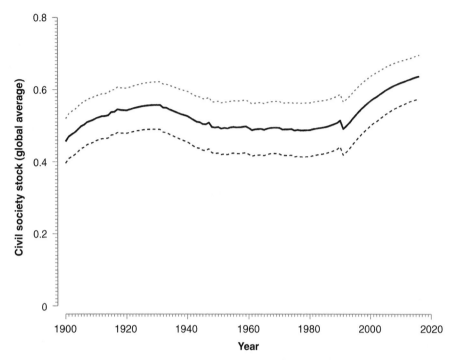

FIGURE 7.A.3 Global trends in civil society stock, 1900–2016. Values based on average of all independent countries observed during that year. Dashed lines show the uncertainty boundaries calculated from the *codelow and *codehigh values

1870s until World War II. As anticipated, we then see a dramatic decline in France's civil society stock, from 0.74 in 1940 to 0.54 in 1946. Afterward, France experienced an initial period of rapid growth until the mid-1950s followed by slow steady increases for the rest of the Cold War. Meanwhile, in the United States, civil society stock grew rapidly from independence but quickly plateaued thereafter until some modest gains from WWI onward. Both France and the United States saw a period of enhanced civil society stock after the end of the Cold War. However, these democracies have seen a slight decline since 2013, perhaps reflecting the third wave of autocratization (Lührmann and Lindberg 2019).

For Kenya, the measure also finds face validity. After an initial period of accumulation from 1900 (when it enters the data) to around 1920, Kenya's stock of civil society is stagnant for the rest of British colonial rule. With independence, it shows a steep upward trend until the late 1960s, when the regime effectively became a one-party state. Afterward, the stock continues to rise, but at a slower annual rate. The restoration of multiparty politics in 1992 precipitated another rapid increase in civil society organizational capacity. This slows considerably following the electoral defeat of the former ruling party, KANU, in 2002 until around 2009, a period when politics in Kenya became especially contentious over the drafting of a new constitution. Thereafter, under the new constitution, civil society stock rises again to present levels.

Finally, for China, after a plateau throughout the 1800s, we see some appreciation during the early years of the Republic of China, rising from 0.51 in 1912 to 0.56 in 1928. However, the Chinese Civil War, Japanese occupation, and World War II precipitated a decades-long decline in civil society stock. The measure declines steadily to 0.50 in 1949, the year of the Chinese Revolution. Following the revolution, the stock measure plummets to 0.21 in 1973. After the mid-1970s, we see a moderate increase in civil society stock as China introduced several liberalizing reforms in its economic and social sectors that allow for more opportunities for civil society to operate outside of the party state. China's civil society stock had increased to 0.43 by 2012. However, like the United States and France, it has seen slight declines since 2013, dropping to 0.41 by 2018.

Because we begin observing countries in a somewhat arbitrary fashion (subject to data availability in V-Dem), we also adjust our model sample in two ways. First, we limit the time period to 1900 and onward. While this allows for stock to accumulate prior to 1900 based on Historical V-Dem, we do not include these country-years because the sample coverage is much smaller. This also allows for stock to accumulate in older polities before they enter the sample frame. Second, we restrict our sample to independent countries but allow colonies and protectorates to develop civil society stock prior to independence. This allows these cases to enter the data with an accumulated civil society stock, despite being non-sovereign in the preceding period. Given what we know about resistance to colonial rule, particularly during the later periods, we think that it is more realistic to account for pre-independence trends even if we do not include colonies in our sample.

Figure 7.A5 provides a histogram of the observation time prior to entry into our sample of 156 countries from 1900 to 2014 (N = 10,205). The darker narrow bars represent discrete time units while the lighter shaded bars are bins of ten-year increments. We also plot a normal distribution curve and report summary statistics. On average, countries accumulated stock for 104 years before entering the sample with a standard deviation of 45.09. The minimum time prior to entry is two years (Belgium and Cameroon) and the maximum is 206 years (Slovakia). The average country had accumulated a civil society stock of 0.45 (out of 1.0) by the time of entry into the sample. For the full sample (i.e., all country-years), the average civil society stock is 0.54.

We present trends for the eight cases that enter the sample before acquiring a generation (thirty years) of civil society stock. Table 7.A2 lists these cases and Figure 7.A6 plots their trajectories before and after they enter the sample. In

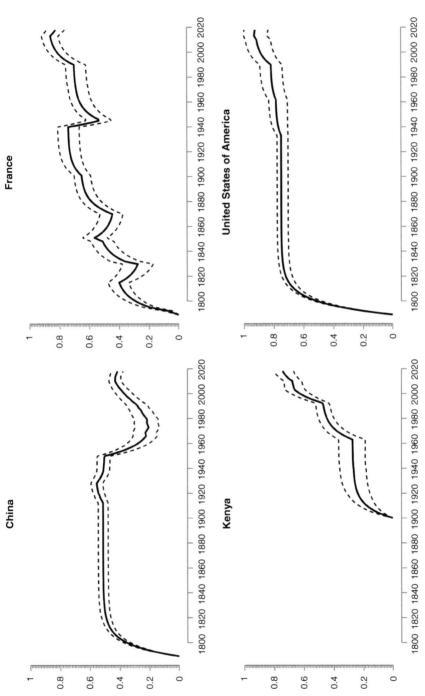

FIGURE 7.A.4 Trends in civil society stock for selected cases. Dashed lines show the uncertainty boundaries calculated from the * codelow and * codehigh values

TABLE 7.A.2 *Cases entering sample with less than thirty years of prior observations*

Country (id)	Time prior to entry
South Africa (8)	11
Nicaragua (59)	22
Cameroon (108)	2
Libya (124)	11
Belgium (148)	2
Israel (169)	4
Singapore (200)	3
United Arab Emirates (207)	24

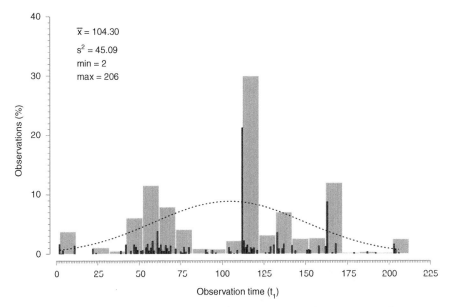

FIGURE 7.A.5 Distribution of entry points for main sample of 156 countries from 1900 to 2014 (N = 10,205). Darker narrow bars represent discrete time units. Lighter wider bars represent bins of ten-year increments. Dashed line is a normal distribution curve

Table 7.B4 we present results with a sample restricted to country-years that have accumulated at least thirty years of civil society stock. The results are fairly similar when the sample is constrained to country-years with at least a generation of civil society stock accumulation.

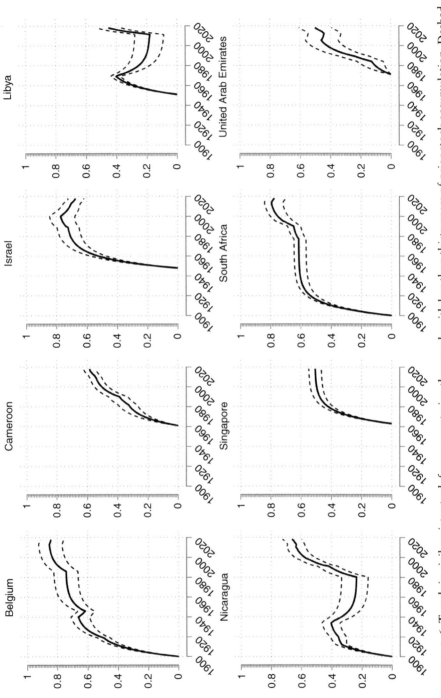

FIGURE 7.A.6 Trends in civil society stock for cases entering the sample with less than thirty years of prior stock accumulation. Dashed lines show the uncertainty boundaries calculated from the *codelow and *codehigh values?

Appendix 7 B Supplemental Tables and Figures

TABLE 7.B.1 *Repression-based depreciation of civil society organizational capacity and procedural democracy*

	(1) Level	(2) Change	(3) Upturns	(4) Downturns
Civil society	1.155***	0.080***	0.048**	0.032**
	(0.098)	(0.019)	(0.016)	(0.012)
GDP per capita (ln)	0.049**	0.006*	0.001	0.006***
	(0.016)	(0.003)	(0.003)	(0.001)
GDP growth (%)	0.045	0.040*	0.006	0.034***
	(0.035)	(0.020)	(0.015)	(0.008)
Oil production (per capita)	−0.003^	−0.000	−0.000	−0.000
	(0.002)	(0.000)	(0.000)	(0.000)
Regional diffusion	0.421***	0.059***	0.033**	0.025**
	(0.086)	(0.015)	(0.012)	(0.008)
Lagged democracy		−0.120***	−0.081***	−0.039***
		(0.012)	(0.008)	(0.005)
Constant	−0.716***	−0.067**	−0.009	−0.058***
	(0.119)	(0.025)	(0.022)	(0.013)
R^2 Overall	0.727	0.043	0.034	0.031
R^2 Within	0.649	0.082	0.071	0.040
R^2 Between	0.740	0.131	0.036	0.072
AIC	−12218.726	−26256.362	−30756.098	−37576.492
BIC	−11358.280	−25388.686	−29895.652	−36716.047

Notes: Estimated coefficients and country-clustered robust standard errors from country and year fixed effects models. Civil society stock is measured using a repression-based depreciation rate from v2csreprss (see Appendix 7A). Dependent variable is the level and annual change in the Munck procedural democracy index (see Hegre et al. 2020). All independent variables are lagged by one year (t–1). N = 10,205; Countries = 156 ^ p < 0.10, * p < 0.05, ** p < 0.01, *** p < 0.001

293

TABLE 7.B.2 *Civil society organizational capacity and procedural democracy using the Schumpeter index*

	(1) Level	(2) Change	(3) Upturns	(4) Downturns	(5) Level	(6) Change	(7) Upturns	(8) Downturns
Civil society	0.635***	0.034**	0.029*	0.005	1.143***	0.081***	0.047**	0.034**
	(0.078)	(0.013)	(0.012)	(0.007)	(0.096)	(0.019)	(0.016)	(0.012)
GDP per capita (ln)	0.088***	0.008**	0.003	0.005***	0.059***	0.007*	0.002	0.005**
	(0.020)	(0.003)	(0.003)	(0.001)	(0.017)	(0.003)	(0.003)	(0.002)
GDP growth (%)	0.068^	0.051*	0.011	0.040***	0.067^	0.051*	0.011	0.040***
	(0.041)	(0.020)	(0.016)	(0.008)	(0.036)	(0.020)	(0.015)	(0.008)
Oil production (per capita)	-0.003*	-0.000	-0.000	-0.000	-0.003^	-0.000	-0.000	-0.000
	(0.001)	(0.000)	(0.000)	(0.000)	(0.002)	(0.000)	(0.000)	(0.000)
Regional diffusion	0.611***	0.075***	0.044***	0.031***	0.431***	0.068***	0.042**	0.027**
	(0.096)	(0.016)	(0.012)	(0.009)	(0.088)	(0.016)	(0.013)	(0.009)
Lagged democracy		-0.114***	-0.079***	-0.035***		-0.126***	-0.084***	-0.042***
		(0.011)	(0.008)	(0.005)		(0.012)	(0.008)	(0.005)
Constant	-0.979***	-0.073^	-0.011	-0.062**	-0.711***	-0.067^	-0.003	-0.064***
	(0.160)	(0.039)	(0.034)	(0.019)	(0.132)	(0.038)	(0.033)	(0.019)
R² Overall	0.654	0.046	0.038	0.034	0.723	0.050	0.039	0.035
R² Within	0.510	0.087	0.076	0.042	0.580	0.090	0.077	0.044
R² Between	0.655	0.118	0.060	0.057	0.755	0.106	0.053	0.048
AIC	-9955.048	-25291.091	-30308.916	-35684.805	-11527.468	-25324.496	-30317.646	-35705.685
BIC	-9094.603	-24423.415	-29441.240	-34824.360	-10667.023	-24464.051	-29449.970	-34845.240
Repression-based?	No	No	No	No	Yes	Yes	Yes	Yes

Notes: Estimated coefficients and country-clustered robust standard errors from country and year fixed effects models. Dependent variable is the level and annual change in the Schumpeter procedural democracy index (see Hegre et al. 2020). Baseline depreciation for civil society stock is 10 percent; regression-based depreciation is calculated using v2csreprss (see Appendix 7A). All independent variables are lagged by one year (t–1). $N = 10,205$; Countries =156 ^ $p < 0.10$, * $p < 0.05$, ** $p < 0.01$, *** $p < 0.001$

TABLE 7.B.3 *Civil society organizational capacity and procedural democracy, linear-log specification*

	(1) Level	(2) Change	(3) Upturns	(4) Downturns	(5) Level	(6) Change	(7) Upturns	(8) Downturns
Civil society (ln)	0.230***	0.014**	0.013***	0.000	0.233***	0.020***	0.019***	0.002
	(0.036)	(0.005)	(0.004)	(0.002)	(0.023)	(0.004)	(0.003)	(0.002)
GDP per capita (ln)	0.079***	0.007**	0.001	0.006***	0.061***	0.006*	0.000	0.006***
	(0.019)	(0.003)	(0.003)	(0.001)	(0.017)	(0.003)	(0.003)	(0.001)
GDP growth (%)	0.036	0.040*	0.005	0.035***	0.039	0.040*	0.005	0.035***
	(0.041)	(0.020)	(0.015)	(0.008)	(0.039)	(0.020)	(0.015)	(0.008)
Oil production (per capita)	-0.003*	-0.000	-0.000	-0.000	-0.003*	-0.000	-0.000	-0.000
	(0.001)	(0.000)	(0.000)	(0.000)	(0.001)	(0.000)	(0.000)	(0.000)
Regional diffusion	0.600***	0.063***	0.033**	0.030***	0.436***	0.054***	0.025*	0.029***
	(0.099)	(0.015)	(0.012)	(0.008)	(0.092)	(0.015)	(0.012)	(0.008)
Lagged democracy		-0.108***	-0.076***	-0.032***		-0.121***	-0.087***	-0.034***
		(0.011)	(0.008)	(0.005)		(0.011)	(0.008)	(0.005)
Constant	-0.484***	-0.044^	0.009	-0.053***	-0.190	-0.021	0.030	-0.051***
	(0.136)	(0.025)	(0.022)	(0.013)	(0.126)	(0.025)	(0.022)	(0.013)
R^2 Overall	0.648	0.039	0.032	0.030	0.705	0.042	0.036	0.030
R^2 Within	0.577	0.080	0.070	0.038	0.630	0.084	0.076	0.038
R^2 Between	0.625	0.138	0.032	0.082	0.713	0.117	0.010	0.078
AIC	-10305.641	-26228.042	-30753.430	-37554.401	-11680.496	-26275.550	-30814.827	-37555.522
BIC	-9445.195	-25367.596	-29892.984	-36693.956	-10820.051	-25407.874	-29947.151	-36695.076
Repression-based?	No	No	No	No	Yes	Yes	Yes	Yes

Notes: Estimated coefficients and country-clustered robust standard errors from country and year fixed effects models. Dependent variable is the level and annual change in the Munck procedural de mocracy index (see Hegre et al. 2020). Baseline depreciation for civil society stock is 10 percent; repression-based depreciation is calculated using v2csreprss (see Appendix 7A). All independent variables are lagged by one year (t–1). N = 10,205; Countries = 156. ^ p < 0.10, * p < 0.05, ** p < 0.01, *** p < 0.001

TABLE 7.B.4 *Civil society organizational capacity and procedural democracy, quadratic specification*

	(1) Level	(2) Change	(3) Upturns	(4) Downturns	(5) Level	(6) Change	(7) Upturns	(8) Downturns
Civil society	0.310	0.069	0.086*	-0.017	1.789***	0.210***	0.239***	-0.029^
	(0.303)	(0.042)	(0.038)	(0.021)	(0.227)	(0.037)	(0.033)	(0.015)
Civil society (sq.)	0.364	-0.036	-0.057	0.020	-0.992**	-0.195***	-0.286***	0.092***
	(0.298)	(0.045)	(0.041)	(0.023)	(0.336)	(0.047)	(0.043)	(0.022)
GDP per capita (ln)	0.080***	0.007**	0.001	0.006***	0.053*	0.007**	0.002	0.005***
	(0.018)	(0.003)	(0.003)	(0.001)	(0.016)	(0.003)	(0.002)	(0.001)
GDP growth (%)	0.051	0.040*	0.005	0.035***	0.041	0.040*	0.005	0.035***
	(0.039)	(0.020)	(0.015)	(0.008)	(0.036)	(0.020)	(0.016)	(0.008)
Oil production (per capita)	-0.003*	-0.000	-0.000	-0.000	-0.003*	-0.000	-0.000	-0.000
	(0.001)	(0.000)	(0.000)	(0.000)	(0.001)	(0.000)	(0.000)	(0.000)
Regional diffusion	0.618***	0.063***	0.033**	0.030***	0.409***	0.058***	0.032**	0.026**
	(0.094)	(0.015)	(0.012)	(0.008)	(0.084)	(0.015)	(0.011)	(0.008)
Lagged democracy		-0.108***	-0.076***	-0.033***		-0.125***	-0.088***	-0.037***
		(0.011)	(0.008)	(0.005)		(0.012)	(0.008)	(0.006)
Constant	-0.904***	-0.079**	-0.028	-0.051***	-0.849***	-0.097***	-0.052*	-0.045***
	(0.171)	(0.028)	(0.024)	(0.013)	(0.129)	(0.027)	(0.024)	(0.012)
R^2 Overall	0.656	0.039	0.031	0.029	0.736	0.043	0.036	0.031
R^2 Within	0.590	0.080	0.071	0.038	0.658	0.086	0.082	0.042
R^2 Between	0.629	0.137	0.025	0.088	0.749	0.107	0.006	0.091
AIC	-10612.012	-26227.858	-30755.500	-37553.970	-12471.321	-26291.937	-30878.951	-37599.723
BIC	-9751.567	-25360.182	-29887.824	-36686.294	-11603.645	-25417.031	-30004.044	-36732.047
Repression-based?	No	No	No	No	Yes	Yes	Yes	Yes

Notes: Estimated coefficients and country-clustered robust standard errors from country and year fixed effects models. Dependent variable is the level and annual change in the Munck procedural democracy index (see Hegre et al. 2020). Baseline depreciation for civil society stock is 10 percent; repression-based depreciation is calculated using v2csreprss (see Appendix 7A). All independent variables are lagged by one year (t−1). N = 10,205; Countries = 156. ^

TABLE 7.B.5 *Civil society organizational capacity and procedural democracy, country-years with at least thirty years prior stock accumulation*

	(1) Level	(2) Change	(3) Upturns	(4) Downturns	(5) Level	(6) Change	(7) Upturns	(8) Downturns
Civil society	0.699***	0.038**	0.037***	0.001	1.177***	0.081***	0.050**	0.032**
	(0.078)	(0.012)	(0.011)	(0.007)	(0.099)	(0.020)	(0.017)	(0.012)
GDP per capita (ln)	0.078***	0.008**	0.001	0.006***	0.048**	0.006*	0.001	0.006***
	(0.019)	(0.003)	(0.003)	(0.001)	(0.016)	(0.003)	(0.003)	(0.002)
GDP growth (%)	0.044	0.040^	0.005	0.035***	0.048	0.040*	0.006	0.034***
	(0.040)	(0.020)	(0.016)	(0.008)	(0.036)	(0.020)	(0.016)	(0.008)
Oil production (per capita)	-0.003^	-0.000	-0.000	-0.000	-0.003	-0.000	-0.000	-0.000
	(0.002)	(0.000)	(0.000)	(0.000)	(0.002)	(0.000)	(0.000)	(0.000)
Regional diffusion	0.589***	0.063***	0.035**	0.029***	0.416***	0.057***	0.033**	0.025**
	(0.092)	(0.015)	(0.012)	(0.008)	(0.087)	(0.015)	(0.013)	(0.008)
Lagged democracy		-0.110***	-0.077***	-0.032***		-0.121***	-0.081***	-0.039***
		(0.011)	(0.008)	(0.005)		(0.012)	(0.008)	(0.005)
Constant	-0.994***	-0.075**	-0.020	-0.056***	-0.713***	-0.068**	-0.009	-0.060***
	(0.148)	(0.026)	(0.023)	(0.013)	(0.120)	(0.025)	(0.023)	(0.013)
R² Overall	0.666	0.040	0.034	0.031	0.730	0.043	0.034	0.032
R² Within	0.591	0.080	0.070	0.038	0.650	0.082	0.070	0.040
R² Between	0.644	0.144	0.041	0.083	0.743	0.130	0.034	0.075
AIC	-10499.687	-25826.870	-30289.408	-37043.870	-12071.857	-25855.872	-30289.730	-37064.765
BIC	-9647.892	-24960.637	-29437.612	-36184.856	-11212.843	-24989.640	-29430.716	-36205.751
Repression-based?	No	No	No	No	Yes	Yes	Yes	Yes

Notes: Estimated coefficients and country-clustered robust standard errors from country and year fixed effects models. Dependent variable is the level and annual change in the Munck procedural democracy index (see Hegre et al. 2020). Baseline depreciation for civil society stock is 10 percent; repression-based depreciation is calculated using v2csreprss (see Appendix 7A). All independent variables are lagged by one year (t–1). $N = 10{,}083$; Countries = 156. ^ $p < 0.10$, * $p < 0.05$, ** $p < 0.01$, *** $p < 0.001$

TABLE 7.B.6 Civil society participation and procedural democracy in the short-run

	(1) Level	(2) Change	(3) Upturns	(4) Downturns	(5) Level	(6) Change	(7) Upturns	(8) Downturns
CSO participation (t−1)	0.089***	0.012***	0.011***	0.000				
	(0.008)	(0.002)	(0.001)	(0.001)				
CSO participation (t−3)					0.078***	0.004**	0.004***	-0.000
					(0.008)	(0.001)	(0.001)	(0.001)
GDP per capita (ln)	0.078***	0.008**	0.002	0.006***	0.078***	0.007*	0.000	0.006***
	(0.017)	(0.003)	(0.002)	(0.001)	(0.018)	(0.003)	(0.002)	(0.001)
GDP growth (%)	0.056	0.041*	0.006	0.035***	0.061	0.045*	0.011	0.034***
	(0.038)	(0.019)	(0.015)	(0.008)	(0.039)	(0.020)	(0.015)	(0.008)
Oil production (per capita)	-0.003*	-0.000	-0.000	-0.000	-0.003*	-0.000	-0.000	0.000
	(0.001)	(0.000)	(0.000)	(0.000)	(0.001)	(0.000)	(0.000)	(0.000)
Regional diffusion	0.538***	0.060***	0.030*	0.030***	0.571***	0.062***	0.032*	0.030***
	(0.087)	(0.015)	(0.012)	(0.008)	(0.089)	(0.014)	(0.011)	(0.008)
Lagged democracy		-0.130***	-0.097***	-0.032***		-0.105***	-0.074***	-0.031***
		(0.011)	(0.008)	(0.005)		(0.010)	(0.007)	(0.005)
Constant	-0.631***	-0.062*	-0.008	-0.054***	-0.632***	-0.048*	0.004	-0.052***
	(0.126)	(0.025)	(0.022)	(0.013)	(0.130)	(0.024)	(0.021)	(0.013)
R^2 Overall	0.691	0.046	0.045	0.030	0.677	0.037	0.031	0.030
R^2 Within	0.634	0.092	0.089	0.038	0.614	0.078	0.067	0.039
R^2 Between	0.668	0.123	0.011	0.082	0.653	0.140	0.011	0.067
AIC	-11774.042	-26360.736	-30959.076	-37554.453	-11203.202	-26544.444	-31077.235	-37769.456
BIC	-10920.827	-25493.060	-30098.631	-36694.008	-10343.283	-25684.525	-30210.089	-36909.536
Observations	10205	10205	10205	10205	10160	10160	10160	10160

Estimated coefficients and country-clustered robust standard errors from country and year fixed effects models. Dependent variable is the level and annual change in the Munck procedural democracy index (see Hegre et al. 2020). All control variables are lagged by one-year. Civil society participation (v2csprtcpt) is lagged in one- and three-year increments. Countries = 156. ^ p < 0.10, * p < 0.05, ** p < 0.01, *** p < 0.001

TABLE 7.B.7 *Strength of anti-system movements and procedural democracy*

	(1) Change	(2) Upturns	(3) Downturns
Anti-system movement strength	−0.000	0.004***	−0.004***
	(0.001)	(0.001)	(0.001)
GDP per capita (ln)	0.008**	0.003	0.005**
	(0.003)	(0.003)	(0.001)
GDP growth (%)	0.041*	0.010	0.031***
	(0.020)	(0.015)	(0.008)
Oil production (per capita)	−0.000	−0.000	0.000
	(0.000)	(0.000)	(0.000)
Regional diffusion	0.069***	0.038**	0.031***
	(0.015)	(0.012)	(0.008)
Lagged democracy	−0.102***	−0.067***	−0.035***
	(0.011)	(0.008)	(0.005)
Constant	−0.054*	−0.012	−0.042***
	(0.025)	(0.023)	(0.012)
R^2 Overall	0.036	0.031	0.034
R^2 Within	0.078	0.071	0.045
R^2 Between	0.132	0.044	0.069
AIC	−26210.819	−30761.326	−37636.595
BIC	−25343.143	−29893.650	−36776.149

Notes: Estimated coefficients and country-clustered robust standard errors from country and year fixed effects models. Dependent variable is the annual change in the Munck procedural democracy index (see Hegre et al. 2020). All independent variables are lagged by one year (t−1). Observations = 10,205; Countries = 156. ^ p<0.10, * p<0.05, ** p<0.01, *** p<0.001

TABLE 7.B.8 *Anti-system strength and democracy, moderated by lagged electoral and procedural democracy*

	(1) Change	(2) Upturns	(3) Downturns	(4) Change	(5) Upturns	(6) Downturns
Anti-system movement strength	0.002^	0.002	0.000	0.003^	0.003*	-0.000
	(0.001)	(0.001)	(0.001)	(0.001)	(0.001)	(0.000)
GDP per capita (ln)	0.003	0.001	0.001	0.006*	0.003	0.003*
	(0.002)	(0.002)	(0.001)	(0.003)	(0.003)	(0.001)
GDP growth (%)	0.032***	0.009	0.024***	0.041*	0.010	0.031***
	(0.010)	(0.007)	(0.005)	(0.020)	(0.015)	(0.008)
Oil production (per capita)	-0.000	-0.000	-0.000	-0.000	-0.000	0.000
	(0.000)	(0.000)	(0.000)	(0.000)	(0.000)	(0.000)
Regional diffusion	0.048***	0.032**	0.016**	0.059***	0.041**	0.019*
	(0.013)	(0.011)	(0.006)	(0.015)	(0.012)	(0.007)
Lagged democracy	-0.072***	-0.042***	-0.031***	-0.109***	-0.066***	-0.043***
	(0.007)	(0.006)	(0.004)	(0.011)	(0.007)	(0.006)
Anti-system * lagged democracy	-0.006**	0.004^	-0.010***	-0.012***	0.003	-0.015***
	(0.002)	(0.002)	(0.002)	(0.003)	(0.003)	(0.003)
Constant	-0.024	-0.002	-0.022*	-0.044^	-0.014	-0.029*
	(0.017)	(0.014)	(0.011)	(0.025)	(0.023)	(0.012)
R^2 Overall	0.046	0.045	0.056	0.038	0.031	0.044
R^2 Within	0.080	0.081	0.066	0.081	0.072	0.058
R^2 Between	0.112	0.027	0.094	0.124	0.048	0.055
AIC	-34600.244	-39583.580	-47003.468	-26238.321	-30763.845	-37765.265
BIC	-33725.337	-38708.673	-46128.561	-25370.645	-29896.169	-36897.589
Outcome	Electoral democracy	Electoral democracy	Electoral democracy	Procedural democracy	Procedural democracy	Procedural democracy

Notes: Estimated coefficients and country-clustered robust standard errors from country and year fixed effects models. Dependent variables are annual changes in the electoral democracy index (v2x_polyarchy) and the Munck procedural democracy index (see Hegre et al. 2020). All independent variables are lagged by one year (t−1). Observations = 10,205; Countries = 156. ^ p < 0.10, * p < 0.05, ** p < 0.01, *** p < 0.001

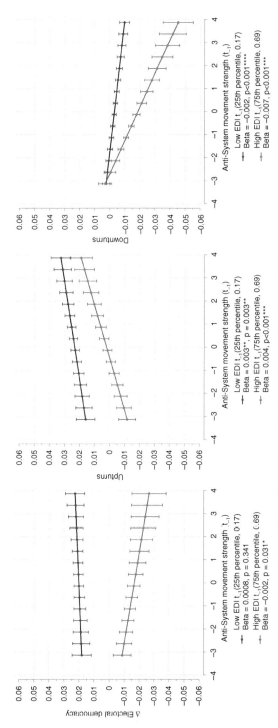

FIGURE 7.B.1 As an alternative to Figure 7.3, this graph shows the predicted annual changes, upturns, and downturns for electoral democracy with 95% confidence intervals as levels of anti-system movement strength increase when lagged levels of electoral democracy are at the twenty-fifth and seventy-fifth percentiles

TABLE 7.B.9 *Anti-system movement character and procedural democracy*

	(1) Change	(2) Upturns	(3) Downturns
Anti-system movement strength	-0.000	0.004**	-0.004***
	(0.001)	(0.001)	(0.001)
Left-wing movements	0.001	-0.003	0.004
	(0.007)	(0.006)	(0.003)
Right-wing movements	-0.003	0.007	-0.011^
	(0.008)	(0.007)	(0.006)
GDP per capita (ln)	0.008**	0.003	0.005**
	(0.003)	(0.003)	(0.001)
GDP growth (%)	0.041*	0.011	0.030***
	(0.020)	(0.015)	(0.008)
Oil production (per capita)	-0.000	-0.000	0.000
	(0.000)	(0.000)	(0.000)
Regional diffusion	0.069***	0.039**	0.030***
	(0.015)	(0.012)	(0.008)
Lagged democracy	-0.102***	-0.068***	-0.033***
	(0.011)	(0.008)	(0.005)
Constant	-0.054*	-0.011	-0.043***
	(0.025)	(0.023)	(0.013)
R^2 Overall	0.036	0.030	0.035
R^2 Within	0.078	0.072	0.047
R^2 Between	0.133	0.042	0.068
AIC	-26207.288	-30763.323	-37646.547
BIC	-25325.151	-29888.416	-36764.410

Notes: Estimated coefficients and country-clustered robust standard errors from country and year fixed effects models. Dependent variable is the annual change in the Munck procedural democracy index (see Hegre et al. 2020). All independent variables are lagged by one year (t–1). Observations = 10,205; Countries = 156.. ^ p < 0.10, * p < 0.05, ** p < 0.01, *** p < 0.001

TABLE 7.B.10 *Anti-system movement character and changes in democracy, moderated by anti-system movement strength*

	(1) Change	(2) Upturns	(3) Downturns	(4) Change	(5) Upturns	(6) Downturns
Anti-system movement strength	0.000	0.004***	-0.003***	0.001	0.005**	-0.004***
	(0.001)	(0.001)	(0.001)	(0.002)	(0.002)	(0.001)
Left-wing movements	-0.000	-0.004	0.003	0.001	-0.004	0.004
	(0.004)	(0.004)	(0.002)	(0.007)	(0.005)	(0.003)
Left-wing * strength	0.000	-0.001	0.001	-0.001	-0.003	0.003
	(0.002)	(0.002)	(0.001)	(0.003)	(0.003)	(0.002)
Right-wing movements	-0.009	0.003	-0.012**	-0.005	0.006	-0.012*
	(0.006)	(0.005)	(0.004)	(0.008)	(0.007)	(0.006)
Right-wing * strength	-0.005	-0.001	-0.004*	-0.006	-0.003	-0.004
	(0.003)	(0.002)	(0.002)	(0.004)	(0.003)	(0.003)
GDP per capita (ln)	0.003^	0.001	0.002*	0.007*	0.003	0.004**
	(0.002)	(0.002)	(0.001)	(0.003)	(0.003)	(0.001)
GDP growth (%)	0.032**	0.009	0.023***	0.040*	0.010	0.030***
	(0.010)	(0.007)	(0.005)	(0.020)	(0.015)	(0.008)
Oil production (per capita)	-0.000	-0.000	-0.000	-0.000	-0.000	0.000
	(0.000)	(0.000)	(0.000)	(0.000)	(0.000)	(0.000)
Regional diffusion	0.053***	0.027*	0.026***	0.069***	0.038***	0.031***
	(0.013)	(0.011)	(0.006)	(0.015)	(0.012)	(0.008)
Lagged democracy	-0.068***	-0.044***	-0.024***	-0.102***	-0.068***	-0.034***
	(0.007)	(0.006)	(0.004)	(0.011)	(0.008)	(0.005)

(continued)

TABLE 7.B.10 (continued)

	(1) Change	(2) Upturns	(3) Downturns	(4) Change	(5) Upturns	(6) Downturns
Constant	-0.028	0.004	-0.032**	-0.052*	-0.011	-0.041**
	(0.017)	(0.014)	(0.011)	(0.026)	(0.023)	(0.013)
R^2 Overall	0.045	0.045	0.047	0.037	0.031	0.035
R^2 Within	0.080	0.081	0.062	0.079	0.072	0.048
R^2 Between	0.108	0.015	0.097	0.127	0.042	0.065
AIC	-34593.752	-39576.562	-46956.587	-26207.757	-30762.817	-37650.925
BIC	-33697.154	-38679.963	-46067.219	-25311.158	-29866.218	-36761.557
Outcome	Electoral democracy	Electoral democracy	Electoral democracy	Procedural democracy	Procedural democracy	Procedural democracy

Notes: Estimated coefficients and country-clustered robust standard errors from country and year fixed effects models. Dependent variables are annual changes in the electoral democracy index (v2x_polyarchy) and the Munck procedural democracy index (see Hegre et al. 2020). All independent variables are lagged by one year (t–1). Observations = 10,205; Countries = 156. ^ $p < 0.10$, * $p < 0.05$, ** $p < 0.01$, *** $p < 0.001$

TABLE 7.B.11 *Anti-system movement character and democracy, moderated by lagged democracy*

	(1) Change	(2) Upturns	(3) Downturns	(4) Change	(5) Upturns	(6) Downturns
Anti-system movement strength	-0.000	0.003***	-0.004***	-0.000	0.004**	-0.004***
	(0.001)	(0.001)	(0.001)	(0.001)	(0.001)	(0.001)
Left-wing movements	-0.009	-0.007	-0.001	-0.009	-0.007	-0.002
	(0.006)	(0.006)	(0.003)	(0.007)	(0.007)	(0.003)
Right-wing movements	-0.003	0.013	-0.016**	0.000	0.009	-0.009^
	(0.009)	(0.010)	(0.005)	(0.012)	(0.012)	(0.005)
GDP per capita (ln)	0.003^	0.001	0.002*	0.008**	0.003	0.005**
	(0.002)	(0.002)	(0.001)	(0.003)	(0.003)	(0.001)
GDP growth (%)	0.032***	0.009	0.024***	0.041*	0.011	0.030***
	(0.009)	(0.007)	(0.005)	(0.020)	(0.015)	(0.008)
Oil production (per capita)	-0.000	-0.000	-0.000	-0.000	-0.000	0.000
	(0.000)	(0.000)	(0.000)	(0.000)	(0.000)	(0.000)
Regional diffusion	0.055***	0.029*	0.026***	0.071***	0.040***	0.031***
	(0.013)	(0.011)	(0.006)	(0.015)	(0.012)	(0.008)
Lagged democracy	-0.075***	-0.044***	-0.031***	-0.115***	-0.074***	-0.041***
	(0.009)	(0.008)	(0.004)	(0.014)	(0.010)	(0.007)
Left-wing * lagged democracy	0.023*	0.011	0.012*	0.037*	0.015	0.021**
	(0.010)	(0.010)	(0.005)	(0.014)	(0.011)	(0.008)
Right-wing * lagged democracy	-0.011	-0.021	0.010	-0.013	-0.006	-0.007
	(0.016)	(0.014)	(0.010)	(0.024)	(0.020)	(0.015)

(continued)

TABLE 7.B.11 (*continued*)

	(1) Change	(2) Upturns	(3) Downturns	(4) Change	(5) Upturns	(6) Downturns
Constant	-0.029	0.002	-0.031**	-0.053*	-0.010	-0.042***
	(0.017)	(0.014)	(0.011)	(0.026)	(0.024)	(0.013)
R^2 Overall	0.044	0.045	0.046	0.036	0.030	0.034
R^2 Within	0.080	0.081	0.063	0.080	0.072	0.048
R^2 Between	0.131	0.024	0.104	0.146	0.050	0.070
AIC	-34596.878	-39583.769	-46957.491	-26220.630	-30763.516	-37660.480
BIC	-33700.279	-38687.170	-46068.123	-25331.262	-29874.149	-36771.112
Outcome	Electoral democracy	Electoral democracy	Electoral democracy	Procedural democracy	Procedural democracy	Procedural democracy

Notes: Estimated coefficients and country-clustered robust standard errors from country and year fixed effects models. Dependent variables are annual changes in the electoral democracy index (v2x_polyarchy) and the Munck procedural democracy index (see Hegre et al. 2020). All independent variables are lagged by one year (t–1). Observations = 10,205; Countries = 156. ^ p < 0.10, * p < 0.05, ** p < 0.01, *** p < 0.001

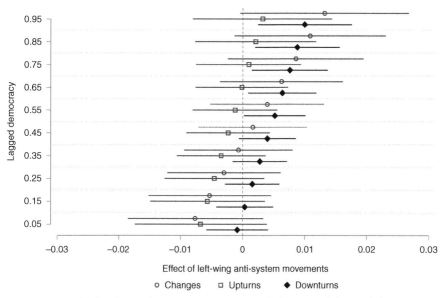

FIGURE 7.B.2 Left-wing anti-system movements and changes to electoral democracy, moderated by existing levels of democracy. Plots include the predicted differences in the marginal effects and 95% confidence intervals on annual changes to democracy for a one-unit change in left-wing anti-system movements (0–1) as lagged levels of electoral democracy increase. Results are based on estimates in Table 7.B11

TABLE 7.B.12 *Anti-system movement character, civil society organizational capacity, and procedural democracy*

	(1) Change	(2) Upturns	(3) Downturns	(4) Change	(5) Upturns	(6) Downturns
Civil society	0.041*	0.019	0.022*	0.080**	0.040*	0.040**
	(0.017)	(0.014)	(0.009)	(0.024)	(0.019)	(0.014)
Anti-system movement strength	−0.001	0.003**	−0.004***	−0.001	0.004**	−0.004***
	(0.001)	(0.001)	(0.001)	(0.001)	(0.001)	(0.001)
Left-wing movements	−0.014	−0.025^	0.011	−0.012	−0.016^	0.005
	(0.017)	(0.014)	(0.008)	(0.011)	(0.010)	(0.006)
Left-wing * civil society	0.027	0.039^	−0.012	0.041	0.044^	−0.003
	(0.028)	(0.022)	(0.015)	(0.030)	(0.025)	(0.016)
Right-wing movements	0.039^	0.029	0.009	0.015	0.019	−0.004
	(0.020)	(0.019)	(0.010)	(0.014)	(0.013)	(0.007)
Right-wing * civil society	−0.079*	−0.042	−0.037	−0.063	−0.041	−0.022
	(0.036)	(0.032)	(0.022)	(0.038)	(0.034)	(0.022)
GDP per capita (ln)	0.007*	0.002	0.004**	0.006*	0.002	0.004**
	(0.003)	(0.003)	(0.001)	(0.003)	(0.003)	(0.001)
GDP growth (%)	0.039*	0.010	0.029***	0.040*	0.010	0.029***
	(0.020)	(0.015)	(0.008)	(0.019)	(0.015)	(0.007)
Oil production (per capita)	−0.000	−0.000	−0.000	−0.000	−0.000	−0.000
	(0.000)	(0.000)	(0.000)	(0.000)	(0.000)	(0.000)

(continued)

Regional diffusion	0.065***	0.037**	0.027***	0.058***	0.033**	0.025**
	(0.015)	(0.012)	(0.008)	(0.015)	(0.012)	(0.008)
Lagged democracy	−0.109***	−0.074***	−0.035***	−0.121***	−0.080***	−0.041***
	(0.011)	(0.008)	(0.005)	(0.012)	(0.008)	(0.006)
Constant	−0.075**	−0.020	−0.056***	−0.067*	−0.016	−0.051***
	(0.028)	(0.024)	(0.013)	(0.026)	(0.024)	(0.013)
R² Overall	0.041	0.034	0.036	0.043	0.035	0.036
R² Within	0.081	0.074	0.048	0.083	0.075	0.050
R² Between	0.146	0.043	0.057	0.138	0.036	0.053
AIC	−26231.306	−30778.699	−37657.803	−26256.119	−30787.838	−37671.433
BIC	−25327.477	−29874.870	−36761.205	−25352.290	−29884.009	−36774.834
Repression-based?	No	No	No	Yes	Yes	Yes

Notes: Estimated coefficients and country-clustered robust standard errors from country and year fixed effects models. Dependent variable is the annual change in the Munck procedural democracy index (see Hegre et al. 2020). Baseline depreciation for civil society stock is 10 percent; repression-based depreciation is calculated using v2csreprss (see Appendix 7A). All independent variables are lagged by one year (t−1). Observations = 10,205; Countries = 156. ^ $p < 0.10$, * $p < 0.05$, ** $p < 0.01$, *** $p < 0.001$.

TABLE 7.B.13 *Ethnic- and religious-based anti-system movements and changes in democracy*

	(1) Change	(2) Upturns	(3) Downturns	(4) Change	(5) Upturns	(6) Downturns
Anti-system movement strength	-0.000	0.003***	-0.004***	-0.001	0.004**	-0.004***
	(0.001)	(0.001)	(0.000)	(0.001)	(0.001)	(0.001)
Left-wing movements	0.000	-0.003	0.003	0.001	-0.003	0.004
	(0.004)	(0.004)	(0.002)	(0.007)	(0.005)	(0.003)
Right-wing movements	-0.006	0.005	-0.011**	-0.002	0.009	-0.011^
	(0.006)	(0.005)	(0.004)	(0.009)	(0.007)	(0.006)
Ethnic-based movements	0.001	-0.003	0.004	0.011	0.004	0.007
	(0.006)	(0.006)	(0.003)	(0.009)	(0.009)	(0.004)
Religious-based movements	-0.012^	-0.012*	-0.000	-0.024**	-0.020*	-0.004
	(0.006)	(0.006)	(0.003)	(0.009)	(0.008)	(0.005)
GDP per capita (ln)	0.003^	0.001	0.003**	0.008**	0.003	0.005**
	(0.002)	(0.002)	(0.001)	(0.003)	(0.003)	(0.001)
GDP growth (%)	0.032***	0.008	0.024***	0.040*	0.010	0.030***
	(0.009)	(0.007)	(0.005)	(0.020)	(0.015)	(0.008)
Oil production (per capita)	-0.000	-0.000	-0.000	-0.000	-0.000	0.000
	(0.000)	(0.000)	(0.000)	(0.000)	(0.000)	(0.000)
Regional diffusion	0.051***	0.025*	0.025***	0.063***	0.035**	0.029***
	(0.013)	(0.011)	(0.006)	(0.015)	(0.012)	(0.008)

(continued)

	Electoral democracy	Electoral democracy	Electoral democracy	Procedural democracy	Procedural democracy	Procedural democracy
Lagged democracy	-0.069***	-0.045***	-0.024***	-0.104***	-0.070***	-0.034***
	(0.008)	(0.006)	(0.004)	(0.011)	(0.008)	(0.005)
Constant	-0.029^	0.006	-0.035**	-0.057*	-0.012	-0.045***
	(0.017)	(0.014)	(0.011)	(0.026)	(0.023)	(0.012)
R^2 Overall	0.045	0.047	0.047	0.037	0.031	0.036
R^2 Within	0.080	0.081	0.061	0.080	0.073	0.047
R^2 Between	0.104	0.010	0.101	0.115	0.029	0.072
AIC	-34594.720	-39586.816	-46945.762	-26218.506	-30772.057	-37646.146
BIC	-33698.121	-38690.217	-46056.394	-25329.138	-29882.689	-36749.548
Outcome	Electoral democracy	Electoral democracy	Electoral democracy	Procedural democracy	Procedural democracy	Procedural democracy

Notes: Estimated coefficients and country-clustered robust standard errors from country and year fixed effects models. Dependent variables are annual changes in the electoral democracy index (v2x_polyarchy) and the Munck procedural democracy index (see Hegre et al. 2020). All independent variables are lagged by one year (t−1). Observations = 10,205; Countries = 156. ^ p < 0.10, * p < 0.05, ** p < 0.01, *** p < 0.001

TABLE 7.B.14 *Violent and nonviolent resistance campaigns and procedural democracy*

	(1) Change	(2) Upturns	(3) Downturns
Violent campaign	−0.002	0.001	−0.003^
	(0.003)	(0.003)	(0.002)
Nonviolent campaign	0.046***	0.048***	−0.001
	(0.011)	(0.011)	(0.003)
GDP per capita (ln)	0.008*	0.002	0.005***
	(0.003)	(0.003)	(0.001)
GDP growth (%)	0.037^	0.005	0.032***
	(0.020)	(0.016)	(0.008)
Oil production (per capita)	−0.000	−0.000	−0.000
	(0.000)	(0.000)	(0.000)
Regional diffusion	0.074***	0.045***	0.029***
	(0.015)	(0.012)	(0.008)
Lagged democracy	−0.097***	−0.066***	−0.031***
	(0.011)	(0.008)	(0.005)
Constant	−0.054*	−0.008	−0.046***
	(0.025)	(0.022)	(0.012)
R^2 Overall	0.048	0.045	0.029
R^2 Within	0.088	0.085	0.037
R^2 Between	0.061	0.044	0.039
AIC	−23773.398	−27765.863	−34265.160
BIC	−22960.122	−26952.587	−33451.884

Notes: Estimated coefficients and country-clustered robust standard errors from country and year fixed effects models. Dependent variable is the annual change in the Munck procedural democracy index (see Hegre et al. 2020). All independent variables are lagged by one year (t–1). Observations = 9,265; Countries = 157. ^ $p < 0.10$, * $p < 0.05$, ** $p < 0.01$, *** $p < 0.001$.

TABLE 7.B.15 *Immediate and long-run relationship between resistance campaigns and democracy*

	(1) Change	(2) Upturns	(3) Downturns	(4) Change	(5) Upturns	(6) Downturns
Post violent campaign	-0.033*	-0.036***	0.003	-0.056**	-0.053***	-0.003
	(0.013)	(0.011)	(0.006)	(0.019)	(0.015)	(0.008)
Post nonviolent campaign	0.015	0.012	0.003	-0.003	0.001	-0.003
	(0.017)	(0.014)	(0.007)	(0.022)	(0.018)	(0.009)
Time (ln)	-0.011**	-0.011***	-0.000	-0.017***	-0.015***	-0.002
	(0.003)	(0.003)	(0.002)	(0.005)	(0.004)	(0.002)
Post violent campaign * time (ln)	0.008*	0.008**	-0.000	0.014**	0.012**	0.001
	(0.003)	(0.003)	(0.002)	(0.005)	(0.004)	(0.002)
Post nonviolent campaign * time (ln)	-0.009^	-0.010*	0.001	-0.005	-0.007	0.002
	(0.005)	(0.004)	(0.002)	(0.006)	(0.005)	(0.003)
Ongoing campaign	0.001	0.007***	-0.006***	0.004	0.011***	-0.007***
	(0.002)	(0.002)	(0.001)	(0.003)	(0.003)	(0.002)
GDP per capita (ln)	0.007**	0.003^	0.003***	0.012***	0.007*	0.005***
	(0.002)	(0.002)	(0.001)	(0.003)	(0.003)	(0.002)
GDP growth (%)	0.033**	0.008	0.025***	0.037^	0.007	0.030***
	(0.010)	(0.008)	(0.005)	(0.020)	(0.016)	(0.008)
Oil production (per capita)	-0.000	0.000	-0.000^	-0.000	-0.000	-0.000
	(0.000)	(0.000)	(0.000)	(0.000)	(0.000)	(0.000)

(continued)

TABLE 7.B.15 (continued)

	(1) Change	(2) Upturns	(3) Downturns	(4) Change	(5) Upturns	(6) Downturns
Regional diffusion	0.064***	0.041***	0.023***	0.081***	0.053***	0.029***
	(0.014)	(0.011)	(0.007)	(0.017)	(0.013)	(0.008)
Lagged democracy	-0.072***	-0.050***	-0.022***	-0.108***	-0.076***	-0.032***
	(0.009)	(0.007)	(0.003)	(0.012)	(0.009)	(0.005)
Constant	-0.051**	-0.010	-0.040***	-0.077**	-0.032	-0.046***
	(0.019)	(0.014)	(0.011)	(0.026)	(0.022)	(0.013)
R^2 Overall	0.071	0.092	0.033	0.051	0.052	0.030
R^2 Within	0.115	0.140	0.047	0.100	0.104	0.040
R^2 Between	0.023	0.015	0.030	0.034	0.043	0.038
AIC	-31668.556	-36364.244	-42404.255	-23889.282	-27951.925	-34287.704
BIC	-30826.744	-35522.432	-41569.577	-23047.470	-27117.247	-33445.892
Outcome	Electoral democracy	Electoral democracy	Electoral democracy	Procedural democracy	Procedural democracy	Procedural democracy

Notes: Estimated coefficients and country-clustered robust standard errors from country and year fixed effects models. Dependent variables are annual changes in the electoral democracy index (v2x_polyarchy) and the Munck procedural democracy index (see Hegre et al. 2020). All independent variables are lagged by one year (t–1). Observations = 9,265; Countries = 157. ^ p < 0.10, * p < 0.05, ** p < 0.01, *** p < 0.001.

TABLE 7.B.16 *Resistance campaigns by class-based coalitions and subsequent procedural democracy*

	(1) Change	(2) Upturns	(3) Downturns	(4) Change	(5) Upturns	(6) Downturns
Luebbert campaign ended	0.057	0.076*	-0.019			-0.011
	(0.040)	(0.031)	(0.020)			(0.014)
Middle-sector campaign ended				0.084**	0.095***	-0.002
				(0.032)	(0.027)	(0.003)
Other campaign ended	0.038***	0.040***	-0.001	0.028**	0.030**	-0.008***
	(0.010)	(0.010)	(0.003)	(0.009)	(0.009)	(0.003)
Ongoing campaign	0.000	0.008**	-0.008***	0.000	0.008**	-0.008***
	(0.004)	(0.003)	(0.002)	(0.004)	(0.003)	(0.002)
GDP per capita (ln)	0.009**	0.004	0.005***	0.008**	0.004	0.005***
	(0.003)	(0.003)	(0.001)	(0.003)	(0.003)	(0.001)
GDP growth (%)	0.035^	0.006	0.030***	0.036^	0.007	0.029***
	(0.020)	(0.016)	(0.008)	(0.020)	(0.016)	(0.008)
Oil production (per capita)	-0.000	-0.000	-0.000	-0.000	-0.000	-0.000
	(0.000)	(0.000)	(0.000)	(0.000)	(0.000)	(0.000)
Regional diffusion	0.073***	0.046***	0.027***	0.074***	0.047***	0.027***
	(0.015)	(0.012)	(0.008)	(0.015)	(0.012)	(0.008)
Lagged democracy	-0.100***	-0.068***	-0.031***	-0.099***	-0.068***	-0.031***
	(0.011)	(0.008)	(0.005)	(0.011)	(0.008)	(0.005)

(continued)

TABLE 7.B.16 (continued)

	(1) Change	(2) Upturns	(3) Downturns	(4) Change	(5) Upturns	(6) Downturns
Constant	-0.061*	-0.020	-0.041***	-0.060*	-0.018	-0.041***
	(0.025)	(0.022)	(0.011)	(0.026)	(0.022)	(0.011)
R^2 Overall	0.044	0.042	0.032	0.046	0.046	0.032
R^2 Within	0.086	0.085	0.040	0.088	0.089	0.040
R^2 Between	0.076	0.075	0.027	0.073	0.069	0.027
AIC	-23749.090	-27762.265	-34293.505	-23770.144	-27798.768	-34289.901
BIC	-22928.680	-26941.855	-33473.095	-22949.734	-26978.358	-33469.491

Notes: Estimated coefficients and country-clustered robust standard errors from country and year fixed effects models. Dependent variable is annual change in the Munck procedural democracy index (see Hegre et al. 2020). All independent variables are lagged by one year (t–1). To qualify for Luebbert's (1991) working class and farmer coalition, the resistance campaign must include industrial workers and peasants, with one of these two groups dominating. To qualify for the middle-sectors thesis, the resistance campaign must include industrial workers and the middle class, with one of these two groups dominating. Data on social group composition of NAVCO campaigns comes from Dahlum et al. (2019). Observations = 9,265; Countries = 157. ^ p < 0.10, * p < 0.05, ** p < 0.01, *** p < 0.001.

TABLE 7.B.17 *Ongoing class-based resistance campaigns and changes in democracy*

	(1) Change	(2) Upturns	(3) Downturns	(4) Change	(5) Upturns	(6) Downturns
Industrial workers	0.039*	0.038**	0.001	0.048*	0.044*	0.003
	(0.017)	(0.014)	(0.003)	(0.021)	(0.019)	(0.004)
Middle class	0.024	0.033**	−0.009	0.018	0.029^	−0.011
	(0.016)	(0.012)	(0.006)	(0.021)	(0.016)	(0.007)
Peasants	−0.011^	−0.005	−0.006*	−0.008	−0.005	−0.003
	(0.006)	(0.004)	(0.003)	(0.007)	(0.005)	(0.003)
Other campaign	0.004	0.009***	−0.005*	0.009^	0.013**	−0.004^
	(0.003)	(0.003)	(0.002)	(0.005)	(0.005)	(0.002)
GDP per capita (ln)	0.004^	0.001	0.003***	0.009**	0.004	0.005***
	(0.002)	(0.002)	(0.001)	(0.003)	(0.003)	(0.001)
GDP growth (%)	0.035**	0.009	0.026***	0.038^	0.006	0.032***
	(0.010)	(0.008)	(0.005)	(0.020)	(0.016)	(0.008)
Oil production (per capita)	−0.000	−0.000	−0.000^	−0.000	−0.000	−0.000
	(0.000)	(0.000)	(0.000)	(0.000)	(0.000)	(0.000)
Regional diffusion	0.059***	0.037**	0.023***	0.077***	0.049***	0.028***
	(0.013)	(0.011)	(0.006)	(0.015)	(0.012)	(0.008)
Lagged democracy	−0.062***	−0.041***	−0.021***	−0.099***	−0.068***	−0.031***
	(0.007)	(0.006)	(0.003)	(0.011)	(0.008)	(0.005)

(continued)

TABLE 7.B.17 *(continued)*

	(1) Change	(2) Upturns	(3) Downturns	(4) Change	(5) Upturns	(6) Downturns
Constant	-0.037*	0.002	-0.039***	-0.062*	-0.017	-0.044***
	(0.018)	(0.014)	(0.010)	(0.026)	(0.022)	(0.012)
R^2 Overall	0.058	0.070	0.033	0.044	0.040	0.030
R^2 Within	0.091	0.103	0.044	0.084	0.082	0.038
R^2 Between	0.062	0.051	0.025	0.068	0.065	0.036
AIC	-31417.602	-35978.124	-42381.098	-23732.423	-27723.890	-34269.535
BIC	-30590.058	-35150.580	-41553.554	-22904.879	-26896.346	-33441.991
Outcome	Electoral democracy	Electoral democracy	Electoral democracy	Procedural democracy	Procedural democracy	Procedural democracy

Notes: Estimated coefficients and country-clustered robust standard errors from country and year fixed effects models. Dependent variables are annual changes in the electoral democracy index (v2x_polyarchy) and the Munck procedural democracy index (see Hegre et al. 2020). All independent variables are lagged by one year (t−1). Data on social group composition of NAVCO campaigns comes from Dahlum et al. (2019). Observations = 9,265; Countries = 157. ^ p < 0.10, * p < 0.05, ** p < 0.01, *** p < 0.001.

TABLE 7.B.18 *Ongoing resistance campaigns by class-based coalitions and electoral democracy*

	(1) Change	(2) Upturns	(3) Downturns	(4) Change	(5) Upturns	(6) Downturns
Luebbert campaign	0.015*	0.023**	-0.008*			
	(0.007)	(0.008)	(0.004)			
Middle-sector campaign				0.030**	0.040***	-0.009*
				(0.010)	(0.008)	(0.004)
Other campaign	0.007*	0.012***	-0.006**	0.003	0.009***	-0.005**
	(0.003)	(0.002)	(0.002)	(0.003)	(0.002)	(0.002)
GDP per capita (ln)	0.004*	0.001	0.003***	0.004^	0.001	0.003***
	(0.002)	(0.002)	(0.001)	(0.002)	(0.002)	(0.001)
GDP growth (%)	0.034**	0.008	0.026***	0.034**	0.008	0.026***
	(0.011)	(0.008)	(0.005)	(0.011)	(0.008)	(0.005)
Oil production (per capita)	-0.000	-0.000	-0.000	-0.000	-0.000	-0.000
	(0.000)	(0.000)	(0.000)	(0.000)	(0.000)	(0.000)
Regional diffusion	0.059***	0.036**	0.022***	0.060***	0.037**	0.022***
	(0.013)	(0.011)	(0.006)	(0.013)	(0.011)	(0.006)
Lagged democracy	-0.065***	-0.044***	-0.021***	-0.063***	-0.042***	-0.021***
	(0.007)	(0.006)	(0.003)	(0.007)	(0.006)	(0.003)
Constant	-0.039*	-0.000	-0.039***	-0.037*	0.002	-0.039***
	(0.018)	(0.015)	(0.010)	(0.018)	(0.014)	(0.010)

(*continued*)

TABLE 7.B.18 (*continued*)

	(1) Change	(2) Upturns	(3) Downturns	(4) Change	(5) Upturns	(6) Downturns
R^2 Overall	0.048	0.054	0.033	0.053	0.064	0.033
R^2 Within	0.082	0.091	0.044	0.086	0.097	0.044
R^2 Between	0.079	0.076	0.023	0.073	0.061	0.024
AIC	-31338.435	-35857.071	-42383.842	-31372.048	-35927.015	-42385.505
BIC	-30525.159	-35043.795	-41570.566	-30558.772	-35113.739	-41572.229

Notes: Estimated coefficients and country-clustered robust standard errors from country and year fixed effects models. Dependent variables are annual changes in the electoral democracy index (v2x_polyarchy). All independent variables are lagged by one year (t–1). To qualify for Luebbert's (1991) working class and farmer coalition, the resistance campaign must include industrial workers and peasants, with one of these two groups dominating. To qualify for the middle-sectors thesis, the resistance campaign must include industrial workers and the middle class, with one of these two groups dominating. Data on social group composition of NAVCO campaigns comes from Dahlum et al. (2019). Observations = 9,265; Countries = 157. ^ p < 0.10, * p < 0.05, ** p < 0.01, *** p < 0.001.

TABLE 7.B.19 *Ongoing resistance campaigns by class-based coalitions and procedural democracy*

	(1) Change	(2) Upturns	(3) Downturns	(4) Change	(5) Upturns	(6) Downturns
Luebbert campaign	0.016^	0.023*	-0.007			
	(0.008)	(0.010)	(0.005)			
Middle-sector campaign				0.032*	0.041***	-0.009^
				(0.014)	(0.012)	(0.005)
Other campaign	0.012*	0.016***	-0.004*	0.008*	0.012**	-0.004*
	(0.005)	(0.004)	(0.002)	(0.004)	(0.004)	(0.002)
GDP per capita (ln)	0.009**	0.004	0.005***	0.009**	0.004	0.005***
	(0.003)	(0.003)	(0.001)	(0.003)	(0.003)	(0.001)
GDP growth (%)	0.038^	0.006	0.032***	0.038^	0.006	0.032***
	(0.020)	(0.016)	(0.008)	(0.020)	(0.016)	(0.008)
Oil production (per capita)	-0.000	-0.000	-0.000	-0.000	-0.000	-0.000
	(0.000)	(0.000)	(0.000)	(0.000)	(0.000)	(0.000)
Regional diffusion	0.075***	0.047***	0.028***	0.077***	0.048***	0.028***
	(0.015)	(0.012)	(0.008)	(0.015)	(0.012)	(0.008)
Lagged democracy	-0.101***	-0.070***	-0.031***	-0.100***	-0.069***	-0.031***
	(0.011)	(0.008)	(0.005)	(0.011)	(0.008)	(0.005)
Constant	-0.065*	-0.020	-0.045***	-0.063*	-0.018	-0.045***
	(0.025)	(0.022)	(0.012)	(0.026)	(0.023)	(0.012)

(continued)

TABLE 7.B.19 (continued)

	(1) Change	(2) Upturns	(3) Downturns	(4) Change	(5) Upturns	(6) Downturns
R^2 Overall	0.039	0.034	0.029	0.041	0.037	0.030
R^2 Within	0.081	0.076	0.038	0.082	0.079	0.038
R^2 Between	0.080	0.080	0.034	0.076	0.073	0.036
AIC	−23701.123	−27676.046	−34270.312	−23713.365	−27703.474	−34271.743
BIC	−22887.847	−26862.770	−33457.036	−22900.089	−26890.198	−33458.467

Notes: Estimated coefficients and country-clustered robust standard errors from country and year fixed effects models. Dependent variable is annual change in the Munck procedural democracy index (see Hegre et al. 2020). All independent variables are lagged by one year (t–1). To qualify for Luebbert's (1991) working class and farmer coalition, the resistance campaign must include industrial workers and peasants, with one of these two groups dominating. To qualify for the middle-sectors thesis, the resistance campaign must include industrial workers and the middle class, with one of these two groups dominating. Data on social group composition of NAVCO campaigns comes from Dahlum et al. (2019). Observations = 9,265; Countries = 157. ^ p < 0.10, * p < 0.05, ** p < 0.01, *** p < 0.001.

TABLE 7.B.20 *Resistance events in the CNTS data and changes in democracy*

	(1) Change	(2) Upturns	(3) Downturns	(4) Change	(5) Upturns	(6) Downturns
Strikes	0.000	0.001	-0.000	0.001	0.001	0.000
	(0.002)	(0.001)	(0.001)	(0.002)	(0.002)	(0.001)
Riots	0.000	0.001*	-0.001**	0.000	0.001*	-0.001*
	(0.001)	(0.001)	(0.000)	(0.001)	(0.001)	(0.000)
Peaceful demonstrations	0.001*	0.001	0.000	0.001*	0.001^	0.000
	(0.000)	(0.000)	(0.000)	(0.001)	(0.001)	(0.000)
GDP per capita (ln)	0.003^	-0.001	0.004***	0.005*	-0.001	0.006***
	(0.002)	(0.002)	(0.001)	(0.003)	(0.002)	(0.002)
GDP growth (%)	0.032**	0.005	0.028***	0.051**	0.012	0.039***
	(0.010)	(0.008)	(0.005)	(0.017)	(0.012)	(0.008)
Oil production (per capita)	-0.000	-0.000	-0.000^	0.000	0.000	-0.000
	(0.000)	(0.000)	(0.000)	(0.000)	(0.000)	(0.000)
Regional diffusion	0.059***	0.037***	0.022**	0.072***	0.045***	0.027**
	(0.014)	(0.011)	(0.007)	(0.015)	(0.011)	(0.009)
Lagged democracy	-0.067***	-0.043***	-0.024***	-0.092***	-0.059***	-0.032***
	(0.007)	(0.006)	(0.003)	(0.011)	(0.008)	(0.005)
Constant	0.008	0.037*	-0.029***	0.017	0.061^	-0.044***
	(0.016)	(0.015)	(0.008)	(0.032)	(0.033)	(0.011)
R^2 Overall	0.040	0.041	0.037	0.035	0.031	0.031

(continued)

TABLE 7.B.20 (*continued*)

	(1) Change	(2) Upturns	(3) Downturns	(4) Change	(5) Upturns	(6) Downturns
R^2 Within	0.073	0.072	0.046	0.074	0.065	0.039
R^2 Between	0.061	0.018	0.055	0.057	0.008	0.054
AIC	−31631.295	−36332.714	−42300.796	−24966.618	−29636.319	−34293.189
BIC	−30947.118	−35648.537	−41616.619	−24282.440	−28952.142	−33609.011
Outcome	Electoral democracy	Electoral democracy	Electoral democracy	Procedural democracy	Procedural democracy	Procedural democracy

Notes: Estimated coefficients and country-clustered robust standard errors from country and year fixed effects models. Dependent variables are annual changes in the electoral democracy index (v2x_polyarchy) and the Munck procedural democracy index (see Hegre et al. 2020). All independent variables are lagged by one year (t–1). Data on number of strikes, riots, and peaceful demonstrations comes from Banks and Wilson (2018). Observations = 9,199; Countries = 157. ^ p < 0.10, * p < 0.05, ** p < 0.01, *** p < 0.001.

Appendix 8 A Structural Equations

Note: The models for each outcome are a system of equations that are estimated simultaneously using maximum likelihood. All models were run with variables previously transformed into deviations from country means so that models would produce country-fixed-effects estimates. All models were run with the SEM suite in Stata 16.

Notation: The alpha_n are the intercepts for each endogenous variable. Rho is the coefficient of the lagged outcome variable. The betas are the coefficients of predictors. The first subscript of coefficients and the epsilons is the order of the equation in the structural model; the second is the order of the term in that equation. Variable subscripts are i for countries, t for years, and d for decades. υ_i is the country-clustered error term and ε_{1it} to ε_{nit} are the residuals for each observation in equations 1 to n.

THE PATH MODEL FOR LEVELS OF POLYARCHY

$\text{Polyarchy}_{it} = \rho_{11} \text{Polyarchy}_{it-1} + \beta_{11}$ Institutionalized parties $_{it-1} + \beta_{12}$ CSO participatory environment $_{it-1} + \beta_{13}$ Rule of law $_{it-1} + \beta_{14}$ Agricultural income $_{it-1}$ + β_{15} ln(GDP per capita) $_{it-1} + \beta_{16}$ Literacy $_{it-1} + \beta_{17}$ Protestant population$_i + \beta_{18}$ Harbor distance$_i + \beta_{19}$ Resource dependence $_{it-1} + \beta_{110}$ European population$_i$ + sum(β_{1d} decade dummies)$_d + \alpha_1 + \upsilon_i + \varepsilon_{1it}$

Institutionalized parties $_{it-1} = \beta_{21}$ Institutionalized parties $_{it-2} + \beta_{22}$ CSO participatory environment $_{it-2} + \beta_{23}$ Rule of law $_{it-2} + \beta_{24}$ Agricultural income $_{it-2} + \beta_{25}$ ln(GDP per capita) $_{it-2} + \beta_{26}$ Literacy $_{it-2} + \beta_{27}$ Protestant population$_i + \beta_{28}$ Harbor distance$_i + \beta_{29}$ Resource dependence $_{it-2} + \beta_{210}$ European population$_i$ + β_{211} Polyarchy $_{it-2} + \alpha_2 + \varepsilon_{2it}$

CSO participatory environment $_{it-1} = \beta_{31}$ Institutionalized parties $_{it-2} + \beta_{32}$ CSO participatory environment $_{it-2} + \beta_{33}$ Rule of law $_{it-2} + \beta_{34}$ Agricultural income $_{it-2} + \beta_{35}$ ln(GDP per capita) $_{it-2} + \beta_{36}$ Literacy $_{it-2} + \beta_{37}$ Protestant population$_i$ + β_{38} Harbor distance$_i$ + β_{39} Resource dependence $_{it-2}$ + β_{310} European population$_i$ + β_{311} Polyarchy $_{it-2}$ + α_3 + ε_{3it}

Rule of law $_{it-1}$ = β_{41} Institutionalized parties $_{it-2}$ + β_{42} CSO participatory environment $_{it-2}$ + β_{43} Rule of law $_{it-2}$ +β_{44} Agricultural income $_{it-2}$ + β_{45} ln(GDP per capita) $_{it-2}$ + β_{46} Literacy $_{it-2}$ + β_{47} Protestant population$_i$ + β_{48} Harbor distance$_i$ + β_{49} Resource dependence $_{it-2}$ + β_{410} European population$_i$ + β_{411} Polyarchy $_{it-2}$ + α_4 + ε_{4it}

Agricultural income $_{it-1}$ = β_{51} Institutionalized parties $_{it-2}$ + β_{52} CSO participatory environment $_{it-2}$ + β_{53} Rule of law $_{it-2}$ +β_{54} Agricultural income $_{it-2}$ + β_{55} ln(GDP per capita) $_{it-2}$ + β_{56} Literacy $_{it-2}$ + β_{57} Protestant population$_i$ + β_{58} Harbor distance$_i$ + β_{59} Resource dependence $_{it-2}$ + β_{510} European population$_i$ + β_{511} Polyarchy $_{it-2}$ + α_5 + ε_{5it}

ln(GDP per capita) $_{it-1}$ = β_{61} Institutionalized parties $_{it-2}$ + β_{62} CSO participatory environment $_{it-2}$ + β_{63} Rule of law $_{it-2}$ +β_{64} Agricultural income $_{it-2}$ + β_{65} ln(GDP per capita) $_{it-2}$ + β_{66} Literacy $_{it-2}$ + β_{67} Protestant population$_i$ + β_{68} Harbor distance$_i$ + β_{69} Resource dependence $_{it-2}$ + β_{610} European population$_i$ + β_{611} Polyarchy $_{it-2}$ + α_6 + ε_{6it}

Literacy $_{it-1}$ = β_{71} Institutionalized parties $_{it-2}$ + β_{72} CSO participatory environment $_{it-2}$ + β_{73} Rule of law $_{it-2}$ +β_{74} Agricultural income $_{it-2}$ + β_{75} ln(GDP per capita) $_{it-2}$ + β_{76} Literacy $_{it-2}$ + β_{77} Protestant population$_i$ + β_{78} Harbor distance$_i$ + β_{79} Resource dependence $_{it-2}$ + β_{710} European population$_i$ + β_{711} Polyarchy $_{it-2}$ + α_7 + ε_{7it}

THE PATH MODEL FOR UPTURNS IN POLYARCHY

Upturn $_{it}$ = ρ_{11} Upturn $_{it-1}$ + β_{11} Agricultural income $_{it-1}$ + β_{12} ln(GDP per capita) $_{it-1}$ + β_{13} Literacy $_{it-1}$ + β_{14} CSO participatory environment $_{it-2}$ + β_{15} Nonviolent campaign$_{it-1}$ + β_{16} Violent campaign $_{it-1}$ + β_{17} Global economic growth$_t$ + sum(β_{1d} decade dummies)$_d$ + υ_i + α_1 + ε_{1it}

ln(GDP per capita) $_{it-1}$ = β_{21} Agricultural income $_{it-2}$ + β_{22} ln(GDP per capita) $_{it-2}$ + β_{23} Literacy $_{it-2}$ + β_{24} Harbor distance$_i$ + β_{25} Resource dependence $_{it-2}$ + β_{26} European population$_i$ + β_{27} Polyarchy $_{it-2}$ + α_2 + ε_{2it}

Literacy $_{it-1}$ = β_{31} Agricultural income $_{it-2}$ + β_{32} ln(GDP per capita) $_{it-2}$ + β_{33} Literacy $_{it-2}$ + β_{34} Harbor distance$_i$ + β_{35} Resource dependence $_{it-2}$ + β_{36} European population$_i$ + β_{37} Polyarchy $_{it-2}$ + α_3 + ε_{3it}

Agricultural income $_{it-1}$ = β_{41} Agricultural income $_{it-2}$+ β_{42} ln(GDP per capita) $_{it-2}$ + β_{43} Literacy $_{it-2}$ + β_{44} Harbor distance$_i$ + β_{45} Resource dependence $_{it-2}$ + β_{46} European population$_i$ + β_{47} Polyarchy $_{it-2}$ + α_4 + ε_{4it}

CSO participatory environment $_{it}$ = β_{51} Agricultural income $_{it-2}$ + β_{52} ln(GDP per capita) $_{it-2}$ + β_{53} Literacy $_{it-2}$ + β_{54} CSO participatory environment$_{it-2}$ + β_{55} Nonviolent campaign$_{it-2}$ + β_{56} Violent campaign $_{it-2}$ + β_{57} Global economic growth$_t$ + β_{58} Polyarchy $_{it-2}$ + α_5 + ε_{5it}

Nonviolent campaign$_{it}$ = β_{61} Agricultural income $_{it-2}$ + β_{62} ln(GDP per capita) $_{it-2}$ + β_{63} Literacy $_{it-2}$ + β_{64} CSO participatory environment $_{it-2}$ + β_{65} Nonviolent campaign$_{it-2}$ + β_{66} Violent campaign $_{it-2}$ + β_{67} Global economic growth$_t$ + β_{68} Polyarchy $_{it-2}$ + α_6 + ε_{6it}

Violent campaign$_{it}$ = β_{71} Agricultural income $_{it-2}$ + β_{72} ln(GDP per capita) $_{it-2}$ + β_{73} Literacy $_{it-2}$ + β_{74} CSO participatory environment $_{it-2}$ + β_{75} Nonviolent campaign$_{it-2}$ + β_{76} Violent campaign $_{it-2}$ + β_{77} Global economic growth$_t$ + β_{78} Polyarchy $_{it-2}$ + α_7 + ε_{7it}

THE PATH MODEL FOR DOWNTURNS IN POLYARCHY

Downturn $_{it}$ = ρ_{11} Downturn $_{it-1}$ + β_{11} Agricultural income $_{it-1}$ + β_{12} ln(GDP per capita) $_{it-1}$ + β_{13} Literacy $_{it-1}$ + β_{14} Resource dependence $_{it-1}$ + β_{15} Polyarchy $_{it-1}$ + β_{16} CSO participatory environment $_{it-1}$ + β_{17} Rule of law$_{it-1}$ + β_{18} Anti-system movement $_{it-1}$ + β_{19} Left-wing campaign $_{it-1}$ + β_{110} Right-wing campaign $_{it-1}$ + β_{111} National economic growth$_{it-1}$ + β_{112} Strict presidentialism$_{t-1}$ + sum(β_{1d} decade dummies)$_d$ + v_i + α_1 + ε_{1it}

ln(GDP per capita) $_{it-1}$ = β_{21} Agricultural income $_{it-2}$ + β_{22} ln(GDP per capita) $_{it-2}$ + β_{23} Literacy $_{it-2}$ + β_{24} Resource dependence $_{it-2}$ + β_{25} Polyarchy $_{it-2}$ + α_2 + ε_{2it}

Literacy $_{it-1}$ = β_{31} Agricultural income $_{it-2}$ + β_{32} ln(GDP per capita) $_{it-2}$ + β_{33} Literacy $_{it-2}$ + β_{34} Resource dependence $_{it-2}$ + β_{35} Polyarchy $_{it-2}$ + α_3 + ε_{3it}

Agricultural income $_{it-1}$ = β_{41} Agricultural income $_{it-2}$ + β_{42} ln(GDP per capita) $_{it-2}$ + β_{43} Literacy $_{it-2}$ + β_{44} Resource dependence $_{it-2}$ + β_{45} Polyarchy $_{it-2}$ + α_4 + ε_{4it}

CSO participatory environment $_{it}$ = β_{51} Agricultural income $_{it-2}$ + β_{52} ln(GDP per capita) $_{it-2}$ + α_n + β_{53} Literacy $_{it-2}$ + β_{54} CSO participatory environment $_{it-2}$ + β_{55} Rule of law $_{it-2}$ + β_{56} Nonviolent campaign$_{it-2}$ + β_{57} Violent campaign $_{it-2}$ + β_{58} Global economic growth$_t$ + β_{59} Polyarchy $_{it-2}$ + α_5 + ε_{5it}

Rule of law$_{it}$ = β_{61} Agricultural income $_{it-2}$ + β_{62} ln(GDP per capita) $_{it-2}$ + β_{63} Literacy $_{it-2}$ + β_{64} Rule of law $_{it-2}$ + β_{65} Polyarchy $_{it-2}$ + α_6 + ε_{6it}

Anti-system movement$_{it}$ = β_{71} Agricultural income $_{it-2}$ + β_{72} ln(GDP per capita) $_{it-2}$ + β_{73} Literacy $_{it-2}$ + β_{74} Anti-system movement$_{it-2}$ + β_{75} Left-wing campaign $_{it-2}$ + β_{76} Right-wing campaign $_{it-2}$ + β_{77} Rule of law $_{it-2}$ + β_{78} National economic growth$_{t-2}$ + β_{79} Polyarchy $_{it-2}$ + α_7 + ε_{7it}

Left-wing campaign $_{it}$ = β_{81} Agricultural income $_{it-2}$ + β_{82} ln(GDP per capita) $_{it-2}$ + β_{83} Literacy $_{it-2}$ + β_{84} Anti-system movement$_{it-2}$ + β_{85} Left-wing campaign $_{it-2}$ + β_{86} Right-wing campaign $_{it-2}$ + β_{87} Rule of law $_{it-2}$ + β_{88} National economic growth$_{t-2}$ + β_{89} Polyarchy $_{it-2}$ + α_8 + ε_{8it}

Right-wing campaign $_{it}$ = β_{91} Agricultural income $_{it-2}$ + β_{92} ln(GDP per capita) $_{it-2}$ + β_{93} Literacy $_{it-2}$ + β_{94} Anti-system movement$_{it-2}$ + β_{95} Left-wing campaign $_{it-2}$ + β_{96} Right-wing campaign $_{it-2}$ + β_{97} Rule of law $_{it-2}$ + β_{98} National economic growth$_{t-2}$ + β_{99} Polyarchy $_{it-2}$ + α_9 + ε_{9it}

National economic growth$_{it}$ = β_{101} Agricultural income $_{it-2}$ + β_{102} ln(GDP per capita) $_{it-2}$ + β_{103} Literacy $_{it-2}$ + β_{104} Rule of law $_{it-2}$ + β_{105} National economic growth$_{t-2}$ + β_{106} Polyarchy $_{it-2}$ + α_{10} + ε_{10it}

Strict presidentialism$_{it}$ = β_{111} Agricultural income $_{it-2}$ + β_{112} ln(GDP per capita) $_{it-2}$ + β_{113} Literacy $_{it-2}$ + β_{114} Polyarchy $_{it-2}$ + α_{11} + ε_{11it}

Appendix 8 B Variable Descriptions

TABLE 8.B.1 *Variable descriptions*

Variable label	Variable name	Source	Mean	S.D.	Min	Max
Polyarchy/Electoral Democracy Index	v2x_polyarchy	V-Dem (v9)	0.274	0.265	0.007	0.948
-Upturn	upturn	V-Dem (v9)	0.077	0.287	0.000	7.020
-Downturn	downturn	V-Dem (v9)	-0.047	0.206	-5.19	0.000
Agricultural income	s_mil_agro	Miller (2015)	51.021	27.66	0.000	96.900
Anti-system movement	v2csantimv	V-Dem (v9)	-0.414	1.291	-3.139	4.015
CSO participatory environment	v2csprtcpt	V-Dem (v9)	-0.281	1.468	-3.532	3.263
Ethnic fractionalization	wim_ethfrac	Chapter 3	0.377	0.274	0.001	0.920
European population/100	eur_pct_est_smooth	Chapter 3	0.206	0.356	0.000	1.000
GDP per capita	e_migdppclni	Chapter 5	8.047	1.141	4.898	12.305
Global economic growth	expand	Based on e_migdppclni	0.004	0.007	0.000	0.045
High state capacity	v2clrspct	V-Dem (v9)	0.217	1.480	-3.685	4.455
Institutionalized parties	v2xps_party	V-Dem (v9)	0.564	0.278	0.004	1.000
Left-wing movement	v2csanmvch_6	V-Dem (v9)	0.222	0.295	0.000	1.000
Literacy	litcyxtend	Chapter 4	53.409	35.308	0.182	100.000
Majoritarian electoral system	elecsys	V-Dem (v9)	0.199	0.399	0.000	1.000
Mean temperature	tmean	Chapter 3	289.868	8.477	266.17	301.459
Middle-sector campaign	midsect_end	DKW*	0.003	0.052	0.000	1.000
National economic growth	ecgrowth	Based on e_migdppclni	0.019	0.074	-0.630	1.737
Natural harbor distance/1000	portdist_natural_km	Chapter 3	0.383	0.372	0.004	1.986

(continued)

TABLE 8.B.1 (*continued*)

Variable label	Variable name	Source	Mean	S.D.	Min	Max
Non-middle-sector campaign	om_end	DKW*	0.011	0.105	0.000	1.000
Nonviolent campaign	navco_nonviol	NAVCO 1.1**	0.018	0.132	0.000	1.000
Non-worker-farmer campaign	ol_end	DKW*	0.012	0.110	0.000	1.000
Ongoing campaign	dkw_ongoing	DKW*	0.071	0.257	0.000	1.000
Protestant population	chrstprotpct	Chapter 3	10.238	20.423	0.000	99.010
Resource dependence/1000	s_mil_resdep2	Miller (2015)	0.004	0.010	0.000	0.100
Right-wing movement	v2csanmvch_7	V-Dem (v9)	0.112	0.212	0.000	1.000
Strict presidentialism	hardpres	Chapter 6	0.328	0.469	0.000	1.000
Violent campaign	navco_viol	NAVCO 1.1**	0.077	0.267	0.000	1.000
Worker-farmer campaign	luebbert_end	DKW*	0.002	0.042	0.000	1.000

*DKW: Dahlum, Knutsen, and Wig 2019 **NAVCO 1.1: Chenoweth 2011; Chenoweth and Stephan 2011

Appendix 8 C Additional Path Models

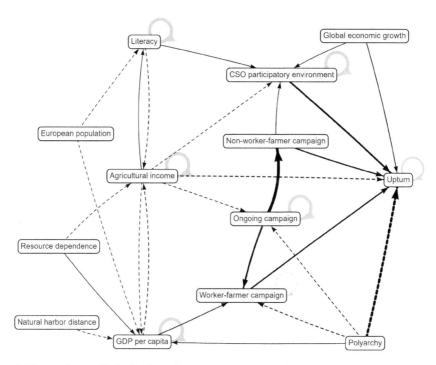

Significant paths are in black. Black line widths are proportional to standardized coefficients. Dashed lines show negative effects. Gray circles show self-lags on a different scale.

FIGURE 8.C.1 Path model of upturns using worker-small farmer campaigns

Appendices

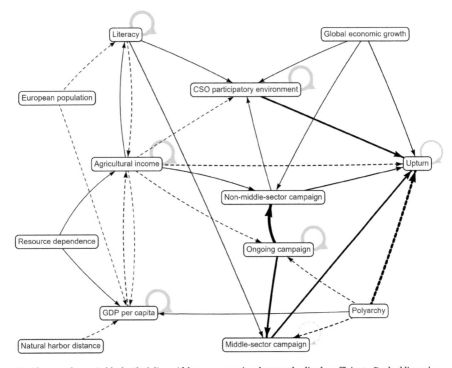

Significant paths are in black. Black line widths are proportional to standardized coefficients. Dashed lines show negative effects. Gray circles show self-lags on a different scale.

FIGURE 8.C.2 Path model of upturns using middle-sector campaigns

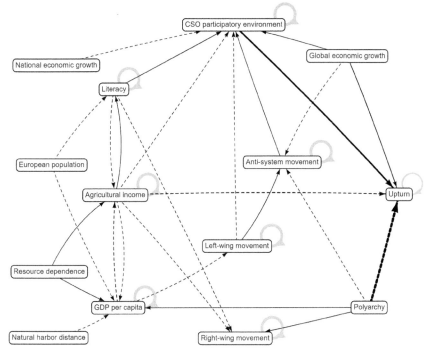

Significant paths are in black. Black line widths are proportional to standardized coefficients. Dashed lines show negative effects. Gray circles show self-lags on a different scale.

FIGURE 8.C.3 Path model of upturns using anti-system and left- and right-wing movements

TABLE 8.C.1 *Path model of upturns using worker-small farmer campaigns*

Endogenous variable	Predictors	unstd. coef.	std. coef.	s.e.	z	p
Upturn$_t$						
	Agricultural income$_{t-1}$	-0.0002***	-0.0696	0.0000	-3.60	0.000
	GDP per capita$_{t-1}$	0.0006	0.0103	0.0011	0.54	0.591
	Literacy$_{t-1}$	0.0001	0.0313	0.0000	1.56	0.120
	CSO participatory environment$_{t-1}$	0.0069***	0.1973	0.0008	9.12	0.000
	Ongoing campaign$_{t-1}$	0.0005	0.0041	0.0017	0.32	0.746
	Worker-farmer campaign$_{t-1}$	0.0822***	0.1312	0.0228	3.61	0.000
	Non-worker-farmer campaign$_{t-1}$	0.0340***	0.1233	0.0074	4.62	0.000
	Polyarchy$_{t-1}$	-0.0066***	-0.3475	0.0006	-11.58	0.000
	Upturn$_{t-1}$	0.2403***	0.2435	0.0194	12.41	0.000
	Global economic growth$_{t-1}$	0.2251*	0.0406	0.0930	2.42	0.015
	1900s	-0.0137***	-0.0646	0.0031	-4.47	0.000
	1910s	-0.0089***	-0.0499	0.0026	-3.40	0.001
	1920s	-0.0069**	-0.0429	0.0026	-2.69	0.007
	1930s	-0.0095***	-0.0612	0.0025	-3.81	0.000
	1940s	-0.0016	-0.0101	0.0025	-0.63	0.528
	1950s	0.0008	0.0061	0.0025	0.32	0.750
	1960s	-0.0030	-0.0255	0.0018	-1.65	0.098
	1970s	-0.0019	-0.0177	0.0021	-0.93	0.355
	1980s	-0.0010	-0.0093	0.0017	-0.57	0.570
	1990s	0.0046***	0.0471	0.0011	4.00	0.000
	intercept	0.0026	0.0719	0.0015	1.75	0.079
Agricultural income$_{t-1}$						
	GDP per capita$_{t-2}$	-0.9067***	-0.0370	0.1440	-6.30	0.000
	Literacy$_{t-2}$	-0.0230***	-0.0282	0.0043	-5.36	0.000
	Agricultural income$_{t-2}$	0.9238***	0.9278	0.0089	103.85	0.000
	Natural harbor distance/1000	-1.2712	-0.0015	2.3063	-0.55	0.581
	Natural harbor distance/1000	13.5804*	0.0060	6.2731	2.16	0.030
	European population$_{t-1}$/100	-1.8042	-0.0031	1.5341	-1.18	0.240
	Polyarchy$_{t-2}$	0.0366	0.0046	0.0257	1.42	0.154
	intercept	-0.4645***	-0.0311	0.0295	-15.77	0.000

(continued)

TABLE 8.C.1 *(continued)*

Endogenous variable	Predictors	unstd. coef.	std. coef.	s.e.	z	p
GDP per capita$_{t-1}$						
	GDP per capita$_{t-2}$	0.9832***	0.9767	0.0031	317.16	0.000
	Literacy$_{t-2}$	0.0001	0.0035	0.0001	1.04	0.300
	Agricultural income$_{t-2}$	−0.0003*	−0.0071	0.0001	−2.21	0.027
	Natural harbor distance/1000	−0.1317*	−0.0037	0.0583	−2.26	0.024
	Resource dependence$_{t-1}$/1000	0.9880***	0.0106	0.2863	3.45	0.001
	European population$_{t-1}$/100	−0.0707**	−0.0030	0.0245	−2.88	0.004
	Polyarchy$_{t-2}$	0.0032***	0.0097	0.0008	3.86	0.000
	intercept	0.0173***	0.0282	0.0012	14.63	0.000
Literacy$_{t-1}$						
	GDP per capita$_{t-2}$	−0.0240	−0.0008	0.0688	−0.35	0.727
	Literacy$_{t-2}$	1.0078***	1.0029	0.0018	547.39	0.000
	Agricultural income$_{t-2}$	0.0080*	0.0065	0.0031	2.55	0.011
	Natural harbor distance/1000	1.0629	0.0010	1.4164	0.75	0.453
	Resource dependence$_{t-1}$/1000	10.0473	0.0036	5.4253	1.85	0.064
	European population$_{t-1}$/100	−1.5660*	−0.0022	0.7634	−2.05	0.040
	Polyarchy$_{t-2}$	−0.0070	−0.0007	0.0164	−0.43	0.670
	intercept	0.6385***	0.0347	0.0366	17.43	0.000
CSO participatory environment$_{t-1}$						
	Global economic growth$_{t-1}$	2.2866**	0.0145	0.8410	2.72	0.007
	GDP per capita$_{t-2}$	0.0005	0.0003	0.0080	0.07	0.947
	Literacy$_{t-2}$	0.0012***	0.0206	0.0003	4.52	0.000
	Agricultural income$_{t-2}$	−0.0010**	−0.0147	0.0003	−2.99	0.003
	Polyarchy$_{t-2}$	0.0010	0.0019	0.0027	0.38	0.703
	CSO participatory environment$_{t-2}$	0.9547***	0.9477	0.0051	185.85	0.000
	Non-worker-farmer campaign$_{t-2}$	0.1296*	0.0164	0.0565	2.29	0.022
	intercept	0.0155***	0.0151	0.0023	6.72	0.000
Ongoing campaign$_{t-1}$						
	Global economic growth$_{t-1}$	−0.5567	−0.0135	0.3090	−1.80	0.072
	GDP per capita$_{t-2}$	−0.0003	−0.0008	0.0052	−0.07	0.948
	Literacy$_{t-2}$	0.0001	0.0087	0.0002	0.72	0.470
	Agricultural income$_{t-2}$	−0.0005*	−0.0303	0.0002	−2.23	0.026
	Polyarchy$_{t-2}$	−0.0051**	−0.0357	0.0018	−2.81	0.005
	CSO participatory environment$_{t-2}$	0.0032	0.0121	0.0031	1.01	0.312

(continued)

TABLE 8.C.I (*continued*)

Endogenous variable	Predictors	unstd. coef.	std. coef.	s.e.	z	p
	Worker-farmer campaign$_{t-2}$	−0.0054	−0.0011	0.0147	−0.37	0.711
	Ongoing campaign$_{t-2}$	0.7416***	0.7407	0.0197	37.64	0.000
	intercept	0.0048***	0.0180	0.0014	3.46	0.001
Worker-farmer campaign$_{t-1}$						
	Global economic growth$_{t-1}$	−0.0643	−0.0073	0.1138	−0.57	0.572
	GDP per capita$_{t-2}$	0.0037**	0.0390	0.0013	2.88	0.004
	Literacy$_{t-2}$	0.0000	0.0104	0.0000	0.94	0.346
	Agricultural income$_{t-2}$	0.0000	−0.0077	0.0001	−0.38	0.705
	Polyarchy$_{t-2}$	−0.0020**	−0.0649	0.0007	−3.01	0.003
	CSO participatory environment$_{t-2}$	0.0008	0.0146	0.0010	0.80	0.423
	Worker-farmer campaign$_{t-2}$	−0.0208***	−0.0205	0.0035	−5.92	0.000
	Ongoing campaign$_{t-2}$	0.0398***	0.1854	0.0085	4.66	0.000
	intercept	0.0001	0.0011	0.0002	0.25	0.800
Non-worker-farmer campaign$_{t-1}$						
	Global economic growth$_{t-1}$	0.4672	0.0232	0.2471	1.89	0.059
	GDP per capita$_{t-2}$	−0.0038	−0.0179	0.0039	−0.99	0.321
	Literacy$_{t-2}$	0.0002	0.0243	0.0001	1.67	0.094
	Agricultural income$_{t-2}$	0.0004	0.0420	0.0002	1.78	0.076
	Polyarchy$_{t-2}$	0.0012	0.0176	0.0016	0.79	0.429
	CSO participatory environment$_{t-2}$	−0.0023	−0.0179	0.0024	−0.94	0.346
	Worker-farmer campaign$_{t-2}$	−0.0132	−0.0057	0.0115	−1.15	0.251
	Ongoing campaign$_{t-2}$	0.2022***	0.4147	0.0186	10.87	0.000
	intercept	−0.0014	−0.0109	0.0008	−1.67	0.094
Error variances						
	Upturn	0.0011	0.8454	0.0001		
	Agricultural income	12.9790	0.0583	1.9953		
	GDP per capita	0.0062	0.0164	0.0006		
	Literacy	1.1807	0.0035	0.1724		
	CSO participatory environment	0.0801	0.0759	0.0075		
	Ongoing campaign	0.0319	0.4429	0.0027		
	Worker-farmer campaign	0.0032	0.9611	0.0007		
	Non-worker-farmer campaign	0.0142	0.8284	0.0015		

* $p < 0.05$, ** $p < 0.01$, *** $p < 0.001$

TABLE 8.C.2 *Path model of upturns using middle-sector campaigns*

Endogenous variable	Predictors	unstd. coef.	std. coef.	s.e.	z	p
Upturn$_t$						
	Agricultural income$_{t-1}$	-0.0002***	-0.0690	0.0000	-3.67	0.000
	GDP per capita$_{t-1}$	0.0005	0.0082	0.0011	0.43	0.665
	Literacy$_{t-1}$	0.0001	0.0302	0.0000	1.52	0.129
	CSO participatory environment$_{t-1}$	0.0070***	0.1998	0.0007	9.47	0.000
	Ongoing campaign$_{t-1}$	0.0006	0.0046	0.0017	0.37	0.710
	Middle-sector campaign$_{t-1}$	0.0934***	0.1889	0.0180	5.20	0.000
	Non-middle-sector campaign$_{t-1}$	0.0239***	0.0812	0.0072	3.29	0.001
	Polyarchy$_{t-1}$	-0.0066***	-0.3428	0.0006	-11.51	0.000
	Upturn$_{t-1}$	0.2380***	0.2409	0.0188	12.63	0.000
	Global economic growth$_{t-1}$	0.2353**	0.0424	0.0915	2.57	0.010
	1900s	-0.0133***	-0.0626	0.0030	-4.38	0.000
	1910s	-0.0087***	-0.0488	0.0026	-3.36	0.001
	1920s	-0.0065**	-0.0406	0.0025	-2.60	0.009
	1930s	-0.0093***	-0.0598	0.0025	-3.74	0.000
	1940s	-0.0011	-0.0073	0.0025	-0.46	0.643
	1950s	0.0012	0.0094	0.0024	0.50	0.614
	1960s	-0.0025	-0.0212	0.0018	-1.42	0.156

(continued)

TABLE 8.C.2 (continued)

Endogenous variable	Predictors	unstd. coef.	std. coef.	s.e.	z	p
	1970s	-0.0014	-0.0134	0.0020	-0.72	0.470
	1980s	-0.0006	-0.0053	0.0017	-0.33	0.739
	1990s	0.0046***	0.0467	0.0011	4.13	0.000
	intercept	0.0023	0.0625	0.0014	1.56	0.118
Agricultural income$_{t-1}$						
	GDP per capita$_{t-2}$	-0.9067***	-0.0370	0.1440	-6.30	0.000
	Literacy$_{t-2}$	-0.0230***	-0.0282	0.0043	-5.36	0.000
	Agricultural income$_{t-2}$	0.9238***	0.9278	0.0089	103.85	0.000
	Natural harbor distance/1000	-1.2712	-0.0015	2.3063	-0.55	0.581
	Resource dependence$_{t-1}$/1000	13.5804**	0.0060	6.2731	2.16	0.030
	European population$_{t-1}$/100	-1.8042	-0.0031	1.5341	-1.18	0.240
	Polyarchy$_{t-2}$	0.0366	0.0046	0.0257	1.42	0.154
	intercept	-0.4645***	-0.0311	0.0295	-15.77	0.000
GDP per capita$_{t-1}$						
	GDP per capita$_{t-2}$	0.9832***	0.9767	0.0031	317.16	0.000
	Literacy$_{t-2}$	0.0001	0.0035	0.0001	1.04	0.300
	Agricultural income$_{t-2}$	-0.0003**	-0.0071	0.0001	-2.21	0.027
	Natural harbor distance/1000	-0.1317***	-0.0037	0.0583	-2.26	0.024
	Resource dependence$_{t-1}$/1000	0.9880***	0.0106	0.2863	3.45	0.001
	European population$_{t-1}$/100	-0.0707**	-0.0030	0.0245	-2.88	0.004

(continued)

Polyarchy_{t-2}	0.0032***	0.0097	0.0008	3.86	0.000
intercept	0.0173***	0.0282	0.0012	14.63	0.000

Literacy_{t-1}

GDP per capita_{t-2}	-0.0240	-0.0008	0.0688	-0.35	0.727
Literacy_{t-2}	1.0078***	1.0029	0.0018	547.39	0.000
Agricultural income_{t-2}	0.0080**	0.0065	0.0031	2.55	0.011
Natural harbor distance/1000	1.0629	0.0010	1.4164	0.75	0.453
Resource dependence_{t-1}/1000	10.0473	0.0036	5.4253	1.85	0.064
European population_{t-1}/100	-1.5660**	-0.0022	0.7634	-2.05	0.040
Polyarchy_{t-2}	-0.0070	-0.0007	0.0164	-0.43	0.670
intercept	0.6385***	0.0347	0.0366	17.43	0.000

CSO participatory environment_{t-1}

Middle-sector campaign_{t-2}	0.2182	0.0155	0.1312	1.66	0.096
Non-middle-sector campaign_{t-2}	0.1211*	0.0145	0.0548	2.21	0.027
Global economic growth_{t-1}	2.3577***	0.0149	0.8474	2.78	0.005
GDP per capita_{t-2}	-0.0007	-0.0004	0.0080	-0.09	0.932
Literacy_{t-2}	0.0011***	0.0201	0.0003	4.37	0.000
Agricultural income_{t-2}	-0.0010**	-0.0144	0.0003	-2.96	0.003
Polyarchy_{t-2}	0.0016	0.0029	0.0026	0.62	0.535
CSO participatory environment_{t-2}	0.9548***	0.9478	0.0050	189.91	0.000
intercept	0.0152***	0.0148	0.0023	6.68	0.000

Ongoing campaign_{t-1}

Global economic growth_{t-1}	-0.5564	-0.0135	0.3087	-1.80	0.072
GDP per capita_{t-2}	-0.0003	-0.0008	0.0052	-0.06	0.949

(continued)

TABLE 8.C.2 (*continued*)

Endogenous variable	Predictors	unstd. coef.	std. coef.	s.e.	z	p
	Literacy$_{t-2}$	0.0001	0.0088	0.0002	0.73	0.465
	Agricultural income$_{t-2}$	-0.0005*	-0.0304	0.0002	-2.24	0.025
	Polyarchy$_{t-2}$	-0.0052**	-0.0359	0.0018	-2.81	0.005
	CSO participatory environment$_{t-2}$	0.0032	0.0121	0.0031	1.01	0.311
	Middle-sector campaign$_{t-2}$	-0.0115	-0.0030	0.0115	-1.00	0.315
	Ongoing campaign$_{t-2}$	0.7416***	0.7407	0.0197	37.62	0.000
	intercept	0.0048***	0.0181	0.0014	3.46	0.001
Middle-sector campaign$_{t-1}$	Global economic growth$_{t-1}$	-0.0484	-0.0043	0.1393	-0.35	0.728
	GDP per capita$_{t-2}$	0.0036	0.0302	0.0020	1.79	0.074
	Literacy$_{t-2}$	0.0001*	0.0332	0.0001	2.44	0.015
	Agricultural income$_{t-2}$	0.0000	-0.0071	0.0001	-0.30	0.768
	Polyarchy$_{t-2}$	-0.0028***	-0.0708	0.0008	-3.28	0.001
	CSO participatory environment$_{t-2}$	-0.0001	-0.0011	0.0012	-0.07	0.946
	Middle-sector campaign$_{t-2}$	-0.0212***	-0.0205	0.0038	-5.59	0.000
	Ongoing campaign$_{t-2}$	0.0657***	0.2412	0.0113	5.83	0.000
	intercept	0.0004	0.0053	0.0004	1.03	0.305
Non-middle-sector campaign$_{t-1}$	Global economic growth$_{t-1}$	0.4571*	0.0242	0.2252	2.03	0.042
	GDP per capita$_{t-2}$	-0.0039	-0.0192	0.0035	-1.10	0.271

(*continued*)

Literacy$_{t-2}$	0.0001	0.0115	0.0001	0.81	0.419
Agricultural income$_{t-2}$	0.0004*	0.0451	0.0002	2.24	0.025
Polyarchy$_{t-2}$	0.0020	0.0303	0.0014	1.41	0.157
CSO participatory environment$_{t-2}$	-0.0014	-0.0117	0.0021	-0.66	0.509
Ongoing campaign$_{t-2}$	0.1762***	0.3844	0.0162	10.89	0.000
Non-middle-sector campaign$_{t-2}$	-0.0054	-0.0054	0.0140	-0.38	0.701
intercept	-0.0017*	-0.0141	0.0008	-2.28	0.023
Error variances					
Upturn	0.0011	0.8342	0.0001		
Agricultural income	12.9790	0.0583	1.9953		
GDP per capita	0.0062	0.0164	0.0006		
Literacy	1.1807	0.0035	0.1724		
CSO participatory environment	0.0799	0.0757	0.0075		
Ongoing campaign	0.0319	0.4429	0.0027		
Middle-sector campaign	0.0050	0.9347	0.0007		
Non-middle-sector campaign	0.0129	0.8534	0.0015		

Log pseudolikelihood = 49,769. N = 8,301. Number of countries: 150. * p < 0.05, ** p < 0.01, *** p < 0.001

TABLE 8.C.3 *Path model of upturns using anti-system and left- and right-wing movements*

Endogenous variable	Predictors	unstd. coef.	coef.	std. s.e.	z	p
Upturn$_t$						
	Agricultural income$_{t-1}$	−0.0002***	−0.0718	0.0000	−3.55	0.000
	GDP per capita$_{t-1}$	0.0002	0.0038	0.0013	0.18	0.858
	Literacy$_{t-1}$	0.0001	0.0328	0.0000	1.57	0.118
	CSO participatory environment$_{t-1}$	0.0071***	0.2027	0.0008	8.47	0.000
	Anti-system movement$_{t-1}$	0.0010	0.0259	0.0007	1.46	0.145
	Left-wing movement$_{t-1}$	−0.0039	−0.0206	0.0028	−1.37	0.171
	Right-wing movement$_{t-1}$	0.0033	0.0126	0.0043	0.76	0.445
	Polyarchy$_{t-1}$	−0.0071***	−0.3689	0.0006	−11.18	0.000
	Upturn$_{t-1}$	0.2473***	0.2503	0.0203	12.16	0.000
	Global economic growth$_{t-1}$	0.2290*	0.0410	0.0970	2.36	0.018
	National economic growth$_{t-1}$	0.0045	0.0099	0.0063	0.71	0.479
	1900s	−0.0160***	−0.0754	0.0031	−5.14	0.000
	1910s	−0.0110***	−0.0617	0.0027	−4.02	0.000
	1920s	−0.0085**	−0.0527	0.0027	−3.13	0.002
	1930s	−0.0111***	−0.0718	0.0027	−4.10	0.000
	1940s	−0.0031	−0.0199	0.0026	−1.19	0.236
	1950s	0.0000	0.0003	0.0026	0.02	0.987

(continued)

1960s	-0.0037	-0.0311	0.0020	-1.86	0.063
1970s	-0.0024	-0.0219	0.0022	-1.04	0.296
1980s	-0.0012	-0.0114	0.0019	-0.62	0.535
1990s	0.0053***	0.0539	0.0012	4.35	0.000
intercept	0.0034*	0.0930	0.0016	2.10	0.036
Agricultural income$_{t-1}$					
GDP per capita$_{t-2}$	-0.9179***	-0.0374	0.1450	-6.33	0.000
Literacy$_{t-2}$	-0.0230***	-0.0281	0.0043	-5.34	0.000
Agricultural income$_{t-2}$	0.9236***	0.9276	0.0089	103.64	0.000
Natural harbor distance/1000	-1.2534	-0.0015	2.3136	-0.54	0.588
Resource dependence$_{t-1}$/1000	13.8740*	0.0061	6.3466	2.19	0.029
European population$_{t-1}$/100	-1.8192	-0.0031	1.5358	-1.18	0.236
Polyarchy$_{t-2}$	0.0371	0.0046	0.0258	1.44	0.151
intercept	-0.4672***	-0.0313	0.0296	-15.80	0.000
GDP per capita$_{t-1}$					
GDP per capita$_{t-2}$	0.9830***	0.9764	0.0030	323.97	0.000
Literacy$_{t-2}$	0.0001	0.0037	0.0001	1.09	0.275
Agricultural income$_{t-2}$	-0.0003*	-0.0070	0.0001	-2.19	0.029
Natural harbor distance/1000	-0.1346*	-0.0038	0.0579	-2.33	0.020
Resource dependence$_{t-1}$/1000	1.0322***	0.0110	0.2803	3.68	0.000
European population$_{t-1}$/100	-0.0713**	-0.0030	0.0240	-2.97	0.003
Polyarchy$_{t-2}$	0.0032***	0.0098	0.0008	3.89	0.000
intercept	0.0171***	0.0279	0.0012	14.67	0.000

(continued)

TABLE 8.C.3 (continued)

Endogenous variable	Predictors	unstd. coef.	coef.	std. s.e.	z	p
Literacy$_{t-1}$						
	GDP per capita$_{t-2}$	-0.0242	-0.0008	0.0695	-0.35	0.728
	Literacy$_{t-2}$	1.0079***	1.0029	0.0018	549.71	0.000
	Agricultural income$_{t-2}$	0.0081**	0.0066	0.0031	2.56	0.010
	Natural harbor distance/1000	1.0716	0.0010	1.4145	0.76	0.449
	Resource dependence$_{t-1}$/1000	10.4612	0.0037	5.4110	1.93	0.053
	European population$_{t-1}$/100	-1.5362*	-0.0021	0.7637	-2.01	0.044
	Polyarchy$_{t-2}$	-0.0070	-0.0007	0.0164	-0.43	0.670
	intercept	0.6371***	0.0346	0.0367	17.38	0.000
CSO participatory environment$_{t-1}$						
	Global economic growth$_{t-1}$	1.9393*	0.0122	0.8797	2.20	0.027
	GDP per capita$_{t-2}$	0.0040	0.0024	0.0084	0.48	0.631
	Literacy$_{t-2}$	0.0012***	0.0216	0.0003	4.76	0.000
	Agricultural income$_{t-2}$	-0.0009*	-0.0125	0.0003	-2.53	0.011
	Polyarchy$_{t-2}$	0.0021	0.0038	0.0029	0.74	0.460
	CSO participatory environment$_{t-2}$	0.9546***	0.9474	0.0051	188.50	0.000
	Anti-system movement$_{t-2}$	0.0101*	0.0095	0.0046	2.19	0.028
	Left-wing movement$_{t-2}$	-0.0410*	-0.0076	0.0208	-1.97	0.049
	Right-wing movement$_{t-2}$	-0.0540	-0.0073	0.0356	-1.51	0.130
	National economic growth$_{t-2}$	-0.1049*	-0.0082	0.0460	-2.28	0.023
	intercept	0.0163***	0.0159	0.0024	6.94	0.000

(continued)

Anti-system movement_{t-1}

Global economic growth_{t-1}	-1.4793*	-0.0099	0.7207	-2.05	0.040
GDP per capita_{t-2}	-0.0046	-0.0029	0.0097	-0.47	0.638
Literacy_{t-2}	-0.0004	-0.0084	0.0003	-1.47	0.140
Agricultural income_{t-2}	-0.0004	-0.0063	0.0004	-1.05	0.295
Polyarchy_{t-2}	-0.0088*	-0.0171	0.0035	-2.53	0.012
CSO participatory environment_{t-2}	0.0096	0.0101	0.0072	1.33	0.184
Anti-system movement_{t-2}	0.9286***	0.9261	0.0072	128.20	0.000
Left-wing movement_{t-2}	0.0632**	0.0125	0.0223	2.84	0.005
Right-wing movement_{t-2}	0.0232	0.0033	0.0367	0.63	0.528
National economic growth_{t-2}	0.1074	0.0089	0.0728	1.47	0.141
intercept	-0.0042	-0.0043	0.0026	-1.58	0.114

Left-wing movement_{t-1}

Global economic growth_{t-1}	-0.0872	-0.0030	0.1772	-0.49	0.623
GDP per capita_{t-2}	-0.0039*	-0.0125	0.0019	-2.10	0.036
Literacy_{t-2}	-0.0001	-0.0057	0.0001	-1.02	0.306
Agricultural income_{t-2}	0.0000	0.0014	0.0001	0.26	0.793
Polyarchy_{t-2}	0.0006	0.0057	0.0006	0.92	0.357
CSO participatory environment_{t-2}	-0.0004	-0.0024	0.0012	-0.36	0.719
Anti-system movement_{t-2}	0.0014	0.0072	0.0011	1.26	0.206
Left-wing movement_{t-2}	0.9364***	0.9379	0.0056	168.51	0.000
Right-wing movement_{t-2}	0.0013	0.0009	0.0062	0.21	0.834
National economic growth_{t-2}	0.0069	0.0029	0.0089	0.78	0.435

(continued)

TABLE 8.C.3 *(continued)*

Endogenous variable	Predictors	unstd. coef.	coef.	std. s.e.	z	p
	intercept	0.0004	0.0022	0.0005	0.93	0.355
Right-wing movement$_{t-1}$						
	Global economic growth$_{t-1}$	0.0332	0.0015	0.1218	0.27	0.785
	GDP per capita$_{t-2}$	−0.0018	−0.0077	0.0015	−1.16	0.248
	Literacy$_{t-2}$	−0.0001**	−0.0169	0.0000	−3.06	0.002
	Agricultural income$_{t-2}$	−0.0001	−0.0140	0.0001	−1.96	0.051
	Polyarchy$_{t-2}$	0.0015*	0.0207	0.0006	2.53	0.012
	CSO participatory environment$_{t-2}$	0.0003	0.0020	0.0008	0.34	0.730
	Anti-system movement$_{t-2}$	−0.0002	−0.0015	0.0009	−0.24	0.807
	Left-wing movement$_{t-2}$	0.0037	0.0051	0.0043	0.86	0.390
	Right-wing movement$_{t-2}$	0.9187***	0.9165	0.0067	137.28	0.000
	National economic growth$_{t-2}$	−0.0050	−0.0029	0.0068	−0.73	0.464
	intercept	0.0007*	0.0048	0.0003	2.21	0.027
Error variances						
	Upturn	0.0011	0.8750	0.0001		
	Agricultural income	13.0412	0.0584	2.0063		
	GDP per capita	0.0061	0.0163	0.0006		
	Literacy	1.1802	0.0035	0.1728		
	CSO participatory environment	0.0801	0.0757	0.0075		
	Anti-system movement	0.1201	0.1283	0.0098		
	Left-wing movement	0.0042	0.1142	0.0004		
	Right-wing movement	0.0030	0.1535	0.0004		

* $p \leq 0.05$, ** $p \leq 0.01$, *** $p < 0.001$

Bibliography

Acemoglu, D., S. Johnson, & J. A. Robinson. 2001. The Colonial Origins of Comparative Development: An Empirical Investigation. *American Economic Review*, 91(5): 1369–1401.

Acemoglu, D., S. Johnson, & J. A. Robinson. 2002. Reversal of Fortune: Geography and Institutions in the Making of the Modern World Income Distribution. *Quarterly Journal of Economics*, 117(4): 1231–1294.

Acemoglu, D., S. Johnson, J. A. Robinson, & P. Yared. 2008. Income and Democracy. *American Economic Review*, 98(3): 808–842.

Acemoglu, D., S. Johnson, J. A. Robinson, & P. Yared. 2009. Reevaluating the Modernization Hypothesis. *Journal of Monetary Economics*, 56(8): 1043–1058.

Acemoglu, D., S. Naidu, P. Restrepo, & J. A. Robinson. 2019. Democracy Does Cause Growth. *Journal of Political Economy*, 127(1): 47–100.

Acemoglu, D. & J. A. Robinson. 2000. Why Did the West Extend the Franchise? Democracy, Inequality, and Growth in Historical Perspective. *Quarterly Journal of Economics*, 115(4): 1167–1199.

Acemoglu, D. & J. A. Robinson. 2006. *Economic Origins of Dictatorship and Democracy*. New York: Cambridge University Press.

Acemoglu, D. & J. A. Robinson. 2019. *The Narrow Corridor: States, Societies, and the Fate of Liberty*. New York: Penguin Press.

Achen, C. 2000. Why Lagged Dependent Variables Can Suppress the Explanatory Power of Other Independent Variables. Paper presented at the Annual Meeting of the Midwest Political Science Association, Chicago.

Ahmed, A. 2014. *Democracy and the Politics of Electoral System Choice*. Cambridge: Cambridge University Press.

Ahmed, A. T. & D. Stasavage. 2020. *Origins of Early Democracy. American Political Science Review*, 114(2): 502–518.

Ahmed, F. Z. 2018. *The Political Legacy of Islamic Conquest*. Unpublished manuscript, Department of Politics, Princeton University.

Aidt, T. S. & P. S. Jensen. 2014. Workers of the World, Unite! Franchise Extensions and the Threat of Revolution in Europe, 1820–1938. *European Economic Review*, 72(November): 52–75.

Aidt, T. S. & G. Leon. 2016. The Democratic Window of Opportunity: Evidence from Riots in Sub-Saharan Africa. *Journal of Conflict Resolution*, 60(4): 694–717.

Albertus, M. 2017. Landowners and Democracy: The Social Origins of Democracy Reconsidered. *World Politics*, 69(2): 233–276.

Alemán, J. & D. D. Yang. 2011. A Duration Analysis of Democratic Transitions and Authoritarian Backslides. *Comparative Political Studies*, 44(9): 1123–1151.

Alemán, E. and Y. Kim. 2015. The democratizing effect of education. *Research & Politics* 2(4): 1-7.

Alesina, A., R. Baqir, & W. Easterly. 1999. Public Goods and Ethnic Divisions. *Quarterly Journal of Economics*, 114(4): 1243–1284.

Alesina, A., A. Devleeschauwer, W. Easterly, S. Kurlat, & R. Wacziarg. 2003. Fractionalization. *Journal of Economic Growth*, 8(2): 155–194.

Alesina, A. & E. LaFerrara. 2005. Ethnic Diversity and Economic Performance. *Journal of Economic Literature*, 63(3): 762–800.

Alexander, M., M. Harding, & C. Lamarche. 2011. Quantile Regression for Time-Series-Cross-Section Data. *International Journal of Statistics and Management System*, 6(1–2): 47–72.

Almond, G. A. & S. Verba. 1963. *The Civic Culture: Political Attitudes and Democracy in Five Nations*. Princeton: Princeton University Press.

Altman, D., F. Rojas-de-Galarreta, & F. Urdinez. 2021. An Interactive Model of Democratic Peace. *Journal of Peace Research*, 58(3): 384–398.

Alvarez, M. 1998. *Presidentialism and Parliamentarism: Which Works? Which Lasts?* Ph.D. Dissertation, Department of Political Science, University of Chicago.

Anckar, C. 2008. Size, Islandness, and Democracy: A Global Comparison. *International Political Science Review*, 29(4): 440–441.

Anckar, C. 2011. *Religion and Democracy: A Worldwide Comparison*. London: Routledge.

Anckar, D. 1999. Homogeneity and Smallness: Dahl and Tufte Revisited. *Scandinavian Political Studies*, 22(1): 29–44.

Anckar, D. 2002. Why Are Small Island States Democracies? *The Round Table*, 91(365): 375–390.

Anckar, D. 2004. Direct Democracy in Microstates and Small Island States. *World Development*, 32(2): 379–390.

Anckar, D. & C. Anckar. 1995. Size, Insularity and Democracy. *Scandinavian Political Studies*, 18(4): 211–229.

Anckar, D. & C. Anckar. 2000. Democracies without Parties. *Comparative Political Studies*, 33(2): 225–247.

Andersen, D., J. Møller, L. L. Rørbæk, & S. E. Skaaning. 2014a. State Capacity and Political Regime Stability. *Democratization*, 21(7): 1305–1325.

Andersen, D., J. Møller, & S. E. Skaaning. 2014b. The State-Democracy Nexus: Conceptual Distinctions, Theoretical Perspectives, and Comparative Approaches. *Democratization*, 21(7): 1203–1220.

Anderson, J. 2004. Does God Matter, and If So Whose God? Religion and Democratization. *Democratization*, 11(4): 192–217.

Anderson, J. 2007. The Catholic Contribution to Democratization's "Third Wave": Altruism, Hegemony or Self-Interest? *Cambridge Review of International Affairs*, 20 (3): 383–399.

Anderson, J. (ed.). 2006. *Religion, Democracy and Democratization*. London: Routledge.

Andersen, J. J. & S. Aslaksen. 2013. Oil and Political Survival. *Journal of Development Economics*, 100(1): 89–106.

Andersen, J. J. & M. L. Ross. 2014. The Big Oil Change: A Closer Look at the Haber–Menaldo Analysis. *Comparative Political Studies*, 47(7): 993–1021.

Ang, J. B., P. G. Fredriksson, & S. K. Gupta. 2020. Crop Yield and Democracy. *Land Economics*, 96(2): 265–290.

Angrist, J. & J. S. Pischke. 2014. *Mastering 'Metrics: The Path from Cause to Effect*. Princeton: Princeton University Press.

Ansell, B. & D. Samuels. 2010. Inequality and Democratization: A Contractarian Approach. *Comparative Political Studies*, 43(12): 1543–1574.

Ansell, B. & D. Samuels. 2014. *Inequality and Democratization: An Elite-Competition Approach*. New York: Cambridge University Press.

Arato, A. 1993 [1981]. *Civil Society and the State, Poland 1980–81, From Neo-Marxism to Democratic Theory*. Armonk: M. E. Sharpe, pp. 171–211.

Aristotle. 1932. *The Politics*, trans H. Rackham. Cambridge, MA: Harvard University Press.

Aronow, P. M. & C. Samii. 2013. Estimating Average Causal Effects under Interference between Units. *The Annals of Applied Statistics*, 11(4): 1912–1947.

Arriol, L. R. 2013. *Multi-Ethnic Coalitions in Africa: Business Financing of Opposition Election Campaigns*. Cambridge: Cambridge University Press.

Aslaksen, S. 2010. Oil and Democracy – More Than a Cross-Country Correlation? *Journal of Peace Research*, 47(4): 421–431.

Bäck, H. & A. Hadenius. 2008. Democracy and State Capacity: Exploring a J-Shaped Relationship. *Governance*, 21(1): 1–24.

Bairoch, P. 1976. Europe's Gross National Product, 1800–1975. *Journal of European Economic History*, 5(2): 273–340.

Baldacchino, G. 2012. Islands and Despots. *Commonwealth and Comparative Politics*, 50(1): 103–120.

Banaszak, L. A. 1996. *Why Movements Succeed or Fail: Opportunity, Culture, and the Struggle for Woman Suffrage*. Cambridge: Cambridge University Press.

Banks, A. S. 1971. *Cross-Polity Time-series Data*. Cambridge: MIT Press.

Banks, A. S. & Kenneth A. Wilson. 2018. Cross-National Time-Series Data Archive. Databanks International. www.cntsdata.com/.

Barbour, S. & C. Carmichael. 2000. *Language and Nationalism in Europe*. New York: Oxford University Press.

Barro, R. 1998. *Determinants of Economic Growth*. Cambridge: MIT Press.

Barro, R. J. 1992. Economic Growth in a Cross Section of Countries. *The Quarterly Journal of Economics*, 106(2): 407–443.

Barro, R. J. 1999. Determinants of Democracy. *Journal of Political Economy*, 107 (6): 158–183.

Barro, R. J. & Xavier Sala-i-Martin. 2004. *Economic Growth*. Cambridge: MIT Press.

Bartolini, S. 2000. *The Political Mobilization of the European Left, 1860-1980*. Cambridge: Cambridge University Press.

Bartusevicius, H. & S. E. Skaaning. 2018. Revisiting Democratic Civil Peace: Electoral Regimes and Civil Conflict. *Journal of Peace Research*, 55(5): 625–640.

Bates, R. 1981. *States and Markets in Tropical Africa: The Political Basis of Agricultural Policy*. Berkeley: University of California Press, series on social choice and political economy.

Bates, R. H. 1983. Modernization, Ethnic Competition and the Rationality of Politics. In D. Rothchild & V. A. Olorunsola, eds., *State versus Ethnic Claims: African Policy Dilemmas*. London: Routledge, pp. 223–250.

Bättig, M. & T. Bernauer 2009. National Institutions and Global Public Goods: Are Democracies More Cooperative in Climate Change Policy? *International Organization*, 63(2): 281–308.

Baum, M. A. & D. A Lake. 2003. The Political Economy of Growth: Democracy and Human Capital. *American Journal of Political Science*, 47(2): 333–347.

Baumgartner, F. R., C. Breunig, C. Green-Pedersen, B. D. Jones, P. B. Mortensen, M. Nuytemans & S. Walgrave. 2009. Punctuated Equilibrium in Comparative Perspective. *American Journal of Political Science*, 53(3): 603–620.

Bayer, M., F. S. Bethke & D. Lambach. 2016. The Democratic Dividend of Nonviolent Resistance. *Journal of Peace Research*, 53(6): 758–761.

Beaulieu, E. 2014. *Electoral Protest and Democracy in the Developing World*. New York: Cambridge University Press.

Beissinger, M. R. 2007. Structure and Example in Modular Political Phenomena: The Diffusion of Bulldozer/Rose/Orange/Tulip Revolutions. *Perspectives on Politics*, 59(2): 259–276.

Bellin, E. 2004. The Robustness of Authoritarianism in the Middle East: Exceptionalism in Comparative Perspective. *Comparative Politics*, 36(2): 139–157.

Benhabib, J. & M. Spiegel. 1994. The Role of Human Capital in Economic Development: Evidence from Aggregate Cross-Country Data. *Journal of Monetary Economics*, 34(2): 143–173.

Benhabib, J., A. Corvalan & M. M. Spiegel. 2011. Reestablishing the Income-Democracy Nexus. Federal Reserve Bank of San Francisco, Working Paper 2011–09.

Bentzen, J. S., N. Kaarsen & A. M. Wingender. 2016. Irrigation and Autocracy. *Journal of the European Economic Association*, 15(1): 1–53.

Berg-Schlosser, D. 2009. Long Waves and Conjunctures of Democratization. In C. W. Haerpfer, P. Bernhagen, R. F. Inglehart & C. Welzel, eds., *Democratization*. Oxford: Oxford University Press, pp.41–54.

Berlin, I. (2002[1958]). Two Concepts of Liberty. In I. Berlin, ed., *Liberty*. Oxford: Oxford University Press, pp. 166–217.

Berman, S. 1997. Civil Society and the Collapse of the Weimar Republic. *World Politics*, 49(3): 401–429.

Bernhard, M. 2016. The Moore Thesis: What's Left after 1989? *Democratization*, 23(1): 118–140.

Bernhard, M. & D. J. Jung. 2017. The Wages of Extrication: Civil Society and Inequality in Postcommunist Eurasia, *Comparative Politics*, 49(3): 373–390.

Bernhard, M. & E. Karakoç. 2007. Civil Society and the Legacies of Dictatorship. *World Politics*, 59(4): 539–567.

Bernhard, M., A. Hicken, C. Reenock. & S. I. Lindberg. 2020. Parties, Civil Society, and the Deterrence of Democratic Defection. *Studies in Comparative International Development*, 55(1): 1–26.

Bernhard, M., T. Nordstrom. & C. Reenock. 2001. Economic Performance, Institutional Intermediation, and Democratic Survival. *Journal of Politics*, 63(3): 775–803.

Bernhard, M., C. Reenock & T. Nordstrom. 2003. Economic Performance And Survival In New Democracies: Is There a Honeymoon Effect? *Comparative Political Studies*, 36(4): 404–431.

Bernhard, M., C. Reenock & T. Nordstrom. 2004. The Legacy of Western Overseas Colonialism on Democratic Survival. *International Studies Quarterly*, 48(1): 225–250.

Bethke, F. S. & J. Pinckney. 2021 Nonviolent Resistance and the Quality of Democracy, *Conflict Management and Peace Science*, 38(5): 503–523.

Benavot, A. 1996. Education and Political Democratization: Cross-National and Longitudinal Findings. Comparative Education Review 40(4): 377–403.

Beyer, P. (ed.). 2001. *Religion in the Process of Globalization*. Würzburg: Ergon Verlag.

Bisbee, J., R. Dehejia, C. Pop-Eleches & C. Samii. 2017. Local Instruments, Global Extrapolation: External Validity of the Labor Supply–Fertility Local Average Treatment Effect. *Journal of Labor Economics*, 35(1): S99–147.

Bizzarro, F., J. Gerring, C. H. Knutsen, A. Hicken, M. Bernhard, S. E. Skaaning, M. Coppedge & S. I. Lindberg. 2018. Party Strength and Economic Growth. *World Politics*, 70(2): 275–320.

Bizzarro, F., A. Hicken & D. Self. 2017. The V-Dem Party Institutionalization Index: A New Global Indicator (1900–2015). V-Dem Working Paper Paper Series 2017–48. The Varieties of Democracy Institute.

Blaug, M. 1966. Literacy and Economic Development. *The School Review*, 74(4): 393–418.

Blaydes, L. 2017. State Building in the Middle East. *Annual Review of Political Science*, 20: 487–504.

Blaydes, L. & E. Chaney. 2013. The Feudal Revolution and Europe's Rise: Political Divergence of the Christian West and the Muslim World before 1500 CE. *American Political Science Review*, 107(1): 16–34.

Bobba, M. & Coviello, D. 2007. Weak Instruments and Weak Identification, In Estimating the Effects of Education, on Democracy. *Economics Letters*, 96(3): 301–306.

Boese, Vanessa A. 2019 How (not) to Measure Democracy. *International Areas Studies Review*, 22(2): 95–127.

Boix, C. 2003. *Democracy and Redistribution*. Cambridge: Cambridge University Press.

Boix, C. 2011. Democracy, Development, and the International System. *American Political Science Review*, 105(4): 809–828.

Boix, C., M. K. Miller & S. Rosato. 2013. A Complete Data Set of Political Regimes, 1800–2007. *Comparative Political Studies*, 46(12): 1523–1554.

Boix, C. & S. C. Stokes. 2003. Endogenous Democratization. *World Politics*, 55(4): 517–549.

Boix, Carles & M. W. Svolik. 2013. The Foundations of Limited Authoritarian Government: Institutions, Commitment, and Power-Sharing in Dictatorships. *The Journal of Politics*, 75(2): 300–316.

Bollen, K. A. & R. W. Jackman. 1985. Political Democracy and the Size Distribution of Income. *American Sociological Review*, 50(4): 438–457.

Bollen, K. A. & R. W. Jackman. 1995. Income Inequality and Democratization Revisited: Comment on Muller. *American Sociological Review*, 60(6): 983–989.

Bollyky, T. J., T. Templin, M. Cohen, D. Schoder, J. L. Dieleman & S. Wigley. 2019. The Relationships between Democratic Experience, Adult Health, and Cause-Specific Mortality in 170 Countries Between 1980 and 2016: An Observational Analysis. *The Lancet*, 393(10181): 1628–1640.

Bolt, J., R. Inklaar, H. de Jong & J. L. van Zanden. 2018. Rebasing "Maddison": New Income Comparisons and the Shape of Long-run Economic Development. Maddison Project Working paper 10.

Bolt, J. & J. L. van Zanden. 2014. The Maddison Project: Collaborative Research on Historical National Accounts. *The Economic History Review*, 67(3): 627–651.

Borcan, O., O. Olsson & L. Putterman. 2018. State History and Economic Development: Evidence from Six Millennia. *Journal of Economic Growth*, 23(1): 1–40.

Brambor, T., A. Goenaga, J. Lindvall & J. Teorell. 2020. The Lay of the Land: Information Capacity and the Modern State. *Comparative Political Studies*, 53(2): 175–213.

Brancati, D. 2016. *Democracy Protests: Origins, Features and Significance*. New York: Cambridge University Press.

Bratton, M. & E. Chang. 2006. State-Building and Democratization in Africa: Forwards, Backwards or Together? *Comparative Political Studies*, 39(9): 1059–1083.

Bratton, M. & N. van de Walle. 1997. *Democratic Experiments in Africa: Regime Transitions in Comparative Perspective*. Cambridge: Cambridge University Press.

Braudel, F. 1972 [1949]. *The Mediterranean and the Mediterranean World in the Age of Philip II*, vols. 1–2. New York: Harper & Row.

Brecke, P. 2001. The Long-Term Patterns of Violent Conflict in Different Regions of the World, in Uppsala Conflict Data Conference, Uppsala.

Brinks, D. & M. Coppedge. 2006. Diffusion Is No Illusion. *Comparative Political Studies*, 39(4): 463–89.

Broadberry, S. 2013. *Accounting for the Great Divergence*. Online. www.nuffield.ox.ac.uk/users/Broadberry/AccountingGreatDivergence6.pdf, accessed November 23, 2016.

Broadberry, S. & A. Klein. 2012. Aggregate and per capita GDP in Europe, 1870–2000: Continental, Regional and National Data with Changing Boundaries. *Scandinavian Economic History Review*, 60(1): 79–107.

Brown, G. G. 1944. Missions and Cultural Diffusion. *American Journal of Sociology*, 50(3): 214–219.

Brownlee, J. 2007. *Authoritarianism in an Age of Democratization*. New York: Cambridge University Press.

Bruce, S. 2004. Did Protestantism Create Democracy? *Democratization*, 11(4): 3–20.

Brumberg, D., L. J. Diamond & M. F. Plattner (eds.). 2003. *Islam and democracy in the Middle East*. Baltimore: Johns Hopkins University Press.

Bueno de Mesquita, B. & A. Smith. 2009. Political Survival and Endogenous Institutional Change. *Comparative Political Studies*, 42(2):167–197.

Buhaug, H. & S. Gates. 2002. The Geography of Civil War. *Journal of Peace Research*, 39 (4) 417–433.

Bunce, V. J. & S. L. Wolchik. 2011. *Defeating Authoritarian Leaders in Postcommunist Countries*. New York: Cambridge University Press.

Burke, E. 1972. Pan-Islam and Moroccan Resistance to French Colonial Penetration, 1900–1912. *The Journal of African History*, 13(1): 97–118.

Burkhart, R. E. 2007. Democracy, Capitalism, and Income Inequality: Seeking Causal Directions. *Comparative Sociology*, 6(4): 481–507.

Burkhart, R. E. 1997. Comparative Democracy and Income Distribution: Shape and Direction of the Causal Arrow. *Journal of Politics*, 59(1): 148–164.

Burkhart, R. E. & M. S. Lewis-Beck. 1994. Comparative Democracy: The Economic Development Thesis. *American Political Science Review*, 88(4): 903–910.

Buruma, I. 2010. *Taming the Gods: Religion and Democracy on Three Continents*. Princeton: Princeton University Press.

Caldwell, J. C., G. E. Harrison & P. Quiggin. 1980. The Demography of Micro-States. *World Development*, 8(12): 953–962.

Campante, F. R. & D. Chor. 2012. Why Was the Arab World Poised for Revolution? Schooling, Economic Opportunities, and the Arab Spring. *Journal of Economic Perspectives*, 26(2): 167–188.

Campante, F. R. & D. Chor. 2014. The People Want the Fall of the Regime: Schooling, Political Protest, and the Economy. *Journal of Comparative Economics*, 42(3): 495–517.

Campbell, A., P. E. Converse, W. E. Miller & D. E. Stokes. 1980. *The American Voter*. Chicago: University of Chicago Press.

Capoccia, G. & D. Ziblatt. 2010. The Historical Turn in Democratization Studies: A New Research Agenda for Europe and Beyond. *Comparative Political Studies*, 43 (8–9): 931–968.

Carbone, G. & V. Memoli. 2015. Does Democratization Foster State Consolidation? *Governance*, 28(1): 5–24.

Cardoso, F. H. & E. Faletto. 1979. *Dependency and Development in Latin America*. *Trans. By Marjory Mattingly Urquidi*. Berkeley: University of California Press.

Carneiro, R. L. 1970. A Theory of the Origin of the State. *Science*, 169(3947): 733–738.

Carneiro, R. L. 1988. The Circumscription Theory: Challenge and Response. *American Behavioral Scientist*, 31(4): 497–511.

Carneiro, R. L. 2012. The Circumscription Theory: A Clarification, Amplification, and Reformulation. *Social Evolution and History*, 11(2): 5–30.

Carothers, T. 2002. The End of the Transition Paradigm. *Journal of Democracy*, 13(1): 5–21.

Carothers, T. & R. Youngs. 2017. Democracy Is Not Dying: Seeing Through the Doom and Gloom. *Foreign Affairs*, 11 April 2017.

Cartledge, P. 2016. *Democracy: A life*. Oxford: Oxford University Press.

Casper, G. & C. Tufis. 2003. Correlation versus Interchangeability: The Limited Robustness of Empirical Findings on Democracy using Highly Correlated Data Sets. *Political Analysis*, 11(2): 196–203.

Castelló-Climent, A. 2008. On the Distribution of Education and Democracy. *Journal of Development Economics*, 87(2): 179–190.

Celestino, M. R. & K. S. Gleditsch. 2013. Fresh Carnations or All Thorn, No Rose? Nonviolent Campaigns and Transitions in Autocracies. *Journal of Peace Research*, 50 (3): 385–400.

Cervellati, M., P. Fortunato & U. Sunde. 2006. Growth and endogenous political institutions. In T. S. Eicher & C. Garcia-Peñalosa, eds., *Institutions, Development and Economic Growth*. Cambridge: MIT Press.

Chaisty, P., N. Cheeseman & T. Power. 2014. Rethinking the "Presidentialism Debate": Conceptualizing Coalitional Politics in Cross-regional Perspective. *Democratization*, 21(1): 72–94.

Chambers, S. & J. Kopstein. 2001. Bad Civil Society. *Political Theory*, 29(6): 837–865.

Chaney, E. 2012. Democratic Change in the Arab World, Past and Present. *Brookings Papers on Economic Activity*, Spring: 363–414.

Che, Y., Y. Lub, Z. Tao & P. Wang. 2013. The Impact of Income on Democracy Revisited. *Journal of Comparative Economics*, 41(1): 159–169.

Cheibub, J. A. 2007. *Presidentialism, Parliamentarism, and Democracy*. Cambridge: Cambridge University Press.

Cheibub, J. A., J. Gandhi & J. Vreeland. 2010. Democracy and Dictatorship Revisited. *Public Choice*, 143(1): 67–101.

Cheibub, J. A. & F. Limongi. 2002. Democratic Institutions and Regime Survival: Parliamentary and Presidential Democracies Reconsidered. *Annual Review of Political Science*, 5(1): 151–79.

Chenoweth, E. 2011. Non-violent and Violent Campaigns and Outcomes Dataset v.1.1. University of Denver. Available at: www.du.edu/korbel/sie/research/chenow_navco_data.html.

Chenoweth, E. & M. J. Stephan. 2011. *Why Civil Resistance Works: The Strategic Logic of Non-violent Conflict*. New York: Columbia University Press.

Chu, L. T. 2011. Unfinished Business: The Catholic Church, Communism, and Democratization. *Democratization*, 18(3): 631–654.

Ciccone, A. 2011. Economic Shocks and Civil Conflict: A Comment. *American Economic Journal: Applied Economics*, 3(4): 215–227.

Claassen, C. 2020. In the Mood for Democracy? Democratic Support as Thermostatic Opinion. *American Political Science Review*, 114(1): 36–53.

Clague, C., S. Gleason & S. Knack. 2001. Determinants of Lasting Democracy in Poor Countries: Culture, Development, and Institutions. *The Annals of the American Academy of Political and Social Science*, 773: 16–41.

Clark, W. R., M. Golder & S. N. Golder. 2017. *Principles of Comparative Politics*. 3rd ed. London: Sage.

Colagrossi, M., D. Rossignoli & M. A. Maggioni. 2020. Does Democracy Cause Growth? A Meta-analysis (of 2000 regressions). *European Journal of Political Economy* 61.

Collier, R. B. 1999. *Paths Towards Democracy: The Working Class and Elites in Western Europe and South America*. Cambridge: Cambridge University Press.

Collier, R. B. & D. Collier. 1991. *Shaping the Political Arena: Critical Junctures, the Labor Movement, and Regime Dynamics in Latin America*. Princeton: Princeton University Press.

Collier, P. & A. Hoeffler. 2004. Greed and Grievance in Civil War. *Oxford Economic Papers*, 56(4): 563–595.

Colomer, J. M. 2007. *Great Empires, Small Nations: The Uncertain Future of the Sovereign State*. London: Routledge.

Congdon Fors, H. 2014. Do Island States Have Better Institutions? *Journal of Comparative Economics*, 42(1): 34–60.

Congleton, R. D. 2011. *Perfecting Parliament: Constitutional Reform, Liberalism, and the Rise of Western Democracy*. New York: Cambridge University Press.

Cook, S. J., J. C. Hays & R. J. Franzese. 2020. "Model Selection and Spatial Interdependence." Chapter 39. In L. Curini. & R. J. Franzese, eds., *The SAGE Handbook for Research Methods in Political Science & International Relations*. Los Angeles: SAGE.

Coppedge, M. 1994. *Strong Parties and Lame Ducks: Presidential Partyarchy and Factionalism in Venezuela*. Stanford: Stanford University Press.

Coppedge, M. 2012. *Democratization and Research Methods*. New York: Cambridge University Press.

Coppedge, M., A. Alvarez & C. Maldonado. 2008. Two Persistent Dimensions of Democracy: Contestation and Inclusiveness. *Journal of Politics*, 70(3): 335–350.

Coppedge, M. & J. Gerring, D. Altman, M. Bernhard, S. Fish, A. Hicken, M. Kroenig, S. I. Lindberg, K. McMann, P. Paxton, H. A. Semetko, S. E. Skaaning, J. Staton & Jan Teorell. 2011. Conceptualizing and Measuring Democracy: A New Approach. *Perspectives on Politics*, 9(2): 247–267.

Coppedge, M., J. Gerring, A. Glynn, C. H. Knutsen, S. I. Lindberg, D. Pemstein, B. Seim, S. E. Skaaning & J. Teorell. 2020. *Varieties of Democracy: Measuring Two Centuries of Political Change*. Cambridge: Cambridge University Press.

Coppedge, M., J. Gerring, S. I. Lindberg, S. E. Skaaning & J. Teorell. 2017. "Comparisons and Contrasts." University of Gothenburg, Varieties of Democracy Institute: Working Paper No. 45.

Coppedge M., B. Denison, L. Tiscornia and S. I. Lindberg, "Varieties of Democratic Diffusion: Neighbors, Trade, and Alliance Networks," Varieties of Democracy Institute Working Paper No. 2 (revised), June 2016.

Coppedge, M., J. Gerring, S. I. Lindberg, S. E. Skaaning, J. Teorell & V. Ciobanu. 2014. V-Dem Country Coding Units v3. Varieties of Democracy (V-Dem) Project.

Coppedge, M., J. Gerring, C. H. Knutsen, S. I. Lindberg, J. Teorell, D. Altman, M. Bernhard, M. S. Fish, A. Glynn, A. Hicken, A. Lührmann, K.L. Marquardt, K. McMann, P. Paxton, D. Pemstein, B. Seim, R. Sigman, S. E. Skaaning, J. Staton, S. Wilson, A. Cornell, L. Gastaldi, H. Gjerløw, N. Ilchenko, J. Krusell, L. Maxwell, V. Mechkova, J. Medzihorsky, J. Pernes, J. von Römer, N. Stepanova, A. Sundström, E. Tzelgov, Y. Wang, T. Wig & D. Ziblatt 2019a. V-Dem Country-Year Dataset v9, Varieties of Democracy (V-Dem) Project.

Coppedge, M., J. Gerring, C. H. Knutsen, S. I. Lindberg, J. Teorell, D. Altman, M. Bernhard, M. S. Fish, A. Glynn, A. Hicken, A. Lührmann, K. L. Marquardt, K. McMann, P. Paxton, D. Pemstein, B. Seim, R. Sigman, S. E. Skaaning, J. Staton, A. Cornell, L. Gastaldi, H. Gjerløw, V. Mechkova, J. von Römer, A. Sundström, E. Tzelgov, L. Uberti, Y. Wang, T. Wig & D. Ziblatt. 2019b. V-Dem Codebook v9, Varieties of Democracy (V-Dem) Project.

Coppedge, M., J. Gerring, C. H. Knutsen, S. I. Lindberg, J. Teorell, V. Ciobanu & L. Gastaldi. 2019c. V-Dem Country Coding Units v9. Varieties of Democracy (V-Dem) Project.

Coppedge, M., J. Gerring, C. H. Knutsen, S. I. Lindberg, J. Teorell, K. L. Marquardt, J. Medzihorsky, D. Pemstein, J. Pernes, J. von Römer, N. Stepanova, E. Tzelgov, Y. Wang & S. Wilson. 2019d. V-Dem Methodology v9 Varieties of Democracy (V-Dem) Project.

Coppedge, M., J. Gerring, C. H. Knutsen, J. Krusell, K. Marquardt, J. Medzihorsky, J. Pernes, N. Stepanova, S. E. Skaaning, J. Teorell, D. Pemstein, E. Tzelgov, Y.Wang,

S. Wilson & S. Lindberg. 2019e. The Methodology of Varieties of Democracy (V-Dem). *Bulletin of Sociological Methodology*, 143(1): 107–133.

Coppedge, M. & D. Kuehn. 2019. Introduction: Absorbing the Four Methodological Disruptions in Democratization Research? *Democratization*, 26(1): 1–20.

Cornell, A. & V. Lapuente. 2014. Meritocratic Administration and Democratic Stability. *Democratization*, 21(7): 1286–304.

Cornell, A., J. Møller & S. E. Skaaning. 2020. *Democratic Stability in an Age of Crisis Reassessing the Interwar Period*. Oxford: Oxford University Press.

Cornell, A., J. Møller, S. E. Skaaning & S. I. Lindberg. 2016. Civil Society, Party Institutionalization, and Democratic Breakdown in the Interwar Period. V-Dem Working Paper 2016:24. Available at https://ssrn.com/abstract=2727717 or http://dx .doi.org/10.2139/ssrn.2727717

Correlates of War Project 2017, State System Membership List, v2016. Available at: http://correlatesofwar.org

Corrin, J. P. 2010. *Catholic Intellectuals and the Challenge of Democracy*. Notre Dame: University of Notre Dame Press.

Cranmer, S. J., Bruce A. Desmarais, & Jason W. Morgan. 2021. *Inferential Network Analysis*. New York: Cambridge University Press.

Cribari-Neto, F. 2004. Asymptotic Inference under Heteroskedasticity of Unknown Form. *Computational Statistics & Data Analysis*, 45(2): 215–233.

Crone, P. 1980. *Slaves on Horses: The Evolution of the Islamic Polity*. Cambridge: Cambridge University Press.

Cuaresma, J. C., H. Oberhofer & P. A. Raschky. 2011. Oil and the duration of dictatorships. *Public Choice*, 148 (3–4): 505–530.

Curtin, P. D. 1989. *Death by Migration: Europe's Encounter with the Tropical World in the Nineteenth Century*. Cambridge: Cambridge University Press.

Curtin, P. D. 1998. *Disease and Empire: The Health of European Troops in the Conquest of Africa*. Cambridge: Cambridge University Press.

Dahl, R. A. 1971. *Polyarchy: Participation and Opposition*. New Haven: Yale University Press.

Dahl, R. A. 1989. *Democracy and Its Critics*. New Haven: Yale University Press.

Dahl, R. A. 1998. *On Democracy*. New Haven: Yale University Press.

Dahlum, S. 2017. *Schooling for dissent? Education, autocratic regime instability and transitions to democracy*. Oslo: University of Oslo. PhD Thesis.

Dahlum, S. 2018. Modernization theory – What Do We Know After 60 Years? *The Annals of Comparative Democratization*, 16(3): 4–6.

Dahlum, S., C. H. Knutsen & T. Wig. 2019. Who Revolts Empirically Revisiting the Social Origins of Democracy. *Journal of Politics*, 81(4): 1494–1499.

Dalgaard, C. J., A. B. Knudsen & P. Selaya. 2020. The Bounty of the Sea and Long-run Development. *Journal of Economic Growth*, 25(3): 259–295.

Davenport, C. 2007. State Repression and Political Order. *Annual Review of Political Science*, 10: 1–23.

Davies, J. C. 1962. Towards a Theory of Revolution. *American Sociological Review*, 27(1): 5–19.

De Juan, A. & J. H. Pierskalla. 2017. The Comparative Politics of Colonialism and Its Legacies: An Introduction. *Politics and Society*, 45(2): 159–172.

De Swaan, A. 2001. *Words of the World: The Global Language System*. Polity.

de Tocqueville, A. 1838. *Democracy in America*. New York: G. Dearborn.

Della Porta, D. 2014. *Mobilizing for Democracy*. Oxford: Oxford University Press.

Denison, B. & M. Coppedge. 2017. *Varieties of Democratic Diffusion in Military Alliance Networks*. Unpublished manuscript. University of Notre Dame.

Diamond, L. 1992. Economic Development and Democracy Reconsidered. *American Behavioral Scientist*, 35(4): 450–499.

Diamond, J. 1992. *Guns, Germs, and Steel: The Fates of Human Societies*. New York: Norton.

Diamond, L. 1999. *Developing Democracy: Toward Consolidation*. Baltimore: John Hopkins University Press.

Diamond, L. 2002. Thinking about Hybrid Regimes. *Journal of Democracy*, 13(2): 21–35.

Diamond, L. 2010. Why are There no Arab Democracies? *Journal of Democracy*, 21(1): 93–112.

Diamond, L. 2016. Democracy in Decline. *Foreign Affairs*, 13 June 2016.

Diamond, L. & L. Morlino. 2004. The Quality of Democracy: An Overview. *Journal of Democracy*, 15(4): 20–31.

Diamond, L. & M. Plattner, eds. 1994. *Nationalism, Ethnic Conflict, and Democracy*. Baltimore: Johns Hopkins University Press.

Diamond, L. & M. Plattner, eds. 2015. *Democracy in Decline?* Baltimore: Johns Hopkins University Press.

Diamond, L., M. F. Plattner & P. J. Costopoulos, (eds.). 2005. *World Religions and Democracy*. Baltimore: Johns Hopkins University Press.

Diamond, L. & S. Tsalik. 1999. Size and Democracy: The Case for Decentralization. In L. Diamond, eds., *Developing Democracy: Towards Consolidation*. Baltimore: Johns Hopkins University Press, pp. 117–160.

Djuve, V. L., C. H. Knutsen & T. Wig. 2020. Patterns of Regime Change Since the French Revolution. *Comparative Political Studies*, 53(6): 923–958.

Dommen, E. 1980. Some Distinguishing Characteristics of Island States. *World Development*, 8(12): 931–43.

Doorenspleet, R. 2000. Reassessing the Three Waves of Democratization. *World Politics*, 52(3): 384–406.

Dorsch, M. T. & P. Maarek. 2014. A Note on Economic Inequality and Democratization. *Peace Economics, Peace Science and Public Policy*, 20(4): 599–610.

Doumenge, F. 1985. The Viability of Small Intertropical Islands. In E. Dommen & P. Hein, eds., *States, Microstates, and Islands*. Dover: Croom Helm, pp. 70–118.

Drake, P. W. 2009. *Between Tyranny and Anarchy: A History of Democracy in Latin America, 1800-2006*. Stanford: Stanford University Press.

Dunning, T. 2012. *Natural Experiments in The Social Sciences: A Design-Based Approach*. New York: Cambridge University Press.

Dworkin, R. 1996. *Freedom's Law: The Moral Reading of the Constitution*. Cambridge: Harvard University Press.

Dyson, T. 2012. On Demographic and Democratic Transitions. *Population and Development Review*, 38 (Supplement): 83–102.

Easterly, W. & R. Levine. 1997. Africa's Growth Tragedy: Policies and Ethnic Divisions. *Quarterly Journal of Economics*, 112(4): 1203–1250.

Economist Intelligence Unit (EIU). 2017. Democracy Index 2016: Revenge of the "Deplorables," Available at: pages.eiu.com/rs/783-XMC-194/images/Democracy_Index_2016.pdf

Edgell, A. B., V. Mechkova, D. Altman, M. Bernhard & S. I. Lindberg. 2018. When and Where Do Elections Matter: A Global Test of the Democratization by Elections Hypothesis. *Democratization*, 24(3): 422–444.

Eisenstadt, S. N. (ed.). 1968. *The Protestant Ethic and Modernization: A Comparative View*. New York: Basic Books.

Ekiert, G. & J. Kubik. 1999. *Rebellious Civil Society*. Ann Arbor: University of Michigan Press.

El Badawi, I. & S. Makdisi. 2007. Explaining the Democracy Deficit in the Arab World. *The Quarterly Review of Economics and Finance*, 46(5): 813–831.

Eldredge, N. & S. J. Gould. 1972. Punctuated Equilibria: An Alternative to Phyletic Gradualism. In T. J. M. Schopf, ed., *Models in Paleobiology*. San Francisco: Freeman Cooper, pp. 82–115.

Elgie, R. (2005). From Linz to Tsebelis: Three Waves of Presidential/Parliamentary Studies? *Democratization*, 12(1): 106–122.

Elis, R., S. Haber & J. Horrillo. 2017. *Climate, Geography, and the Evolution of Economic and Political Systems*. Unpublished manuscript, Stanford University.

Elkins, Z. 2013. The Weight of History and the Rebuilding of Brazilian Democracy. *Lua Nova: Revista de Cultura e Política*, 88: 257–303.

Engerman, S. L. & K. L. Sokoloff. 2012. *Economic Development in the Americas since 1500: Endowments and Institutions*. Cambridge: Cambridge University Press.

Englebert, P. 2000. Solving the Mystery of the Africa Dummy. *World Development*, 28(10): 1821–1835.

Epstein, D. L., R. Bates, J. Goldstone I. Kristensen & S. O'Halloran. 2006. Democratic Transitions. *American Journal of Political Science*, 50(3): 551–569.

Epstein, D. L., B. Leventoglu & S. O'Halloran. 2012. Minorities and Democratization. *Economics and Politics*, 24(3): 259–278.

Esposito, J. L., & J. O. Voll. 1996. *Islam and Democracy*. Oxford: Oxford University Press.

Faria, H., H. Montesinos-Yufa & D. Morales. 2014. Should the Modernization Hypothesis Survive Acemoglu, Johnson, Robinson, and Yared? Some More Evidence. *Econ Journal Watch*, 11(1): 17–36.

Fariss, C. J., C. D. Crabtree, T. Anders, Z. M. Jones, F. J. Linder, & J. N. Markowitz. 2017. *Latent Estimation of GDP, GDP per capita, and Population from Historic and Contemporary Sources*. Unpublished manuscript, Department of Political Science, University of Michigan.

Fayad, G., R. H. Bates. & A. Hoeffler. 2012. Income and Democracy: Lipset's Law Inverted. OxCarre Research Paper 61.

Fernandes, T. & R. Branco. 2017. Long-Term Effects: Social Revolution and Civil Society in Portugal, 1974–2010. *Comparative Politics*, 49(3): 411–431.

Fernando B., J. Gerring, C. H. Knutsen, A. Hicken, M. Bernhard., S. E. Skaaning, M. Coppedge. & S. I. Lindberg. 2018. Party Strength and Economic Growth. *World Politics*, 70(2): 275–320.

Fieldhouse, D. K. 1966. *The Colonial Empires: A Comparative Study from the Eighteenth Century*. London: Macmillan.

Findley, M. G., K. Kikuta & M. Denly. 2021. External Validity. *Annual Review of Political Science*, 24: 365–393.

Finkel, S. E., A. Pérez-Liñan & M. A. Seligson. 2007. The Effects of U.S. Foreign Assistance on Democracy Building, 1990–2003. *World Politics*, 59(3): 404–439.

Fish, M. S. 2002. Islam and Authoritarianism. *World politics*, 55(1): 4–37.

Fish, S. 2006. Stronger Legislatures, Stronger Democracies. *Journal of Democracy*, 17(1): 5–20.

Fishman, R. 2017. How Civil Society Matters in Democratization: Setting the Boundaries of Post-Transition Political Inclusion. *Comparative Politics*, 49(3): 391–409.

Fjelde, H., C. H. Knutsen. & H. M. Nygård. 2021. Which Institutions Matter? Re-Considering the Democratic Civil Peace. *International Studies Quarterly*, 65(1): 223–237.

Fortin, J. 2012. Is There a Necessary Condition for Democracy? The Role of State Capacity in Postcommunist Countries. *Comparative Political Studies*, 45(7): 903–930.

Fox, J. 2008. *A World Survey of Religion and the State*. New York: Cambridge University Press.

Franzese, R. J., Jr. 2018. Sessions 3–6: Estimating, Evaluating, Interpreting, and Presenting Models of Spatial and Spatiotemporal Interdependence. Lecture slides for Spatial-Econometric Analysis of Interdependence, ICPSR Summer Program, Ann Arbor, MI (July, 9–13).

Franzese, R. J., Jr. & J. C. Hays. 2008a. Interdependence in Comparative Politics: Substance, Theory, Empirics, Substance. *Comparative Political Studies*, 41(4–5):742–780.

Franzese, R. J., Jr. & J. C. Hays. 2008b. *Empirical Models of Spatial Interdependence*. In J. Box-Steffensmeier, H. Brady & D. Collier, eds., *Oxford Handbook of Political Methodology*, Oxford: Oxford University Press, pp. 570–604. Corrected web version accessed May 18, 2019 from www-personal.umich.edu/~franzese/FranzeseHaysSpatial InterdepOxfordHandbook.Corrected.pdf: p. 24.

Freeman, J. R. & D. P. Quinn. 2012. The Economic Origins of Democracy Reconsidered. *American Political Science Review*, 106(1): 58–80

Fukuyama, F. 2004. The Imperative of State-Building. *Journal of Democracy*, 15(2): 17–31.

Fukuyama, F. 2014. States and Democracy. *Democratization*, 21(7): 1326–1340.

Gandhi, J. 2008. *Political Institutions under Dictatorship*. New York: Cambridge University Press.

Gandhi, J. & A. Przeworski. 2007. Authoritarian Institutions and the Survival of Autocrats. *Comparative Political Studies*, 40(11): 1279–1301.

Gasiorowski, M. J. 1995. Economic Crisis and Political Regime Change: An Event History Analysis. *American Political Science Review*, 89(4): 882–897.

Gasiorowski, M. J. & T. J. Power. 1998. The Structural Determinants of Democratic Consolidation: Evidence from the Third World. *Comparative Political Studies*, 31(6): 740–771.

Gassebner, M., J. Gutmann & S. Vogt. 2016. When to expect a coup d'etat? An Extreme Bounds Analysis of Coup Determinants. *Public Choice*, 169(3): 293–313.

Gassebner, M., M. J. Lamla & J. R. Vreeland. 2009. Extreme Bounds of Democracy. Working Paper 224. Zurich: KOF Swiss Economic Institute.

Gassebner, M., M. J. Lamla & J. R. Vreeland. 2013. Extreme Bounds of Democracy. *Journal of Conflict Resolution*, 57(2): 171–195.

Geddes, B. 1999. What Do We Know About Democratization After Twenty Years? *Annual Review of Political Science*, 2: 115–144.

Geddes, B. 2003. *Paradigms and Sand Castles: Theory Building and Research Design in Comparative Politics*. Ann Arbor: University of Michigan Press.

Geddes, B. 2007. What Causes Democratization. In R. E. Goodin, eds., *The Oxford Handbook of Political Science*. Oxford: Oxford University Press.

Geddes, B., J. Wright & E. Frantz. 2014. Autocratic Breakdown and Regime Transitions: A New Data Set. *Perspectives on Politics*, 12(2): 313–331.

Gerring, J. 2012. Mere Description. *British Journal of Political Science*, 42(4): 721–746.

Gerring, J. 2012. *Social Science Methodology: A Unified Framework*. Cambridge: Cambridge University Press.

Gerring, J., B. Apfeld., T. Wig. & A. F. Tollefsen. 2022. *The Deep Roots of Modern Democracy*. Cambridge: Cambridge University Press.

Gerring, J., P. Bond., W. T. Brandt. & C. Moreno. 2005. Democracy and Economic Growth: A Historical Perspective. *World Politics*, 57(3): 323–364.

Gerring, J., A. Hicken., D. Weitzel. & L. Cojocaru. 2018. Electoral Contestation: A Comprehensive Polity-Level Analysis. V-Dem Working Paper 2018:73. V-Dem Institute.

Gerring, J., M. Hoffman. & D. Zarecki. 2018. The Diverse Effects of Diversity on Democracy. *British Journal of Political Science*, 48(2): 283–314.

Gerring, J., S. C. Thacker. & R. Alfaro. 2012. Democracy and Human Development. *Journal of Politics*, 74(1): 1–17.

Gerring, J. & W. Veenendaal. 2020. *Population and Politics: The Impact of Scale*. Cambridge: Cambridge University Press.

Gerring, J., T. Wig., W. Veenendaal., D. Weitzel., J. Teorell. & K. Kikuta. 2021. Why Monarchy? The Rise and Demise of a Regime Type. *Comparative Political Studies*, 54 (3–4): 585–622.

Gerring, J. C. H. Knutsen., M. Maguire., S. E. Skaaning., J. Teorell. & M. Coppedge. 2021. Electoral Democracy and Human Development: Issues of Conceptualization and Measurement. *Democratization*, 28(2): 308–332.

Gibler, D. M. 2009. *International Military Alliances, 1648–2008*. CQ Press.

Giuliano, P. & N. Nunn. 2013. The Transmission of Democracy: From the Village to the Nation-State. *American Economic Review*, 103(3): 86–92.

Gjerløw, H. & C. H. Knutsen. 2019. Leaders, Private Interests, and Socially Wasteful Projects: Skyscrapers in Democracies and Autocracies. *Political Research Quarterly*, 72(2): 504–520.

Gjerløw, H., C. H. Knutsen., T. Wig. & M. C. Wilson. 2018. Stairways to Denmark: Does the Sequence of State-building and Democratization Matter for Economic Development. Working Paper 2018:72. Varieties of Democracy Institute.

Glaeser, E. L., G. A. M. Ponzetto. & A. Shleifer. 2007. Why Does Democracy Need Education? *Journal of Economic Growth*, 12(2): 77–99.

Gleditsch, K. S. 2002. Expanded Trade and GDP Data. *Journal of Conflict Resolution*, 46(5): 712–724.

Gleditsch, N. P., P. Wallensteen., M. Eriksson., M. Sollenberg. & H. Strand. 2002. Armed Conflict 1946–2001: A New Dataset. *Journal of Peace Research*, 39(5): 615–637.

Gleditsch, K. S. & M. D. Ward. 1999. Interstate System Membership: A Revised List of the Independent States since 1816. *International Interactions*, 25(4): 393–413.

Gleditsch, K. S. & M. D. Ward. 2006. Diffusion and the International Context of Democratization. *International Organization*, 60(4): 911–933.

Go, J. 2003. A Globalizing Constitutionalism? Views from the Postcolony, 1945–2000. *International Sociology*, 18(1): 71–95.

Goertz, G. 2003. *International Norms and Decision Making: A Punctuated Equilibrium Model*. Rowman & Littlefield.

Goldring, E. & S. C. Greitens. 2019. Rethinking Democratic Diffusion: Bringing Regime Type Back In. *Comparative Political Studies*, 53(2): 319–353.

Goldthorpe, J. H. 2001. The Uses of History in Sociology: Reflections on Some Recent Tendencies. *British Journal of Sociology*, 42(2): 211–230.

González Ocantos E. 2016. *Shifting Legal Visions: Judicial Change and Human Rights Trials in Latin America*. New York: Cambridge University Press.

Goodliffe, J. & D. Hawkins. 2015. Dependence Networks and the Diffusion of Domestic Political Institutions. *Journal of Conflict Resolution*, 61(4): 903–929.

Gould, A. 1999. *Origins of Liberal Dominance: State Church, and Party in Nineteenth Century Europe*. Ann Arbor: University of Michigan Press.

Graham, B. A. T., M. K. Miller. & K. R. Strøm. 2017. Safeguarding Democracy: Powersharing and Democratic Survival. *American Political Science Review*, 111(4): 686–704.

Gu, M. Li. & E. Bomhoff. 2012. Religion and Support for Democracy: A Comparative Study for Catholic and Muslim Countries. *Politics and Religion*, 5(2): 280–316.

Gundlach, E. & M. Paldam. 2009. A Farewell to Critical Junctures: Sorting Out Long-Run Causality of Income and Democracy. *European Journal of Political Economy*, 25(3): 340–354.

Gunitsky, S. 2014. From Shocks to Waves: Hegemonic Transitions and Democratization in the Twentieth Century. *International Organization*, 68(3): 561.

Gunitsky, S. 2017. *Aftershocks: Great Powers and Domestic Reforms in the Twentieth Century*. Princeton: Princeton University Press.

Gurr, T. R. 1970. *Why Men Rebel*. Princeton: Princeton University Press.

Haber, S. & V. Menaldo. 2011. Do Natural Resources Fuel Authoritarianism? A Reappraisal of the Resource Curse. *American Political Science Review*, 105(1): 1–26.

Habermas, J. 1996. *Between Facts and Norms: Contributions to a Discourse Theory on Law and Democracy*. Cambridge: MIT Press.

Hadenius, A. 1992. *Democracy and Development*. Cambridge: Cambridge University Press.

Hadenius, A. & J. Teorell. 2005. Cultural and Economic Prerequisites of Democracy: Reassessing Recent Evidence. *Studies in comparative international development*, 39(4), 87–106.

Hadenius, A. & J. Teorell. 2007. Pathways from Authoritarianism. *Journal of Democracy*, 18(1): 143–156.

Haggard, S. & Kaufman, R. R. 1995. *The Political Economy of Democratic Transitions*. Princeton: Princeton University Press.

Haggard, S. & R. Kaufman. 2016. *Dictators and Democrats: Elites, Masses, and Regime Change*. Princeton: Princeton University Press.

Hanson, J. K. & R. Sigman. 2011. Leviathan's Latent Dimensions: Measuring State Capacity for Comparative Political Research. Available at: https://papers.ssrn.com/sol3/papers.cfm?abstract_id=1899933

Hariri, J. G. 2012. The Autocratic Legacy of Early Statehood. *American Political Science Review*, 106(3): 471–94.

Hariri, J. G. 2015. A contribution to the Understanding of Middle Eastern and Muslim Exceptionalism. *The Journal of Politics*, 77(2): 477–490.

Hayek, F. A. 1960. *The Constitution of Liberty*. Chicago: University of Chicago Press.

Hays, J. C., A. Kachi. & R. J. Franzese Jr. 2010. A Spatial Model Incorporating Dynamic, Endogenous Network Interdependence: A Political Science Application. *Statistical Methodology*, 7(3): 406–428.

Hechter, M. 1975. *Internal Colonialism: The Celtic Fringe in British National Development*. Transaction Publishers.

Heckman, J. J. 1979. Sample Selection Bias as a Specification Error. *Econometrica*, 47(1): 153–161.

Hefner, R. W. (ed.). 2009. *Remaking Muslim politics: Pluralism, contestation, democratization*. Princeton University Press.

Hegre H. 2014. Democracy and Armed Conflict. *Journal of Peace Research*, 51(2): 159–172.

Hegre, H., M. Bernhard. & J. Teorell. (2020). Civil Society and the Democratic Peace. *Journal of Conflict Resolution*, 64(1): 32–62.

Hegre, H. & N. Sambanis. 2006. Sensitivity Analysis of Empirical Results on Civil War Onset. *Journal of Conflict Resolution*, 50(4): 508–535.

Heid, B., J. Langer. & M. Larch. 2012. Income and Democracy: Evidence from System GMM Estimates. *Economics Letters*, 116(2): 166–169.

Held, D. 2006. *Models of Democracy*. Redwood City: Stanford University Press.

Hendrix, C. S. & S. Haggard. 2015. Global Food Prices, Regime Type, and Urban Unrest in the Developing World. *Journal of Peace Research*, 52(2): 143–157.

Hendrix, C. S. & I. Salehyan. 2012. Climate Change, Rainfall, and Social Conflict in Africa. *Journal of Peace Research*, 49(1): 35–50.

Hensel, P. R. 2018. ICOW Colonial History Data Set, version 1.1. Available at www .paulhensel.org/icowcol.html.

Herbst, J. 2009. *Population Change, Urbanization, and Political Consolidation*. In R. E. Goodin. & C. Tilly, eds., *The Oxford Handbook of Contextual Political Analysis*. Oxford: Oxford University Press.

Hiroi, T. & S. Omori. 2009. Perils of Parliamentarism? Political Systems and the Stability of Democracy Revisited. *Democratization*, 16(3): 485–507.

Hobsbawm, E. J. 1973. Peasants and Politics. *The Journal of Peasant Studies*, 1(1): 3–22.

Hochschild, A. 2018. *Strangers in Their Own Land: Anger and Mourning in the American Right*. The New Press.

Hoffman, M. & A. Jamal. 2014. Religion in the Arab Spring: Between Two Competing Narratives. *Journal of Politics*, 76(3): 593–606.

Honaker, J. & G. King. 2010. What to Do about Missing Values in Time-Series Cross-Section Data. *American Journal of Political Science*, 54(2): 561–581.

Howard, M. M. 2002. The Weakness of Postcommunist Civil Society. *Journal of Democracy*, 13(1): 157–169.

Horowitz, D. L. 1985. *Ethnic Groups in Conflict*. Berkeley: University of California Press.

Horowitz, D. L. 1990. *Comparing Democratic Systems. Journal of Democracy* 1(4): 73–9.

Houle, C. 2009. Inequality and Democracy: Why Inequality Harms Consolidation but Does Not Affect Democratization. *World Politics*, 61(4): 589–622.

Houle, C., M. A. Kayser. & J. Xiang. 2016. Diffusion or Confusion? Clustered Shocks and the Conditional Diffusion of Democracy. *International Organization*, 70(4): 687–726.

Hunt, R. C. 1989. Appropriate Social Organization? Water User Associations in Bureaucratic Canal Irrigation Systems. *Human Organization*, 48(1): 79–90.

Huntington, S. P. 1968. *Political Order in Changing Societies.* New Haven: Yale University Press.

Huntington, S. P. 1991. *The Third Wave: Democratization in the Late Twentieth Century.* Norman: University of Oklahoma Press.

Huntington, S. P. 1993. The Clash of Civilizations? *Foreign Affairs*, 72(3): 22–49.

Huntington, S. P. 1996. *The Clash of Civilizations and the Remaking of World Order.* New York: Simon & Schuster.

Hyde, S. D. 2007. The Observer Effect in International Politics: Evidence from a Natural Experiment. *World Politics*, 60(1): 37–63.

Imbens, G. W. & D. B. Rubin. 2015. *Causal Inference for Statistics, Social, and Biomedical Sciences: An Introduction.* New York: Cambridge University Press.

Infra, C. 2016. Reconstructing Global Inequality. Available at: www.clio-infra.eu /#datasets.

Inglehart, R., R. Foa., C. Peterson. & C. Welzel. 2008. Development, Freedom, and Rising Happiness. *Perspectives on Psychological Science*, 3(4): 264–285.

Inglehart, R. & C. Welzel. 2005. *Modernization, Cultural Change, and Democracy: The Human Development Sequence.* New York: Cambridge University Press.

Jackman, R. W. 1973. On the Relation of Economic Development and Democratic Performance. *American Journal of Political Science*, 17(3): 611–21.

Jamal, A. A. 2012. *Of Empires and Citizens: Pro-American Democracy or No Democracy at All?* Princeton: Princeton University Press.

Jensen, J. L., P. B. Mortensen. & S. Serritzlew. 2019. A Comparative Distributional Method for Public Administration Illustrated Using Public Budget Data. *Journal of Public Administration Research and Theory*, 29(3): 460–473.

Jones, E. L. 1981. *The European Miracle: Environments, Economies and Geopolitics in the History of Europe and Asia.* 2nd ed. Cambridge: Cambridge University Press.

Jones-Correa, M. A. & D. L. Leal. 2001. Political Participation: Does Religion Matter? *Political Research Quarterly*, 54(4): 751–770.

Joseph, J. 2004. *Language and Identity: National, Ethnic, Religious.* Springer.

Kalyvas, S. 1996. *The Rise of Christian Democracy in Europe.* Ithaca: Cornell University Press.

Karakoç, E. 2017. A Theory of Redistribution in New Democracies: Income Disparity in New Democracies in Europe. *Comparative Politics*, 49(3): 311–330.

Katz, J. N. 2014. Causal Inference with Panel and TSCS Data. Lecture at the workshop on Advanced Causal Inference, Duke University Law School, August 15.

Keck, M. E. & K. Sikkink. 1998. *Activists beyond Borders: Advocacy Networks in International Politics.* Ithaca: Cornell University Press.

Kennedy, R. 2010. The Contradiction of Modernization: A Conditional Model of Endogenous Democratization. *Journal of Politics*, 72(3): 785–798.

Kim, M. 2008. Spiritual Values, Religious Practices, and Democratic Attitudes. *Politics and Religion*, 1(2): 216–236.

Klaas, B. 2016. *The Despot's Accomplice: How the West is Aiding and Abetting the Decline of Democracy.* London: C. Hurst.

Klerman, D. M., P. G. Mahoney., H. Spamann. & M. I. Weinstein. 2011. Legal Origin or Colonial History? *Journal of Legal Analysis*, 3(2): 379–409.

Knutsen, C. H. 2011. Democracy, Dictatorship and Protection of Property Rights. *Journal of Development Studies*, 47(1): 164–182.

Knutsen, C. H. 2012. Democracy and Economic Growth: A Review of Arguments and Results. *International Area Studies Review*, 15(4): 393–415.

Knutsen, C. H. 2014. Income Growth and Revolutions. *Social Science Quarterly*, 95(4): 920–937.

Knutsen, C. H. 2015. Reinvestigating the Reciprocal Relationship between Democracy and Income Inequality. *Review of Economics and Institutions*, 6(2): Article 1.

Knutsen, C. H. 2021. A Business Case for Democracy: Regime Type, Growth, and Growth Volatility. *Democratization* Online First. www.tandfonline.com/doi/pdf/10 .1080/13510347.2021.1940965

Knutsen, C. H., J. Teorell., T. Wig., A. Cornell., J. Gerring., H. Gjerløw., S. E. Skaaning., D. Ziblatt., K. Marquardt., D. Pemstein. & B. Seim. 2019a. Introducing the Historical Varieties of Democracy Dataset: Political Institutions in the Long 19th Century. *Journal of Peace Research*, 56(3): 440–451.

Knutsen, C. H., J. Gerring., S. E. Skaaning., J. Teorell., M. Maguire., S. I. Lindberg. & M. Coppedge. 2019b. Economic Development and Democracy: An Electoral Connection. *European Journal of Political Research*, 58(1): 292–314.

Knutsen, C. H., A. Kotsadam., E. H. Olsen. & T. Wig. 2017. Mining and Local Corruption in Africa. *American Journal of Political Science*, 61(2): 320–334.

Knutsen, C. H. & H. M. Nygård. 2015. Institutional Characteristics and Regime Survival: Why Are Semi-Democracies Less Durable Than Autocracies and Democracies? *American Journal of Political Science*, 59(3): 656–670.

Knutsen, C. H., H. M. Nygård. & T. Wig. 2017b. Autocratic Elections: Stabilizing Tool or Force for Change? *World Politics*, 69(1): 98–143.

Kopstein, J. & J. Wittenburg. 2010. Beyond Dictatorship and Democracy: Rethinking National Minority Inclusion and Regime Type in Interwar Eastern Europe. *Comparative Political Studies*, 43(8–9): 1089–1118.

Korotayev, A. V. 1995. Mountains and Democracy: An Introduction. In N. N. Kradin & V. A. Lynsha., eds., *Alternative Pathways to Early State*. Vladivostoik: Dal'nauka, pp. 60–74.

Krieckhaus, J. T. 2006. *Dictating Development: How Europe Shaped the Global Periphery*. Pittsburgh: University of Pittsburgh Press.

Kuran, T. 1995. *Private Truths, Public Lies: The Social Consequences of Preference Falsification*. Cambridge: Harvard University Press.

Kuran, T. 2011. *The Long Divergence: How Islamic Law Held Back the Middle East*. Princeton: Princeton University Press

Kurlantzick, J. 2014. *Democracy in Retreat: The Revolt of the Middle Class and the Worldwide Decline of Representative Government*. New Haven: Yale University Press.

Kuru, A. T. 2014. Authoritarianism and Democracy in Muslim Countries: Rentier States and Regional Diffusion. *Political Science Quarterly*, 129(3): 399–427.

La Porta, R., F. Lopez-de-Silanes., A. Shleifer. & R. W. Vishny. 1998. Law and finance. *Journal of Political Economy*, 106(6): 1113–1155.

La Porta, R., F. Lopez-de-Silanes., A. Shleifer. & R. W. Vishny. 1999. The Quality of Government. *Journal of Economics, Law and Organization*, 15(1): 222–279.

Lai, B. & R. Melkonian-Hoover. 2005. Democratic Progress and Regress: The Effect of Parties on the Transitions of States to and Away from Democracy. *Political Research Quarterly*, 58(4): 551–564.

Lake, D. A. and M. A. Baum. 2001. The Invisible Hand of Democracy: Political Control and the Provision of Public Services. *Comparative Political Studies* 34(6): 587–621.

Lambert, P. J. 2001. *The Distribution and Redistribution of Income*. New York: Palgrave.

Land, K. & G. Deane. 1992. On the Large-Sample Estimation of Regression Models with Spatial or Network-Effects Terms: A 2-Stage Least Squares Approach. *Sociological Methodology*, 22: 221–248.

Lange, M., J. Mahoney. & M. vom Hau. 2006. Colonialism and Development: A Comparative Analysis of Spanish and British Colonies. *American Journal of Sociology*, 111(5): 1412–1462.

Lankina, T. & L. Getachew. 2012. Mission or Empire, Word or Sword? The Human Capital Legacy in Postcolonial Democratic Development. *American Journal of Political Science*, 56(2): 465–483.

Lankina, T. & L. Getachew. 2013. Competitive Religious Entrepreneurs: Christian Missionaries and Female Education in Colonial and Post-Colonial India. *British Journal of Political Science*, 43(1): 103–131.

Lauth, H. J. 2016. The Internal Relationships of the Dimensions of Democracy: The Relevance of Trade-offs for Measuring the Quality of Democracy. *International Political Science Review*, 37(5): 606–617.

Leach, E. R. 1960. The Frontiers of "Burma". *Comparative Studies in Society and History*, 3(1): 49–68.

Lee, A. & J. Paine. 2020. Colonialism and Democracy: Origins of Pluralism and Authoritarianism in the Non-European World. Unpublished manuscript, University of Rochester.

Leeds, B., J. Ritter., S. Mitchell. & A. Long. 2002. Alliance Treaty Obligations and Provisions, 1815-1944. *International Interactions*, 28(3): 237–260.

Leeson, P. T. & A. M. Dean. 2009. The Democratic Domino Theory: An Empirical Investigation. *American Journal of Political Science*, 53(3): 533–551.

Lepsius, M. R. 2017. From Fragmented Party Democracy to Government by Emergency Decree and National Socialist Takeover: Germany. In C. Wendt., ed., *Max Weber and Institutional Theory*. Springer.

LeSage, J. & K. Pace. 2009. *Introduction to Spatial Econometrics*. Boca Raton: CRC Press, Taylor & Francis Group.

Levitsky, S. 1998. Institutionalization and Peronism. *Party Politics*, 4(1): 77–92.

Levitsky, S. & L. A. Way. 2006. Linkage versus Leverage: Rethinking the International Dimension of Regime Change. *Comparative Politics*, 38(4): 379–400.

Levitsky, S. & L. Way. 2015. The Myth of Democratic Recession. *Journal of Democracy*, 26(1): 45–58.

Levy, J. S. 1981. Alliance Formation and War Behavior: An Analysis of the Great Powers, 1495–1975. *Journal of Conflict Resolution*, 25(4): 581–613.

Lewis, B. 1993. Islam and Liberal Democracy. *Atlantic Monthly*, 271(2): 89–98.

Lewis, B. 2002. *What Went Wrong? Western Impact and Middle Eastern Response*. Phoenix, London.

Li, P. Y. R. & W. Thompson. 1975. The 'Coup Contagion' Hypothesis. *Journal of Conflict Resolution*, 19(1): 63–84.

Li, Q. & R. Reuveny. 2006. Democracy and Environmental Degradation. *International Studies Quarterly*, 50(4): 935–956.

Lieberman, E. S. 2009. *Boundaries of Contagion: How Ethnic Politics have shaped Government Responses to AIDS*. Princeton: Princeton University Press.

Lijphart, A. 1977. *Democracy in Plural Societies: A Comparative Exploration*. New Haven: Yale University Press.

Lijphart, A. 1984. *Democracies: Patterns of Majoritarian and Consensus Government in Twenty-One Countries*. New Haven: Yale University Press.

Lijphart, A. 1999. *Patterns of Democracy {Government Forms and Performance in Thirty-Six Countries*. New Haven: Yale University Press.

Lindberg, S. I. 2006a. *Democracy and Elections in Africa*. Baltimore: Johns Hopkins University Press.

Lindberg, S. I. 2006b. The Surprising Significance of African Elections. *Journal of Democracy*, 17(1): 139–151.

Lindberg, S. I. eds. 2009. *Democratization by Elections: A New Mode of Transition*. Baltimore: Johns Hopkins University Press.

Linz, J. 1978. Crisis, Breakdown, and Reequilibration. In J. Linz & A. Stepan, eds., *The Breakdown of Democratic Regimes*. Baltimore: Johns Hopkins University Press, pp. 1–130

Linz, J. 1990. The Perils of Presidentialism. *Journal of Democracy*, 1(1): 51–69.

Linz, J. 1990. The Virtues of Parliamentarism. *Journal of Democracy*, 1(4): 84–91.

Linz, J. & A. Stepan. 1996. *Problems of Democratic Transition and Consolidation*. Baltimore: Johns Hopkins University Press.

Linz, J. & A. Valenzuela., eds. 1994. *The Failure of Presidential Democracy*. Baltimore: Johns Hopkins University Press.

Linz, J. J. 1994. Introduction: Presidential or Parliamentary Democracy: Does It Make a Difference? In J. J. Linz. & A. Valenzuela., eds., *The Failure of Presidential Democracy*. Baltimore: Johns Hopkins University Press.

Linz, J. J. & A. Stepan. 1996. *Problems of Democratic Transition and Consolidation*. Baltimore: Johns Hopkins University Press.

Liou, Y. M. & P. Musgrave. 2014. Refining the Oil Curse: Country-Level Evidence from Exogenous Variations in Resource Income. *Comparative Political Studies*, 47(11): 1584–1610.

Lipset, S. M. 1959. Some Social Requisites for Democracy: Economic Development and Political Legitimacy. *American Political Science Review*, 53(1): 69–105.

Lipset, S. M. 1960. *Political Man: The Social Bases of Politics*. Garden City: Doubleday.

Lipset, S. M., K. R. Seong. & J. C. Torres. 1993. A Comparative Analysis of the Social Requisites of Democracy. *International Political Science Review*, 45(2): 154–175.

Lohmann, S. 1994. The Dynamics of Informational Cascades: The Monday Demonstrations in Leipzig, East Germany, 1989–91. *World Politics*, 47(1): 42–101.

Londregan, J. R. & K. T. Poole. 1996. Does High Income Promote Democracy? *World Politics*, 49(1): 1–30.

López-Córdova, J. E. & C. M. Meissner. 2008. The Impact of International Trade on Democracy: A Long-Run Perspective. *World Politics*, 60(4): 539–575.

Luebbert, G. 1991. *Liberalism, Fascism, or Social Democracy: Social Classes and the Political Origin of Regimes in Interwar Europe*. Oxford: Oxford University Press.

Lührmann, A. 2021. Disrupting the Autocratization Sequence: Towards Democratic Resilience. *Democratization*, 28(5): 1017–1039.

Lührmann, A. & S. I. Lindberg. 2019. A Third Wave of Autocratization is Here: What Is New About It? *Democratization*, 26(7): 1095–1113.

Lührmann, A., V. Mechkova., S. Dahlum., L. Maxwell., M. Ohlin., C. S. Petrarca., R. Sigman., M. Wilson. & S. I. Lindberg. 2018. State of the World 2017: Autocratization and Exclusion? *Democratization*, 25(8): 1321–1340.

Lührmann, A., M. Tannenberg. & S. I. Lindberg. 2018. Regimes of the World (RoW): Opening New Avenues for the Comparative Study of Political Regimes. *Politics and Governance*, 6(1): 60–77.

Lust, E. 2011. Missing the Third Wave: Islam, Institutions, and Democracy in the Middle East. *Studies in Comparative International Development*, 46(2): 163–190.

Maddison, A. 2001. *The World Economy: A Millennial Perspective*. Paris: OECD.

Madrid, R. L. 2003. *Retiring the State: The Politics of Pension Privatization in Latin America and Beyond*. Palo Alto: Stanford University Press.

Maeda, K. 2010. Two Modes of Democratic Breakdown: A Competing Risks Analysis of Democratic Durability. *The Journal of Politics*, 72(4): 1129–1143.

Magaloni B. 2006. *Voting for Autocracy: Hegemonic Party Survival and its Demise in Mexico*. Cambridge: Cambridge Univ. Press.

Magaloni, B. & R. Kricheli. 2010. Political Order and One-Party Rule. *Annual Review of Political Science*, 13(1): 123–143.

Mahoney, J. 2010. *Colonialism and Postcolonial Development: Spanish America in Comparative Perspective*. Cambridge: Cambridge University Press.

Mainwaring, S. 1993. Presidentialism, Multipartism, and Democracy: The Difficult Combination. *Comparative Political Studies*, 26(2): 198–228.

Mainwaring, S., eds. 2018. *Party Systems in Latin America: Institutionalization, Decay, and Collapse*. New York: Cambridge University Press.

Mainwaring, S. & A. Pérez-Liñán. 2013. *Democracies and Dictatorships in Latin America: Emergence, Survival, and Fall*. New York: Cambridge University Press.

Mainwaring, S. & M. Torcal. 2006. Party System Institutionalization and Party System Theory After the Third Wave of Democratization. In R. S. Katz and W. Crotty, eds., *Handbook of Political Parties*. London: Sage, pp. 204–227.

Mainwaring, S. & T. Scully, eds. 1995. *Building Democratic Institutions: Party Systems in Latin America*. Stanford: Stanford University Press.

Mainwaring, S. & M. S. Shugart. 1997. Juan Linz, Presidentialism and Democracy. A Critical Appraisal. *Comparative Politics*, 29(4): 449–471.

Malthus, T. 1798. *An Essay on the Principle of Population*. London: J. Johnson, in St. Paul's Church-Yard.

Mankiw, N. G., D. Romer. & D. N. Weil. 1992. A Contribution to the Empirics of Economic Growth. *The Quarterly Journal of Economics*, 107(2): 407–437.

Mann, M. 1986. *The Sources of Social Power, Volume I: A History of Power from the Beginnings to 1760 AD*. Cambridge: Cambridge University Press.

Mann, M. 2004. *Fascists*. New York: Cambridge University Press.

Mansfield, E. D. & J. L. Snyder. 2007. The Sequencing 'Fallacy'. *Journal of Democracy*, 18(3): 5–10.

Mantilla, L. F. 2010. Mobilizing Religion for Democracy: Explaining Catholic Church Support for Democratization in South America. *Politics and Religion*, 3(3): 553–579.

Maoz, Z. & E. A. Henderson. 2013. The World Religion Dataset, 1945-2010: Logic, Estimates, and Trends. *International Interactions*, 39(3): 265–291.

Maoz, Z. & B. Russett. 1993. Normative and Structural Causes of Democratic Peace. *American Political Science Review*, 87(3): 640–654.

Marquardt, K. L. 2018. Identity, Social Mobility, and Ethnic Mobilization: Language and the Disintegration of the Soviet Union. *Comparative Political Studies*, 51(7): 831–867.

Marquardt, K. L. & D. Pemstein. 2018. IRT Models for Expert-Coded Panel Data. *Political Analysis*, 26(4): 431–456.

Marshall, M. G., T. R. Gurr. & K. Jaggers. 2013. POLITY IV PROJECT: Political Regime Characteristics and Transitions, 1800-2013. Center for Systemic Peace.

Matloff, J. 2017. *No Friends but the Mountains: Dispatches from the World's Violent Highlands*. New York: Basic Books.

Mayoral, L. & O. Olsson. 2019. *Pharoah's Cage: Environmental Circumscription and Appropriability in Early State Development*. Working paper. Online: https://papers .ssrn.com/sol3/papers.cfm?abstract_id=3496225

Mayshar, J., O. Moav. & Z. Neeman. 2017. Geography, Transparency, and Institutions. *American Political Science Review*, 111(3): 622–636.

Mayshar, J., O. Moav., Z. Neeman. & L. Pascali. 2019. *The Origin of the State: Land Productivity or Appropriability?* Unpublished manuscript, Hebrew University.

Mazzuca, S. L. & G. L. Munck. 2014. State or Democracy First? Alternative Perspectives on the State-Democracy Nexus. *Democratization*, 21(7): 1221–1243.

McConnaughy, C. M. 2014. *The Woman Suffrage Movement in America: A Reassessment*. New York: Cambridge University Press.

McDonald, P. J. 2015. Great Powers, Hierarchy, and Endogenous Regimes: Rethinking the Domestic Causes of Peace. *International Organization*, 69(3): 557–588.

Mechkova, V., A. Lührmann. & S. I. Lindberg. 2017. How Much Backsliding? *Journal of Democracy*, 28(4): 162–169.

Mellinger, A. D., J. D. Sachs. & J. Gallup. 2000. Climate, Coastal Proximity, and Development. In G. L. Clark., M. S. Gertler. & M. P. Feldman., eds., *The Oxford Handbook of Economic Geography*. Oxford: Oxford University Press, pp. 169–194.

Meltzer, A. H. & S. F. Richard. 1981. A Rational Theory of the Size of Government. *Journal of Political Economy*, 89(5): 914–927.

Menaldo, V. 2012. The Middle East and North Africa's Resilient Monarchs. *Journal of Politics*, 74(3): 707–722.

Michael C., B. Denison, L. Tiscornia & S. I. Lindberg 2016. *Varieties of Democratic Diffusion: Neighbors, Trade, and Alliance Networks*, Varieties of Democracy Institute Working Paper No. 2 (revised).

Michalopoulos, S. 2012. The Origins of Ethnolinguistic Diversity. *American Economic Review*, 102(4): 1508–39.

Mickey, R. 2015. *Paths Out of Dixie: The Democratization of Authoritarian Enclaves in America's Deep South, 1944-1972*. Princeton: Princeton University Press.

Midlarsky, M. I. 1995. Environmental Influences on Democracy: Aridity, Warfare, and a Reversal of the Causal Arrow. *Journal of Conflict Resolution*, 39(2): 224–262.

Migdal, J. 1988. *Strong Societies, Weak States*. Princeton: Princeton University Press.

Mill, J. S. 1861/1958. *Considerations on Representative Government*. New York: Liberal Arts Press.

Miller, M. K. 2012. Economic Development, Violent Leader Removal, and Democratization. *American Journal of Political Science*, 56(4): 1002–1020.

Miller, M. K. 2015. Democratic Pieces: Autocratic Elections and Democratic Development since 1815. *British Journal of Political Science*, 45(3): 501–530.

Miller, M. K. 2016. Democracy by Example? Why Democracy Spreads When the World's Democracies Prosper. *Comparative Politics*, 49(1): 83–116.

Miller, M. K., M. Joseph. & D. Ohl. 2018. Are Coups Really Contagious? An Extreme Bounds Analysis of Political Diffusion. *Journal of Conflict Resolution*, 62(2): 410–441.

Milner, H. & K. Kubota. 2005. Why the Move to Free Trade? Democracy and Trade Policy in the Developing Countries. *International Organization*, 59(1): 107–143.

Milner, H. V. & B. Mukherjee. 2009. Democratization and Economic Globalization. *Annual Review of Political Science*, 12: 163–181.

Møller, J. & S. E. Skaaning. 2011. *Requisites of Democracy: Conceptualization, Measurement, and Explanation*. London: Routledge.

Møller, J. & S. E. Skaaning. 2011. Stateness First? *Democratization*, 18(1): 1–24.

Møller, J. & S. E. Skaaning. 2013. *Democracy and Democratization in Comparative Perspective: Conceptions, Conjunctures, Causes, and Consequences*. London: Routledge.

Montalvo, J. G. & M. Reynal-Querol. 2005a. Ethnic Diversity and Economic Development. *Journal of Development Economics*, 76(2): 293–323.

Montalvo, J. G. & M. Reynal-Querol. 2005b. Ethnic Polarization, Potential Conflict, and Civil Wars. *American Economic Review*, 95(3): 796–816.

Montesquieu, Charles-Louis de Secondat. 1748 [1989]. *The Spirit of the Laws*. Cambridge: Cambridge University Press.

Moore, B. 1966. *Social Origins of Democracy and Dictatorship: Lord and Peasant in the Making of the Modern World*. Boston: Beacon Press.

Moral-Benito, E. 2013. Likelihood-Based Estimation of Dynamic Panels With Predetermined Regressors. *Journal of Business & Economic Statistics*, 31(4): 451–472.

Moral-Benito, E. & C. Bartolucci. 2012. Income and Democracy: Revisiting the Evidence. Banco de Espana Working Paper No. 1115

Muller, E. N. 1988. Democracy, economic development, and income inequality. *American Sociological Review*, 53(1): 50–68.

Muller, E. N. 1995. Economic Determinants of Democracy. *American Sociological Review*, 60 (4): 966–982.

Munck, G. L. 2009. *Measuring Democracy: A Bridge between Scholarship and Politics*. Baltimore: Johns Hopkins University Press.

Munck, G. L. 2019. *The Quest for Knowledge About Societies: How Advances in the Social Sciences Have Been Made*. Book manuscript, University of Southern California.

Munck, G. L. & J. Verkuilen. 2002. Conceptualizing and Measuring Democracy: Evaluating Alternative Indices. *Comparative Politics Studies*, 35(1): 5–34.

Murdie, A. & D. Peksen. 2014. Women and Contentious Politics: A Global Event-Data Approach to Understanding Women's Protest. *Political Research Quarterly*, 68(1): 180–192.

Murshed, S. M., Bergougui, B., Badiuzzaman, M., & Pulok, M. H. 2020. Fiscal Capacity, Democratic Institutions and Social Welfare Outcomes in Developing Countries. *Defence and Peace Economics*, Online first https://doi.org/10.1080/10242694.2020.1817259.

Murtin, F. & R. Wacziarg. 2014. The Democratic Transition. *Journal of Economic Growth*, 19(2): 141–181.

Myerson, R. B. 2006. Federalism and Incentives for Success of Democracy. *Quarterly Journal of Political Science*, 1: 3–23.

Narizny, K. 2012. Anglo-American Primacy and the Global Spread of Democracy: An International Genealogy. *World Politics*, 64(2): 341–373.

Nasr, S. V. R. 2005. The Rise of 'Muslim Democracy'. *Journal of Democracy*, 16(2): 13–27.

Negretto, G. 2006. Minority Presidents and Democratic Performance in Latin America. *Latin American Politics and Society*, 48(3): 63–92.

Neumayer, E. & T. Plümper. 2016. W. *Political Science Research and Methods*, 4(1): 175–193.

Noland, M. 2008. Explaining Middle Eastern Political Authoritarianism I: The Level of Democracy. *Review of Middle East Economics and Finance*, 4(1): 1–30.

Norris, P. 2012. *Making Democratic Governance Work: How Regimes Shape Prosperity, Welfare, and Peace*. Cambridge: Cambridge University Press.

Norris, P. & R. Inglehart. 2011. *Sacred and Secular: Religion and Politics Worldwide*. New York: Cambridge University Press.

North, D. C. 1990. *Institutions, Institutional Change and Economic Performance*. Cambridge: Cambridge University Press

Nunn, N. & D. Puga. 2012. Ruggedness: The Blessing of Bad Geography in Africa. *Review of Economics and Statistics*, 94(1): 20–36.

O'Donnell, G. 1973. *Modernization and Bureaucratic-Authoritarianism: Studies in South American Politics*. Berkeley: Institute of International Studies, University of California.

O'Donnell, G. & P. C. Schmitter. 1986. *Transitions from Authoritarian Rule, Vol. 4: Tentative Conclusions about Uncertain Democracies*. Baltimore: Johns Hopkins University

O'Loughlin, J., M. D. Ward., C. L. Lofdahl., J. S. Cohen., D. S. Brown. & D. Reilly. 1998. The Diffusion of Democracy, 1946–1994. *Annals of the Association of American Geographers*, 88(4): 545–574.

Olson, M. 1965. *The Logic of Collective Action*. Cambridge: Harvard University Press.

Olsson, O. 2005. Geography and Institutions: A Review of Plausible and Implausible Linkages. *Journal of Economics*, 86(1): 167–194.

Olsson, O. 2009. On the Democratic Legacy of Colonialism. *Journal of Comparative Economics*, 37(4): 534–551.

Ott, D. 2000. *Small is Democratic: An Examination of State Size and Democratic Development*. New York: Garland.

Owolabi, O. 2010. Forced Settlement, Colonial Occupation and Divergent Political Regime Outcomes in the Developing World, 1946–2004. Paper presented at the American Political Science Association Annual Conference, Washington DC, 2–5 September.

Owolabi, O. 2012. *The Colonial Origins of Development and Underdevelopment, Democracy and Authoritarianism: Forced Settlement, Occupation and the Divergent Consequences of Colonial Rule in the West Indies and Sub-Saharan Africa*. Doctoral Dissertation, Department of Political Science, University of Notre Dame.

Paine, J. 2019. Democratic Contradictions in European Settler Colonies. *World Politics*, 71(3): 542–585.

Paxton, P. 2000. Women's Suffrage in the Measurement of Democracy: Problems of Operationalization. *Studies in Comparative International Development*, 35(3): 92–111.

Paxton, P., M. M. Hughes. & J. L. Green. 2006. The International Women's Movement and Women's Political Representation, 1893–2003. *American Sociological Review*, 71(6): 898–920.

Peattie, R. 1936. *Mountain Geography*. Cambridge: Harvard University Press.

Pelke, L. & P. Friesen. 2019. Democratization Articles Dataset: An Introduction. *Democratization*, 26(1): 140–160.

Pemstein, D., K. L. Marquardt., E. Tzelgov., Y. Wang., J. Medzihorsky., J. Krusell., F. Miri. & J. von Römer. 2019. The V-Dem Measurement Model: Latent Variable Analysis for Cross-National and Cross-Temporal Expert-Coded Data. V-Dem Working Paper No. 21. 4th edition. University of Gothenburg: Varieties of Democracy Institute.

Pemstein, D., S. Meserve. & J. Melton. 2010. Democratic Compromise: A Latent Variable Analysis of Ten Measures of Regime Type. *Political Analysis*, 18(4): 426–449.

Persson, T. & G. Tabellini. 2009. Democratic Capital: The Nexus of Political and Economic Change. *American Economic Journal: Macroeconomics*, 1(2): 88–126.

Pettersson, T. 2019. UCDP/PRIO Armed Conflict Dataset Codebook v 19.1. Available at: https://ucdp.uu.se/downloads/.

Pettersson, T., S. Högbladh. & M. Öberg. 2019. Organized violence, 1989-2018 and peace agreements. *Journal of Peace Research*, 56(4): 589–603.

Pevehouse, J. C. 2002. With a Little Help from My Friends? Regional Organizations and the Consolidation of Democracy. *American Journal of Political Science*, 46(3): 611–626.

Philpott, D. 2004. Christianity and Democracy: The Catholic Wave. *Journal of Democracy*, 15(2): 32–46.

Platteau, J. P. 2008. Religion, politics, and development: Lessons from the lands of Islam. *Journal of Economic Behavior & Organization*, 68(2): 329–351.

Plattner, M. F. 2019. Illiberal Democracy and the Struggle on the Right. *Journal of Democracy*, 30(1): 5–19.

Ponticelli, J. & H. J. Voth. 2011. Austerity and Anarchy: Budget Cuts and Social Unrest in Europe, 1919-2009. Working Paper. Online: https://papers.ssrn.com/sol3/papers.cfm?abstract_id=1908561

Potrafke, N. 2012. Islam and Democracy. *Public Choice*, 151 (1–2): 185–192.

Power, T. J. & M. J. Gasiorowski. 1997. Institutional Design and Democratic Consolidation in the Third World. *Comparative Political Studies*, 30(2): 123–155.

Przeworski, A. 1991. *Democracy and the Market: Political and Economic Reforms in Eastern Europe and Latin America*. New York: Cambridge University Press.

Przeworski, A. 2004. Institutions Matter? *Government and Opposition*, 39(2): 527–540.

Przeworski, A. 2010. *Democracy and the Limits of Self-Government*. Cambridge: Cambridge University Press.

Przeworski, A., M. Alvarez., J. A. Cheibub. & F. Limongi. 2000. *Democracy and Development: Political Institutions and Well-Being in the World, 1950–1990*. New York: Cambridge University Press.

Przeworski, A. & F. Limongi. 1997. Modernization: Theories and Facts. *World Politics*, 49(2): 155–183.

Puddington, A. & T. Roylance. 2017. The Freedom House Survey for 2016: The Dual Threat of Populists and Autocrats. *Journal of Democracy*, 28(2): 105–119.

Putnam, R. D. 2000. *Bowling Alone: The Collapse and Revival of American Community*. New York: Simon and Schuster.

Putnam, R. D., R. Leonardi. & R. Nanetti. 1994. *Making Democracy Work: Civic Traditions in Modern Italy*. Princeton: Princeton University Press.

Rabushka, A. & K. A. Shepsle. 1972. *Politics in Plural Societies: A Theory of Political Instability*. Columbus: Merrill.

Rahman, A. & R. Venhoven. 2018. Freedom and Happiness in Nations: A Research Synthesis. *Applied Research on Quality of Life*, 13(2): 435–456.

Rapport. M. 2008. *1848: Year of Revolution*. London: Little.

Rawls, J. 1971. *A Theory of Justice*. Oxford: Oxford University Press.

Reenock, C., M. Bernhard, & D. Sobek. 2007. Regressive Socioeconomic Distribution and Democratic Survival. *International Studies Quarterly*, 51(3): 677–699.

Reenock, C., J. K. Staton. & M. Radean. 2013. Legal Institutions and Democratic Survival. *Journal of Politics*, 75(2): 491–505.

Reilly, B. 2012. Institutional Designs for Diverse Democracies: Consociationalism, Centripetalism and Communalism Compared. *European Political Science*, 11(2): 259–270.

Reynal-Querol, M. 2002. Ethnicity, Political Systems, and Civil Wars. *Journal of Conflict Resolution*, 46(1): 29–54.

Richards, J. 1982. Politics in Small Independent Communities: Conflict or Consensus? *Journal of Commonwealth & Comparative Politics*, 20(2): 155–171.

Riggs, F. 1993. Fragility of the Third World Regimes. *International Social Science Journal*, 136; 199–243.

Riley, D. 2010. *The Civic Foundations of Fascism in Europe: Italy, Spain, and Romania 1870–1945*. Baltimore: Johns Hopkins University Press.

Roberts, K. M. 1998. *Deepening Democracy? The Modern Left and Social Movements in Chile and Peru*. Stanford University Press.

Roberts, T. L. 2015. The Durability of Presidential and Parliament-Based Dictatorships. *Comparative Political Studies*, 48(7): 915–948.

Rød, E. G., C. H. Knutsen. & H. Hegre et al. 2020. The Determinants of Democracy: A Sensitivity Analysis. *Public Choice*, 185(1–2): 87–111.

Ross, M. 2015. What Have We Learned About the Resource Curse? *Annual Review of Political Science*, 18: 239–259.

Ross, M. & P. Mahdavi. 2015. *Oil and Gas Data, 1932–2014*. Harvard Dataverse.

Ross, M. L. 2001. Does Oil Hinder Democracy? *World Politics*, 53(3): 325–361.

Ross, M. L. 2012. *The Oil Curse: How Petroleum Wealth Shapes the Development of Nations*. Princeton: Princeton University Press.

Rothstein, B. 1998. *Just Institutions Matter: The Moral and Political Logic of the Universal Welfare State*. Cambridge: Cambridge University Press.

Rothstein, B. & R. Broms. 2013. Governing Religion: The Long-Term Effects of Sacred Financing. *Journal of Institutional Economics*, 9(4): 469–490.

Rousseau, J. J. (1993[1762]). The Social Contract. In J. J. Rousseau, ed., *The Social Contract and Discourses*. London: Dent, pp. 180–309.

Rowley, C. K. & N. Smith. 2009. Islam's Democracy Paradox: Muslims Claim to Like Democracy, So Why Do They Have So Little? *Public Choice*, 139(3): 273–299.

Royle, S. A. 2001. *A Geography of Islands: Small Island Insularity*. London: Routledge.

Rudolph, S. H. 1997. Introduction: Religion, States, and Transnational Civil Society. In S. H. Rudolph. & J. Piscatori., eds., *Transnational Religion and Fading States*. Boulder: Westview Press.

Rudra, N. 2005. Globalization and the Strengthening of Democracy in the Developing World. *American Journal of Political Science*, 49(4): 704–730.

Rueschemeyer, D., E. H. Stephens. & J. D. Stephens. 1992. *Capitalist Development and Democracy*. Chicago: University of Chicago Press.

Rummel, R. 1997. *Death by Government*. New Brunswick: Transaction Publishers.

Rustow, D. 1970. Transitions to Democracy: Toward a Dynamic Model. *Comparative Politics*, 2(3): 337–363.

Sadowski, Y. 2006. Political Islam: Asking the Wrong Questions? *Annual Review Political Science*, 9: 215–240.

Saghaug Broderstad, T. 2018. A Meta-Analysis of Income and Democracy. *Democratization*, 25(2): 293–311

Saideman, S. M., D. J. Lanoue., M. Campenni. & S. Stanton. 2002. Democratization, Political Institutions, and Ethnic Conflict: A Pooled Time-Series Analysis, 1985–1998. *Comparative Political Studies*, 35(1): 103–129.

Sambanis, N. 2001. Do Ethnic and Non-Ethnic Civil Wars Have the Same Causes? A Theoretical and Empirical Inquiry (Part I). *Journal of Conflict Resolution*, 45(3): 259–282.

Sanborn, H. & C. L. Thyne. 2014. Learning democracy: Education and the fall of authoritarian regimes. *British Journal of Political Science*, 44(4): 773–797.

Sarkees, M. R. & F. Wayman. 2010. *Resort to War: 1816 – 2007*. Washington: CQ Press.

Sartori, G. 1976. *Parties and Party Systems*. Cambridge: Cambridge University Press.

Sawer, M. 2012. *Marxism and the Question of the Asiatic Mode of Production, (Vol. 3)*. Springer Science & Business Media. DOI: 10.1007/978-94-009-9685-4

Schattschneider, E.E. 1942. *Party Government*. New York: Rinehart and Company.

Schimmelfennig, F. 2007. European Regional Organizations, Political Conditionality, and Democratic Transformation in Eastern Europe. *East European Politics & Societies*, 21(1): 126–141.

Schönholzer, D. 2020. *The Origin of the Incentive Compatible State: Environmental Circumscription*. Unpublished manuscript, Stockholm University.

Schulz, J., D. Barahmi-Rad., J. Beauchamp. & J. Henrich. 2018. *The Origins of WEIRD Psychology*. Online: https://papers.ssrn.com/sol3/papers.cfm?abstract_id=3201031

Schumpeter, J. 1949. *Capitalism, Socialism, and Democracy*. 3rd ed. New York: Harper.

Schumpeter, J. A. 1942. *Capitalism, Socialism, and Democracy*. New York: Harper & Brothers.

Scott, J. C. 2009. *The Art of Not Being Governed: An Anarchist History of Upland Southeast Asia*. New Haven: Yale University Press.

Scott, J. C. 2017. *Against the Grain: A Deep History of the Earliest States*. New Haven: Yale University Press.

Selway, J. & K. Templeman. 2012. The Myth of Consociationalism? Conflict Reduction in Divided Societies. *Comparative Political Studies*, 45(12): 1542–1571.

Sen, A. 1993. Capability and Well-Being. In M. Nussbaum. & A. Sen., eds., *The Quality of Life*. Oxford: Oxford University Press, pp. 30–53.

Seul, J. 1999. "Ours Is the Way of God": Religion, Identity, and Intergroup Conflict. *Journal of Peace Research*, 36(5): 553–569.

Sharabi, H. 1988. *Neopatriarchy: A Theory of Distorted Change in Arab Society*. Oxford: Oxford University Press.

Shugart, M. S. & J. M. Carey. 1992. *Presidents and Assemblies. Constitutional Design and Electoral Dynamics*. Cambridge: Cambridge University Press.

Sing, M. 2010. Explaining Democratic Survival Globally (1946–2002). *The Journal of Politics*, 72(2): 438–455.

Singer, D. J., S. Bremer, and J. Stuckey (1972). Capability Distribution, Uncertainty, and Major Power War, 1820-1965. In B. Russett (ed.), *Peace, War, and Numbers*, pp. 19–48. Beverly Hills: Sage.

Siverson, R. M. & J. Emmons. 1991. Birds of a Feather Democratic Political Systems and Alliance Choices in the Twentieth Century. *Journal of Conflict Resolution*, 35(2): 285–306.

Skaaning, S. E. 2020. Waves of Autocratization and Democratization: A Critical Note on Conceptualization and Measurement. *Democratization*, 27(8): 1533–1542.

Skaaning, S. E., J. Gerring. & H. Bartusevičius. 2015. A Lexical Index of Electoral Democracy. *Comparative Political Studies*, 48(12): 1491–1525.

Skaaning, S. E. & M. Jeminez. 2017. The Global State of Democracy, 1975–2015. In International IDEA, *The Global State of Democracy: Exploring Democracy's Resilience*. Stockholm: International Institute for Democracy and Electoral Assistance, pp. 2–33.

Slater, D. & S. Fenner. 2011. State Power and Staying Power: Infrastructural Mechanisms and Authoritarian Durability. *Journal of International Affairs*, 65(1): 15–29.

Slater, D., B. Smith. & G. Nair. 2014. Economic Origins of Democratic Breakdown? The Redistributive Model and the Postcolonial State. *Perspectives on Politics*, 12(2): 353–374.

Smith, B. 2004. Oil Wealth and Regime Survival in the Developing World, 1960–1999. *American Journal of Political Science*, 48(2): 232–246.

Smith, B. 2006. The Wrong Kind of Crisis: Why Oil Booms and Busts Rarely Lead to Authoritarian Breakdown. *Studies in Comparative International Development*, 40(4): 55–76.

Snyder, J. 2000. *From Voting to Violence: Democratization and Nationalist Conflict*. New York: Norton.

Solt, F. 2009. Standardizing the World Income Inequality Database. *Social Science Quarterly*, 90(2): 231–242.

Srebrnik, H. 2004. Small Island Nations and Democratic Values. *World Development*, 32(2): 329–341.

Stamatov, P. 2010. Activist Religion, Empire, and the Emergence of Modern Long-distance Advocacy Networks. *American Sociological Review*, 75(4): 607–628.

Starr, H. 1991. Democratic Dominoes Diffusion Approaches to the Spread of Democracy in the International System. *Journal of Conflict Resolution*, 35(2): 356–381.

Starr, H. & C. Lindborg. 2003. Democratic Dominoes Revisited: The Hazards of Governmental Transitions, 1974-1996. *Journal of Conflict Resolution*, 47(4): 490–519.

Stasavage, D. 2016. Representation and Consent Why They Arose in Europe and Not Elsewhere. *Annual Review of Political Science*, 19: 145–62.

Stasavage, D. 2020. *The Decline and Rise of Democracy: A Global History from Antiquity to Today*. Princeton: Princeton University Press.

Stepan, A. 1985. State Power and the Strength of Civil Society in the Southern Cone of Latin America. In P. B. Evans., D. Rueschemeyer. & T. Skocpol., eds., *Bringing the State Back*. Cambridge: Cambridge University Press, pp. 317–346.

Stepan, A. & C. Skach. 1993. Constitutional Frameworks and Democratic Consolidation. Parliamentarism versus Presidentialism. *World Politics*, 46(1): 1–22.

Stepan, A. C. 2000. Religion, Democracy, and the "Twin Tolerations". *Journal of Democracy*, 11(4): 37–57.

Stepan, A. C. & G. B. Robertson. 2003. An "Arab" More than a "Muslim" Democracy Gap. *Journal of Democracy*, 14(3): 30–44.

Stockton, H. 2001. Political Parties, Party Systems, and Democracy in East Asia Lessons from Latin America. *Comparative Political Studies*, 34(1): 94–119.

Strøm, K. 2000. Delegation and Accountability in Parliamentary Democracies. *European Journal of Political Research*, 37(3): 261–289.

Sutton, P. 2007. Democracy and Good Governance in Small States. In E. Kisanga & S. J. Danchie., eds., *Commonwealth Small States: Issues and Prospects*. London: Commonwealth Secretariat.

Sutton, P. & A. Payne. 1993. Lilliput Under Threat: The Security Problems of Small Island and Enclave Developing States. *Political Studies*, 41(4): 579–593.

Svolik, M. 2008. Authoritarian Reversals and Democratic Consolidation. *American Political Science Review*, 102(2): 153–168.

Svolik, M. 2012. *The Politics of Authoritarian Rule*. New York: Cambridge University Press.

Svolik, M. 2015. Which Democracies Will Last? Coups, Incumbent Takeovers, and the Dynamic of Democratic Consolidation. *British Journal of Political Science*, 45(4): 715–738.

Templeman, K. A. 2012. The Origins and Decline of Dominant Party Systems: Taiwan's Transition in Comparative Perspective. PhD dissertation, University of Michigan.

Teorell, J. 2010. *Determinants of Democratization: Explaining Regime Change in the World, 1972-2006*. Cambridge: Cambridge University Press.

Teorell, J., N. Charron., S. Dahlberg., S. Holmberg., B. Rothstein., P. Sundin. & R. Svensson. 2013. The Quality of Government Dataset, version 15. University of Gothenburg: The Quality of Government Institute, Available at: www.qog.pol.gu.se.

Teorell, J., M. Coppedge., S. I. Lindberg. & S. E. Skaaning. 2019. Measuring Polyarchy across the Globe, 1900–2017. *Studies in Comparative International Development*, 54 (1): 71–95.

Teorell, J. & A. Hadenius. 2009. Elections as Levers of Democracy: A Global Inquiry. In S. I. Lindberg, ed., *Democratization by Elections: A New Mode of Transition*. Baltimore: Johns Hopkins University Press.

Teorell, J. & S. I. Lindberg. 2019. Beyond Democracy-Dictatorship Measures: A New Framework Capturing Executive Bases of Power, 1789–2016. *Perspectives on Politics*, 17(1): 66–84.

Tessler, M. 2002. Islam and democracy in the Middle East: The impact of religious orientations on attitudes toward democracy in four Arab countries. *Comparative Politics*, 34(3): 337–354.

Tierney, B. 1988. *The Crisis of Church and State, 1050–1300*. Toronto: University of Toronto Press.

Tilly, C. 1975. Reflections on the History of European State-Making. In C. Tilly, ed., *The Formation of National States in Western Europe*. Princeton: Princeton University Press, pp. 3–84.

Tobler, W. R. 1970. A Computer Movie Simulating Urban Growth in the Detroit Region. *Economic Geography*, 46: 234–40.

Tocqueville, Alexis de. 1988[1835/40*Democracy in America*. New York: Harper and Row.

Tollefsen, A. F., H. Strand. & H. Buhaug. 2012. PRIO-GRID: A Unified Spatial Data Structure. *Journal of Peace Research*, 49(2): 363–374.

Treier, S. & S. Jackman. 2008. Democracy as a Latent Variable. *American Journal of Political Science*, 52(1): 201–217.

Treisman, D. 2015. Income, Democracy, and Leader Turnover. *American Journal of Political Science*, 59(4): 927–942.

Treisman, D. 2020. Economic Development and Democracy: Predispositions and Triggers. *Annual Review of Political Science*, 23: 241–257.

Tripp, A. M. 2001. The New Political Activism in Africa. *Journal of Democracy*, 12(3): 141–155.

Troy, J. 2009. "Catholic Waves" of Democratization? *Roman Catholicism and Its Potential for Democratization*. *Democratization*, 16(6): 1093–1114.

Tsebelis, G. 1995. Decision Making in Political Systems: Veto Players in Presidentialism, Parliamentarism, Multicameralism and Multipartyism. *British Journal of Political Science*, 25(3): 289–325.

Tsui, K. K. 2010. Resource Curse, Political Entry, and Deadweight Costs. *Economics & Politics*, 22(3): 471–497.

Tullock, G. 2005. *The Social Dilemma of Autocracy, Revolution, Coup D'État, and War*. Indianapolis: Liberty Fund.

Tusalem, R. F. 2009. The Role of Protestantism in Democratic Consolidation among Transitional States. *Comparative Political Studies*, 42(7): 882–915.

Ufen, A. 2008. Political Party and Party System Institutionalization in Southeast Asia: Lessons for Democratic Consolidation in Indonesia, the Philippines and Thailand. *The Pacific Review*, 21(3): 327–350.

van Ham, C. & B. Seim. 2018. Strong States, Weak Elections? How State Capacity in Authoritarian Regimes Conditions the Democratizing Power of Elections. *International Political Science Review*, 39(1): 49–66.

Vanhanen, T. 1999. Domestic Ethnic Conflict and Ethnic Nepotism: A Comparative Analysis. *Journal of Peace Research*, 36(1): 55–73.

Vanhanen, T. 2003. Democratization and Power Resources 1850-2000 [computer file]. FSD1216, version 1.0 (2003-03-10). Tampere: Finnish Social Science Data Archive [distributor]. Available at: www.fsd.uta.fi/en/data/catalogue/FSD1216/meF1216e.html

Varshney, A. 2007. Ethnicity and Ethnic Conflict. In C. Boix. & S. Stokes, eds., *Oxford Handbook of Comparative Politics*. Oxford: Oxford University Press, pp. 274–295.

Vasselai, F., S. Baltz. & A. Hicken. 2019. Presidents and/or Prime Ministers: A Historical Dataset. Working paper presented at the American Political Science Association Conference.

Veenendaal, W. P. 2013. Political Representation in Microstates: St. Kitts and Nevis, Seychelles, and Palau. *Comparative Politics*, 45(4): 437–456.

Veenendaal, W. P. 2014. A Big Prince in a Tiny Realm: Smallness, Monarchy, and Political Legitimacy in the Principality of Liechtenstein. *Swiss Political Science Review*, 21(2): 333–349.

Wallace, J. 2013. Cities, Redistribution, and Authoritarian Regime Survival. *The Journal of Politics*, 75(3): 632–645.

Wallerstein, I´. 1974. *The Modern World-System, vol. I: Capitalist Agriculture and the Origins of the European World-Economy in the Sixteenth Century.* New York: Academic Press.

Wang, Y., P. Lindenfors., A. Sundström., F. Jansson., P. Paxton. & S. I. Lindberg. 2017. Women's Rights in Democratic Transitions: A Global Sequence Analysis, 1900–2012. *European Journal of Political Research*, 56(4): 735–756.

Wang, Y., V. Mechkova. & F. Andersson. 2019. Does Democracy Enhance Health? New Empirical Evidence 1900–2012. *Political Research Quarterly*, 72(3): 554–569.

Waylen, G. 2007. *Engendering Transitions: Women's Mobilization, Institutions, and Gender Outcomes.* Oxford: Oxford University Press.

Weber, M. 1965. *Politics as a Vocation.* Philadelphia: Fortress Press.

Weber, M. 1968 [1922]. *Economy and Society.* 2 Vols. Berkeley, CA: University of California Press.

Weber, M. 2013 [1909]. *The Agrarian Sociology of Ancient Civilizations.* London: Verso.

Weart, S. R. 1998. *Never at War.* New Haven: Yale University Press.

Weingast, B. 1997. The Political Foundations of Democracy and the Rule of Law. *American Political Science Review*, 91(2): 245–263.

Welzel, C. 2013. *Freedom Rising: Human Empowerment and the Quest for Emancipation.* Cambridge: Cambridge University Press.

Welzel, C. 2014. Evolution, Empowerment, and Emancipation: How Societies Climb the Freedom Ladder. *World Development*, 64: 33–51.

Welzel, C. 2015. *Freedom Rising: Human Empowerment and the Quest for Emancipation.* Cambridge: Cambridge University Press.

Weyland, K. G. 2007. *Bounded Rationality and Policy Diffusion. Social Sector Reform in Latin America.* Princeton: Princeton University Press.

Weyland, K. 2014. *Making Waves: Democratic Contention in Europe and Latin America since the Revolutions of 1848.* New York: Cambridge University Press.

Whitehead, L. 1986. International Aspects of Democratization. In G. O'Donnell., P. C. Schmitter. & L. Whitehead, eds., *Transitions from Authoritarian Rule: Comparative Perspectives.* Baltimore: Johns Hopkins University Press, pp. 3–46.

Whitehead, L. 2001. Three International Dimensions of Democratization. In L. Whitehead., eds., *The International Dimensions of Democratization: Europe and the Americas.* Oxford: Oxford University Press, pp. 3–27.

Wigley, S., J. L. Dieleman., T. Templin., J. E. Mumford. & T. J. Bollyky. 2020. Autocratisation and Universal Health Coverage: Synthetic Control Study. *British Medical Journal*, 371: m4040.

Wilkinson, S. I. 2009. Riots. *Annual Review of Political Science*, 12: 329–343.

Wilson, M. C. & C. H. Knutsen. 2020. Geographical Coverage in Political Science Research. *Perspectives on Politics*, FirstView: 1–16.

Wimmer, A., L. E. Cederman. & B. Min. 2009. Ethnic Politics and Armed Conflict. A Configurational Analysis of a New Global Dataset. *American Sociological Review* 74(2): 316–337.

Wittfogel, K. A. 1957. *Oriental Despotism: A Comparative Study of Total Power*. New Haven: Yale University Press.

Wolf, E. 1982. *Europe and the People without History*. Berkeley: University of California Press.

Woodberry, R. D. 2012. The Missionary Roots of Liberal Democracy. *The American Political Science Review*, 106(4): 244–274.

World Bank. 2013. *World Development Indicators 2013*. Washington: World Bank.

World Bank. 2016. *World Development Indicators 2016*. Washington: World Bank.

Yashar, D. 2005. *Contesting Citizenship in Latin America: The Rise of Indigenous Movements and the Postliberal Challenge*. New York: Cambridge.

Zhukov, Y. M. & B. M. Stewart. 2013. Choosing Your Neighbors: Networks of Diffusion in International Relations. *International Studies Quarterly*, 57(2): 271–287.

Ziblatt, D. 2008. Does Landholding Inequality Block Democratization? A Test of the Bread and Democracy Thesis and the Case of Prussia. *World Politics*, 60(4): 610–641.

Ziblatt, D. 2017. *Conservative Parties and the Birth of Democracy*. Cambridge: Cambridge University Press.

Printed by Printforce, United Kingdom